D1597186

POSITIVE VIBRATIONS

POSITIVE VIBRATIONS

POLITICS, POLITRICKS
AND THE STORY OF REGGAE

STUART BORTHWICK

REAKTION BOOKS

This book is dedicated to Rachel, Lily and Seán. Thank you for coming with me on this journey. Also to Mum and Dad (Janice and Brian) – thanks for everything.

Published by Reaktion Books Ltd
Unit 32, Waterside
44–48 Wharf Road
London N1 7UX, UK
www.reaktionbooks.co.uk

First published 2022
Copyright © Stuart Borthwick 2022

Printed and bound in Great Britain
by Bell & Bain, Glasgow

A catalogue record for this book is available from the British Library

ISBN 978 1 78914 569 4

CONTENTS

PROLOGUE *7*

INTRODUCTION *9*

PART I

1 'LOOK TO AFRICA': THE POLITICS OF THE RASTAFARI *15*

2 'MISS JAMAICA': MUSIC AND POLITICS, 1945–70 *33*

3 'BETTER MUST COME': ROOTS REGGAE AND THE POLITICS OF JAMAICA IN THE 1970S *66*

4 'INGLAN IS A BITCH': REGGAE CROSSOVER IN THE UK *113*

PART II

5 'RING THE ALARM': THE 1980S AND THE DECADE OF DANCEHALL *147*

6 'YUH NUH READY FI DIS YET': WOMEN AND THE POLITICS OF DANCEHALL AND REGGAE, 1990–2010 *195*

7 'NOBODY CAN SING "BOOM BYE BYE" FOR ME': MEN AND THE POLITICS OF DANCEHALL AND REGGAE, 1990–2010 *214*

PART III

8 'DON'T TOUCH THE PRESIDENT': DANCEHALL AND
THE TIVOLI GARDENS MASSACRE *257*

9 'NICE UP THE DANCE': THE REGGAE REVIVAL *279*

EPILOGUE *333*

REFERENCES *347*
SELECT BIBLIOGRAPHY *370*
SELECT DISCOGRAPHY *372*
ACKNOWLEDGEMENTS *381*
INDEX *382*

PROLOGUE

Elmina Castle

Elmina, Ghana, 2004

R achel and I are walking towards the gates of Elmina Castle, a former fort built on the coast of what is now Ghana in West Africa – where Africans were bought and sold and shipped out to other colonies. A place of horror, darker than any place I have ever visited. I hear my name.

'Stuart?'

The voice sounds unsure, but I turn around instinctively and scan the faces behind me. I see among them a former student and quickly explain this to my wife, who is as intrigued as I am to discover how I have been spotted in Ghana, of all places. We are on holiday, although Rachel had arrived before me, having spent the previous few months working in the Volta region in the east of the country. On my arrival, and without really thinking about it, I had agreed to visit Elmina Castle and the better-known Cape Coast Castle, both originally developed by the Portuguese as trading posts but then used in the transatlantic slave trade.

'What are *you* doing *here?*' my student exclaims.

As I stand before her, our eyes meet and I ask myself the same question, but with a different emphasis. What *am* I doing here?

I try and answer, but I struggle beyond the pleasantries of 'hello' and 'wow' and 'where are you staying?' In reality, I didn't have an answer. Why does anyone visit a place such as this? It took me a long time to find an answer to my student's question, and it was only on a further trip to Ghana some fifteen years later that I came to understand why I was so fascinated by this aspect not only of Ghana's history, but of Jamaica's and the UK's too. Without knowing it, my first visit to Ghana's castles had made me wonder whether this is where reggae originated all those years ago.

By the time of my next visit, I had learned that amid the depths of man's brutality, humanity lives on, and with that humanity comes music and rhythm. So I returned to Ghana to try and find out why I was haunted by reggae, which by then I had found to be the most intoxicating thing imaginable, sometimes made of little other than sweetness and light, yet at other times pure storm and thunder. By this point, I had learned that at the centre of reggae is both a distinctive rhythm and a melancholy that carries with it pain and suffering. Here is also a rhythm that has travelled numerous times backwards and forwards across the Atlantic Ocean since its first journey west out of Ghana, with the passage of the music picking up speed as we hurtle into the future. On this most recent visit, I also began to ask: if reggae can be traced back to here, how did the politics of history shape it in the following centuries, and, conversely, how has reggae shaped the politics of the societies in which it is played and listened to?

INTRODUCTION

I suppose it could be called sunshine music. Jamaican music
is crying out for social and economic freedom and for justice
and it all involves politics. That's not because music is involved
with politics but because politics is involved with everything.

BOB ANDY[1]

60 per cent of reggae is the frustration of oppressed people
... They're just fighting to get out from under that heavy
weight. They know that pie-in-the-sky is a fake. But still,
40 per cent of it is fantasy. The music is happy; we sing a happy
melody, but it's sad underneath. You can sing a happy song and
underneath you're really hungry.

JIMMY CLIFF[2]

As the famous aphorism goes, writing about music is like
dancing about architecture. For this reason, this book is not
an economic or political history of reggae in a conven-
tional sense but is an attempt to tell the story of the journey of a
rhythm and a sound from a bygone age. This is the story of how a
rhythm was imbued with terror and dread as it travelled across an
ocean, and how it was then nurtured and held tight by an enslaved
and oppressed people before being sold around the world in the
past half a century or so. *Positive Vibrations* is also the story of
how reggae is special, a sacred music inextricably connected to
a uniquely twentieth-century religion, and a musical form that
has been buffeted by local and global political forces since its
development around sixty years ago.

In his book *The Black Atlantic: Modernity and Double Consciousness*, Paul Gilroy observes that racial slavery was central to the development of Western civilization, and that modern civilization is the product of what he describes as a Black Atlantic, yet little is known of this history. Starting out from this premise, one chapter in Gilroy's book examines the significance of music within our understanding of the Black Atlantic, and how a focus on Black music challenges the view that language and writing are the pre-eminent expressions of human consciousness. Gilroy explores the notion of Black Atlantic music as a distinctive counterculture of modernity, and how Black popular culture articulates the experience of being both within and without 'the West'. Importantly, he emphasizes that Black Atlantic culture is hybridized, the inevitable product of a creolization, and that modern Black music is the product of a melding of styles from Africa, the Caribbean, the United States and Europe. Without wishing to offer any sort of comparison between my book and Gilroy's groundbreaking study, *Positive Vibrations* picks up from Gilroy's chapter and explores a form of music that has its roots in both Africa and the slave trade, and which developed out of a form of Black nationalism and Black communitarianism that was both of this world and outside it, both material and metaphysical. In this way, *Positive Vibrations* traces the development of reggae and how it was shaped by, and helped also to shape, the politics of Jamaica and the post-colonial politics of 'the West', showing how reggae articulated the experience of a racial majority at a crucial point in the development of a tiny Caribbean island, leading to Jamaica punching well above its weight in both musical and commercial terms.

Positive Vibrations argues that modern reggae contains a unique fusion of religious and secular styles that were peculiar to Jamaica, and shows how, as the genre evolved, it played a significant role in the development of new musical forms in the global North, with a hybridized global pop now carrying with it both the trebly assonance of dancehall and the rumbling bass of reggae's dub side. 'Dancehall', that most English of terms yet also a Jamaican phrase, is a musical form controversial for its perceived commercialism, misogyny and homophobia, but also a sound that has conquered the world with huge-selling singles and albums. Finally, this book explores how, at just the point when it seemed that Jamaican music was about to merge with R&B, soul and hip-hop within a new global pop music, we would see not the gradual extinction of reggae but its rebirth. The twenty-first-century 'Reggae Revival' sees a new generation spearheading the rejuvenation of what is now one of the world's most recognizable genres of popular music. Accompanying the heartbeat of reggae in this new modern form is also a new politics and the return of the Afrocentrism heard during reggae's earlier development. Almost all of this new generation of musicians share a religion with their musical forebears, with the distinctive world-view of the Rastafari born out of the experiences of ancestors of the enslaved. It is here, then, among the Rastafari, that the story begins.

PART I

PART 1

1

'LOOK TO AFRICA': THE POLITICS OF THE RASTAFARI

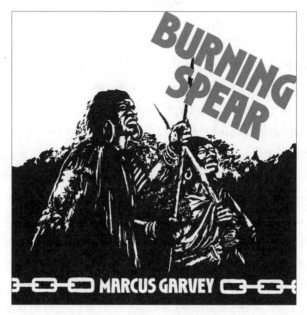

Burning Spear, *Marcus Garvey* (1975)

Look to Africa, when a black king shall be crowned, for the day
of deliverance is near.

ATTRIBUTED TO MARCUS GARVEY

Wi Faada we iina evn, mek piipl av nof rispek fi yu an yu niem.

The Jamaican New Testament[1]

The Rastafari frequently object to the characterization of their
movement as a religion, while also objecting to the suffix
'-ism' being appended to Ras Tafari, the name taken by Lij
Tafari Makonnen when he became Prince Regent and heir to the

throne of Ethiopia in September 1916. For many Rastafari, the phrase 'Rastafarianism', along with any reference to their world-view as a religion, is the language of Babylon, that ancient evil empire from which all subsequent oppressive regimes draw their sustenance.

In objecting to the classification of their beliefs as a religion, the Rastafari do have a point: their way of thinking is contradictory and slippery to the intellectual touch. Once you think you have grasped it, its language shifts and melts away. Their beliefs are founded in an anti-colonial movement in the Caribbean, yet they venerate an African emperor who largely spurned his Jamaican followers. Their worldview can be seen to be politically anti-capitalist, yet adherents say that their belief in a oneness with God pre-dates the modern era. Theologically, the faith combines elements of African spirituality, Coptic Christianity, Judaism, Ethiopianism, Revivalism and Western Protestantism, although the Rastafari do not see it like this. Controversially, the Rastafari rail against the racism of Babylon, yet within the history of their movement is enough racial supremacism to make a Western liberal blush.

The faith of the Rastafari is an ancient yet modern brew, born out of the speeches of Marcus Mosiah Garvey (1887–1940), a Jamaican-born Black nationalist, activist and global leader who introduced Afrocentrism to an exiled diaspora hungry for change. Garvey was born in St Ann's Bay on the island's north coast in 1887 in a British colony still reeling from the Morant Bay Rebellion of 1865, when a courthouse was attacked by a crowd led by the preacher Paul Bogle. The response of the authorities was devastating, with several hundred shot on site and several hundred more executed afterwards.[2]

Initially a trade unionist and ardent traveller, Garvey's devel-oping political consciousness was piqued by what he saw while searching for work in Costa Rica, Panama, Guatemala, Nicaragua,

Ecuador, Chile, Peru and, eventually, England, where he attended lectures at Birkbeck College and worked in the docks of London, Cardiff and Liverpool.[3] As a writer and orator, Garvey was beginning to develop a devastating style that combined hard-edged political militancy with spirituality and prophecy. Upon his return to Jamaica in 1914, and despite his young age, Garvey rapidly became one of the island's best-known Black leaders, establishing the Universal Negro Improvement Association (UNIA) as a global confraternity among Africans and those of African descent. Heady stuff for a 27-year-old, whose mixture of self-belief and a driving desire for change led him to leave Jamaica again only two years later, this time bound for the United States. Garvey arrived in New York, where he mixed with scholars and Black radicals before his restlessness took hold again and he embarked on a tour of 38 of America's states. Finally returning to New York at the start of what became known as the Harlem Renaissance, Garvey refocused his energies on developing the American branch of the UNIA, which was soon to become the headquarters of an international movement for Black self-help, salvation and liberation.[4]

While in New York, Garvey began work on several money-making ventures, none of which captured the imagination more than his Black Star Line, a commercial shipping line formed to assist in the repatriation of the Black diaspora to Africa. Self-determination of Africans, 'at home and abroad', came to sit in the centre of Garvey's consciousness and political position, and he continued to employ his oratorial brilliance in set-piece speeches throughout his own growing empire. UNIA-owned printing presses in Costa Rica, Panama, Harlem and Jamaica helped to spread the word further.

By June 1919, Garvey was claiming that his organization had 2 million members worldwide, making him the world's first truly global Black leader.[5] Local and national branches of the UNIA were semi-independent of their parent body and organized educational activities, debates, concerts and dances, while collecting local dues, paying out sickness benefits and sending a percentage of income to the UNIA HQ in New York. There and in other American cities, UNIA women met once a week to practise military drills, eventually forming the UNIA Motor Corps.

As a young man, Garvey had asked himself:

'Where is the black man's government?' 'Where is his King and his kingdom?' 'Where is his President, his country, his ambassador, his army, his navy, his men of big affairs?' I could not find them, and then I declared, 'I will help to make them.'[6]

In July 1921, at the age of 33, Garvey fleshed out his vision:

As you are aware, the world in which we live today is divided into separate race groups and distinct nationalities. Each race and each nationality is endeavouring to work out its own destiny, to the exclusion of other races and other nationalities. We hear the cry of 'England for the Englishman', of 'France for the Frenchman', of 'Germany for the German', of 'Ireland for the Irish', of 'Palestine for the Jew', of 'Japan for the Japanese', of 'China for the Chinese'. We of the Universal Negro Improvement Association are raising the cry of 'Africa for the Africans', those at home and those abroad.[7]

A recording of this speech is one of only two of Garvey in existence and is treasured by his followers, and 'Africa for the Africans' is a recurring theme in the Black liberation movements that Garvey inspired.

Expanding exponentially, the UNIA soon attracted the unwanted attention of the Federal Bureau of Investigation (FBI). In 1922,

Garvey was charged with fraud for seeking funding for a ship that the UNIA did not yet own. After a delayed trial, the UNIA's figurehead was imprisoned and the Black Star Line collapsed. After serving two years in prison, Garvey was deported to Jamaica.[8] By then, his organization was fragmented and economically moribund. After a failed attempt to form a political party, he moved to London in 1935 and attempted to revive the UNIA, but he died in 1940 following a series of strokes, never having set foot in Africa.

Originally buried in West London, Garvey was largely forgotten for decades, and even as late as 1975, the Jamaican Rasta musician Burning Spear was singing 'no one remember old Marcus Garvey.' However, it was not the Rastafari who brought Garvey back to prominence following his long-forgotten death, but the Pan-Africanism of Kwame Nkrumah. In 1957, Nkrumah became the first president of the newly independent country of Ghana and in his autobiography, published in the same year, wrote, 'I think of all the literature that I studied, the book that did more than any other to fire my enthusiasm was *Philosophy and Opinions of Marcus Garvey*.'[9] Accompanying Ghanaian independence was a flag for the new nation that incorporated the black star of the UNIA's shipping line, along with the pan-Africanist colours of red, yellow and green. With his posthumous reputation rising, Garvey's remains were exhumed in 1964 and returned to Jamaica before being reinterred in Kingston's National Heroes Park.

Garvey's vision was of an organized African diaspora seeking their own liberation, but in the end, his legacy was far more quixotic than he could have imagined. Prior to his departure from Jamaica in 1916, Garvey is supposed to have made his most famous proclamation: 'Look to Africa, when a black king shall be crowned, for the day of deliverance is near.'[10] Robert Hill, the most pre-eminent Garvey scholar, states that no evidence has been found to demonstrate that Garvey ever made this assertion, but irrespective of this,

Garveyites take the quotation as being Garvey's own, as do many contemporary Rastafari.[11]

Later, while in America, Garvey fleshed out his spiritual vision:

> If the white man has the idea of a white God, let him worship his God as he desires. If the yellow man's God is of his race let him worship his God as he sees fit. We, as Negroes, have found a new ideal. Whilst our God has no colour, yet it is human to see everything through one's own spectacles, and since the white people have seen their God through white spectacles, we only now started out (late though it be) to see our God through our own spectacles. The God of Isaac and the God of Jacob. We Negroes believe in the God of Ethiopia, the everlasting God – God the Father, God the Son and God the Holy Ghost, the One God of all ages. That is the God in whom we believe, but we shall worship Him through the spectacles of Ethiopia.[12]

Garvey's declaration drew on Ethiopianism for its spiritual succour, a religious tradition born out of independent African-led churches of the eighteenth and nineteenth century that deviated from colonial religious authorities and which developed an Afrocentric spiritual worldview. Using the King James translation of the Bible, adherents declared that Ethiopia was the birthplace of humanity, providing worshippers with an alternative to white Christianity, while also predicting the fall of slavery and the redemption of Africans. 'Princes shall come out of Egypt; Ethiopia shall soon stretch out her hands unto God' (Psalms 68:31) is a particularly important verse for Garveyism, Ethiopianism and the Rastafari. As we will shortly see, it is important to reggae as well.

Later, in a speech delivered at Madison Square Garden in New York on 16 March 1924, Garvey combined spirituality and politics:

The Universal Negro Improvement Association represents the hopes and aspirations of the awakened Negro. Our desire is for a place in the world; not to disturb the tranquillity of other men, but to lay down our burden and rest our weary backs and feet by the banks of the Niger and sing our songs and chant our hymns to the God of Ethiopia.[13]

When Garvey's supposed prediction came to pass and a Black king was crowned Negusa Nagast (King of Kings) in Ethiopia in November 1930, Garvey became a prophet in the eyes of the more spiritually minded of his followers, part John the Baptist and part Black Moses. On becoming monarch, Ras Tafari took the name Haile Selassie (which translates as 'Might of the Trinity'),[14] while his full title was 'By the Conquering Lion of the Tribe of Judah, Haile Selassie I, King of Kings, Lord of Lords, Elect of God', with Ethiopian dynastic tradition also declaring that Selassie was a direct descendent of King Solomon and the Queen of Sheba.

For the emerging Rastafari, Selassie's long list of titles came as a revelation. Here was the Black king that Garvey had foreseen, an emperor no less, within the only part of Africa that was then outside of Western control, and a king descended from David and Solomon, too. Even the name Ethiopia carried great symbolism over and above that of an East African kingdom, with its original Greek usage referring to the entirety of sub-Saharan Africa. The God of Ethiopia that Garvey foresaw had arrived, and he would surely lead the African diaspora to redemption.

Further sparking the development of the new religious movement was an article by Garvey in the UNIA's *Black Man* magazine concerning Selassie's coronation, referred to by many Rastafari as 'the Prophecy':

The Psalmist prophesied that Princes would come out of Egypt and Ethiopia would stretch forth her hands unto God. We have no doubt that the time has now come. Ethiopia is now really stretching forth her hands. This great kingdom of the East has been hidden for many centuries, but gradually she is rising to take a leading place in the world and it is for us of the Negro race to assist in every way to hold up the hand of Emperor Ras Tafari.[15]

Within a few short years, a messianic cult had developed around the figure of Selassie, yet it was treated with disdain by Garvey, who retained the Christianity of his upbringing.[16] In a sense, the arrival of the Rastafari split what was left of the UNIA's 'Back to Africa' movement in Jamaica. The more affluent Garveyites were hopeful that Selassie's rule would be positive for their movement, but nothing more than that, whereas the dispossessed were more fervent and worshipful. Among these stood Leonard Howell, Joseph Hibbert, Archibald Dunkley, Robert Hinds and Altamont Reid, who would go on to become the leading preachers of the new movement, and who proclaimed Selassie as the Lord.

While Garvey's speeches led the Rastafari to believe that repatriation to 'Ethiopia' was imminent, this was tempered by a later warning from Garvey: 'we are going to emancipate ourselves from mental slavery because whilst others might free the body, none but ourselves can free the mind.'[17] Used with devastating effect in Bob Marley's 'Redemption Song' (1980), this aphorism has been debated endlessly by the Rastafari, yet its meaning remains clear: the upliftment of the African diaspora can only be achieved by themselves.

At the time of Garvey's warning, Selassie was no longer in Ethiopia, having fled the country after the Italian Army, under the control of the fascist dictator Benito Mussolini, crossed the

Mareb River from Eritrea and marched into Ethiopia with a view to creating a new Italian empire. Initially, Garvey was horrified by Mussolini, viewing him as 'a barbarian compared to Haile Selassie, the Emperor of Abyssinia . . . one man is a tyrant, a bully, an irresponsible upstart, whilst the other is a sober, courteous and courageous gentleman.'[18] However, in the following years, Garvey's position began to shift as he criticized Selassie's leadership and unpreparedness for the invasion.

Garvey was convinced that technology and progress would prove the salvation of his movement, and faithful to modernity, he was dismissive of Haile Selassie's reliance on prayer and belief that God would come to the aid of the Ethiopian nation.[19] The reality proved that Garvey was right: Selassie's army was quickly crushed, and the emperor fled to England, where he was met by Garvey and others at Waterloo Station in London. Colin Grant, Garvey's most recent biographer, has Selassie snubbing the delegation by walking past them, and Grant suggests that it was this incident that finally turned Garvey against Selassie.[20] It is certainly the case that within a year, Garvey was referring to the emperor as a man 'of limited intellectual calibre and weak political character' and a 'feudal Monarch who looks down upon his slaves and serfs with contempt'.[21]

Making such criticisms meant that Garvey lost the confidence of many of the remaining UNIA members in Jamaica, and although his views on race came to sit at the centre of the worldview of the Rastafari, Garvey's new-found opinions on Haile Selassie were largely ignored. While Garvey's assessment of Selassie had changed, his views on racial supremacism remained dangerously close to the fascism of the emperor's Italian foe. In a 1937 interview, Garvey stated that 'we were the first fascists . . . Mussolini copied fascism from me.'[22] Like Mussolini, Garvey had come to preach a doctrine of racial purity: 'I believe in a pure black race just as how all self-respecting whites believe in a pure white race, as far as that can be.'[23]

Following the victory of British forces over Mussolini's army in 1941, Selassie returned to Ethiopia as its leader, presiding over a feudal land-tenure system and a largely rural peasantry. For the next thirty years, during a time when Western powers were relinquishing their imperial possessions, Ethiopia remained an empire of its own, although with little economic power. Slowly but surely the population became restless for change and especially for land reform. A famine between 1972 and 1974 weakened Selassie's grip on power and rioting in the capital Addis Ababa in February 1974 was followed by an Army mutiny. Selassie was deposed seven months later and placed under house arrest. On 28 August 1975, it was announced that the emperor had died at the age of 83, with the cause of death reported to have been due to an earlier prostate operation.[24] His eldest son, Crown Prince Asfaw Wossen Haile Selassie, accused his father's usurpers of murder.[25] It was not until after the fall of the Marxist regime of the People's Democratic Republic of Ethiopia in 1991 that Selassie's last resting place was found, underneath a concrete slab in the Palace grounds. In 2000, his remains were disinterred and given a funeral in the Holy Trinity Cathedral in Addis Ababa. For many Rastas, the legend of Selassie continues – like Christ, he has not died but lives on for the salvation of Africans everywhere, omnipresent, omnipotent and omniscient.

If Garveyism is the intellectual foundation of the Rastafari, the spiritual heart of the movement can be found in both the worship of Selassie and the beliefs and cultural practices that enslaved Africans had brought with them to Jamaica, combined with aspects of Christianity and Judaism. The kidnapped Africans who arrived in Jamaica were largely from the West-African Akan people, and in particular the Fante and Ashanti tribes in what is now Ghana. Whereas religious practices of African origin were suppressed in other Caribbean colonies and Christianity was enforced, in Jamaica the English planters refused to 'share' their religion and there was little attempt to Christianize the enslaved. This allowed the continuation of African practices such as ancestor worship and animism until the arrival of Moravians, Methodists and Baptists in the eighteenth century, and Presbyterians in the nineteenth century, many of whom attempted to convert their slaves, albeit without being able to stamp out entirely those social and religious practices that were African in origin. It is also worth bearing in mind that the exuberance of much worship among Nonconformist Protestantism was not as antithetical to ancestor worship or animism as initial appearances might suggest, with many religious denominations in Jamaica taking on an Afro-Christian form.

Following emancipation in 1834 came the arrival of Kumina, a form of worship brought to Jamaica by those free Africans who arrived from Congo between the 1840s and 1860s and who settled in the parish of St Thomas. Kumina provides scholars and onlookers with some powerful clues as to the religious and social customs of Central Africa at the time. While it can be controversial to say so, Kumina's focus on dancing, singing and drumming clearly influenced the Rastafari of the following century, who took its musical elements and combined them with aspects of Christianity, Judaism and Zionism.[26]

Regarding the development of a form of Zionism within Rastafarian belief, the role of Marcus Garvey is again crucial, with a speech in Harlem in 1920 helping to explain his thinking: 'other races were engaged in seeing their cause through – the Jews through their Zionist movement and the Irish through their Irish movement – and I decided that, cost what it might, I would make this a favourable time to see the Negro's interest through.'[27]

Within Judaic Zionism, God's chosen people are the Jews, descendants of the ancient Israelites who are destined to return to

their ancient homeland. For the Rastafari, it is the Africans who
will return to their ancient Promised Land of Zion. For many
Rastafari, Ethiopia, Zion and Israel are one and the same, and they
see themselves as both Ethiopians and Israelites, living in exile in
Babylon.[28] Within Rastafarian reggae, a longing for Zion is central,
both as an idealized and mythologized pre-colonial state and as a
future utopia. Outside of Zion, life in Babylon is characterized by
suffering, an important term within the language of the Rastafari.

Armed with both the New and Old Testament, the early Rastafari
saw Garvey's predictions as prophesies and began to view key passages
of the Bible through the lens of Ras Tafari's coronation. In Jamaica,
Selassie gained another name to add to the Rasta lexicon, Jah, an
abbreviation of Jahweh (or Yahweh) found in the Hebrew Bible or
Tanakh and in certain translations of Psalms 68:4: 'Sing unto God,
sing praises to his name: extol him that rideth upon the heavens
by his name JAH, and rejoice before him.' Horace Andy's 'Psalm 68'
(1976) is perhaps the best-known recording within reggae to refer
explicitly to this Psalm, with God returning in a new name and with
the chorus making it clear that his name 'must be Jah'.

Other key biblical passages for the Rastafari can be found in
the Book of Revelation, that Apocalyptic and prophetic testimony
of John the Baptist. 'And he hath on his vesture and on *his* thigh a
name written, KING OF KINGS, LORD OF LORDS' (Revelation 19:16)
is confirmation for Garveyite spiritualists and for the Rastafari that
Christ had returned in the form of Ras Tafari. Yet there was more
to be found in Revelation:

And I saw in the right hand of him that sat on the throne a
book written within and on the backside, sealed with seven
seals. And I saw a strong angel proclaiming with a loud
voice, Who is worthy to open the book, and to loose the seals
thereof? And no man in heaven, nor in earth, neither under

the earth, was able to open the book, neither to look thereon. And I wept much, because no man was found worthy to open and to read the book, neither to look thereon. And one of the elders saith unto me, Weep not: behold, the Lion of the tribe of Juda, the Root of David, hath prevailed to open the book, and to loose the seven seals thereof. (Revelation 5:1–5)

Who else could this be other than Selassie? Jamaican preacher Leonard Howell, considered by many to be the first Rasta, certainly thought so. Within three years of Selassie's coronation, Howell was evangelizing across Jamaica and proclaiming Selassie as the Lord, with particular success in St Thomas, to the east of Kingston and the site of the ill-fated Morant Bay Rebellion. Leonard E. Barrett Sr, the foremost researcher of the Rastafari during its early development, attributes six principles to Howell:

> Hatred for the White race;
> the complete superiority of the Black race;
> revenge on Whites for their wickedness;
> the negation, persecution, and humiliation of the government
>   and legal bodies of Jamaica;
> preparation to go back to Africa; and
> acknowledging Emperor Haile Selassie as the Supreme Being
>   and only ruler of Black people.[29]

For his book *The Rastafarians*, published in 1997, Barrett Sr drafted a more contemporary summary of 'uniquely Rastafarian beliefs':

> Haile Selassie is the living god;
> the Black person is the reincarnation of ancient Israel, who,
>   at the hand of the White person, has been in exile
>   in Jamaica;

the white person is inferior to the Black person;

the Jamaican situation is a hopeless hell; Ethiopia is heaven;

the Invincible Emperor of Ethiopia is now arranging for
   expatriated persons of African origin to return to Ethiopia;

in the new future Blacks shall rule the world.[30]

Within both of Barrett's summaries, one cannot help but notice the elements of racial supremacism. The origin of this can be traced back to Garveyism, with specific statements by Garvey having the power to shock when they rub up against twenty-first-century liberalism. A flavour is provided by Garvey's views on 'miscegenation': 'for a Negro man to marry someone who does not look like his mother or is not a member of his race is to insult his mother, nature and God, who made his father.'[31] The fact that Garvey followed this with the instruction to 'never trust a Jew . . . Whisper all the time that the Jew is bad. Flatter him as he robs you,' marks Garvey down not merely as a racial supremacist but as an antisemite.[32] No wonder Garvey felt the need to warn his followers that 'in preaching race purity, be very careful because it is a delicate subject.'[33]

Garvey largely escaped censure for his revolutionary ways but was imprisoned for allegedly corrupt business practices. The opposite was the case with Leonard Howell, who funded his evangelism through the sale of photographs of Selassie that purported to be passports, but who was arrested, charged and imprisoned for seditious activities rather than fraud. Upon his release, Howell, by then known as Gong, fled to the hills of Jamaica to found a commune entitled Pinnacle on a former plantation estate that he had purchased with others.[34] It was here that believers grew their hair into locks, founding another key practice of the Rastafari, one born of a Garveyite celebration of blackness, accompanied by scriptural justification, with Leviticus 21:5 containing the Lord's instruction to Moses: 'They shall not make baldness upon their head, neither shall they shave off the corner of their beard, nor make any cuttings in their flesh.'

Following the rapid foundation of the Rastafarian faith in the 1930s came a period that Barrett Sr refers to as 'routinization' as different collectives began to propagate their own versions of the faith.[35] The oldest of these 'mansions' of the Rastafari is the Haile Selassie I Theocratic Order of the Nyahbinghi Reign, named after a legendary East African tribal queen who inspired anti-colonial movements in the region,[36] and a name attributed to an East African secret society said to be led by Haile Selassie.[37] The most significant event within the order is the Grounation (occasionally spelt Groundation), a holy day of prayer, drumming and ganja, the Hindi-in-origin name given to cannabis by most Jamaicans. Central to the Nyahbinghi order is the principle that food should be 'ital': naturally grown, shorn of additives (especially salt) and largely unprocessed. Many Rastafari are vegetarian or vegan as a result. References to ital within reggae are numerous, notable examples being Horace Andy's 'Ital Vital' (1974), Niney the Observer's 'Ital Correction' (1972), Prince Jazzbo's 'Ital Natty Dread' (1977), Tappa Zukie's 'Ital Pot' (1978), as well as Dub Specialist's *Ital Sound Dub* (1974) and Augustus Pablo's *Ital Dub* (1974) albums. Ital is also a central component of the Rasta notion of 'livity', where a positive diet and a faith in Selassie provides for both physical and spiritual enrichment.

Another Rasta mansion, the Bobo Ashanti, was formed by Emmanuel Charles Edwards, or Prince Emmanuel I to his followers, who in 1958 called a Universal Convention of the Rastafari and founded the Ethiopia Africa Black International Congress Church of Salvation. Followers of Emmanuel, who died in 1994, worship him as divine, alongside Garvey as a prophet and Selassie as king, in a new Rasta trinity, with Emmanuel seen as an incarnated Black Christ. The Bobo Ashanti have a dress code involving the wearing of turbans for men, and the covering of arms and legs for women. Largely segregationist and often living communally, the Bobo Ashanti can seem isolated from the broader societies in which they are situated (mostly in the Caribbean). Despite being referred to as empresses, women are viewed as subordinate to men and male children. Black supremacy is a core belief, and the Bobo Dreads take a particularly confrontational approach to Babylon.[38] Much of this can be found in the uncompromising musical messages of a new breed of modern reggae artist that includes Anthony B, Capleton, Sizzla, Lutan Fyah and Fantan Mojah.

In contrast to the Nyahbinghi and the Bobo Dreads is the Twelve Tribes of Israel, perhaps the best known of the mansions of the Rastafari, not least due to Bob Marley's membership. Formed in 1968 at 83 Hope Road, Kingston, by Vernon Carrington, known as the Prophet Gad, the Twelve Tribes developed in the 1970s one block from Tuff Gong, Marley's main residence at 56 Hope Road. Carrington had been a member of the Ethiopian World Federation, established in 1937 to support Ethiopia after the Italian invasion, with his branch becoming the Twelve Tribes. Followers must read the Bible each day; adherents are given a name and colour based on the date of their birth within the ancient Egyptian calendar; like Jehovah's Witnesses and the Unification Church, adherents believe that the chosen few are limited to 144,000; Haile Selassie represents the second coming of Jesus Christ; repatriation is a goal; ganja is smoked; Gad is revered as a Prophet; music is central; membership is open to all races (and some members are white); and, finally, the number twelve has particular significance.[39] Unlike Bob Marley, not all Twelve Tribes Rastafari are dreadlocked. Barrett Sr views the Twelve Tribes as being the most Christian of the Rastafari and a reverence for Christ was confirmed by Carrington himself in a rare and final media interview.[40]

If the Nyahbinghi order ensured the centrality of sacred rhythms to the Rastafari through their development of a form of drumming seen as being deeply spiritual, it was the Twelve Tribes of Israel who took the roots-reggae genre and popularized it as a global religious form. In addition to Bob Marley, other notable members have included Dennis Brown, Freddie McGregor, Rita Marley, Judy Mowatt and Fred Locks, as well as members of the band Israel Vibration.[41] Other smaller Rastafari mansions include the Haile Selassie I School of Vision, the Royal Ethiopian Judah Coptic Church, the International Peace Makers, the Leonard P. Howell Foundation, the Haile Selassie I Theocracy Government, Camp David and the Rastafari Centralization Organization.

The point at which Haile Selassie became aware that he had followers in Jamaica who were worshipping him as a God is unclear. When Selassie received a delegation in 1961 that consisted of both Rastafari and others, his courtiers advised the visitors against mentioning that some of them worshipped him as a God, stating that this would be contrary to Selassie's role as head of the Ethiopian Orthodox Church. Nonetheless, Selassie was seen to have offered hope to the mission, with the emperor quoted as saying:

> Tell the brethren be not dismayed, I personally will give my assistance in the matter of their repatriation. I want not only men but women and children. I do not want you to suffer any difficulties. It will take some time for careful study and planning.[42]

This message was seen as an unambiguous statement by those Rastafari who were already aware that Selassie had provided a plot of land at Shashamane, 240 kilometres (150 mi.) south of Addis Ababa, for occupation by those Western Blacks who had supported Ethiopia during the Italian occupation. The first settlers were African American Jews, most of whom were to resettle eventually in Israel, followed by a small number of Rastafari.

By the time of Selassie's only visit to Jamaica in April 1966, the emperor cannot have failed to be aware of his status in the eyes of the Rastafari. On the day of his arrival, his plane was met by tens of thousands of Rastas and Selassie was reported to have wept upon seeing the massed reception party.[43] His visit led to an increasing number of Rastafari travelling to Shashamane, where the Rastafari sometimes have a strained relationship with their Ethiopian hosts, due largely to the Rastafari's continued veneration of a leader seen by many contemporary Ethiopians as being deeply flawed.[44]

Despite Barrett Sr's attempts at a summary, the Rastafari have little in the way of dogma, other than a belief in the divinity of Haile Selassie. On occasions, even a reverence for Selassie is peripheral to other beliefs. When in Ghana, I met Rastafari who have much less interest in Selassie than their Jamaican-born brethren, and whose spirituality is focused on a more abstract theism. Some Ghanaian Rastas view Selassie not as Jah made flesh, but as God's emissary, 'like Kwame Nkrumah'.[45] For these Rastafari, Ghana is Ethiopia and Ethiopia is Ghana. Or as Rocky Dawuni, Ghana's pre-eminent Rastafarian musician, puts it, 'Ghana is the current gateway to Africa, the New Jerusalem and the Western Wall of Ethiopia – Africa. The whole continent is one entity and geographical locations created by colonial demarcations are of little relevance in the big picture.'[46] It is this idealization of Africa that unites all Rastafari and Garveyites in a belief that Africans will never achieve their maximum potential in Babylon. When the time came in Jamaica for a new musical form to rise out of the country's folk culture, Afrocentrism and Black pride sat at its centre, as did the Rastafari, who developed a musical form that spoke to them about their contemporary enslavement and spoke to the rest of the world about the continuation of imperialism even within a supposedly post-colonial world.

2

'MISS JAMAICA': MUSIC AND POLITICS, 1945–70

Millie Small, 'My Boy Lollipop' (1964)

The Prime Minister once said that if you want to know what's going on in Jamaica, look at what's in the charts, listen to the words of the songs.

JIMMY CLIFF[1]

That song all right. I think we can use it.
When it going to be released, huh?
Hold on a minnute, read this first.
What's the meaning of this?
That means you get twenty dollars for the record.
Twenty dollars, sir? That don't sound right.

How much do you think it's worth, then?

I don't really know, sir.

Come on, you must have an idea. What do you think it's worth?

Well, I think at least about 200 dollars you know, sir. I don't think
I'm signing this for twenty dollars you know, sir.

I see. Looks like you have a new producer. I wish you luck.

The Harder They Come, DIR. PERRY HENZELL[2]

While all musical forms are intricately connected to the economic, cultural and historical contexts of the societies in which they develop, the evolution of reggae is unique in being intricately connected not just to the Rastafari, but to Jamaican party politics, from the growth of the music out of ska and rock-steady in the 1960s to the present day. Never has a popular musical form been so intricately bound up in the affairs of a nation state, and never have a nation's leaders been quite so bound up in the development of a form of popular music.

As with many of the colonies of Europe, the end of the Second World War brought to Jamaica a period of relative stability, if not prosperity. As elsewhere, there were two large parties that dominated politics. The People's National Party (PNP) was founded in 1938 and first led by Norman Manley, a barrister born to mixed-heritage parents in the Jamaican parish of Manchester. The Jamaica Labour Party (JLP) was formed in 1943 by Alexander Bustamante, a former PNP member and a distant cousin of Manley, whose source of wealth was his work as a moneylender but who was also a trade unionist and activist against the colonial power, leading to a prison term in 1940 for subversion.

In the first elections under universal adult suffrage in 1944, the JLP and PNP stood on what ostensibly looked like similar tickets, but with a difference of emphasis. While Bustamante focused on economics as a way of improving the lot of Jamaican workers, Manley looked to political solutions, seeing colonial rule as the source of Jamaica's ills. Bustamante's approach was the more successful. The JLP won 22 of the 33 seats in the House of Representatives in an election campaign where the JLP founder presented himself as being the Jamaican leader who was on the side of working-class Blacks, who began to refer to him as 'chief'.[3] Manley responded with an aggressive move onto Bustamante's turf, founding the Jamaican Trade Union Congress (TUC) and putting himself in direct competition with the Bustamante Industrial Trade Union (BITU). The JLP would go on to win the 1949 elections, but with a reduced majority, before the PNP won power in 1955 with Norman Manley becoming Chief Minister.

By the late 1950s, nationalist sentiment in Jamaica was growing as both the JLP and PNP campaigned for the country to throw off the shackles of colonial rule. The post-war Labour government in the UK had begun a process of decolonization, with British India partitioned into the independent dominions of India and Pakistan in 1947. Despite the Conservative governments of 1951 suspending further decolonization, victory for the Tory pragmatist Harold Macmillan in the general election of 1959 saw the new prime minister bow to the seemingly inevitable continuation of the process. In a symbolically loaded speech, delivered in Cape Town, South Africa, Macmillan declared that 'the wind of change is blowing through this continent. Whether we like it or not, this growth of national consciousness is a political fact.'[4] The wind of change was so strong it could also be felt in Jamaica, and it would only be a matter of time before Jamaica was to be given its independence.

During this period, several figures were coming into prominence within the nascent Jamaican music industry who would go on to play significant roles in the following years. In 1947, Ken Khouri purchased a disc-based recording device in Miami and used it to record Jamaican bands, sending discs to London for duplication. Awakened to the commercial potential of selling recordings, he purchased further equipment and set up Times Record Limited, Jamaica's first label, in 1954, recording calypsos and releasing American records under licence. Later he built Federal Records, Jamaica's first fully fledged recording studio.[5]

In competition with Khouri was Stanley Motta, the owner of an electrical store in Kingston, who set up a studio in the early 1950s to record mento, a Jamaican folk music form that brought together African rhythms and European-in-origin instrumentation, with Motta sending acetates to London for duplication. This led to the simultaneous release of records in both Jamaica and the UK, with Melodisc in London and MRS (Motta's Recording Studios) in Kingston releasing 'Glamour Gal' by the Ticklers in 1952.[6] Stanley Motta left the music industry in 1957, leaving Ken Khouri with a recording monopoly until Radio Jamaica Rediffusion (RJR) opened a studio facility a year later.

Born in 1937, Chris Blackwell was the English-born son of a wealthy white Anglo-Jamaican family, who had returned to Jamaica in 1955 following a public-school education and accountancy training in England. Following a brief military career as a major in the Jamaican army, Blackwell began working as aide-de-camp to Sir Hugh Foot, the colonial Governor General of Jamaica, before leaving the sphere of government to emerge as a musical entrepreneur, founding Island Records in 1959 with Jamaican producer Leslie Kong and Australian-born sound engineer Graeme Goodall, who had built both the RJR studio and the Federal Records facility.[7] In May 1962, Blackwell collected JA$5,400 from backers and established himself as a UK-based licensing agent and distribution outlet for leading Jamaican recordings.[8] A year later, Island Records had their first hit with 'Boogie in My Bones' by the Cuban-born Laurel Aitken, which Blackwell had produced himself with assistance from Graeme Goodall.[9]

Former police officer Arthur 'Duke' Reid ran a mobile sound system in the 1950s originally called 'Duke Reid's the Trojan', playing predominantly American R&B to audiences across Jamaica. Branching out into record production, Reid founded his own Treasure Isle studio and record label, and gradually moved away from American music to focus on developing ska, a musical form that would slowly evolve into rocksteady and reggae as the 1960s progressed. Later, in what was Duke Reid's most successful move, the producer began to license Jamaican music to UK record labels, thus starting a UK chart boom in early reggae.

One of ska's purported origins is in a meeting in 1959 between Reid's great rival, Clement Seymour 'Coxsone' Dodd, owner of the Downbeat Sound System since 1954, and Cluett Johnson and Ernest Ranglin from the band the Blues Blasters. During their meeting, Dodd suggested that the band should develop a variant of American R&B that emphasized an offbeat within the music. After being introduced to Dodd, the band began their rhythmic experimentation at the studios of the Jamaica Broadcasting Corporation (JBC), formed in 1959. Coxsone used the recording on an exclusive 'dubplate', a one-off pressing of relatively poor quality, for his sole use as operator of the Downbeat Sound System. The track was subsequently re-recorded by the band, with Ken Richards rather than Ranglin on guitar.[10] The result was 'Easy Snappin'' (1959) by Clue J. and His Blues Blasters, considered by many to be the first ska release due to its distinctive offbeat piano and guitar. Others suggest that the origins of ska were in an 'upside-down R&B' sound said to be influenced by the popularity of U.S. radio stations that could be picked up in Jamaica, with the rhythm of American R&B recordings occasionally matching the warping of long-wave radio signals as they phased in and out of tune.

Contesting the view of ska as a Jamaican inversion of an African American musical form are those who point to one of the music's roots in mento, often perceived to be a Jamaican form but in reality a hybridized sound consisting of Trinidadian calypso, *son Cubano*, the music of Kumina and the fife-and-drum accompaniment to many quadrille dances of the nineteenth century.[11] In the 1940s and '50s, mento was popular at least partly due to it being the preferred form of the early troubadours in Jamaica who carried news in a musical form, with lyrical messages accompanied by home-made drums, bamboo fifes and fiddles.[12] Importantly for the eventual development of what became known as Nyabinghi drumming, mento carried within it a call-and-response styling derived from African folk song and an emphasis on polyrhythmic drumming that sat in stark contrast to the European and New World focus on melody and harmony.[13] Also important in the development of ska was the work of Prince Buster (Cecil Bustamante Campbell) following his departure from Coxsone Dodd's sound system in 1959, particularly the singles 'African Blood' and 'Time Longer than Rope', which had a rhythmic emphasis on the offbeat. Whatever its origins, by the time a sixteen-year-old Bob Marley laid down 'Judge Not', his first recording, at Federal Records in 1962, the sound of ska had settled into its 4/4 time signature, with a walking bassline and a snare backbeat, and with the offbeat dominated by piano and saxophone.

Coxsone Dodd had been sourcing popular R&B records from the U.S. for many years, selling them to several sound systems, and his next step would be to open his own facility, Studio One, where he began recording hit records by the likes of the Maytals and the Skatalites. As well as recording tracks for general release, both Duke Reid and Coxsone Dodd continued to record dubplate 'specials' for exclusive use on their own sound systems, competing against each other to produce the most popular recordings.

After Reid and Dodd, the third most significant sound system of the era was that owned and run by Vincent 'King' Edwards, who released tracks on his own record label. In most reggae histories, Edwards's role is overshadowed by that of Coxsone Dodd and Duke Reid, but in the late 1950s and early 1960s it was Edwards's system that was the most popular, with the selector Red Hopeton at the controls. Edwards's musical career was relatively short-lived, as he joined the PNP and entered politics, winning a seat in Jamaica's parliament in the general election of 1962.

Also beginning a career in music in the late 1950s was Edward Seaga, an earnest Jamaican scholar of African, Scottish, Indian and Lebanese heritage who would go on to be a pivotal figure in the development of Jamaican music as well as serving as the country's prime minister from 1980 to 1989. Following his graduation from Harvard after submission of a thesis on folk culture in West Kingston, Seaga retained an anthropological interest in the religious cults of the Trench Town district, who spoke their own language and who combined elements of Protestantism and Animism with Revivalism and Kumina (the former being a more Europeanized religious form and the latter more African). As part of his research, Seaga began recording Revival Zion and Kumina rituals involving dancing, drumming, singing and spirit possession, sending recordings to the Ethnic Folkways record label in New York. Specialists in archiving folk recordings, the label eventually released Seaga's *Folk Music of Jamaica* (1956) album, which he distributed to local shops. The demand for such recordings was minimal, though, with the Jamaican record-buying public preferring imported American R&B.

While his ethnographic recordings in West Kingston were a commercial failure, Seaga hit on the idea of importing master recordings of American songs for manufacture at a new pressing plant of his at 13 Bell Road in Kingston. Flushed with success, Seaga's West Indies Recording Ltd (WIRL) turned towards local recordings and became the first organization to record Jamaican songs onto vinyl rather than shellac or acetate, developing a truly mass-produced consumer item for the first time. WIRL's first Jamaican hit was 'Manny, Oh' by Joe Higgs and Roy Wilson, recorded at the RJR studio with Graeme Goodall on engineering duties. While the *Jamaica Observer* has repeatedly insisted that this release sold over 50,000 copies,[14] Seaga played down such claims in his memoirs, stating that no records from the early 1960s sold anything like that number.[15] Either way, 'Manny, Oh' was a big hit, and demonstrated the commercial possibilities of recording and releasing Jamaican music.

Following Seaga, there were new entrants to the market, all using unique combinations of equipment and acoustics – ensuring that each new producer had a specific sound, accentuated by the use of in-house bands. The best known of these were the Skatalites' recordings for Coxsone Dodd, the Upsetters' recordings for Lee 'Scratch' Perry (Rainford Perry) and, later in the 1970s, the work of the Aggrovators for Bunny 'Striker' Lee, the Harry J All Stars for Harry Johnson at his own recording facility, the Revolutionaries for Joseph Hoo Kim at his Channel One studio (partly built by Graeme Goodall) and Roots Radics for Henry 'Junjo' Lawes's Volcano label and sound system.[16] Bunny Lee and Harry J were not sound-system owners, but producers who plugged directly into the recording and distribution businesses that were beginning to spring up. Meanwhile, Lee Perry was originally an employee of Coxsone Dodd before the pair fell out, with Perry recording 'I Am the Upsetter' as an attack on Dodd before naming his own house band the Upsetters.

Popularizing each studio's product were Jamaica's two main radio stations, the JBC and the RJR networks, who played ska somewhat begrudgingly.[17] Sometimes, backing bands would change their names to suit the producer they were working for at the time, who would most often be seen as the auteur of the end product, even though they rarely composed the music played by the musicians. These were not producers in the Anglo-American mould, who worked with musicians to arrange songs and had a powerful influence in the playing and recording of music. With some famous Jamaican recordings, the producer was not even in the building when the recording was made. Nonetheless, each producer maintained a proprietorial control over not merely the recording premises and record labels that they owned, but over the house musicians employed to provide backing tracks and over the master tapes emanating from each session.

Throughout the following decades, little or no attention was paid to the notion of intellectual property. If you owned a recording of a song, it was yours to exploit in any way you saw fit, including onward sale to any interested party inside or outside of Jamaica. At the time, no thought was given to songwriting royalties. With one eye out for a bargain, Edward Seaga was the first to sense that there was money to be made in obtaining the intellectual property rights of Jamaican compositions, and he eventually registered the copyrights of a number of songs that had become hits, but he had limited success due to his retrospective approach.[18] Seaga's experience did not exactly inspire musicians or producers to consider intellectual property, and producers continued to pay musicians to record tracks whose financial involvement ended as soon as they left the studio.

Within the political sphere, Seaga had been working for Alexander Bustamante, who in 1959 had nominated Seaga to serve in the Upper House of the Jamaican Parliament. Following this, Seaga began to play a significant role in shaping Jamaica's relationships with its immediate neighbours. Norman Manley's PNP government had settled on a policy of Jamaican membership of the West Indies Federation, believing that a federal Caribbean would be the most appropriate constitutional unit to seek independence from Britain. Federal elections were organized, with the newly formed West Indies Federal Labour Party led by Manley and the

Democratic Labour Party led by Bustamante. Jamaican discontent with their relatively small share of seats in a federal parliament that sat in Trinidad and Tobago was harnessed by the JLP, who led calls for Jamaica to withdraw. The popularity of the JLP's position eventually forced Norman Manley's hand, and he bowed to popular opinion and called a referendum for September 1961. In an early example of a Jamaican popular music song being used by a political party, the JLP made extensive use of Clancy Eccles's 'Freedom' as the soundtrack to their referendum campaign.[19] Building on the success of Eccles's earlier single 'River Jordan', 'Freedom' uses a biblical metaphor that compares Jamaica's journey to that of the Israelites crossing the River Jordan to get to their Promised Land. Eccles himself objected to the JLP's use of his song, but was powerless to prevent the party from adopting it: 'The politicians used it as an escape route to bring things back to order . . . but we were thinking about a Rastafarian movement. It got to me by seeing the Rastamen out there preaching in different districts in Jamaica, trying to let the word reach people.'[20]

The referendum on 19 September 1961 saw a narrow victory for the JLP, who won a 54.1 per cent majority in favour of Jamaica leaving the Federation, which collapsed as a result. Released shortly afterwards, Lord Creator's 'Independent Jamaica' references the result, with the narrator declaring that the people voted wisely and 'everybody is happy' now that the Federation is no more. Perhaps more significantly for the intertwined histories of reggae and the Rastafari was the release of Winston and Roy's 'Babylon Gone', which featured the drummer Count Ossie on a track that celebrated the collapse of the Federation.

The referendum paved the way for Jamaica to gain independence not merely from the West Indies Federation, but from the United Kingdom; however, a general election was required to ascertain whether the PNP or the JLP would oversee the process. Clancy

Eccles's 'Freedom' continued to be used within the JLP's election-eering, and at the election of 10 April 1962, the momentum of the referendum victory led to the JLP beating the PNP, taking 26 of the 45 available seats. One of the successful JLP candidates was Edward Seaga, standing for the constituency of Kingston Western, the poorest in Jamaica and the site of a Rastafarian stronghold at Back o'Wall. Seaga had originally chosen to seek election to the constitu-ency as he wished to continue his anthropological work, while life in Jamaica's capital would enable him to combine his two careers as a music producer and politician. Following the election, Seaga began to use his new political base to nurture a range of musicians on his WIRL label, including Dennis Brown, Laurel Aitken, Byron Lee, and the Victors, who would go on to become the Techniques.

Following the JLP's election victory, the UK granted formal inde-pendence to Jamaica on 6 August 1962. As the newly appointed Minister of Development, Seaga was responsible for a Festival of Independence encompassing a celebration of Jamaican literature, fine arts and popular music.[21] Within this, Seaga set himself the task of assisting in the development of a new Jamaican popular cul-ture that would build upon a folk culture that had suffered what Seaga referred to as 'benign neglect' within a society that did not wish to be reminded too frequently of its African origins.[22]

Outside of the independence festival, ska was also developing and now incorporated some aspects of the Jamaican folk music loved by Seaga, but melded to the increasingly popular rhythms of American R&B. The evolution of ska was built upon several tech-nological progressions, including new amplification technology, which was also essential for the development of the outdoor sound systems of Duke Reid, Coxsone Dodd and King Edwards, who would play ska alongside jive, boogie, rhythm and blues, and rock and roll. Seaga describes the economic processes at work:

sound system operators . . . vied for crowd attendance by 'discovering' little-known gems in archives abroad, chiefly boogie and rhythm and blues records, which had had little or no previous exposure in Jamaica. They dusted them off in the warehouses of record companies, brought them to Jamaica, removed the labels and gave them new lives with new names. The marketing strategy was to create heavy demand by excessive turntable play and by creating a shortage of supply, which allowed them to hike prices based on scarcity. Eventually, as the popularity of each record waned, prices would decrease and quantities of sale would increase. Within this strategy, a few 'producers' controlled the market.[23]

If there was one vinyl release that encapsulated the mood of Jamaica in the immediate post-independence era, it was Jimmy Cliff's 'Miss Jamaica', a rootsy number with the distinctive emphasis on the offbeat that would come to define much Jamaican music. The metaphor within the song, between the love of the narrator for a beauty-pageant competitor and the love of Jamaicans for their new nation, is well delivered by Cliff. In the song, the narrator explains that while Jamaica might not have 'a fabulous shape', it suits him just fine.

'Miss Jamaica' was not the only political song of the era, with other tracks hoping to both reflect and shape the popular mood. Al T. Joe's 'Independence Time Is Here' and Derrick Morgan's 'Forward March' were further attempts to express the nationalist sentiment of the time, although, beneath the surface, both spoke of political conflict as well as the supposed unity of newly independent Jamaica. Al T. Joe's track instructs the listener to forget the past amid this time of national celebration, for 'it is equality that we will enjoy.' This seemed a stretch; equality was not promised by either the JLP or PNP, and deep divisions between rich and poor remained in Jamaican society. After the abolition of slavery, land and property ownership was retained by a small, privileged elite, much to the chagrin of the poor workers courted by both Bustamante and Manley. Importantly, neither was full independence on offer, as Queen Elizabeth II was to continue as head of state while Jamaica's legal system would remain yoked to that of the UK.

Derrick Morgan's post-independence 'Forward March' was vaguer than Al T. Joe's track. Following a call-and-response first verse promising 'we're independent, we're independent', the song's chorus then promises that the Lord was still with Jamaican brothers and sisters, who should give joy and praise. Here, God was being called to anoint a secular development, almost as if Morgan realized that the march from independence to true freedom would be along a rocky road, and one that might not necessarily lead to spiritual salvation. Without the invocations to the Lord, similar sentiments can be heard in Joe White and Chuck's 'One Nation', Prince Buster and the Blue Beats' 'Independence Song' and Basil Gabbidon's 'Independent Blues'. A typically up-tempo track with a lightweight feel, the Joe White and Chuck recording speaks of a united nation of people who should jump for joy, join hands together and march to independence. With vocals very much in the foreground, the Prince Buster track also tries to bring a nation together. Instructing his followers to 'put the shoulders to the wheel', Buster is unquestioning in his suggestion that independence would lead to great changes for Jamaica. Meanwhile, Basil Gabbidon's 'Independent Blues' was more uplifting than the title might initially suggest – the reference to blues is musicological rather than inferring melancholy.

Listening to this 'independence ska' now, one would be harsh to criticize it for its naivety. Nonetheless, it can sound syrupy when compared to the undiluted anger of much Jamaican music in the following decade. Independence ska promised the listener 'no more slaving', while in the roots reggae that was to follow, slavery continues and will not end until Babylon falls. Nonetheless, ska eventually came to be seen as the national music of Jamaica, although before it was able to be so, it would need to conquer not merely the downtown sound systems operated by the likes of Duke Reid and Coxsone Dodd, but also the uptown house parties of Jamaica's elite.

The number that united all of Jamaica was 'My Boy Lollipop' (1964) by Jamaican teenager Millie Small, a song that also helped to ensure that Chris Blackwell had a solid foundation on which a future music empire could be built. 'My Girl Lollipop' was originally written by Bobby Spencer, the brother of doo-wop veteran Carl Spencer, but shortly after penning what would become the best-selling release from Jamaica in the 1960s, Spencer gave away the rights of the song during a game of poker.[24] New York recording mogul Morris Levy contacted the winner of the bet and purchased the rights – an astute move, considering the subsequent sales.[25] Originally a number that leaned more towards R&B, the song was re-recorded by Small in London's Olympic Studios at Island's request. It is this second recording that reached the top ten in the USA and the UK, and while it was a release aimed at the U.S. and European markets, it was taken by Jamaica as being recorded by one of their own, even if, barring Millie Small herself, the only other Jamaican performer involved was the guitarist Ernest Ranglin, who supervised the recording in London.[26]

In many ways, 'My Boy Lollipop' was an anomaly. Ska sounded joyous and celebratory, as that was the popular mood in Jamaica at that time. However, the music was not universally popular on the island, as home-grown Jamaican forms were largely shunned by a Jamaican middle class who denigrated ska as 'downtown music'. It would take the success of 'My Boy Lollipop' in the UK before ska became popular in uptown Kingston. Edward Seaga explains how:

It was easy to export recordings to England, where they became known as Blue Beat. Popularity in London jumped. Millie Small's hit pushed popularity further. Jamaicans began to take note and uptowners became more inclined to listen to the downtown products once London was registering its approval. The journey to popularity for ska was from downtown Kingston, to London, to uptown Kingston, an unnecessary social re-routing of 6,000 miles.[27]

The 'Blue Beat' referred to by Seaga was Blue Beat Records, a sub-label of London-based independent Melodisc, who licensed Jamaican recordings for sale in the UK. The label's first release was 'Boogie Rock' (1960) by Laurel Aitken and the Boogie Cats, followed by 'Dumplins' by Byron Lee and the Dragonnairs and Edward Seaga's 'Manny, Oh' production. With Blue Beat releases increasingly popular in the UK, particularly among Jamaican migrants, this changed the dynamic within Jamaica.

Although 'My Boy Lollipop' was a Chris Blackwell release that Seaga could not gain credit for, he did have a hand in uniting Jamaica behind ska by inviting uptown bandleader Byron Lee to watch ska bands perform at Kingston's Chocomo Lawn, which Seaga had purchased as a base for his political headquarters in Kingston. Introduced to ska for the first time, Byron Lee's band then took the offbeat rhythms of downtown Kingston and incorporated them into uptown performances in the city's more desirable neighbourhoods. Now that ska was popular uptown, it became a unifying force within Jamaica, symbolizing and encapsulating a brief era. Seaga would go on to claim that 'Jamaican music had reached its pinnacle, riding very largely on the talents of downtown inner-city youths whose creations were part of the rejected culture but in the new wave of the post-independence cultural explosion, it became central to the identity that was being moulded.'[28] Despite his success, for Seaga the lure of a career as a politician was stronger than that of an entrepreneur, and following his independence festival, he effectively retired from the music industry. Later, the WIRL studio was purchased by Byron Lee who renamed it Dynamic Sounds.

No sooner had ska conquered all of Jamaica than the socio-musical dynamic began to move away from up-tempo celebrations towards something more ambivalent lyrically and darker in musical style. Disillusionment and confusion came first, and then anger. Within a year of the release of Prince Buster and the Blue Beats' 'Independence Song' came Buster's famous track 'Madness' (1963), which warned 'propaganda ministers' that 'it's gonna be tougher.' In the same year, Delroy Wilson released 'Lion of Judah' and Jimmy Cliff released 'King of Kings', both clear pointers of the direction of spiritual travel. A year later, the Wailers, backed by the Skatalites recorded 'Simmer Down' for Coxsone Dodd, eventually reaching number one in the JBC singles chart. The Wailers had foreseen that tempers would get out of control if Jamaican independence did not lead to change, and they were right. Justin Hinds and the Dominoes' 'Carry Go Bring Home' (1964), recorded in Duke Reid's Treasure Isle studios, performed a similar role. To the outsider, the track speaks of the misery and oppression of contemporary existence, with the wicked oppressing the weak, while hinting at where salvation will arrive ('in Mount Zion high'). To the more knowledgeable, the Jezebel of the lyrics was Gladys Longbridge, the wife of Alexander Bustamante.[29]

The Wailers and Justin Hinds had identified a rising temperature within Jamaica's political culture and had begun to point the blame for a lack of social cohesion on Jamaica's political class. Others looked outwards. In 1963, the Skatalites released the instrumental 'Fidel Castro' on Coxsone Records. This took an uneasy look 260 kilometres (160 mi.) north of Jamaica at the unfolding of a geo-political crisis, sparked by the Soviet Union stationing nuclear missiles in Cuba, only 145 kilometres (90 mi.) from the shores of the United States. The track may have come about because both Tommy McCook and Roland Alphonso from the Skatalites were born in Cuba. Looking in the same direction and fearing a nuclear apocalypse was Prince Buster with '100 Ton Megaton' (1963) and Lester Sterling with 'Air Raid Shelter' (1963), both ska instrumentals. Following the assassination of u.s. president John F. Kennedy on 22 November 1963, the Skatalites quickly recorded 'Lee Harvey Oswald' (released under Roland Alphonso's name) before looking further afield to assess the situation, recording 'Addis Ababa' in the following year.

Edward Seaga went on to view his independence festival as being only partially successful. Old moulds were broken, and Jamaica developed a more positive relationship with its African and folk heritage, but other than ska there was not the rise of new cultural forms as Seaga had anticipated. More successful was Seaga's realization that an independent Jamaica would need a new national hero, with Seaga alighting on Marcus Garvey as the prime candidate. Having led a global movement early in his life, Garvey had died in London as a largely forgotten figure interred in the catacombs of Kensal Green Cemetery. With a keen sense of the importance of the moment, Seaga arranged for Garvey's remains to be exhumed and reinterred as Jamaica's first national hero in a shrine within Jamaica's new National Heroes Park. From this moment onwards, Garvey's influence returned to Jamaican politics, and to Black politics nationally and internationally. He was the first Black nationalist, the first to speak of Black pride, yet he had been forgotten, but not for long. 'Marcus Garvey', the B-side to the Skatalites' 'Guns of Navarone' (1964), was the first of numerous recordings to venerate Jamaica's new national hero.

With Jamaican music changing apace, the political scene also saw a significant shift. In 1965, Alexander Bustamante had a stroke that weakened his political power if not his position at the head of his party. While Bustamante remained leader of the JLP, Sir Donald Sangster took the position of Acting Prime Minister. Sangster went on to win the general election of 1967, only to die two months later of a brain haemorrhage. Within West Kingston, Edward Seaga's ethnographic work among the religious cultures of the area was standing him in good stead, deepening his understanding of his constituents and leading him to a position where he could harness his understanding of the electorate for political gain. From this point onwards, Seaga was very much a JLP leader in waiting.

Occupying a dual role as both the district's MP and Minister of Development, Seaga began work redeveloping West Kingston, leading to the destruction of the Rasta encampment at Back o' Wall and its replacement with a newly built district that would become known as Tivoli Gardens. While the stated reason for the bulldozing of Back o' Wall was its lack of infrastructure and poor sanitation, the fact that it also contained a large Rastafarian commune sealed its fate, as there were considerable fears within Jamaica regarding the revolutionary potential of the new cult. Seaga himself denied that a fear of the Rastafari was his motivation, using his memoirs to characterize Back o' Wall as a '40-acre den of the most notorious criminals in Jamaica'.[30]

Irrespective of whether it was a commune or a nest of vipers, in managing the rebuilding of Tivoli Gardens as a more modern development, Seaga ensured that the required construction work was undertaken by JLP supporters, providing them with both valuable employment and a further reason to vote for Seaga in the future. Following the area's redevelopment, the entirety of the new housing stock was allocated exclusively to JLP supporters.[31] Again, Seaga denies that this was by design, claiming that the eventual domination of Tivoli Gardens by JLP-supporting residents was because those PNP supporters who previously resided in Back o' Wall did not wish to return and live in an area dominated by the JLP.

It is here in West Kingston that we see the beginnings of what would become known as 'garrison politics', where the granting of economic and other favours to constituents led to the creation of political fiefdoms where voters were expected to show their gratitude come election time. Whether by accident or design, Labourite activists soon made West Kingston a cold house for supporters of the PNP, and by the 1970s, Michael Manley, son of Norman Manley and his successor as party leader, began to refer to Tivoli Gardens as a one-party state.[32] Manley Jr had a point; Seaga reaped the benefits of JLP domination of West Kingston over successive decades, with an astonishing 99.6 per cent of voters selecting him as their preferred candidate in the general election of 1980. On his retirement from politics in 2005, Seaga's successor as party leader would also be given the Kingston Western constituency, and the circle would be completed when this new MP became prime minister of Jamaica in 2007. Kingston Western is the only Jamaican constituency not to have changed hands since independence and it remains a JLP seat until this day.[33]

Through the 1960s and '70s, other garrisons developed, as houses, jobs, contracts, land and cash were exchanged for political support. Party supporters used whatever means necessary, including violence, to maintain their privileges. Soon, the fiercely loyal local gangs who protected sound-system operators from the attention of troublemakers would also take on a political character as they gradually became aligned to either the JLP or PNP. In time, politicians would provide these gangs with firearms to ensure that their mutual grip on each constituency was maintained. The garrisons would eventually be fortified with improvised checkpoints manned by these foot soldiers. Many took on colloquial names derived from global trouble spots, such as Tel Aviv, Zimbabwe and Belfast, and all would take on a distinct colour coding, with PNP strongholds using orange and JLP strongholds using green within murals and graffiti.

At the dawn of the era of garrison politics, a speech by Seaga at an event to mark the centenary of the Morant Bay Rebellion served as an announcement of how things would work from hereon in. In response to unruly heckling, Seaga issued the following threat: 'If they think they are bad, I can bring the crowds of West Kingston. We can deal with you in any way at any time. It will be fire for fire, and blood for blood.'[34] Within a decade, each garrison would have a so-called 'Don' who controlled the neighbourhood, a term said to be derived from Martin Scorsese's *Godfather* films. In exchange for corralling political support, each Don would be free to conduct his business as he saw fit.

Running concurrently with the emergence of garrison politics was the development of a partially mythical figure who would have a significant impact on subsequent lyrical developments, namely the 'rude boy'. An anti-establishment and unemployed Jamaican ghetto youth, and often an economic émigré from the countryside, the figure of the rude boy quickly captured both the attention of Jamaica's emerging tabloid press and the imagination of musicians and ska fans in Jamaica and beyond.

Predecessors for the rude boys were Jamaican gangs that had formed in the 1940s and '50s, such the Phantom, Vikings, Spangler, Phoenix, Skill, Pigeon and Mau Mau.[35] By the 1960s, many of these gangs were aligned to either the PNP or JLP, with the Spanglers, who protected Duke Reid's sound-system operation, connected to the PNP, and the originally apolitical Phoenix gang soon becoming aligned with the JLP.[36] A line can also be drawn from the outlaw status of the rural Maroons (escapees from slavery who had taken to the mountains and forest of Jamaica) through to the emergence of the urban rude boys. Marx would have called the rude boys *lumpenproletariat*, dispossessed and never possessed. Syracuse University's Erin Mackie describes them as so:

> Kingston youths, descendants of those slaves, looking to get some of the goods back for themselves, follow the models of success handed down to them ... The rude boys in twentieth-century Kingston act like pirates for the same reasons that young men in the seventeenth and eighteenth centuries did: because it offers an available and potentially lucrative, if sometimes lethal, opportunity in a life with too few chances. They turn pirate because pirates eat better, are paid better, and pack more heat than legitimate workers.[37]

Following their emergence, Jamaica's music scene maintained a love–hate relationship with real and metaphorical rude boys. The central figure within the Wailers' 'Simmer Down' is a rude boy in all but name, and the message of the song is clear: the rude boys should modify their behaviour. Another early use of the phrase is on the B-side of Eric Morris's 'What a Man Doeth', an instrumental titled 'Rude Boy' and credited to Duke Reid's Group, aka the Skatalites, with Roland Alphonso's saxophone appearing prominently. On 'Rude Boy', a Studio One A-side by the Wailers from 1965, the rude boy is characterized as wanting what he cannot get and getting what he does not want. Released in the following year were 'Don't Be a Rude Boy' by the Rulers, 'Rude Boy Charlie' by Charlie Organaire, 'Rude Boy Gone to Jail' by Desmond Baker and the Clarendonians, 'Let Him Go (Rude Boy Get Jail)' by the Wailers and 'Rock Fort Rude Boy' by Karl Walker. Quickly following these were Desmond Dekker's 'Rude Boy Train', Prince Buster All Stars' 'Rude Boy Rude', Little Grant and Eddie's 'Rudy's Dead' and perhaps the most famous of the rude-boy tracks of the 1960s, '007 (Shanty Town)' by Desmond Dekker and the Aces.

Released in 1967 and mixing up imagery from James Bond films and 1960's *Ocean's 11*, '007' was Dekker's response to reports of political violence following a student demonstration:

> The students had a demonstration and it went all the way around to Four Shore Road [*sic*] and down to Shanty Town. You got wildlife and thing like that because it down near the beach. And the higher ones wanted to bulldoze the whole thing down and do their own thing and the students said no way. And it just get out of control . . . Is just a typical riot 'cause I say – 'Them a loot, them a shoot, them a wail'.[38]

'007 (Shanty Town)' also demonstrated that Jamaican music had undergone significant change. By now, the frenetic tempo of ska had dropped significantly, and a different musical style was emerging in the new-found aural space between the beats. Rocksteady was the name used for this comparatively languid form, with legend having it that the drop in tempo was determined by the demands of the unusually hot summer in Jamaica in 1966. This is apocryphal, though, as data provided by the West Indies Meteorological Service for 1966 shows that temperatures in Jamaica in the summer of that year were only slightly above normal, and certainly not as high as some have suggested.[39] Rather than the climate, a far more likely influence on the musical development of rocksteady was the sound of the electric bass guitar, newly imported from the United States and played in a different style, with brass then taking a step back within a newly expanded stereo picture that replaced mono recordings.

The new sound can be heard on Lloyd Williams's 'Rocksteady People' (the first single to use the phrase, and one played and recorded at a noticeably sedate pace), Hopeton Lewis's 'Take It Easy', Alton Ellis's 'Rocksteady' and on Derrick Morgan's 'Tougher Than Tough', a rude-boy anthem. While the Lloyd Williams, Hopeton Lewis and Alton Ellis tracks are lyrically light, 'Tougher Than Tough' is far darker in theme. On the Derrick Morgan track, a piano figure is accompanied by a prominent bass guitar, not yet dominant but heading in that direction. Lyrically, the song is very much typical rude-boy fayre. With rudies in court, a series of defendants are asked by the presiding judge to account for themselves, and their response is that they are fearless in the face of justice. On a later rudie track, 'Johnny (Too) Bad' by the Slickers, a lilting organ introduces the melody and accompanies the tale of a ratchet-blade-wielding protagonist seen as the author of his eventual, inevitable demise. French journalist Thibault Ehrengardt has 'Johnny (Too) Bad' as depicting the life of Trevor 'Batman' Wilson (brother of the singer Delroy Wilson), a protégé and protector of producer Bunny Lee.[40] The weapon makes further appearances on 'Ratchet Knife' by Amiel Moodie and the Dandemites and 'Drop the Ratchet' by Stranger Cole and the Conquerors. In other songs, the preferred weapon is the pistol, as on Jackie Edwards's softly sung 'Johnny Gunman', 'Blam Blam Fever' by the Valentines, 'Guns Fever' by Baba Brooks, 'Gunmen Coming to Town' by the Heptones and 'Guns Town' by Clancy Eccles.

In many of the rude-boy recordings of the 1960s, young men meet their demise on the streets or in jail, with a rash of songs featuring court appearances. Lee Perry and the Sensations' 'Don't Blame the Children' begins with the spoken words of a defence barrister, making a plea for mercy based on the suggestion that society is responsible for the actions of his defendant. On one release of 'Don't Blame the Children', the song is paired with 'Set Them Free' on its B-side, where the analogy is continued with a prominent spoken-word dialogue between the same barrister ('Lord Defend') and judge. Here, the barrister pleads that the sentence of five hundred years is unfair; the defendants are uneducated, from a poor background and forced to rob by unemployment. On 'Court Dismiss', another spoken-word number, this time by Derrick Morgan, the 'rough, tough' rude boy is found guilty and taken away to jail. On Honey Boy Martin and the Voices' 'Dreader Than Dread', the spoken-word narrator is the rude boy himself, and when he finds himself sentenced to 1,000 years in jail, he is confident that he will win his appeal and that the judge will be forced to pay for his punitive sentencing. On Prince Buster's 'Judge Dread', the narrator is 'Judge 1,000 years', otherwise known as 'Judge Dread', who sentences the 'rough and tough' defendants on trial. When one of the defendants, voiced by Lee Perry, talks back to the judge, he is given an additional four hundred years as a punishment.

From this moment onwards, Jamaican music maintained an ambivalent relationship with the figure of the rude boy, part fascination, part horror, as some praised the rudies and others condemned them. On 'Tougher Than Tough', Derrick Morgan was lauding the rude boys as 'strong like lion', while the Wailers, who had originally instructed the rude boys to 'simmer down', became so enamoured with Jamaica's new-found outlaws that they briefly styled themselves as the Wailing Rudeboys. On their track 'Jailhouse', released in 1966, the rude boy is presented as being wise in his judgement and a future ruler of Jamaica, with the political system seen as unable to deal with him. At the other end of the spectrum, the Valentines' 'Stop the Violence' criticizes the rudies for beating and stealing from their fellow ghetto dwellers, and equally clear in its condemnation is Alton Ellis's rocksteady classic 'Dancecrasher', which attacks those rudies who break up dances, encouraging them instead to get fit 'like Mr Bunny Grant', a Jamaican boxing champion.

Skinhead Moonstomp: Reggae in England

While Coxsone Dodd and Duke Reid had considerable success in Jamaica, the label that is most associated with the rocksteady era is an English one. Trojan Records was formed in London in 1962 by Chris Blackwell and Jamaican-born Lee Gopthal, who had emigrated to London in 1952 after his father, Sikarum, had boarded the *Empire Windrush* for her maiden voyage from Jamaica to Tilbury Docks, transporting Jamaicans who had responded to job adverts and who paid £28 to travel.

Sikarum Gopthal was a 28-year-old Indian-Jamaican emigrating to take up work as a mechanic, and giving his future address as the International Club, East Croydon. Within a few years, he had retrained as a tailor and set up a shop in Kilburn, north London. In November 1952, Gopthal sent for his thirteen-year-old son Lee. While Sikarum returned to Jamaica in 1960, his son remained in Kilburn, working as an accountant and occupying a flat above the premises that his father had previously occupied. Eventually, Lee Gopthal advertised for a tenant for the basement below the shop, and received a response from a Sonny Roberts, who made use of the subterranean nature of the accommodation to build what was at the time Britain's only Black-owned recording studio.[41]

At this point, Britain had several independent music labels, including Melodisc Records, established in 1946 and specializing in importing jazz, blues and R&B as well as music from Africa and Jamaica, with founder Emil Shalit believing that he could develop and supply music to niche markets quicker than the corporate major labels. In 1960, Shalit set up Blue Beat, and such was the popularity of subsequent releases among the emerging cognoscenti of English youth culture that the label's name came to be synonymous with Jamaican blues and ska. A Blue Beat night at London's famous Marquee Club became popular, and Blue Beat releases were played at soul clubs elsewhere, including at the influential Twisted Wheel in Manchester. In an interview in 1964, the music journalist Siggy Jackson introduced the label to the public:

the blue beat rhythm itself was started by Prince Buster. He had been singing in Kingston for a while, then he invented this new rhythm. His success since then has been phenomenal. He has packed halls in Brixton and his 'Madness' has sold over 120,000 copies. That's our best seller that's top of our own little chart. Other good discs for us are 'Carolina' by the Folkes Brothers and our new one 'Tom Hark Goes Blue Beat'. Although Buster invented the blue beat rhythm, I invented the name for our label.[42]

By 1962, Chris Blackwell had relocated from Jamaica to London to try and increase the profile of Island Records, aiming to cherry pick the very best Jamaican releases and obtain the necessary permission to sell them in the UK. In the autumn of 1962, Lee Gopthal's first tentative steps into the music industry were boosted when Blackwell's partner, David Betteridge, called Gopthal to state that Blackwell wished to inspect his premises with a view to renting the empty ground-floor shop.

Having formed Island Records UK, Blackwell set himself up downstairs from Gopthal and flitted between Jamaica and Kilburn, cutting deals to sell Jamaican recordings in the UK. Gradually drawing his London landlord into his business, Blackwell suggested that Gopthal might be interested in starting a mail-order company to sell vinyl pressed by Island Records. Gopthal proposed putting together a network of agents instead, who would sell records door-to-door to Jamaican customers across London, eventually forming Beat & Commercial Records, or B&C, to distribute Blackwell's product. While this was still a niche business that would not yet trouble the major record labels, the seeds of future developments were sown. But the problem for Blackwell and Gopthal was that it was all very well to license records for sale door-to-door, but to hit it big, an independent record label would require the distribution clout of a major label to make an impact on the charts. This was Chris Blackwell's route to market when he found himself sitting on a smash hit with Millie Small's 'My Boy Lollipop'. A deal cut by Blackwell with Fontana, a subsidiary of the Dutch giant Phillips, meant that the emerging label boss had the distribution channels to ensure that the release was widely stocked throughout the UK. The result was that 'My Boy Lollipop' reached number two in the UK sales chart in March 1964. Having witnessed Chris Blackwell's success, Gopthal relinquished his career as an accountant to open a record shop off Kilburn High Road, selling releases licensed and pressed by Blackwell. Eventually, Gopthal expanded to develop a chain of shops known as Musicland, while Blackwell grew his record wholesaling business, with David Betteridge as marketing manager.

Both Island Records and B&C quickly outgrew their Kilburn base, leading to Gopthal, Blackwell and Betteridge renting in nearby Harlesden. By now working full time as a record distributor and having a decent knowledge of Jamaican music, Gopthal took a leaf out of Blackwell's book and began to approach Jamaican producers, enquiring about the possibility of licensing recordings to B&C Records. The end result was UK releases for products that originated in the studios of Coxsone Dodd and Duke Reid, with Gopthal using the label names Studio One, Coxsone and Tabernacle for releases produced by Dodd, and Treasure Isle and Trojan for music purchased from Reid. The first release on the newly formed Trojan imprint was 'Judge Sympathy' in July 1967, credited to Duke Reid but performed by the Freedom Singers.[43]

With Chris Blackwell at the helm of Island Records and Lee Gopthal managing B&C, both parties began to see how shared interests and co-working might enable them to counter the sharp business practices of wily Jamaican producers, who would often attempt to sell the same recording on an exclusive basis to both

POSITIVE VIBRATIONS

Island and B&C. Working surreptitiously, Island Records and B&C would counter this by informing each other whenever they were approached by a Jamaican producer, ensuring that neither was put in the position of outbidding the other. Finding that the partnership was increasingly beneficial, Gopthal and Blackwell eventually formed Trojan Records Ltd in a 50/50 business deal, with the earlier Trojan label folded into the new firm.

Initially, the new partnership worked a dream – Blackwell's connections in Jamaica meant that Trojan got the best music, while B&C's retail outlets ensured that UK releases found their way to market. If a release threatened to break out of the Jamaican community and go mainstream, distribution would shift to the established nationwide retail chains. At times, Trojan would press so-called 'white-labels', releases that often bore few artist details, selling them to emerging English selectors – reggae DJs – and sound-system operators. If the recording broke through, more would be pressed for release under the Trojan Records brand or a sub-label. This would become a tried-and-tested method of marketing and audience development from this point onwards, particularly for music popular in nightclubs.

Trojan continued the practice of developing sub-labels for individual producers or artists, with Harry J used for Harry Johnson's productions, Song Bird for productions by Derrick Harriott, and Upsetter for the work of Lee Perry. As well as releasing Jamaican productions, Trojan began to work with artists based in the UK, most notably Jamaican-born Dandy Livingstone (Robert Thompson), who was given his own Down Town label, and the Rudies, another Jamaican act later renamed as Greyhound following a move to London and a change in personnel. But whether on Treasure Isle, Harry J, Song Bird, Upsetter or Down Town, these were all Trojan releases, the only difference being the different paper labels printed by Gopthal and shipped to pressing plants for fixing onto each record prior to their eventual distribution.[44]

60

Although Trojan Records was now working as a full partnership between Blackwell's Island and Gopthal's B&C, the label remained prey to the old practice of Jamaican producers playing UK licensees off against each other. In particular, Trojan Records competed with Pama, a London-based record company formed to release U.S. soul music, but which by 1967 was releasing ska and rocksteady. At times, Trojan would purchase a recording and arrange for a pressing, but would end up shelving the records if they became aware that the track had just been released by Pama. At other times, both companies released recordings of the same song, as happened in 1972 with 'Lively Up Yourself' by Bob Marley and the Wailers. Such were the perils of dealing with Jamaican producers.

Having developed a successful business, Gopthal continued to stimulate demand among the burgeoning youth culture of the swinging sixties. One way of doing this was to purchase advertising slots on Radio Caroline and Radio London, both pirate radio stations based on small shipping vessels anchored in the North Sea. The strategy paid off with a big hit: Desmond Dekker's '007 (Shanty Town)' released on Graeme Goodall's Pyramid label, in which Gopthal had invested. Further offshore radio play for the likes of Baba Brooks's 'Girl Town Ska' and the Skatalites' 'Guns of Navarone' saw ska and rocksteady begin to become popular not merely with Londoners of Jamaican origin but also among Britain's latest and much-feared youth cult, the skinheads. Thus began an intriguing relationship between Jamaican music and a youth subculture that would come to be seen by many as irredeemably racist and right wing, but which in the 1960s was a trailblazer for a new form of multiculturalism, with white working-class men adopting Jamaican musical and sartorial styles. Eventually, the Trojan label became synonymous with both the Jamaican pop music of the 1960s and the English skinheads who listened to it.

The origin of the skinheads was in the 'mod' movement that had emerged out of the coffee-house culture of the beatniks. Once mod became more popular around 1964, internal friction began to emerge between the elitism of the original mods, whose love of expensive clothes and the accoutrements of their subculture required a certain level of income, and those newcomers who could not afford the extravagant lifestyles of their forebears. By 1966, the tensions between elitism and popularism saw mods split two ways: 'smooth' mods grew longer hair and leaned towards the paisley patterns of the swinging sixties, while the 'hard' mods cut their hair short and began to focus less on European tailoring and more on an eclectic mix of American and British workwear, particularly button-down shirts, denim jeans and work boots. In 1968 the split was complete, with the skinheads becoming a mass working-class movement.

Like all of the youth subcultures of the 1960s and '70s, the skinheads required their own form of music, and it was here that Jamaican rocksteady and the first hints of reggae came into their own. The appeal was not immediately obvious to outsiders, but to the skinheads, Jamaican rude boys embodied an insouciance that they could emulate, while rocksteady and early reggae contained more than enough rhythm to keep them rocking on the dance floor. There was also more than a hint of violence attached to the rude-boy ethos, deepening the attraction for a rough and tough English youth culture.

While B&C Records was formed to sell music to Jamaican migrants, it would be the skinheads who bought Trojan recordings in bulk. Unlike the Windrush generation, who most often purchased their records in small independent outlets or direct from door-to-door salesmen, the skinheads were more likely to buy their music from one of the 6,000 or so 'chart-return' shops that sent sales figures through to the British Market Research Bureau, who developed the first official UK chart from February 1969 onwards.

As a result, the most quintessential of skinhead reggae tracks, the Hammond-organ driven 'Liquidator' by the Harry J All Stars, spent twenty weeks in the UK charts through the summer and autumn of 1969. The track was so popular with skinheads that from that moment onwards it would be used as the walk-out music at their west London haunt, Chelsea's Stamford Bridge football ground.

A year later, the skinhead love affair with Trojan Records reached its apogee with the release of the album *Skinhead Moonstomp* by Symarip, a UK-based act formed by Jamaican migrants. With a title track based on Derrick Morgan's 'Moon Hop' (about the Apollo 11 Moon landing of July 1969), the album also contains 'Skinhead Girl', 'Skinhead Jamboree' and a rocksteady cover of Nancy Sinatra's 'These Boots Are Made for Walking'. The album became an instant hit and has been re-released on numerous occasions since. On most releases, the album features a distinctive cover, not of the band, as might be expected, but of five English skinheads in denim jackets, jeans and work boots.

Such was the financial draw of a licensing deal with Trojan that several Jamaican artists were lured from the island to record in London. This was not entirely successful, either financially or artistically. Many artists moved from Jamaica to the UK once they had tasted chart success, only to find themselves homesick and cut adrift from the cultural currents that led them to produce music that was of interest to the English market in the first place.

Having had their fingers burned, Trojan then considered how they could refine Jamaican releases, making them more appealing to a broader section of English youth. With this in mind, the label began to take Jamaican recordings and overdub them with orchestral strings and soul-style brass recorded in London. However, the use of overdubs split the by now sizeable Trojan fanbase, with some seeing them as smoothing out the rougher edges of Jamaican recordings that they prized. In a set of unique ironies, just at the point where the skinheads were developing a reputation as racist nationalists, they were also rejecting Trojan's attempts to anglicize Jamaican-recorded reggae even if, paradoxically, one of the styles that was being mimicked was Black American soul music, the skinheads' other great musical love.

This is not to say that the use of overdubs was not, on occasion, commercially successful. The Pioneers' first UK hit was the Leslie Kong-produced 'Long Shot Kick de Bucket', concerning an unsuccessful Jamaican racehorse put out of its misery at the Caymanas Park racecourse near Kingston, with the track using a rhythm originally heard on an earlier unsuccessful single by the band entitled 'Long Shot (Bust Me Bet)', which was produced by Joe Gibbs and arranged by Lee Perry, with the rhythm then featuring on 'People Funny Boy' by Perry himself, considered by many to be the first reggae record. 'People Funny Boy' was a thinly veiled attack on studio boss Joe Gibbs, who Perry accused of not paying him for his services. While Perry complained of being underpaid by Gibbs, the boot was on the other foot when Perry made the move from recording artist to producer himself, with the Wailers grumbling at their meagre payslips and Max Romeo accusing Perry of refusing to pay him royalties for his *War ina Babylon* album.

'Long Shot Kick de Bucket' reached number 21 in the UK charts in October 1969 and it was only after this release that Trojan came up with the idea of overdubs. For their long-awaited follow-up, the Pioneers recorded the Jimmy Cliff number 'Let Your Yeah Be Yeah', with the rhythm track laid down at Byron Lee's Dynamic Sounds studio in Kingston and the vocals and strings added at a session in a studio in Chalk Farm, north London. The song reached number five in the UK singles chart in July 1971, at least partially vindicating Trojan's approach. In between the two Pioneers' hits, string and/or brass overdubs were added to Bob Andy and Marcia Griffiths's cover version of Nina Simone's 'Young, Gifted and Black', Nicky

Thomas's 'Love of the Common People' and Greyhound's 'Black and White', all of which reached the top ten.

But were the overdubs needed for chart success? Not necessarily. Trojan's first number one was Dave and Ansel Collins's 'Double Barrel' (released on the label's Techniques imprint), an uncompromising number without strings that hit the top of the charts in May 1971. The only thing added to the master tapes were the vocals of Dave Barker, who did not meet Collins until after the record's release. Barker's vocals were delivered in the new deejay style popular in the Jamaican dancehalls, giving the track an improvised feel (in the UK, the term 'toasting' is generally used to describe this vocal style). Perhaps unwittingly, Trojan had stumbled upon a production technique that would soon come to dominate much of Jamaican music in subsequent decades.

In terms of cultural impact, the biggest of the Trojan releases would be 'Young, Gifted and Black', which became an anthem for the sons and daughters of the Windrush generation, situated culturally somewhere between the Jamaica of their parents (which the majority of the second generation had never fully experienced) and the UK of their white peers. Here, the use of brass and strings helped to ensure that the song broke out of the confines of the emerging reggae form and had an appeal beyond skinheads and rudies. Trojan's approach to the augmentation of Jamaican recordings did not necessarily make them inauthentic, but there was certainly a time and place, and the times were changing, for back in Jamaica reggae was turning away from its pop side and beginning to encompass the dread and anger of the Rastafari.

3

'BETTER MUST COME': ROOTS REGGAE AND THE POLITICS OF JAMAICA IN THE 1970S

Joe Gibbs and the Professionals, *State of Emergency* (1976)

Tell you the truth, any political party in Jamaica would love our support, and they might not come fe it just like that, but it come sometime. But the beauty about it, we don't support it. See what we figure outta politics, all we see outta politics what happen in Jamaica is that a lot of youths, youths that can't even vote, die. And we know that a folly-tician never know you until it is either you can throw a stone fe him or you can dip your finger. 'Caw him no business about your personal life. Maybe you sick, maybe you want to see a doctor, but him

don't care about that, him want a vote. After that, anything
happen to you, great. So me no defend politics.

BOB MARLEY[1]

> One little bwoy come blow im horn
> an me look pon im wid scorn
> an me realize how me five bwoy-picni
> was a victim of de trick
> dem call partisan politricks

MICHAEL SMITH[2]

Their words are corruption, and where there's corruption, there
must be an eruption. Ya no see? Politricks! Politicians been
promising the most good but doing the most dangerous evil.
And all the people get is promises.

PETER TOSH[3]

B y the start of the 1970s, rocksteady had morphed into the
organ-driven shuffle of reggae, named after the Maytals' 'Do
the Reggay' (1968). Following this, the tempo of Jamaican
music fell dramatically with Rasta themes becoming increasingly
evident. To distinguish itself from the fast-paced sound of the previous decade, the new style of the 1970s would come to be known
as roots reggae. Despite the Rastafari rejecting much mainstream
political ideology, both the People's National Party (PNP) and the
Jamaica Labour Party (JLP) began to use the new form in their
campaigning. By this time, Hugh Shearer had replaced Donald
Sangster as JLP party leader and prime minister, while the retirement
of Norman Manley shortly before his death in 1969 precipitated a
leadership election in the PNP that was eventually won by his son
Michael, who had entered politics in his twenties and who won the
seat of Kingston Central at the 1967 general election.

With both the JLP and PNP adapting to life under new leaders, attention turned to the next general election, scheduled for spring 1972. Under Michael Manley, the PNP twinned their traditional anti-colonial rhetoric with musical references, employing the memorable catchphrase 'look deh now' from the Ethiopians' 'Everything Crash' (1968) to highlight brewing social unrest. The song references a series of strikes by police officers, firefighters, water engineers and telephone workers that collectively rocked Jamaica's economy in 1968, before warning that, in the future, 'everything crash'. The track was banned by the Shearer-led JLP government, providing a fillip for the opposition.[4] At the same time, the JLP also began courting the Rastas and circulated photographs of party members standing next to Selassie during his 1966 visit to the island.[5]

To complement the increased electoral interest in the Rastafari, emerging reggae musicians began to record explicitly political tracks, with Max Romeo recording 'Labor Wrong' and 'Ginalship' as direct attacks on the JLP. By this point, Michael Manley had come to draw heavily on the nickname of Joshua, originally given to him when he led an industrial dispute in the 1960s. Coincidentally, or perhaps not, the name Joshua was also highly prized by the Rastafari for its biblical reference to the leader of the Israelites following the death of Moses. Like Joshua, would Manley lead the Rastas to the Promised Land? Junior Byles thought so, and promptly recorded 'Joshua's Desire' as a tribute to Manley. And if Manley was Joshua, who was the Rastas' oppressor; who was the pharaoh? Despite being named in honour of Alexander Bustamante, the founder of the JLP, Prince Buster pointed the finger at Hugh Shearer in a cover version of 'Everything Crash', accusing Shearer of being the Pharaoh, while Junior Byles recorded 'Pharaoh Hiding' as a nursery-rhyme attack on the sitting prime minister.[6]

Along with Max Romeo's 'Let the Power Fall on I', it was Delroy Wilson's 'Better Must Come', produced by Bunny Lee and a number-one hit in Jamaica in 1971, that would soundtrack the PNP's election campaigning. Both tracks turn a narrator's desire for personal advancement into a political rallying cry, and following their release Michael Manley constructed an elaborate reading of the lyrics:

> When a man sings 'Better Must Come' he means no sedition, he means no violence. He only means that he is suffering and looking forward to a better day. 'Let the Power Fall on I' means every man who can't find a job and goes and sees others with opportunity and privilege, and who says if there is a God, 'Let the Power Fall on I.' It means every woman who says 'me find some way to send my child to school in a way that I would like.' 'The Rod of Correction' says that a man looks around and realizes that graft and corruption abound and henchmen grow rich, and that it takes a rod of correction to bring justice, then justice must come. When Junior Byles sings 'Beat Down Babylon' he is not talking about the police. The police are honest people with a job to do. 'Beat Down Babylon' says: remove oppression, oppression in Babylon, and let justice rise in the land.[7]

Whether Junior Byles agreed with Michael Manley's analysis is moot, but Max Romeo subsequently commented on the use of 'Let the Power Fall on I' by saying: 'It wasn't intended to be a protest song, but Michael Manley heard it and thought it would be a good slogan for the party and I said yeah, go ahead. He was a good man. There was a lot of suffering in Jamaica and he was aware of it.'[8]

Elsewhere, the PNP's use of the Wailers' track 'Small Axe' turned a Rasta-driven critique of the music industry into an attack on the JLP government (the song was originally seen as an attack on Coxsone Dodd, Ken Khouri and Byron Lee), while the same party's adoption of Peter Tosh's 'Them a, fi Get a Beaten' accurately predicted the election outcome.[9] Thibault Ehrengardt has the JLP employing a Peter Tosh soundalike to record a pro-JLP version of the song,[10] with a B-side consisting of a reworked 'Beat Down Babylon' that took aim at 'the comrade man' of Manley, hinting at what would later become an explicit accusation: that Manley was turning communist. All these songs, from 'Let the Power Fall on I' to 'Better Must Come' and 'Beat Down Babylon', were banned from radio play by a state nervous of the potential role that radio might perform in determining the election outcome.[11]

During this period, the PNP's Beverley Anderson approached Clancy Eccles, a stalwart socialist, to organize a national tour that was to feature Dennis Alcapone, Ken Boothe, Junior Byles, Inner Circle, Max Romeo, the Chosen Few, the Wailers and Delroy Wilson.[12] The plan was for Jamaica's leading artists to play at a series of free or low-cost concerts, dubbed a 'caravan of stars', in an attempt to harness the anger at the government's banning of their music from radio play. Many were suspicious of the PNP's motives and Bunny Livingston of the Wailers only agreed to play once he had been promised a fee of JA$150 per show.[13] Others, though, were supporters of the PNP, with Clancy Eccles explaining his own personal motivation:

> I have a belief in socialism, because capitalism, one set get rich while one set get poor, and if it was divided equally, half would be rich and half would be poor ... I believe that the distribution of wealth of the world should be given to everyone equally for their amount of work.[14]

Each gig on the tour was to be filmed by the up-and-coming director Perry Henzell, who would come to international attention with *The Harder They Come*, filmed in the election year of 1972.

A fictionalized depiction of the musical Wild West of the Jamaican recording industry of the time, *The Harder They Come* revolves around the character of Ivanhoe 'Ivan' Martin, a young rude-boy singer played by Jimmy Cliff. In search of work, Martin moves from the country to the city, where he meets a record producer who offers him a pitiful $20 for his song, the film's title track, written and recorded by Jimmy Cliff. Henzell initially envisaged that Cliff's role in the film would be limited to recording the soundtrack, but the producer eventually asked Chris Blackwell to approach Cliff to find out whether he was interested in playing the main character (Blackwell had been introduced to Cliff by Edward Seaga at the 1964 World Fair in New York).[15] Henzell's fictional record producer eventually wins the signature of the young singer and puts him in a recording studio, with these scenes filmed at Dynamic Sounds in Kingston. Following this, Cliff's character turns from hero to anti-hero, becoming a marijuana dealer and cop killer while on the run from the police. The unnamed record producer eventually releases 'The Harder They Come' on the back of Martin's notoriety, who at the end of the film is killed by the police in a one-sided duel.

In addition to being a generic rude boy, Jimmy Cliff's character was also based on Vincent 'Ivanhoe' Martin, known as Rhyging, a Jamaican gangland figure who became a popular anti-hero after representing himself in a trial in 1946 before escaping from prison. While on the run, Rhyging committed a series of violent robberies and murders, taunting his pursuers in a series of open letters.[16] Mike Thelwell, who wrote the novelized version of *The Harder They Come*, describes Rhyging as 'a supernatural figure, who stole from the rich and represented the frustrations, aspirations, and resentments of the poor, black working class'.[17]

Jimmy Cliff was an Island Records artist, and the success of the film inspired Chris Blackwell to turn away from his increasing interest in English prog rock and return to Jamaica. In October 1972, Island and B&C ended their partnership amid what were described as 'policy differences', with B&C taking full control of Trojan Records and Island Records focusing on the development of album-length artists.[18] While at Island, Jimmy Cliff was marketed as a serious artist working in an entirely different *oeuvre* from Trojan's pop-oriented releases.

By this time, there was a sharp polarization between the string-laden pop releases of Trojan and the angrier sounds coming out of Jamaica, but the latter was not necessarily to the liking of Jimmy Cliff, who was not keen on Blackwell's vision of him as a roots-reggae rebel, and who left Island Records for EMI as a result.[19] Continuing to be inspired by *The Harder They Come*, Blackwell began the search for a new signing, alighting on the Wailers as the act that he would make into international stars. The label boss and the vocal trio were not strangers. Blackwell had already licensed more than a dozen Wailers recordings for sale in the UK, but when Brent Clarke, a freelance promoter in London, approached Blackwell to see if he could help rescue the band from a tour of secondary schools in the English Midlands, Blackwell began to consider the impact that he might have with Bob Marley, Bunny Livingston and Peter Tosh. Explaining the appeal of Marley in particular, Blackwell said:

> He came in right at the time when in my head there was this idea that this rebel type of character could really emerge. And that I could break such an artist. I was dealing with rock music, which was really rebel music. I felt that would really be the way to break Jamaican music. But you needed somebody who could be that image. When Bob walked in, he really was that image, the real one that Jimmy had created in the movie.[20]

Blackwell and the Wailers agreed on an advance of £4,000 and the band flew back to Jamaica for sessions in Dynamic Sounds. Notably, only Marley, Livingston and Tosh were signatories to the contract, with touring and studio mainstays such as bassist Aston 'Family Man' Barrett and his drumming brother Carlton frozen out of the deal.[21] Around the same time, there was another visitor to the studio, as Michael Manley was joined by Clancy Eccles on 'Power for the People', a spoken-word speech set to a lilting reggae beat.

'Let the Power Fall on I':
The 1972 Election and the Rise of Michael Manley

With many of the leading reggae musicians on board the PNP's campaign, not least because they were being paid for their services, the scene was set for both reggae and the Rastafari to play significant parts in the forthcoming general election. If anything, it was Michael Manley's use of the image of a 'Rod of Correction' that electrified the campaign. The rod itself was a walking stick reportedly given to Manley by Haile Selassie during a formal visit to Ethiopia by Manley and his PNP colleague P. J. Patterson. Patterson was another PNP politician with a bright future, who rose to prominence in a by-election in 1969 when he used 'Young, Gifted and Black' as his campaign slogan.[22] Manley's rod was given its symbolic name by Claudius Henry, a Rasta who in 1960 had been charged with treason and sentenced to ten years' imprisonment with hard labour.[23] Within Proverbs 22:15, King Solomon recommends the use of a 'rod of correction' to punish children for foolishness, and beyond that, photographs were in circulation in Jamaica of Ethiopian priests carrying sticks, enhancing the aura of Manley's cane.

Within a year of it being presented to him, Manley started to make a connection between his rod and the lyrics of Junior Byles's

'Beat Down Babylon', with the latter's promise to whip wicked men. Seizing upon this idea, Clancy Eccles, whose 'Freedom' had been used by the JLP in the referendum campaign of 1961, was commissioned by the PNP to write a song, and 'Rod of Correction' (1971) was quickly pressed into political service at rallies and party functions. In the song, two biblical metaphors are conflated, with a mention of Lot's wife turning to salt as she looks back at the burning city of Sodom placed alongside a reference to the stick brandished by Moses to part the sea, allowing the Israelites to escape and drowning the Egyptian army. It soon became clear to listeners that the pharaohs of the Egyptian army were the JLP, and it was Manley who was attempting to part an electoral ocean. Accompanying 'Rod of Correction' on the campaign trail was another number that the PNP commissioned from Eccles, 'Power to the People', used alongside 'Let the Power Fall on I' to dramatic effect. Responding in opposition to Eccles was the lesser-known Billy Gentiles singing 'Take the Rod Off from Our Backs' over Max Romeo's rhythm, blaming 'Joshua' for Jamaican poverty.[24]

Under the ownership of Michael Manley, the rod of correction came to be used metaphorically as part of a promise to rid the country of JLP corruption, its supposedly magical powers containing a cure for economic ills. At political rallies, Michael Manley would begin by saying 'The Word Is Love', while the rod would be placed in a box, centre stage, waiting for Manley to fall silent and lift it in dramatic fashion. One witness described how 'he wouldn't say anything at all . . . he didn't have to. The crowds would just go wild.'[25] Edward Seaga was outraged. As a former researcher into the folk religions of West Kingston, it might have been expected that it would have been he who would employ such mystical imagery, not Manley. As the JLP's rising star, Seaga's response was to commission a series of newspaper advertisements that questioned the providence of Manley's rod, with one featuring a photograph of Seaga with a similar stick, and Seaga claiming: 'I have it now!'[26] The *Daily Gleaner*, which at the time was owned by a former chairman of the JLP, ran a piece on how Manley had dropped the rod and that it was now in Seaga's possession.[27] At a rally in West Kingston, Seaga declared that Manley was now 'a shepherd without his staff – a Joshua without his rod – and a leader without power'.[28] Manley responded with a claim that he had been burgled by those looking for the rod.[29] Manley's use of the rod is depicted in Winston Scotland's 'Power Skank', with Manley depicted as Joshua, 'a lion who will devour you'.

As well as being the source of useful imagery, the Rastafari were an increasingly important part of the electorate, particularly in the poorer constituencies. In her work on Jamaican politics in the 1970s, one of sociologist Anita Waters's respondents states that by the 1972 election, the Rastafari had 'to some degree taken over the urban *lumpen* areas',[30] while another, a campaign manager for the PNP, noted that the numbers of Rastafari had swelled and that:

> a lot of middle-class kids became Rastas. It is also true that by that time, their image had improved. Many were into art, doing creative things. Their language was gaining currency amongst the middle classes and school children. We had the feeling that Rasta talk was understood across the country.[31]

The reappraisal of the Rastafari was not limited to the PNP and Waters notes a JLP election candidate as saying, 'I respected the Rasta thing. They have a very proud, positive attitude toward blackness.'[32]

The election of 2 March 1972 resulted in a landslide PNP victory, with the party gaining 37 parliamentary seats and the JLP falling to its lowest vote share since 1955. The JLP's attempt to use music to capture a greater electoral share had ended in failure, and leader-in-waiting Edward Seaga eventually admitted that 'there was no positive, attractive slogan or song for the JLP 1972 campaign, both essential for effective campaigning.'[33] No sooner had Michael Manley won the election for the PNP than he lifted the ban on political recordings, enabling Jamaica's two radio stations to play Ken Lazarus's 'Hail the Man' (1972), penned by Ernie Smith in celebration of the victory of 'Joshua', while Clancy Eccles released 'Halilujah [*sic*] Free at Last', to celebrate the PNP victory.[34]

During the period of its early development, the faith of the Rastafari had been largely criminalized, with Leonard Howell jailed for sedition and his Pinnacle commune raided on numerous occasions before the police forced out the few remaining residents in 1958. In the years following the general election of 1972, Michael Manley and his government began to develop a more liberal policy towards the Rastafari, resulting in the PNP gaining some support among the faithful. Following the JLP's defeat, Hugh Shearer stood down as leader, making way for Edward Seaga. Both Manley and Seaga were populist in their approach, and both set out to appeal to the instincts of the electorate, as Manley attempted to pit the populace against Jamaica's elite while Seaga began to whip up anti-communist sentiment by accusing Manley of flirting with political extremism.

Changes were also afoot at Island Records. The Wailers had emerged from their sessions at Dynamic Sounds with a set of tracks that would form the bedrock of their inaugural album for Island, 1973's *Catch a Fire*. Before the final mix, Chris Blackwell exerted his authority on the master tapes, insisting that the band add new instrumentation to the original recordings to make the music more appealing to rock audiences. The Wailers were despatched to Island Records' Basing Street Studios in west London, with famed Muscle Shoals guitarist Wayne Perkins drafted in to overdub guitar licks on top of the Jamaican recordings. At Basing Street, the music's tempo was increased on Blackwell's request, and further additional guitar, slide guitar, clavinet, electric piano and keyboards added, although it is said that Bob Marley supervised each overdub.[35] While Blackwell's vision was of a roots-reggae rebel, the sound of the Wailers would need to be fleshed out to make it more palatable to rock audiences outside of Jamaica. In the UK at least, reggae was seen as a form of pop music that was very different to the serious progressive rock of the era, and by this time, Trojan was heading towards bankruptcy as its hits dried up. However, there was a swan song: Ken Boothe's astonishing number one 'Everything I Own', a cover version of a ballad by the American rock band Bread, recorded at Federal Records and a UK number one in 1974.

With the decline in popularity of Trojan-style reggae in the UK, the time was ripe for Island to seize the moment with their release of *Catch a Fire*. This album is seen by many as beginning the era of authentic roots reggae, even though the album contains a series of recordings whose fidelity is moot, with a mid-Atlantic sound somewhere between Jamaica and the UK. Meanwhile, Trojan would steal a march on Island Records by releasing the Wailers' *African Herbsman*, a compilation of tracks recorded in Jamaica and licensed for release in the UK. In a supreme irony, here was an overdub-free Trojan album seen as more authentic than the competition. It would take an appearance by the Wailers on the BBC's rock show *The Old Grey Whistle Test* to turn the situation around, suggesting to British audiences that reggae had both depth and soul – the elements perceived to be missing from Trojan's singles. A divide had opened up between the direction in which reggae had gone so far, as epitomized by the big Trojan hits, and the direction in which it would go, towards a political militancy and a rebel sensibility. Trojan Records folded shortly afterwards, although it has lived on under several guises since, with its back catalogue passed from pillar to post until it was sold by the Universal Music Group to BMG Rights Management in 2012.

Following the release of *Catch a Fire*, an Island-orchestrated press blitz raised the Wailers' profile outside of Jamaica, leading to concern from uptown Kingston that the best-known Jamaican was not a statesman but a Rasta who was attempting to bring about their downfall. Meanwhile, tensions within the Wailers boiled over as Peter Tosh and Bunny Livingston argued with Marley about money and refused to play at American 'freak clubs'. This latter attitude can be detected in 'Midnight Ravers', the album's closer, where the Wailers decry the position where you can no longer tell the difference between men and women.

With the Wailers constantly fighting, the band's follow-up album, *Burnin'* (1973), would be their last before they split. A support slot for Marvin Gaye in Kingston on 21 May 1974 was the band's final gig, where Marley met Don Taylor, who would go on to be his manager. Once Livingston and Tosh had departed, the band was rechristened as Bob Marley and the Wailers. The Barrett brothers remained with Marley, joined on backing vocals by the I Threes (Rita Marley, Judy Mowatt and Marcia Griffiths). Livingston blamed Chris Blackwell for the split, referring to him as 'Chris Whiteworst', and when he left the band he took as much of the Wailers' name with him as he could, referring to himself as Bunny Wailer from that moment onwards.

Buoyed by global success and back in love with Jamaican music, Blackwell remained on the island and attempted to replicate his success with the Wailers by signing Burning Spear, Third World, Inner Circle and Max Romeo. Burning Spear (Winston Rodney) was signed in the wake of the local success of his *Marcus Garvey* album, which Island then remixed for an international audience, much to the artist's annoyance.[36] Burning Spear promptly left Island for his own label, where he would have complete creative control, although subsequent releases were licensed to Island for international distribution.

Formed in 1973, Third World coalesced around the nucleus of Michael 'Ibo' Cooper and Stephen 'Cat' Coore, two former members of Inner Circle, the latter of whom was the son of the barrister David Coore, said to be Michael Manley's best friend and deputy prime minister from 1972 until 1978.[37] After signing to Island, the band toured before releasing their eponymous debut *Third World* (1976), the first of five albums recorded for Island before the band moved to the American giant cbs. Once Cooper and Coore had split from Inner Circle, the latter band reformed around the nucleus of brothers Ian and Roger Lewis, who recruited Jacob Miller as lead vocalist before signing to Island in 1978. Miller was killed in a car accident in 1980, leading the band to split up, although they reformed in 1986 with the Lewis brothers employing Calton Coffie on vocal duties.

Max Romeo is as well known as Third World or Inner Circle for a body of work, although Romeo's career alighted on Blackwell's Island empire for only two albums. *War ina Babylon* (1976) arrived at just the right time to have significance, soundtracking the politics of Jamaica as it began to destabilize. Backing Romeo in the studio were the Upsetters, with the album produced by Lee Perry. Romeo was to shift to Island's Mango sub-label for the less successful follow-up, *Reconstruction* (1977), but he soon fell out with Chris Blackwell concerning the perennial issue of intellectual property rights. In an interview with the Jamaican press in early 2019, Romeo was asked what Blackwell could do to make it up to him for concentrating so much of his attention on promoting Bob Marley to the detriment of other acts. Romeo responded:

What Chris Blackwell could do for Max Romeo is give him a statement for the sales of *War Ina Babylon*. And let him have some money instead of coming with this story that I was stupid to sign a contract [as a] 'writer for hire.' Even a seven-year-old kid would know that a 'writer for hire' contract don't cut it. And he used that over my head from 1976 until today. That I was just merely a 'writer for hire.' So Island Records owns the whole product.[38]

Away from the machinations of the music industry, in January 1976 Michael Manley continued to reach out to the Rasta electorate, telling the *Daily Gleaner* that it was wrong for the security forces to persecute those with dreadlocks.[39] Following dialogue between Manley and both the Jah Rastafari Hola Coptic Church and the Centralizing Committee of the Rastafarian Selassie I Divine Theocratic Government,[40] some Rastas viewed their faith as having at least something in common with Manley's Afrocentric democratic socialism, but this was not a universal view among Rasta musicians.[41] Although Max Romeo had written 'Press Along Joshua', 'Joshua Row the Boat Ashore', 'Joshua Gwan' and 'Socialism Is Love' to express support for Manley, he eventually penned 'No, Joshua, No' (1974), accusing Manley of canvassing for support from the Rastafari at election time, only to abandon them once victory was assured. Romeo described his thinking as:

> Hey, you say you wanted us to vote PNP. Now we've voted PNP there's nothing happening. So I did the song 'No Joshua No'. He [Manley] summoned me to Jamaica House and said he had a cut of that song three times on one cassette playing in his car and that's what inspired him to do all the social programmes that he brought in.[42]

Joining Romeo in criticism of Manley's government was Junior Byles with 'When Will Better Come?' and Bob Andy with 'Fire

Burning'. In an interview, Andy stated that his opposition to Manley was because the politician had adopted a Moses-like persona but had failed to live up to his promises.[43]

Before the 1972 election, rumours swirled that the PNP had promised to legalize cannabis, and while this was not actually the case, the perceived lack of action by the PNP government damaged them in the eyes of the Rastafari.[44] More broadly, whether it was wise for Manley to vow that 'Better Must Come' is questionable. Economic and social change was always going to be slow in the making, although Manley advised the electorate that he was putting multinational corporations 'under heavy manners', employing an evocative turn of phrase also used as the title of two recordings in the mid-1970s by Derrick Morgan and Prince Far I.[45] Also in circulation at the time was Lord Laro's 'Foreign Press', the B-side to 'Budget Debate' (1976), a calypso-inflected number with a spoken-word introduction that accused Jamaica's press of focusing on the ephemeral and exaggerating the negative aspects of life under the PNP.

Whereas the 1972 election was seen as 'joyous', 'warm' and a 'carnival', by 1976 rude-boy garrison politics had returned to the fore, made more lethal by an influx of firearms into Jamaica.[46] The change in mood from hope to fear was heralded by Max Romeo, with the apocalyptic 'War ina Babylon' capturing the moment on a track that sat at the centre of Romeo's album of the same name. In the opening track, the title 'One Step Forward' is followed by the lyric 'two steps backward' and the track goes on to criticize what the narrator perceives as Manley's craven attitude to Uncle Sam. Also making an impact was Junior Murvin's 'Police and Thieves', backed by the Upsetters and produced by Lee Perry in his Black Ark studio, which warns the nation of the repercussions of gang war. Meanwhile Leroy Smart's 'Ballistic Affair', recorded at Channel One, called on ghetto youth to throw away their guns and knives and unite as one.

Following a dramatic increase in ghetto violence, Manley claimed political sabotage, declaring that sinister forces were destabilizing Jamaica in the hope of overthrowing the democratically elected PNP government. An upsurge in gun violence led to 130 killings in the first six months of 1976, while the discovery of a significant cache of arms and a series of unexplained fires led to alarm.[47] In June 1976 the Governor-General declared a state of emergency, with Manley stating that he had received a warning from the security forces of a planned escalation of violence.[48]

The state of emergency was to last twelve months as 593 Jamaicans were detained without charge, with some interned for many months.[49] This included a significant number of senior JLP figures such as Pearnel Charles, the JLP Deputy Leader; Peter Whittingham, a former Jamaica Defence Force officer and the JLP candidate for East Central St Catherine;[50] and Olivia 'Babsy' Grange, who would go on to become a minister in all subsequent JLP governments (she remains a cabinet minister today).[51] The PNP claimed that the violence had started in Edward Seaga's West Kingston constituency and that swift action had stopped the overthrow of Jamaica's elected government, with JLP gunmen now said to be under heavy manners. Naturally, Seaga denied this.

When Whittingham was detained, Manley stated that he had been arrested in possession of a briefcase containing documents demonstrating that figures within the JLP had taken up arms against the PNP.[52] The JLP countered with the suggestion that the state of emergency was a transparent attempt by Manley to manipulate the outcome of the forthcoming election, scheduled for 1977. In his memoirs, Seaga acknowledges the violence that led up to the state of emergency but claims that it was instigated by the PNP.[53] Manley subsequently referred to this allegation as 'the most disgraceful single case of political and journalistic dishonesty that I have witnessed in my long years in public life'.[54] With political tension at an all-time high, reggae performed its usual role as clarion, with the release of records by Jah Baba and Joe Gibbs and the Professionals, both with the title 'State of Emergency', alongside Burning Spear's 'No More War' and Bob Marley and the Wailers' 'War'.

Under Heavy Manners: The 1976 General Election

In December 1976, Bob Marley headlined a large-scale musical event that was to have significant political ramifications within Jamaica. The origins of the event, which became known as the Smile Jamaica concert, are wrapped up in competing narratives. Bob Marley's manager Don Taylor and Colin Grant, biographer of the Wailers, both claim it was Marley's idea, while others such as Timothy White, another biographer, state that the idea only came to fruition after a group of PNP 'bad men' visited Marley and persuaded him to perform at a concert 'for the people'.[55] Putting flesh on the bones of this narrative, White claims that in October 1976 Marley received a delegation of PNP heavies at his Hope Road residence who were eager to ask him whether he was a democratic socialist or merely a 'hip dread capitalist'. If Marley was the former, would he be prepared to play a free concert 'for the people' on the lawn of Jamaica House, the prime minister's official residence?[56] Rita Marley's memoirs support this view, saying that the PNP government had approached her husband to bring stability to the country, saying 'Bob, it's only you who can say it through your music. Let us have a concert.'[57] Chris Salewicz, another Marley biographer, claims that Marley only agreed to the concert because he was in political debt to the PNP's Anthony Spaulding, the minister for housing and MP for Trench Town, who had set up Rita Marley and the couple's children in a new home in Bull Bay, with Bob Marley then living a partially separate existence at Hope Road.[58]

Irrespective of whether the planned concert was Bob Marley's idea or that of the PNP, the singer was clearly enamoured with the idea of a large-scale event that not only would unite the politically affiliated gangsters that he remained friends with, but which might also unite the divided Rastafarian movement along with the rest of Jamaica. At the time, 56 Hope Road was a hangout for both PNP- and JLP-affiliated rude boys, including Claudie Massop, Edward Seaga's chief enforcer and the leading JLP Don and leader of the Shower Posse gang of West Kingston, and Aston 'Bucky Marshall' Thompson of the Spanglers Posse, based in the PNP stronghold of Arnett Gardens in Trench Town, along with Milton 'Red Tony' Welsh, a PNP-aligned fixer for Anthony Spaulding. Nicknamed 'Concrete Jungle', Arnett Gardens was built by the PNP in 1972, with Spaulding using the Tivoli Gardens garrison as his template. The building of Arnett Gardens meant that Spaulding had up to 40,000 new homes at his disposal, allowing him to build up a fiefdom to the immediate north of Seaga's powerbase.[59]

One of the PNP enforcers in Arnett Gardens was Winston 'Burry Boy' Blake, Michael Manley's personal bodyguard, who accompanied the PM on an official government trip to Cuba in 1975 and who was on the receiving end of several government contracts. When Blake was shot dead in March 1975, Manley led the mourners as the funeral cortège was shot at as it passed Tivoli Gardens on its way to May Pen Cemetery.[60] Gang researcher Laurie Gunst claims that Manley's prominent role in the funeral was in acknowledgement of an incident when Manley and his wife, Beverley Anderson, were shot at by a JLP gunman. Reports suggest that Blake threw Manley and Anderson to the ground just in time to save their lives.[61] When Manley resigned as prime minister and leader of the PNP, after having served another term in high office from 1989 to 1992, he admitted that his biggest political error was attending the funeral of Blake, acknowledging that it sent out the wrong message regarding his views on political violence.[62]

Manley's involvement with Winston Blake came at a time when the politically aligned gangs of Jamaica were increasing their grip on their respective territories. In Tivoli Gardens, the Shower Posse had gained considerable control over the neighbourhood. It is said that there are two etymological origins of the gang's name. One is that they were named after a speech reputed to have been given by Edward Seaga in West Kingston, where Seaga promised that 'blessings will shower from the sky and money going jingle in your pockets'.[63] The second purported origin is more prosaic in nature, with the observation that the group were prepared to shower their victims with automatic gunfire.[64]

All the different versions of how the Smile Jamaica concert came about are united in one aspect: that Marley was keen to use the opportunity to try to bring peace between the two competing blocs in Jamaica's gang war. By the time of the public announcement of the gig, plans for the event had snowballed. Marley had agreed to fund what would be the largest free musical event ever seen in Jamaica, billed as 'a concert presented by Bob Marley in association with the Cultural Department of the Government of Jamaica' and relocated away from the partisan site of Jamaica House to the National Heroes Park, site of the grave of Marcus Garvey. Don Taylor organized a press conference to unveil the event, but shortly after 5 December was announced as the date of the concert, the PNP government announced that the general election would be held only ten days later, on 15 December, rather than in February of the following year as was originally planned. Bob Marley's initial enthusiasm gave way to anger at what the concert had become, a PNP promotional tool designed to gain them votes at the ballot box. If Marley was displeased, the JLP gunmen who had befriended the singer were furious, and if reports are correct,

Marley received several death threats following the announcement of the event. Don Taylor also has Marley being visited by the CIA, who warned him of the repercussions of continuing with the concert.[65]

Fearful of an impending attack on Marley, an armed cadre of PNP vigilantes named the Echo Squad began to keep guard at Hope Road, but on 3 December 1976, they had mysteriously disappeared as a number of armed men in two cars entered the premises. The British music journalist Vivien Goldman was an eyewitness to the events and describes three intruders, one of whom 'brandished two automatics like he was Jimmy Cliff in *The Harder They Come*'.[66] Rita Marley was shot in the head and Don Taylor was seriously wounded after being shot numerous times. Bob Marley was lucky to escape with only superficial wounds from a bullet that had grazed his chest before entering his arm, with the bullet remaining there until his death.[67]

With Rita Marley staying in hospital to have a bullet removed from her skull, Bob Marley was whisked away to a hideout in the Blue Mountains while Chris Blackwell chartered a private jet and fled the island. The concert began on time the following day, but with Marley and his band absent. Eventually, Anthony Spaulding visited the singer in his refuge and persuaded him that it was safe to go ahead with the concert, although some of Marley's fearful band refused to take to the stage while Rita Marley performed in her hospital gown. During the band's performance, Michael Manley joined Marley on stage uninvited, shaking his hand before the singer addressed the crowd, stating: 'when me decided to do dis yere concert two anna 'alf months ago, me was told dere was no politics. I jus' wanted ta play fe da love of da people.'[68] The following day, Marley left Jamaica, and while he did eventually return to the island, notably for another political concert in 1978, he had, in effect, gone into self-imposed exile, in fear for his life.

In the days after the shooting, the PNP alleged that the incident was political and involved the JLP, claiming that the situation presented Jamaica with a choice between 'violence or heavy manners'.[69] The JLP responded with the claim that the Smile Jamaica concert was an example of naked political opportunism on the part of the PNP.

Carnage followed the attempted assassination of Marley. In televised interviews, the singer claimed that he soon became aware of the identity of the protagonists. Don Taylor said the same, stating that the motives of those responsible were partly political and partly revenge for the erroneous perception that Marley was involved in a horse-race-fixing scam at Caymanas Park that had gone badly wrong. In explaining what happened to the alleged assassins, Taylor went on to tell a New York court that 'they were hanged. I saw them hung.' A lawyer for Danny Sims, Marley's former music publisher, then asked Taylor: 'the government of Jamaica hung them?', to which Marley's manager responded: 'No, our friends down in the ghetto tried them and hung them.'[70] Later, Taylor would explain that after the shooting, he and Marley were driven by Earl 'Tek Life' Wadley, a JLP enforcer and a fixture at Hope Road, to a gully at which a kangaroo court tried three men, who confessed to being CIA (U.S. Central Intelligence Agency) agents before two were hanged and the third was shot. Taylor recounts: 'I still recall how the ghetto generals offered the gun to Bob before shooting the last victim. They turned to him and said, "Skip, yuh waan shoot the blood claat here?" I sat and watched as Bob refused, showing no emotion whatsoever.'[71]

Don Taylor claims that after the shooting, Michael Manley visited Bob Marley in London to inform him that it was a joint plot by the JLP and CIA to kill him, a view that was widespread at the time.[72] Whether true or not, allegations of JLP involvement in an attempted assassination of Marley damaged Edward Seaga, who was consistent in denying JLP involvement, most recently in a Netflix documentary film shot shortly before his death in 2019.

In the years following the shooting at Hope Road, Marley seems to have confided in others that the attack was led by a man he subsequently met, Lester 'Jim Brown' Coke, who was Claudie Massop's second in command and who was identified by several eyewitnesses as being one of the gang members, although Coke was not among the men that Don Taylor claimed to have seen hanged in retribution.[73] In 1983, in response to a request under the U.S. Freedom of Information Act, the U.S. state released a four-paragraph wire on the attempt on Marley's life, which concluded with:

> Rumors abound as to the motivation for the shooting. Some see the incident as an attempt by JLP gunmen to halt the concert which would feature the 'politically progressive' music of Marley and other reggae stars. Others see it as a deep-laid plot to credit a progressive, youthful Jamaica martyr – to the benefit of the PNP.[74]

Irrespective of who the protagonists were, the shooting of Bob Marley, Rita Marley and Don Taylor electrified the last ten days of political campaigning before the general election. As in 1972, this was a vote soundtracked by reggae, with many artists playing on the clear enmity between Michael Manley and Edward Seaga. For the PNP, Neville Martin used the chorus of his single 'The Message' to report that 'my leader born ya'. By omission, the listener was left to conclude that Edward Seaga was not 'born ya' (Seaga was born in Boston, Massachusetts). Seaga responded that while he could not help his place of birth, he had given up his American citizenship to serve Jamaica.[75] Elsewhere in the song, Neville Martin draws attention to PNP policies on land reform, free education, equal pay for women and a minimum wage. JLP activists responded with the claim that the song was, in effect, racist.[76] The PNP also used Pluto Shervington's similar track, 'I Man Born Ya', to ram home the message, even if Shervington's song was less explicit and, in all possibility, not concerned with either Manley's or Seaga's place of birth. It is claimed that following the release of his song, Shervington was forced to relocate to Florida due to threats on his life, although he says himself that this narrative is overplayed.[77] The JLP countered the PNP's use of 'The Message' and 'I Man Born Ya' with 'Turn Dem Back' and 'Jump and Shout' by the JLP Deputy Leader Pearnel Charles, along with the Ethiopians' 'Promises' and Ernie Smith's 'Jah Kingdom Gone to Waste'.[78] In a later twist, in 2017, the JLP co-opted 'The Message' and used it against Shane Alexis, a Canadian-born PNP election candidate who faced questions about his citizenship.[79]

What the furore over both 'The Message' and 'I Man Born Ya' ignored was that, irrespective of which leader was in charge, the legacy of slavery meant that a pale-skinned elite ruled over a majority Black population. The phrase 'pigmentocracy' is often used to describe Jamaica's ethno-class relations, even though the phrase was originally coined to describe the apartheid policy of the South African state from 1948 onwards. While Manley and Seaga quarrelled over who was more faithful to Jamaica, Rastas could not help but notice that both the JLP and PNP were led by mixed-heritage metropolitans educated at leading universities outside of Jamaica, and this presented yet another reason for roots-reggae musicians to remain above the fray and condemn 'politricks'.

By the time of the general election on 15 December 1976, the PNP's courting of a disenfranchised working class was a success and the PNP maintained their grip on power, winning 47 out of 60 parliamentary seats on a broadly similar vote share to 1972. But no sooner had the PNP won the election than the political tide began to turn away from them. From this point onwards, the JLP argued successfully that the PNP's stewardship of the economy was increasingly inept.

Like most left-leaning governments of the 1970s, nationalization formed a central policy plank for the PNP, along with state investment in housing and education. Meanwhile, the JLP had turned from being a traditional party of unionized labour into something quite different: a party that maintained an orientation towards the working class of Jamaica (it had no choice if it was ever to win an election), but also one that adopted the rhetoric of the emerging 'new right', specifically the notion that economic liberalism would bring freedom. In contrast to the JLP's new emphasis on macroeconomic theory, the PNP government became increasingly focused on foreign policy, supporting liberation struggles in Africa.

The new Afrocentric mood of the PNP was replicated within reggae. In 1975, Count Ossie and the Mystic Revelation of Rastafari released their second album, *Tales of Mozambique*, and a year later the Jah Wally Stars released the single 'Mozambique', with the flip side 'Frelimo' namechecking the Frente de Libertação de Moçambique (Mozambique Liberation Front), a nationalist liberation movement turned Marxist–Leninist political party. Following this, Channel One's the Revolutionaries, featuring the noted rhythm section of Sly Dunbar and Robbie Shakespeare, co-opted the melody from the Beatles' 'Norwegian Wood' on 'Angola' (1976), while Pablo Moses recorded 'We Should Be in Angola' and Joe Gibbs released 'Angola Crisis', based on his version of Alton Ellis's 'I'm Still in Love with You'. Reggae also turned to the issue of Rhodesia, where a predominantly white government had issued a unilateral declaration of independence in a move designed to thwart majority Black rule. A number of recordings were designed to shine a light on the situation, including tracks by Bob Marley and the Wailers, the Soul Syndicates, the Rebels, Big Youth and Alton Ellis. Meanwhile, Peter Tosh's album *Equal Rights* took a swipe at South African apartheid, while 'Namibia' by Liberation Group focused on South Africa's illegal occupation of its neighbour to the west. In 1976 Tappa Zukie released his album *MPLA*, named after the Movimento Popular de Libertação de Angola, which fought a war of independence against the Portuguese army from 1961 until 1974 and formed one side in a civil war fought from 1975 onwards. Demonstrating that Jamaican internationalism of the 1970s was not all PNP-led, Tapper Zukie (David Sinclair) was a former PNP supporter who had turned to the JLP. As a teenager, Zukie had worked on the mic at PNP events before Bunny Lee and Sinclair's mother packed him off to London to keep him out of trouble, with the deejay only returning to Jamaica as an adult.[80]

Although Rasta-led roots reggae welcomed the PNP's new focus on Africa, the picture was more complicated where Ethiopia was concerned. In September 1961, Haile Selassie had attended a Conference of the Heads of State of Government of Non-Aligned Countries in Belgrade, Yugoslavia, now considered to be the founding conference of the Non-Aligned Movement in which Michael Manley positioned Jamaica. Within less than fifteen years, Selassie was dead, most likely killed by the Marxist regime of 'the Derg', more formally the Coordinating Committee of the Armed Forces, Police and Territorial Army, a group of low-ranking Ethiopian Army officers who overthrew Selassie and abolished the monarchy. The new Ethiopian regime received significant military aid from the Soviet Union, North Korea and Cuba, while Fidel Castro attempted to seize control of the Non-Aligned Movement and shift it leftwards, with some support from Michael Manley. Sensing the importance of the move, the JLP began to suggest that the PNP had turned communist. Naturally, this view alienated those Rastas who were aware that their deity had met his demise at the hands of the Cuban-funded Derg.

Stuck in the middle of this debate was Bob Marley. Born in the JLP stronghold of St Ann's, but raised from the age of twelve in the mixed neighbourhood of Trench Town, Marley was seen initially as being broadly left wing, however Gayle McGarrity, a professor at Florida Atlantic University and a former friend of Marley, argues that Marley moved steadily rightwards as the 1970s progressed. In particular, McGarrity argues that Marley was swept up in Seaga's anti-communist rhetoric, partly due to the influence of the Jamaican high society that the singer now lived in, and especially due to the role played by his extra-marital muse Cindy Breakspeare, a staunch supporter of the JLP.[81] An expert on relations between Jamaica and Cuba, McGarrity suggests that the shift in Marley's politics can be measured by his changing views on Cuba:

> By the time I went to Cuba it was already known, the role of the Cuban military in supporting the Ethiopian military. So I remember Bob saying that he used to think that Cuba was really a great place, and that they had eliminated capitalism, and blah blah blah, but they clearly were doing the Devil's work now, because they had this role in Ethiopia . . . He saw Communism as godless and that it was an 'ism' – you know, his whole thing about Rasta don't deal with ism.[82]

As well as alarming Bob Marley, the PNP's foreign policy also began to concern the U.S. establishment, exacerbated by the personal closeness of Michael Manley to Fidel Castro. The ire of the United States was also raised by a well-publicized speech in which Manley informed the electorate that 'Jamaica has no room for millionaires. If you want to be a millionaire, there are five flights a day to Miami.'[83] Manley issued a quick clarification that he was merely referring to those whose mission was 'the selfish desire to become a millionaire overnight' and who 'refused to regard themselves as part of the Jamaican society and owing an obligation of service like the rest of us'.[84] But it was too late and the press had a field day, with the *Daily Gleaner*, ever faithful in their support of the JLP, leading the charge. PNP activists countered allegations that Manley was drawn to communism with the suggestion that the CIA were responsible for attempts to overthrow the democratically elected PNP government.[85] At a constituency meeting in central Kingston, Manley was to say: 'I cannot prove in a court of law that the CIA is here. What I have said is that certain strange things are happening in Jamaica which we have not seen before.'[86]

In *Jamaica: Struggle in the Periphery*, Manley defines destabilization as a phenomenon where 'some source – or perhaps two sources in concert, one outside and one inside – set out to create a situation of instability and panic *by design* [Manley's emphasis]'.[87] While he does not specifically name the 'inside' and 'outside' parties, Manley was alleging that the JLP worked in concert with the CIA to destabilize Jamaica and so ensure that the electorate lost all faith in the PNP's ability to govern the island. In the 1980s, Philip Agee and John Stockwell, two former CIA officers who would go on to be vocal critics of the USA's covert operations abroad, corroborated Manley's claim.[88] Elsewhere in his memoir, Manley alleges that the CIA bankrolled the JLP in the late 1970s:

> making every allowance for what the JLP could raise from the local oligarchy and the overseas migrant population, it is simply not on the cards that they could have raised money by ordinary means to match the level of their expenditure. They obviously had a godfather or godfathers somewhere in the international system.[89]

Others have made similar allegations, with, for example, Kevin Edmonds of the University of Toronto alleging that the CIA shipped arms to JLP garrisons as part of a covert destabilization campaign.[90]

Seaga soon gained the nickname 'Edward CIAga', and the theme of CIA involvement in Jamaica quickly made its way on to vinyl. 'Rat Race' by Bob Marley and the Wailers suggests that 'Rasta no work for no CIA' while Jacob Miller's 'Roman Soldiers of Babylon' alleges that the CIA , 'coming from the North', were behind an influx of weapons that found their way into the hands of JLP activists, stating that Selassie will 'blow away' the CIA. Seaga went on to deny that the CIA was at work in Jamaica in the 1970s: 'If it was, it was well hidden.'[91] In the Netflix documentary *Who Shot the Sheriff?* Seaga was very careful with his words. Answering a question as to whether the CIA were involved in Jamaican affairs, he responded that *he* had never spoken to the CIA, leaving open the possibility that others in the JLP had.

Although the PNP won the 1976 election, there was little time for euphoria as wave after wave of economic crises hit Jamaica. A foreign exchange crisis led Manley to seek the support of the U.S.-dominated International Monetary Fund (IMF), leading to wage and pension controls. But this move failed as growth stalled, unemployment increased and government borrowing from overseas debt markets ballooned. Following the international oil crisis of 1972–4, the increased cost of imported oil was particularly deleterious to the Jamaican economy and led to unprecedented price increases. Tourism, seen as one of the few potential growth areas in the Jamaican economy, was now in decline. By the end of 1977, the IMF announced that the Jamaican government had failed to devalue the Jamaican currency by 40 per cent and had therefore not adhered to their side of a deal that had allegedly been struck in the previous year.

With the IMF insisting on the imposition of austerity measures, it was clear to all that the joy of Jamaican independence, only fifteen years earlier, had evaporated. Who could now say that Jamaica was truly independent when its economic policy was determined by the IMF? A further agreement with the IMF was drawn up in May 1978. Manley referred to this as 'one of the most savage packages ever imposed on any client government by the IMF'.[92] Reggae sat up and took notice, with 'IMF Rock' by the Revolutionaries and 'IMF' by Jah Lloyd.

The PNP was split on the issue of IMF involvement, while political violence continued, including allegations that the army and police were involved in political assassinations. In what became known as the Green Bay Massacre of January 1978, five activists from downtown Kingston were shot dead after they and seven other JLP gunmen were lured into an ambush by members of the Jamaica Defence Force (JDF) armed with pistols, rifles and machine guns. One of those killed was Glenroy Richards, an aspiring singer who had released the song 'Wicked Can't Run Away' only months earlier. The JLP cried PNP involvement in state murder, although a trial of ten soldiers collapsed due to insufficient evidence. The PNP national security minister Dudley Thompson was blunt in his assessment of the events: 'no angels died in Green Bay.'[93] John Holt had already warned what the JDF were capable of in his single 'Up Park Camp' (1974), referring to the army's headquarters as a place that schoolchildren are warned about. After the killings, reggae's response included Tappa Zukie's 'Green Bay Murder', Big Youth's 'Green Bay Killing', Jah Lloyd's 'Green Bay Incident' and 'Green Bay Incident' by Lord Sassafrass and Debra Keys.

It is said that the Green Bay Massacre influenced the emergence of a peace treaty between the warring JLP and PNP blocs, heralded within reggae by the spring 1978 release of 'Peace Treaty Special' by Jacob Miller, sung to the tune of 'When Johnny Comes Marching Home Again'. The truce led to one of the most celebrated events at the interface of reggae and Jamaican party politics, the One Love Peace Concert at the National Stadium in Kingston on 22 April 1978, headlined by Bob Marley and the Wailers and featuring Big

Youth, Dillinger, Beres Hammond, the Meditations, Althea and Donna, the Mighty Diamonds, Culture and Peter Tosh.

The peace treaty and concert were the work of Claudie Massop and his opposite number, Aston 'Bucky Marshall' Thompson, who had both been interned during the state of emergency. Upon their release in early 1977, Massop and Thompson agreed that guns would fall silent in the districts they controlled. Later that year, both parties requested the assistance of Vernon Carrington of the Twelve Tribes of Israel to intercede with Bob Marley and persuade him to return to Jamaica to headline a concert. With the vibes seeming to be good, Massop and Thompson headed to London with Milton 'Red Tony' Welsh and Earl 'Tek Life' Wadley to persuade Marley that it would be safe for him to return to the island. At the time, Marley was recording the album *Exodus* at Island's studios in Notting Hill. Upon this album's eventual release, Jamaican listeners were surprised to hear the lyric 'we know where we're going' within its title track. Whether by coincidence or not, this was one of Michael Manley's sayings from the general election of 1976, and its use by Marley was a dangerous move considering the attempt on his life only eighteen months earlier.

On the day of the concert, an early set by Jacob Miller set the tone, with Miller calling Massop, Thompson, Welsh and Wadley to the stage as he sung his 'Peace Treaty Special', praising the four gang leaders for their role in bringing about the truce.[94] While the concert was organized by Massop, Thompson, Wadley and Welsh, it was attended by both Michael Manley and Edward Seaga in a rare sign of cross-party unity. Third World's Stephen 'Cat' Moore sets the scene:

> We were surrounded by guns, all brand-new guns! Hundreds and hundreds of them, machine guns! And I took Mick Jagger down there and we were on the side of the stage. Manley

and Seaga were there, but they weren't in the first seats, they were in the second row for protection.[95]

After a full musical programme in front of an audience of over 30,000, Marley encouraged Manley and Seaga to the stage:

> Could we have over here on stage the presence of Mr Michael Manley and Mr Edward Seaga? I just want to shake hands and show the people that we're gonna make it right, we're going to unite, we're going to make it right … The moon is right over my head, and I give my love instead.[96]

In footage from the concert, a thunderclap breaks out as lightning strikes, but this was added afterwards for dramatic effect. Seaga took to the stage first and stood nervously directly behind Marley. Marley embraced Seaga and held him with his right arm around his back, and as Manley approached, Marley shook hands with the PM and embraced him with his left arm. With Marley now stood between the two political leaders, they shook hands awkwardly and held hands above Marley's head as the singer cried 'Love, prosperity, be with us all Jah, Rastafari, Selassie.' If the idea of a concert organized by a gangland elite being attended by the prime minister and leader of the opposition was not strange enough, a respondent of gang researcher Laurie Gunst makes a far more damning allegation: that the concert was used as a convenient cover for Seaga's men to import a shipment of guns into the country.[97]

Following the concert, calls for peace continued, from Althea and Donna's 'Make a Truce' and 'No More Fighting' to Johnny Clarke's 'Peace and Love in the Ghetto'. Even Coxsone Dodd got in on the act, adding additional percussion and bass to an old Delroy Wilson track 'Peace with Your Neighbour', while John Holt and George Nooks recorded versions of Little Roy's 'Tribal War', with Dillinger also recording a version with deejay talk-over vocals. In the end, so many would record versions of 'Tribal War' that it became a pan-reggae anthem.

Also prominent at the time was Tapper Zukie's *Peace in the Ghetto*. Zukie was one of Virgin Records' new signings and the album was used to launch the company's new Front Line imprint. Containing tracks such as 'Peace in the Arena' and 'Peace in the City', the album namechecked Bucky Marshall and Claudie Massop in a call for 'peace pon di corner'. By this point, Richard Branson's Virgin had already released Peter Tosh's *Legalize It* and *Equal Rights*, fleshing out Branson's vision of a British reggae imprint. Following these releases was a slew of albums by the likes of I-Roy, U-Roy and Prince Far I, all of whom were deejays who recorded half-sung, half-spoken vocals in the style popular in Jamaican dancehalls. Along with the deejays' collective efforts, Front Line also released a long list of roots-reggae albums by the likes of Sly Dunbar, Culture, the Mighty Diamonds and the Twinkle Brothers. Zukie's *MPLA* had already gained popularity among the London punk cognoscenti, and, flushed with success, Zukie formed his own label, Stars, and released a further nine albums in the 1970s, including *Tapper Roots* for Front Line. For a brief moment, it looked like Front Line might rival Island Records, but Branson soon tired of reggae and ended up folding his label.

With Virgin closing their Front Line operation, the stage was clear for Island Records to continue as the premier Anglo-Jamaican record label, with a roster that included Bob Marley and the Wailers, Bunny Wailer (who had made his peace with Blackwell), Inner Circle, Third World, the Revolutionaries, Burning Spear, Black Uhuru and England's Steel Pulse. By 1979 it was Black Uhuru who were the leading contenders. Originally called Uhuru, Swahili for 'freedom', the band had gained international attention with their single 'Shine Eye Gal', featuring Keith Richards on guitar, before the band signed to Island and released 1980's *Sinsemilla*, recorded at Channel One and featuring Sly and Robbie alongside Ansel Collins. *Sinsemilla* was followed by three further albums for Island: *Red* (which charted in the UK), *Chill Out* and *Anthem*. By the end of the band's tenure at Island, they had fallen out with the label over the latter's continuing insistence on remixing Jamaican recordings to cater for international tastes. While *Anthem* received the inaugural Grammy for best reggae album in 1985, seemingly vindicating the label's approach, the band remained dissatisfied. Following the success of *Anthem*, lead singer Michael Rose left to pursue a solo career, following which the band recruited Junior Reid as vocalist and left Island Records for RAS Records, a U.S.-based reggae-focused independent. Black Uhuru were originally lined up to be the next Wailers, uncompromisingly militant yet prepared to do what it would take to become international stars and spread the message of Jah, but it was not to be, and their career never regained the heights obtained with Island Records.

In February 1979 Claudie Massop, who had returned to Jamaica two months previously having accompanied Bob Marley on an international tour, was in a car that was stopped by the Jamaican Constabulary. Massop was killed in a hail of bullets. Newspaper reports stated that he was shot as many as forty times.[98] The JLP had claimed that a PNP-led death squad had been formed to assassinate official and unofficial JLP leaders, and for the JLP faithful the police killing of Massop was ample evidence of this. Edward Seaga referred to Massop as 'one of the most popular young men throughout the inner city and the music world' and claimed that his killing was 'a blatant act of state murder'.[99] Those close to Seaga also accused the PNP's Dudley Thompson of having set up Massop for assassination. Whether true or not, the truce inaugurated in 1978 broke down completely, and in May 1979 Aston Thompson was shot dead in a nightclub in Brooklyn, New York, possibly in reprisal for the killing of Massop. While Massop's reign over Tivoli Gardens had ended, he would soon be replaced at the head of the Shower Posse by Lester 'Jim Brown' Coke, a former bodyguard to Edward Seaga and the man that Bob Marley had told confidants had led the attempt on his life at Hope Road.[100] Few believed that Claudie Massop would have tried to assassinate his friend, but plenty believed that Lester Coke would have done so.

With both Claudie Massop and Bucky Marshall now dead, there was no let-up in Jamaica's political warfare. During the months leading to the next election, gun violence and arson attacks killed hundreds. Within the Kingston metropolitan area, murder became the leading cause of death and the ghettoes increasingly resembled a warzone.[101] Estimates suggest that as many as 1,000 were killed by political violence in the run-up to the general election of October 1980.[102] Both the PNP and JLP blamed each other for the violence, but irrespective of its origins, the violence played into the hands of the JLP, who were able to portray Jamaica as a society out of control.

In terms of policy and rhetoric, several issues remained in play, including continuing allegations of Soviet and Cuban involvement in Jamaican affairs as well as criticisms of the PNP's stewardship of an ailing economy. This was just at the point when globalization began to severely limit the opportunities for any Jamaican government to intervene in the economy. At the time, the PNP blamed the IMF for the state of the country while the JLP blamed the PNP, who they accused of being increasingly focused on international affairs to the neglect of economic issues in Jamaica. The PNP responded with the view that there were parallels between the state of Jamaica's economy and that of other countries. Reggae saw these parallels too. Released in 1979, *Survival* by Bob Marley and the Wailers has a distinctly international feel, with 'Zimbabwe' (written in

Shashamane, Ethiopia) and 'Africa Unite' melding newer struggles to traditional pan-Africanism. The album also features 'Ambush in the Night', where Marley speaks of how a 'brother' opened fire on him while politicians fought for power and bribed voters with guns and money. In the song, Marley only survives the attempt on his life due to protection from His Majesty. From the relative safety of London, Marley could afford to pen explicitly political tracks; however, the dangers for those closer to the ground in Jamaica were great. From this point on, the Rastafari would continue to chant down Babylon, but in traditional biblical terms as the era of explicitly political reggae drew to a close. Unsurprisingly, musicians were fearful of the repercussions of any further involvement in party political affairs.

Rastafarian Themes in the Roots Reggae of the 1970s

By the end of the 1970s, roots reggae had established itself as a stable genre, with a number of lyrical themes sitting at its centre. In particular, most roots recordings had a focus on sufferation, struggle and liberation, although the route to liberation was contested, specifically around whether a 'repatriation of the mind' and a spiritual liberation in Jamaica should take precedence over the struggle for physical repatriation to Africa. Either way, themes concerning both redemption and repatriation dominated roots reggae.

It was Marcus Garvey who had first introduced the notion that redemption would only be achieved when Africans had returned to Africa, saying that 'no one knows when the hour of Africa's Redemption cometh. It is in the wind. It is coming. One day, like a storm, it will be here.'[103] This millenarian aspect of Garveyism is represented in roots reggae, where adherents not only preach of the necessity of salvation and the struggle to obtain redemption, but speak of the inevitability of an apocalyptic end of times for Babylon. Here we see Garvey's role as a modern-day John the Baptist in full effect. In particular, Barry Chevannes of the University of the West Indies pointed to the role that Garveyite mythology played in the 1970s, with one of his respondents claiming that Garvey had said that 'anyone who passed through the seventies would be able to pass through anything.'[104] Whether Garvey made this prophecy is almost irrelevant; what matters is that many Rastafari believed it.

As 1977 approached, a myth intensified around the year 'when the sevens clash' and this is immortalized in Culture's celebrated album *Two Sevens Clash*. It is said that on 7 July 1977, when four sevens clashed, the streets of Jamaica were deserted.[105] The final verse of the album's title track outlines the origins of another aspect of the myth, dating from a period when Garvey served a sentence in Spanish Town Prison following a conviction for contempt of court for alleging that Jamaican judges took bribes. Garvey was said to have prophesied that once he left the jail, nobody else would enter, and this is faithfully represented in the album's title track. The titles of other songs on the album are also instructive in providing an insight into the Rasta worldview: 'Calling Rasta Far I', 'I'm Alone in the Wilderness', 'Pirate Days', 'I'm Not Ashamed', 'Get Ready to Ride the Lion to Zion', 'Black Starliner Must Come', 'Jah Pretty Face', 'See Them a Come' and the final track of the album, 'Natty Dread Taking Over'.

In addition to generalized themes of struggle, repatriation and liberation, specific themes of Africa, Zion and Ethiopia permeate much of the roots reggae of the era. The Four Gees's 'Ethiopia', an early example from 1967, uses the melody of *Strawberry Fields Forever* by the Beatles, only here it is Ethiopia that the narrator wishes to return to. In many subsequent recordings, Zion is used interchangeably with Ethiopia and Africa to refer to the Promised Land of the Rastafari. Early examples include Clancy Eccles's 'Mount Zion'

(1969), the Westmorlites' 'Zion' (1970), Junior Byles's 'A Place Called Africa' (1970) and 'Deliver Us to Africa' (1971), and 'Back to Africa' (1971) by Alton Ellis. Later in the 1970s, Cedric Brooks's yearning 'Ethiopia' (1976) is light on lyrics, but the theme is clear and repeated on Prince Francis's deejay talk-over version of the track. Horace Andy's 'Children of Israel' (1974), Dennis Brown's 'Children of Israel' (1978), Aswad's 'Back to Africa' (1976) and Junior Delgado's 'Sons of Slaves' (1977) all make the same point, with the latter saying that enslaved Africans were the children of Israel and they should have the right to return to their Promised Land. If a Rasta is not in Ethiopia or Zion, he must be in Babylon, as Big Youth's 'Dread in a Babylon' (1973) makes clear. According to roots reggae, Jamaicans of African descent should either adhere to Johnny Clarke's injunction to 'Move Out of Babylon, Rastaman' (1974) or, if this is not possible, they should 'Beat Down Babylon', as Junior Byles sang in 1971.

Naturally, a further theme of much roots reggae in the 1970s was the ancestry and wisdom of Haile Selassie, which for the Rastafari remained undimmed by his passing in 1975. In the former category are references to Selassie's claimed lineage from David and Solomon, including Derrick Harriott's 'Solomon & Selassie' (1976), Junior Murvin's 'Solomon' (1977) and Rod Taylor's 'Ethiopian Kings' (1978). In the latter category are references to Selassie's role as a statesman and leader, with the most prominent being Bob Marley and the Wailers' 'War' on *Rastaman Vibration*. The lyrics of 'War' are based on a translation of a speech delivered by Selassie in Amharic to the United Nations in 1963 and published in 1972 with the injunction that the speech could be reproduced freely without prior permission. In his speech, Selassie declares that

> until the philosophy which holds one race superior and another
> inferior is finally and permanently discredited and abandoned;
> That until there are no longer first-class and second-class

citizens of any nation; That until the color of a man's skin is of no more significance than the color of his eyes; That until the basic human rights are equally guaranteed to all without regard to race; That until that day, the dream of lasting peace and world citizenship and the rule of international morality will remain but a fleeting illusion, to be pursued but never attained; And until the ignoble and unhappy regimes that hold our brothers in Angola in Mozambique and in South Africa in subhuman bondage have been toppled and destroyed; Until bigotry and prejudice and malicious and inhuman self-interest have been replaced by understanding and tolerance and good-will; Until all Africans stand and speak as free beings, equal in the eyes of all men, as they are in the eyes of Heaven; Until that day, the African continent will not know peace.[106]

Bob Marley's version appended a pithier ending to that originally provided by Selassie, observing that 'until that day – war'.

While the Rastafari debated whether they would be able to achieve salvation in Jamaica or whether repatriation was a must, all were united in the view that the Bible sat at the centre of their theology, although particular significance was granted to both the Judaic Old Testament Psalms and the apocalyptic Revelation, as well as the *Kebra Nagast*, the 'lost Bible of the Rastafari', written in Ethiopia during the fourteenth century and telling the story of the relationship between King Solomon and the Queen of Sheba.

The best-known example of a track based on a Psalm remains 'Rivers of Babylon' by the Melodians, an almost instant reggae classic and one much covered by both devout and secular artists. The opening line of the song is close to a direct reading of the opening line of Psalms 137, King James Version, 'By the rivers of Babylon, there we sat down, yea, we wept, when we remembered Zion,' while the following lines are close to verses 3 and 4, 'For there they that carried us away captive required of us a song . . . How shall we sing the Lord's song in a strange land?' For the Rastafari, the strange land of exile was Jamaica. The song's bridge then adapts Psalms 19:14: 'Let the words of my mouth, and the meditation of my heart, be acceptable in thy sight, 'O, LORD, my strength, and my redeemer.'

If 'Rivers of Babylon' was a song based on a single Psalm, five years later Prince Far I would go one better with his debut album *Psalms for I*, in which the baritone-voiced deejay chanted nine sets of Psalmic verses over a range of rhythms played by the Aggrovators. In the same year, Lee Perry's 'Dreadlocks in Moonlight' used the analogy in Psalms 125:1 of the Lord's trust being 'as mount Zion', while 'Night Shift' by Bob Marley and the Wailers used 'The sun shall not smite thee by day, nor the moon by night' from Psalms 121 as its opening line. In the end, all three of the original Wailers would record tracks with lyrics based on the Psalms, including Peter Tosh's 'Arise Blackman' and Bunny Wailer's 'Psalms'.

If roots reggae's use of the Psalms demonstrates how the Rastafari incorporated Old Testament imagery into their worship of Jah, an examination of the use of the Book of Revelation in roots reggae explains the origins of much of the Rastafari's 'dread'. It was from Revelation that Selassie drew his symbolic names of 'King of Kings, Lord of Lords' and 'the Lion of the Tribe of Judah', and it is here where Babylon is finally punished for its wickedness and where there is a gathering of armies at the mythical location of Armageddon. On the Wailer's 'Rasta Man Chant', the narrator hears the angel with the seven seals, a reference to the symbolic seals that secured the book that John of Patmos saw in an apocalyptic vision in Revelation, where the opening of the seals marked the Second Coming of Christ. Later, Bunny Wailer's 'Armageddon' (1976) is another example of a reggae release containing imagery and themes from Revelation, including the notion of the gates of doom leading to a bottomless pit, drawing comparisons between contemporary wars and the final battlefield of Armageddon itself. Four years later, 'the bottomless pit' returned in 'Redemption Song' on Bob Marley's final studio album *Uprising*, only here it is a dungeon in a slave castle from which kidnapped Africans are plucked before being forced to make their transatlantic voyage. Meanwhile, Armageddon also appears in recordings by Augustus Pablo, Creation Rebel and Freddie McGregor.

Metaphors of war, be they contemporary conflicts in Babylon or more ancient biblical wars, are a running theme through much of the roots reggae of the 1970s, perhaps unsurprising considering that Jamaica was itself heading towards a dangerous conflagration. A further reason for the notion of conflict being so central to reggae in this period was the almost perpetual battle between the Jamaican state and the Rastafari regarding the latter's use of ganja (illegal in Jamaica from 1913 onwards) as a religious sacrament. Like so much else within their faith, ganja use is justified through reference to several specific verses within the Bible, including:

And the earth brought forth grass, *and* herb yielding seed after his kind, and the tree yielding fruit, whose seed *was* in itself, after his kind: and God saw that it *was* good (Genesis 1:12)

... thou shalt eat the herb of the field (Genesis 3:18)

... eat every herb of the land (Exodus 10:12)

Better *is* a dinner of herb where love is, than a stalled ox and hatred therewith (Proverbs 15:17).

He causeth the grass to grow for the cattle, and herb for the service of man (Psalms 104:14).

> In the midst of the street of it, and on either side of the river, *was there* the tree of life, which bare twelve *manner of* fruits, *and* yielded her fruit every month: and the leaves of the tree *were* for the healing of the nations (Revelation 22:2).

Such is the significance of ganja that Leonard Barrett Sr views the real centre of Rastafarian religiosity as being the 'revelatory dimensions' of 'the holy herb', rather than worship of Selassie.[107] Within roots reggae, ganja themes are numerous, but most focus on spiritual rather than recreational use, with Linval Thompson's 'I Love Marijuana' (1978) drawing a distinction between the Black man who cultivates and smokes ganja for meditative purposes and the white man whose usage is merely recreational. Of the secular approaches to ganja, Peter Tosh's 'Legalize It' (1975) is the best known. Originally banned in Jamaica, Tosh's track focuses on opposing the criminal status that possession of marijuana brings with it, while also pointing out its use across the class spectrum from musicians to doctors and nurses to lawyers and judges. Since 2015, possession of modest amounts of ganja goes unpunished in Jamaica and it is smoked openly, a significant step in the decriminalization of the Rastafari. Notably, it was a JLP government that initiated this move rather than the PNP, but not before moves to decriminalize cannabis in the United States had signalled its international acceptability.

One further aspect of the lifestyle of the Rastafari marked them as outlaws, namely their view that hair should be unshorn. Again, there are biblical justifications for the wearing of dreadlocks, with Numbers 6:5 warning that: 'All the days of the vow of his separation there shall no razor come upon his head: until the days be fulfilled, in the which he separateth *himself* unto the LORD, he shall be holy, *and* shall let the locks of the hair of his head grow.'

In addition to theological reasons, the wearing of locks was influenced by Ethiopian depictions of the mythical Lion of Judah, along with pictures of African warriors circulating in Jamaica in the 1940s, identified by some as Gallas, Somalis or Maasai,[108] and by others as the anti-colonial freedom fighters of Jomo Kenyatta's Kenya African Union (KAU).[109] Later, in December 1970, the *National Geographic* published a photograph of two dreadlocked Ethiopian monks, further popularizing the style.[110] Irrespective of its origins, dreadlocked hair became synonymous with the Rastafari and many musicians adopted the style, including Alton Ellis, Bob Andy, Winston Rodney, Horace Andy, Johnny Clarke and Jimmy Cliff.[111] Lyrically, the most prominent promotion of the Nazarite vow was 'Natty Dread' (1974) by Bob Marley and the Wailers, but there are other notable examples, including the Heaven Singers' 'Rasta Dreadlocks', released in the same year, the Diamonds 'Jah Jah Bless the Dreadlocks' (1975), Linval Thompson's 'Don't Cut Off Your Dreadlocks' (1976), Lee Perry's 'Dreadlocks in Moonlight' (1976), Dr Alimantado's 'Can't Conquer Natty Dreadlocks' (1978) and the Gladiators' 'Dreadlocks the Time Is Now' (1978). In Britain, the reggae band Brown Sugar released the single 'I'm in Love with a Dreadlocks' (1977), helping to popularize, if not normalize, the look in the UK.

If the lyrics of roots reggae focused on the Afrocentric worldview of the Rastafari, a similar story can be heard within the music's rhythm, particularly when considering the Nyabinghi drumming heard on many of the more spiritual reggae releases of the era. If the worldview of the Rastafari is syncretic in a theological sense, Nyabinghi drumming is also a synthesis of disparate pre-existing elements, including the musical elements of Kumina and Burru drumming. A major feature of the Kumina cult is a form of ritual dancing to rhythms played on the *Kbandu* and Playing Cast drums, augmented by graters, shakers and claves.[112] While many Rastas object to the notion of a connection between Kumina and their faith, both Kumina and the Rastafari are sites of the evolution of African drumming in Jamaica.[113]

Another significant influence on the Nyabinghi style of drumming is the music that accompanied Burru, a fertility masquerade that originated in the Ashanti kingdom of what is now Ghana and which was popular among those who settled in the Jamaican parish of Clarendon. Burru music is said to be derived from the praise songs of African tradition, and the survival of Burru music has been attributed to slave masters allowing its continuation because of its function as a work metronome.[114] After their emancipation, Burru drummers found themselves without work and gradually migrated from the Jamaican countryside to the towns. It was in West Kingston that the early Rastafari would come into contact with adherents of Burru and began to adopt and adapt their drumming, using the three-part akete drum ensemble of bass, mid-pitched *funde* and high-pitched repeater (or 'peta). However, whereas the Burru played melody on the repeater, rhythm on the bass drum and syncopation on the funde, within Nyabinghi drumming, the funde plays rhythm, the bass drum follows a similar pattern to the funde but varying in pitch and tone, and the repeater leads or improvises.[115]

Within the immediate pre-history of reggae, perhaps the earliest use of Nyabinghi drumming are the Laurel Aitken compositions 'Nebuchnezer' and 'Ghana Independence' from 1957. Three years later, Prince Buster made effective use of the Nyabinghi percussion of Count Ossie Williams and four Burru drummers on his production of the Folkes Brothers' 'Oh Carolina!', a foundational text in the development of the reggae rhythm and a big influence on 1970s' roots reggae. Born in St Thomas and influenced by the Kumina drumming he heard in his youth, Count Ossie had also been observing the drumming of the Burru. In his recording of 'Oh Carolina!', his band the Mystic Revelation of Rastafari use the three akete drums of bass, repeater and a large flat slack funde to weave in and out of each other's path, while the track has an authentic shuffling ska sound due to the emphasis on the off-beat in the piano playing of Owen Gray and the guitar work of Jerome Hines.

Nyabinghi drumming, with the bass, repeater and funde at its core, is first and foremost a sacred music, but is also found within more secular reggae, and many recordings in the 1970s fuse rock drumming with Nyabinghi percussion. Nyabinghi drumming can also be heard on a triple album by Count Ossie and the Mystic Revelation of Rastafari entitled *Grounation* (1973), and on albums by Ras Michael and the Sons of Negus, including their debut *Peace and Love – Wadadasow* (released under the name Dadawah, Amharic for peace and love) and the follow-up *Nyahbinghi*.

Although not a musicologist, Barrett Sr's description of the rhythmic structure of Nyabinghi drumming in the hands of Count Ossie goes some way to capturing its spirit: 'The down beat of the drummer symbolizes the death of the oppressive society but it is answered by the akete drummers, a resurrection of the society through the power of Ras Tafari . . . it is a call to Africa.'[116]

Elsewhere, Nyabinghi drumming was prominent on 'Satta Amassa Gana' by the Abyssinians. The song had been recorded for Coxsone Dodd in 1969, but Dodd refused to release it due to its religious lyrics sung in Amharic, with the producer instructing the band to record something secular for the dancehall instead. This pinnacle of devout Rastafarian reggae would only see the light of day when the song was re-recorded before forming the title track of an album that sold well in Jamaica and internationally.

While the sound of unadorned Nyabinghi drumming was limited to a handful of releases, its structure continued to determine the form of roots reggae in subsequent decades, where lead guitar, keyboards and horns imitate the repeater, and where the bass guitar follows the bass rhythms of the Nyabinghi. Writing in the 1970s, the musicologist Verena Reckord describes the way that roots reggae incorporates the feel of Nyabinghi drumming as well as its sound:

> There is greater freedom at present in the bass ridim of reggae. Whilst this behavior need not be directly attributed to the tradition of the Rasta bass drum, it brings to mind the fact that on occasion, in the heat of playing Rasta music, the sedate bass drum takes off on its own, playing triplets and other unprecedented patterns according to the emotional dictates of the player.[117]

By the end of the 1970s, roots reggae was fully formed, and while there were further lyrical and musical turns as the genre progressed through following decades, its basic structure has remained in place from the 1970s to the present date, surviving the global music industry's transition from analogue to digital technology and newly reinvigorated in the twenty-first century by a self-named Reggae Revival movement. However, this bright future was unknown at the dawn of the 1980s, when many were saying that the days of reggae were over, with the music starting to be overshadowed by the rise of a new musical form christened dancehall.

While the roots of the dancehall form were found in the same sound systems that gave birth to reggae, this was a music that was different from reggae – sonically, thematically and politically. Both its polar opposite and its distant cousin, dancehall began the 1980s in ascendancy over roots reggae, heralding social and economic changes as Michael Manley's experimentation with Third-World democratic socialism was replaced by Edward Seaga's brand of neo-liberal economics after the JLP won the October 1980 election by a landslide. But before we can explore dancehall, we must look at how reggae was received outside of the Caribbean. During the late 1970s and into the 1980s, Britain continued to play an important role in popularizing Jamaican music. Here, black and white youth took reggae to their hearts and allowed it to speak of their experiences. In doing so, England in particular produced some fantastic music, including the music of a reggae band that sold over 70 million records but whose members, as we shall see, ended up almost penniless.

4

'INGLAN IS A BITCH': REGGAE CROSSOVER IN THE UK

Promotional image for The Specials, *The Specials* (1979)

Inglan is a bitch
Dere's no escapin it
Inglan is a bitch
Y'u bettah face up to it.

LINTON KWESI JOHNSON[1]

We're on the same side as the Rastas. People think they're
as loony as us. But it's because they're their own people,
projecting their own image.

'WILLIE', PUNK[2]

By the end of the 1970s both Jamaica's dream of independence and the post-war social and economic consensus in Britain were being swept aside by the same global economic forces. Michael Manley's vision of an independent socialist Jamaica had been permanently derailed by the 1973 energy crisis and the inevitable balance-of-payments crisis that followed, while the response of the UK government to the quadrupling of the oil price was to enforce a three-day working week to conserve electricity use. In a marked increase in industrial militancy, and sensing that the moment was theirs, the National Union of Mineworkers (NUM) demanded a series of wage increases from the British government, and when in January 1974 their demands were refused, the union voted to strike. Outraged, the Conservative prime minister Ted Heath called a general election for 10 October 1974 and campaigned with the slogan 'Who Governs Britain?', asking voters to choose between his government and the NUM. The electorate's answer to Heath's rhetorical question was 'not you', and the government fell.

From this moment onwards, a quarter of a century of cross-political consensus as to how the economy should be run unravelled amid industrial unrest, rising unemployment, racial tension and the rise of the same 'new-right' economics and politics as found in Jamaica. The cultural theorist Stuart Hall, born in Kingston, Jamaica, and by the mid-1970s Director of the Centre for Contemporary Cultural Studies at the University of Birmingham, describes the moment as one of 'a fully fledged capitalist recession, with extremely high rates of inflation, a toppling currency, cuts in the social wage and in public spending, a savaging of living standards, and a sacrifice of the working class to capital'.[3] Hall could have been depicting events in Jamaica but was instead describing a first-world country buffeted by the swollen tides of global capital. In Jamaica, the cultural response was Rasta belligerence and roots reggae, whereas in Britain, it was a decline in happy-go-lucky glam pop and the rise of punk rock.

Pointing a finger at a metaphorical map and locating the precise point of origin of a fast-moving cultural phenomenon such as punk is a thankless task, for there always seems to be something earlier that indicates the general direction of travel. Sometimes, though, it seems appropriate to suggest that a particular event was at least a tipping point, and the rioting that occurred in Notting Hill, west London, in August 1976 was surely that. This riot was by no means the birth of punk – that could be located at least a decade earlier in American garage rock – but it was almost certainly the origin of what Bob Marley went on to dub a 'Punky Reggae Party'.

The Notting Hill Carnival had begun in the mid-1960s as an attempt by the Windrush generation to carve out a space for their music and culture, but its location was a response to something darker, a series of earlier race riots in August 1958 when the houses of newly arrived Caribbean residents were attacked by three or four hundred white men. In 1976 the rioting was sparked by heavy-handed policing of that year's carnival, with more than a hundred police officers injured and sixty arrests.[4] In the thick of it were members of the newly formed punk band the Clash, who responded to finding themselves in the centre of a Black-led riot with the song 'White Riot', where chief lyricist Joe Strummer articulates his desire for a 'riot of my own'. Within weeks of the events in Notting Hill, the Clash were wearing clothes adorned with slogans from Jamaica including 'Rockers', 'Heavy Manners' and 'Heavy Duty Discipline'.

In the following years, one of the many strands of punk was a reggae crossover, as British reggae acts joined punks on the line-ups of gigs and festivals, and with several punk-rock acts incorporating reggae rhythms and Jamaican symbolism within their music. Music writer Jon Savage puts it well:

> reggae transmitted the experience of England's most visible outsiders, those Rastas who, confronted with prejudice, totally refused to enter England's dream. The Clash had seen how Reggae had acted as a soundtrack for social resistance at the Notting Hill Carnival and, with their use of drop-out and stencilled slogans, they were attempting to create their own white Rasta in Punk – a new cultural resistance.[5]

Sensing the new vibe, the Clash quickly recorded a cover version of Junior Murvin's 'Police and Thieves' for their debut album, and this caught the attention of both Lee 'Scratch' Perry and Bob Marley as a result. Marley was in London recording *Exodus*, effectively living in exile after the assassination attempt of the previous year. Vivien Goldman, who had been present when Marley was shot, introduced Marley and Perry to the Clash, and captured the moment when she asked the pair for their views on the band's version of 'Police and Thieves':

> 'Well, what do you think?' I eagerly asked. Originally a Scratch production sung by Junior Murvin, the track's cynical realism had helped it become a punk anthem. At first listen, Bob and Scratch were startled by Joe Strummer's harsh bark, compared to Murvin's mellifluous falsetto. 'It is different, but me like 'ow 'im feel it,' was Marley's verdict, though. He liked the link between the two tribes of alienated, angry youth – punks and Rastafari. 'Punks are outcasts from society. So are the Rastas. So they are bound to defend what we defend,' Marley concluded. Shortly thereafter, they began recording the single Punky Reggae

Party, and by naming an underground social phenomenon, helped further it.[6]

The eventual release of 'Punky Reggae Party', written by both Marley and Perry and appearing as a B-side to 'Jamming', saw Marley intoning a 'new wave, new rave' and criticizing 'boring old farts'. Elsewhere in the song, Marley name-checked the Damned, the Jam, the Clash and Doctor Feelgood, alongside the Wailers and the Maytals. Following the release of 'Punky Reggae Party', Perry went on to co-produce the Clash's 'Complete Control' single, which saw punk's influence rub off on the producer, who by then had a photo of the Clash in pride of place as the only white artists to adorn a wall of his Black Ark studio back in Jamaica.

A year after 'Police and Thieves', the Clash's '(White Man) in Hammersmith Palais' deepened the band's relationship with reggae, articulating lead singer Joe Strummer's experience of attending a reggae showcase starring Dillinger, Leroy Smart and Delroy Wilson. The song was, in effect, a criticism of the Trojan pop sound of the earlier era, articulating the band's disappointment that the Hammersmith Palais all-nighter 'ain't got no roots rock rebel'.

Punk rock's fascination with reggae was more than musical tourism and went beyond similar basslines; these were two outsider subcultures, both concerned with an existential crisis before the end of times. Importantly, punk did not require reggae to be shorn of its Rasta roots for it to be accepted by its largely white audience – quite the opposite, as the outré nature of Rasta was central to its appeal. Even though the first wave of punk rock would not last more than a couple of years, the connection to and affinity with reggae extended into the subsequent musical era as a post-punk aesthetic formed. Again, the Clash were on the front line, with their third album *London Calling* capturing the moment with its mix of punk rock, ska, reggae and Americana. Following this hybridity came 'Bankrobber', the band's standalone single from 1979, which was pure reggae. The single featured a deejay version on the B-side with vocals from Jamaica's Mikey Dread, while the expansive 'Robber Dub' was also scheduled for release on twelve-inch before the band's new label CBS pulled the plug at the last minute.

By this time, a diverse range of musical styles was following in punk's wake. This provided more space for reggae, with a move away from the mono-dimensional guitar-led sound of punk rock towards a new eclecticism seen on a range of releases. A good example would be punk band the Ruts, best known for the single 'Babylon's Burning' and debut album *The Crack*. Later, recording as Ruts DC, the band's 1981 album *Rhythm Collision, Vol. 1* was pure reggae, produced by Mad Professor, a London-based producer and mixer who would go on to become known as one of Britain's finest reggae engineers.

While Jamaican roots reggae was a largely male affair, the gender diversity of punk provided a space for female musicians, with the Slits being the best-known all-women band on the scene. Signed to Island Records, the band's debut album *Cut* was produced by the Barbados-born Londoner Dennis Bovell, the head honcho of his own Jah Sufferer sound system and a reggae musician in his own right, recording under the name Blackbeard. The Slits singer Ari Up was passionate about reggae and a full-on Rasta in an underground reggae scene in London that revolved around unlicensed 'blues' parties:

> I was not just the only white girl but the only one with dreads. In fact, I was the first person to have the tree – I had my locks up in a tree-type shape. But I got away with it because I was dancing the hell out of their blues parties. Back then the style of dancing was called 'steppers' and I was such a good stepper.[7]

Although the likes of the Clash, the Ruts and the Slits incorporated reggae within their recorded output, it was on stage that the punky reggae party was best observed, particularly at festivals and events organized by the Anti-Nazi League (ANL) and Rock against Racism (RAR) organizations.

The impetus for the formation of Rock against Racism was a drunken on-stage rant by the British blues guitarist and singer Eric Clapton, who in August 1976 had declared support for the overt racism of Enoch Powell at a concert held in a venue directly opposite where Powell had made his infamous 'Rivers of Blood' speech eight years earlier. Clapton's support for Powell was mystifying considering that the songwriter had a lifelong debt to American rhythm and blues and had recorded a cover version of the Wailers' 'I Shot the Sheriff' only two years previously.[8] Indeed, it was the fact that Clapton was so clearly in debt to Black music that raised the ire of campaigners – racism might be expected from others, but not from Clapton. Meanwhile, the ANL were formed by the Socialist Workers Party as a front organization designed to broaden the appeal among young people of the party's brand of left-wing politics.

The ANL and RAR were built by activists keen to stop punk rock from turning Nazi during a period when there was a noticeable increase in support for the openly fascist National Front (NF) and British Movement (BM). Both organizations were picking up support among a skinhead youth culture that had, by the end of the 1970s, divided into competing factions. Anti-racist skins held on to what they referred to as 'the Spirit of '69', while some of their younger cousins turned to fascism while embracing Oi!, a second-wave punk-rock offshoot shorn of any Jamaican elements and refocused on shouty vocals, lead guitar and rock rhythms.

By late 1977, the message concerning British fascism had spread as far as Jamaica, with Dillinger recording the track 'Rockers', where he warns starkly 'beware of the National Front'. Within

months, Rock against Racism and the reggae bands they promoted were up against the wall, and events at a gig at the Central
London Polytechnic on 24 February 1978 are a good example of
the problems they faced. The gig itself was to be headlined by
Oi! aficionados Sham 69, with Misty in Roots, a roots-reggae
act from Southall, west London, in support. With no discern-
ibly right-wing lyrics, Sham 69 had nevertheless picked up a
sizeable following of fascist skinheads, despite attempts by the
band to discourage this, not least through their work with RAR.
The gig itself was dubbed 'Smash Race Hate', and a fascist ram-
page was only narrowly avoided due to the actions of a group of
dockers who were acting as stewards at the gig and who, armed
with club hammers and other assorted tools, confronted those
fascist trouble-makers who had gained access to the venue. RAR
organizer Red Saunders captures the mood:

> The atmosphere was extraordinary. There I am on stage doing
> a bit of compering, for lack of a better word, just shouting
> at the audience who were Sieg-Heiling. People were going,
> 'Why have we let them in?' I was going, 'This is what we're
> about. This is the fucking real world, mate. Here's the white
> working class and here's a reggae band and we've brought
> them all together.'[9]

The gig ended with a show of anti-fascist unity when Sham 69's
lead singer Jimmy Pursey joined Misty in Roots on stage for a
reversioning of Desmond Dekker's 'Israelites'.

Later in 1978, following a carnival in Trafalgar Square jointly
organized by RAR and the ANL, the Clash headlined a free concert
in Victoria Park in London, attended by an estimated 100,000.
Also on the bill was the reggae band Steel Pulse, from Handsworth,
Birmingham. By the end of 1978, RAR had organized over three

hundred concerts, including a big event in October in Brockwell Park, south London, featuring Misty in Roots, who were joined on the bill by Aswad, another London-based roots-reggae band. Also featured was Elvis Costello, who the previous year had released the *noir* reggae single 'Watching the Detectives'.

The cadre of black British artists who performed at RAR and ANL gigs ended up forming the backbone of British reggae in the 1980s. Steel Pulse's first single, 'Kibudu-Mansatta-Abuku', called for an increased focus on African culture within black British culture, while their first single for Island, 'Ku Klux Klan', set out their anti-racist stall. However, it was the band's long-playing debut *Handsworth Revolution* that brought critical acclaim, with the album articulating a politicized pan-Africanist and Rastafarian worldview, drawing comparisons between Apartheid in South Africa and the racial relations of the Handsworth district of Birmingham.

Like Steel Pulse, Misty in Roots were also deeply political and beginning to reject the roles cast for them by both British society and their parents' generation. Lead singer Poko (Walford Tyson) is quoted as saying that from the outset, the band 'no longer wanted to sing about love and women. We wanted to do progressive protest music.'[10] In 1979 the band's manager Clarence Baker was badly injured in a police raid on a community centre in Southall, west London, that was being used as an anti-fascist headquarters set up to counter a planned election meeting by the National Front. The Ruts penned the dub-influenced 'Jah War' as a tribute to Baker, with the track going on to have a significant influence upon a strand of punk reggae that was developed within an anarchist squatting scene in England in the 1980s and which went on to influence the American singer Henry Rollins and his band Black Flag. Misty in Roots and The Ruts went on to play a 'Southall Kids are Innocent' benefit gig, along with the Clash, Aswad, the Pop Group and Pete Townsend of the Who.

Reggae often sat at the centre of punk gigs, and there was undoubtedly a reggae element to some of punk rock's recordings. However, the notion that punk was a unity movement of black and white is often overplayed in accounts that gloss over the development of a right wing within the second generation of punk acts, and which also often neglect to mention that punk's audience was largely white. It should be acknowledged, too, that, putting Marley and Perry to one side, the direction of musical influence was almost entirely one way, from reggae to punk, with the likes of Aswad, Steel Pulse and Misty in Roots refusing to budge a musical inch to accommodate punk audiences. Indeed, Aswad walked off a tour with Eddie and the Hot Rods due to conflict with the audience, particularly the spitting and overt aggression that was common at punk gigs.[11] Irrespective of any sense of political affinity between punk and reggae, the approach of both movements to musicianship was radically different, as Steel Pulse's Mykaell Riley acknowledges:

> Reggae and punk were oil and water. We were busy learning our instruments to be as proficient as possible and they were going, 'Just pick it up and play.' Punk was going in the absolute opposite direction that we were going in. We were practising harmonizing and delivering a performance. Punk was a revolution that we couldn't engage with the mindset at all. Culturally, it just jarred at first. We were rebelling in a different way by talking about politics and by the way we dressed and by having politicized lyrics. Punk was just saying, 'fuck off'.[12]

The Sex Pistols were particularly good at saying 'fuck off', but their lead singer, Johnny Rotten (John Lydon), was also a huge reggae fan, although he would have to wait until his band split before he could incorporate reggae within his recorded output. In

1978, with the Sex Pistols on the rocks and Lydon under pressure, he fled to Jamaica with the journalist Chris Salewicz and Don Letts, the punk film-maker and Clash acolyte who had introduced many punks to reggae in his role as resident selector at London venue the Roxy. With reggae music now in his blood, and following the Sex Pistols' inevitable split, Lydon, shorn of his Rotten sobriquet, formed Public Image Limited with guitarist Keith Levine, drummer Jim Walker and bassist Jah Wobble (John Wardle), all of whom were more than capable of ensuring that Jamaican sounds were at the forefront of PIL's post-punk brew. The end result was the band's debut *First Issue* and the follow-up *Metal Box*, both of which featured deep reggae basslines and spidery guitar lines, seeming to define a new post-punk ethos. Jah Wobble eventually left the band but continued to experiment with reggae, both with his band Invaders of the Heart and as a solo artist, including on the album *Chinese Dub*, recorded with his wife Zi Lan Liao.

Elsewhere within the post-punk fallout, reggae formed an element of numerous other acts' music, often alongside a postmodern melee of other Black Atlantic musical forms. Scritti Politti's debut single, 'Skank Bloc Bologna' (1978), melded angular guitar riffs with a reggae bassline in a stew of post-structuralist theory influenced by Italian autonomism and events in Bologna when an uprising shook the communist mayor and threatened to replace orthodox communism with a form of libertarian leftism, before the rebellion was crushed.[13]

Equally as avant garde were Bristol's the Pop Group, who incorporated jazz and funk into their angry dissonance, topped off with politically charged lyrics. Notable releases included the Dennis Bovell-produced single 'She Is beyond Good and Evil' and debut album *Y*, while the band's first tour featured dub poet Linton Kwesi Johnson as support. By this time, Johnson was well known among music fans in the UK, with the music newspaper *Sounds* featuring him on their front cover in 1978 with the strapline 'The Voice of Black Britain'.[14] Meanwhile, in the mainstream, the Police's 'Walking on the Moon', the band's second number one, featured an unmistakably reggae groove.

On the other side of the Atlantic, in the United States, Pere Ubu had developed a quintessentially post-punk sound before punk had even burned out, with a reggae bassline to 'Heaven', on the album *The Modern Dance* (1978), and further reggae archaeology buried beneath noise and funk on their follow-up *Dub Housing*. This signalled the moment when American post-punk took on the same musical influences as its English variant. It was no surprise, then, when Anglo-American band the Pretenders recorded the reggae track 'Private Life', subsequently covered by Grace Jones with Sly and Robbie on the back line. Eventually, the band's Ohio-born singer Chrissie Hynde fell so in love with reggae that she chose the then unknown Birmingham act UB40 as support for her band's 1979 tour. Also hailing from Ohio were Devo, who mined a seam of art rock within punk and post-punk and who recorded a cover version of the Rolling Stones' '(I Can't Get No) Satisfaction' in something approximating a reggae style. By this time, the Rolling Stones had themselves developed an interest in reggae, recording Eric Donaldson's 'Cherry Oh Baby' in 1976 and their own composition, 'Hey Negrita', in 1976.

What all the British and American post-punk acts had in common was that they rejected the 'rockism' they saw within the canon of rock and roll. The privileged role of the lead singer or lead guitarist at the front of the stage, with one foot on a floor monitor speaker, idolized by all before him, was anathema to this new scene. Like post-punk, reggae had little place for onstage rockist heroics. Unlike rock's privileging of the lead singer and lead guitarist, within reggae there is an equilibrium between guitar, bass and drums, with vocals that often weave between them. It is this ideology that came to be shared with other Black Atlantic music forms such as soul, funk and disco, and later rap, house, techno and rave.

'Ghost Town': Post-Punk and a Ska Revival

At the turn of the 1970s, punk and post-punk's notions of musical equality, breaking down barriers between audience and band, began to be shared by a somewhat unlikely ska revival that drew in an army of British teenagers and popularized Jamaican music for a new generation. At its centre was a record label that would embody the original punk ethos of anti-racism and combine it with the music of an earlier generation to produce something both authentic and quintessentially English. Unlike post-punk, the story of 2 Tone Records begins and ends with ska, although there were sufficiently Anglocentric stylings to ensure a widespread popularity and a series of chart hits. It was this deft combination of a naturally energetic Jamaican musical form with an English sensibility that propelled 2 Tone releases to the top of the charts.

The 2 Tone roster was quickly formed as a neat capsule collection of English ska. Announcing the arrival of the label was a double-headed seven-inch single, with the Specials' 'Gangsters' on one side and the Selecter's eponymous debut on the other, with neither track privileged with 'A-side' status. The label's black-and-white iconography by label founder Jerry Dammers proved almost as influential as the music. The enduring appeal of the image of 'Walt Jabsco', Dammers's hand-drawn rude boy, was that it so neatly captured the multiracial 'Spirit of '69' ethos of the band. It was all there in monochrome: the crisp trousers, tight to the leg and finishing a little higher than normal to show off white socks; the long jacket, with shirt cuffs protruding from the sleeve; the skinny tie, wrap-around shades and pork-pie hat. A sartorial history lesson wrapped in a clearly symbolic black-and-white chequerboard. The band's Horace Panter, now a fine artist, explains its appeal: 'It's really easy to reproduce – clean lines, black and white, you can draw it on the cover of your rough book at school or your satchel. The logo really summed up what The Specials were about at the time – the shoes and the hats and the suits.'[15]

If the bands that made up the 2 Tone stable brimmed with a righteous anger at racism and the state of the nation, this provided a lyrical contrast to the upbeat rhythm of ska, played at a break-neck tempo. This was not the deep and devastating roots reggae of the Rastafari but the sound of its earlier secular cousin, reinvigorated by the collision of English and Jamaican youth cultures. In the music of 2 Tone, the aesthetic of the original Kingston rude boys is filtered through 'Spirit of '69' skinheads and given a proto-feminist twist in the Selecter's Pauline Black and the all-women Bodysnatchers, 2 Tone's least well-known act, but one of its most important. Even the all-male line-up of the Beat managed to capture the new gender politics of the time with the monochrome imagery of their 'Beat Girl' matching 2 Tone's mythical Walt Jabsco. Signed to 2 Tone for a one-off ska cover of Smokey Robinson's 'Tears of a Clown', the Beat's lead singer Dave Wakeling had been at the Eric Clapton gig in Birmingham in 1976 and was shocked by what he heard:

> Here's this bloke singing Bob Marley songs telling every-body to get the 'wogs out'. It seemed like he had had a few, so some of the speech was more gargling than pontificating but the thrust of it was 'Enoch was right' and that 'we should all vote for him' and that 'England was a white country' and then a lot of saying 'get 'em out'.[16]

Formed in response to Clapton's outburst, it was no surprise to find that the Beat were political in their outlook. The band's other vocalist, Ranking Roger, whose style leaned very much towards that of the Jamaican deejay, explains:

> The Beat was definitely a political band but we had love songs and a commercial side too. It was a balance ... We saw racism; we wrote about it. We saw unemployment; we wrote about it. We saw war; we wrote about it. We were singing about realities, like punk and the reggae acts from the past. We just updated it to what was happening to us.[17]

The role of women in 2 Tone was crucial in bringing to the fore a view from the other side of life. The young age of both the 2 Tone bands and their audiences was also of note. Whereas Jamaican reggae would laud both young and old, combining experience, wisdom and vitality in equal measure, 2 Tone ska was all about the naivety and energy of an English youth culture at the sharp edge of rising youth unemployment. The music of 2 Tone might sound joyous, but there was an anger here too, in lyrics that decried the state of a nation turning rightward under new prime minister Margaret Thatcher. 2 Tone fans would not be living the life of Riley sold to them by older brothers and sisters, who had lived their youthful years in the full employment of the 1960s. The youthful naivety of 2 Tone was not shared by all, though, with Steel Pulse's David Hinds arguing that:

> 2 Tone came with a style of music that said, 'We've been there, done that and worn the T-shirt.' God, man, my brothers came with ska music in 1962. Why bring it back? We saw it as a revival and a lot of old musicians ... We didn't see the musicians as that talented because of the chords they were jumping to. We were going onto minor and major seventh and eleventh and thirteenth chords; those chords were unheard

of in the kind of music they were playing. We didn't think they played it that well and thought the singing was off-key and the energy too fast. It was punk wired up to the point where everybody's gone off their rocker, especially coming from people like Madness with all their gimmicks.[18]

Madness were a north London act initially signed to 2 Tone, whose debut single, 'The Prince', a tribute to Prince Buster, was a top-twenty hit. The single was followed by a succession of hits that climbed ever higher in the charts before the band finally hit the number-one spot with 'House of Fun' in 1982. On the way, Madness were criticized in much the same way as Sham 69 were, with a focus on what the band should have been doing to rid themselves of openly fascistic fans. While Sham 69 had performed for Rock against Racism and had spoken out against the significant right-wing element of their support, Madness initially seemed reticent to confront their fascist fans, before relenting in musical form with their fifth hit 'Embarrassment', released in November 1980. Musically, the track was a typically jaunty number, yet beneath the nutty-boy image lay a critique of the racism of an older white generation, informed by their saxophone player Lee Thompson's experience of his family's reaction to his teenage sister's relationship with a Black man.[19] The message was clear, but not clear enough for the fascists who had attached themselves to the band. In the end, Madness had to spell it out in black and white in a press statement that acknowledged their debt to Jamaican ska and reggae, and which encouraged their fans to reject racism.[20] Having jumped ship from 2 Tone to fellow indie Stiff, by this point the band was moving away from Jamaican rhythms towards a broader pop sound with a hint of English music hall, just as the ska revival was running out of steam.

Once Madness left 2 Tone, the band headed in a commercial direction and had 22 consecutive top-forty hits as a result.

The Specials, led by the quixotic Jerry Dammers, had a shorter period in the charts before a change in musical direction led to the break-up of the band. Following their debut 'Gangsters' was an epochal cover version of Dandy Livingstone's rocksteady anthem 'Rudy, a Message to You', which saw Dammers co-opt Cuban-born Rico Rodriguez into the band. A follower of Count Ossie, who had played trombone on Livingstone's original, Rodriguez would stay with the Specials through a series of shifting line-ups until Dammers dissolved the band.

Increasingly political, the Specials' follow-up was an EP featuring 'Too Much Too Young' as its title track, a song loosely based on 'Birth Control' (1969) by Jamaican singer Lloyd Charmers. Charmers's original is risqué, but musically light and airy and recorded at a sedate pace, so when the narrator requests his lover to take the newly released contraceptive pill, as 'me no want no picni' [children], this is a plaintive call. In contrast, the Specials' 'Too Much Too Young' is shot through with aggression and bitterness, a tale of teenage pregnancy and early marriage. Lead singer Terry Hall spits bile at a young married woman with children, a potential lover 'who could be having fun with me'.

An unlikely number-one hit, the 'Too Much Too Young' EP also included a quartet of cover versions from the Trojan era: 'Guns of Navarone', 'Long Shot Kick de Bucket', 'The Liquidator' and 'Skinhead Moonstomp', introducing rocksteady and Trojan-style reggae to a younger generation. Top-ten follow-ups continued, casting an unflinching eye on what by then was being called 'Thatcher's Britain'. 'Rat Race', written by the Specials' guitarist Roddy Byers, saw the band reflect on what was then the middle-class privilege of a university education, with a musical soundtrack drawing on Linton Kwesi Johnson's earlier release 'Me Wan' fi Go Rave'. 'Stereotype' saw the band depart from the ska template, foreshadowing an eventual adoption of easy listening 'muzak', while 'Do Nothing', their final single for 1980, saw them return to ska with the kitchen-sink realism of a lyric that proclaimed, 'living a life without meaning'.

Collected together, the Specials' early singles were influential, but it would be 'Ghost Town', their first single of 1981 and their second number one, that would come to define a particular moment of political and social torment. In a moment of prescience, the recording went on to become the soundtrack for a series of riots that spread through those areas of England's cities that had relatively large Black populations. The track was recorded in two recording sessions in the English Midlands. The day after the first session, in the late afternoon of 10 April 1981, Michael Bailey, a young Black man in Brixton, south London, who was heavily bleeding from a stab wound, was followed by the police into a local house before being taken by them to a minicab, ostensibly to transport him to hospital. A crowd of around thirty to forty gathered and, thinking that Bailey was being arrested, argued for his release. The injured man was eventually taken by the crowd and despatched to hospital in a private car. By this time, rumours were circulating that the police had attacked Bailey and prevented him from going to hospital. At a hastily organized community meeting later that evening, the Metropolitan Police tried to dispel the rumours, but to little effect. The following day, there was a heavy police presence in Brixton, which only inflamed tensions. That evening, arson and violence ripped apart any semblance of normality. More than 7,000 police officers were drafted in to try to quell the disorder, and over that weekend they arrested 247 members of the public, while 401 officers were injured along with at least 48 civilians, with 117 police cars either damaged or destroyed.[21] Brixton was already a tinderbox, and the Michael Bailey incident was a lit match.

On the Saturday after the Brixton uprising, Satnam Singh Gill, a twenty-year-old student, was stabbed to death by racist skinheads in the Specials' home town of Coventry. The band announced a

gig to promote racial unity to be held on 12 June 1981, the scheduled release date for 'Ghost Town'. Ominously, the National Front
announced a march for the same day.[22] In the end, the day went
largely without incident, but the same cannot be said for the following months. 'Ghost Town' was to spend three weeks at number one
and ten weeks on the charts, during which time there was rioting
in Handsworth in Birmingham, Chapeltown in Leeds, Toxteth in
Liverpool and Moss Side in Manchester, all areas with large African
and Afro-Caribbean populations. Race relations in England's cities
would never be the same. Tom Watson, a future Deputy Leader
of the Labour Party, explains how 'Ghost Town' shone a light not
merely on Brixton, but on other towns and cities, too:

> Every kid in the Midlands lived in a ghost town. There were
> kids I knew who literally didn't get work for five years. It was
> a direct result of the 1981 budget which Peter Tapsell, the
> Tory grandee, said was 'the most illiterate budget in history'.
> It wiped out a third of the West Midlands manufacturing
> base in two or three years. We hated the government and
> we hated Thatcher. It added to our sense of powerlessness as
> teenagers, but songs brought people together.[23]

If 'Ghost Town' captured the general mood, it would take a
reggae artist close to the ground to help explain and explore the
specifics of what went on in Brixton that spring. Linton Kwesi
Johnson was born in 1952 in Chapelton, Jamaica, before his family
moved to Brixton in 1963, with Johnson eventually studying soci-
ology at Goldsmiths College in nearby New Cross. Coming to
prominence in the journal *Race Today*, Johnson is best known as
a dub poet, using the rhythms of reggae within the metre of his
poetry and drawing upon Jamaican speech and patois in both the
poetry's orthography and delivery. Johnson describes his style as

'poetry rooted in the orality of the Caribbean and in the music of Jamaica', with his dramatic work, *Voices of the Living and the Dead*, published by *Race Today* in 1974, followed by *Dread Beat an' Blood*, a collection of poetry, a year later.[24] In 1978 Johnson worked with Dennis Bovell to set *Dread Beat an' Blood* to music on what was the first of a series of albums that cemented his place within the reggae canon. Following *Dread Beat an' Blood* was 1979's *Forces of Victory* and the twin header of *Bass Culture* and *LKJ in Dub* in 1980, all for Island Records. Also signing to Island Records and recording for Dennis Bovell was the Jamaican dub poet Michael Smith. A big influence on Johnson, Smith's one and only album, *Mi C-YaaN beLieVe iT* (1982), was recorded in London with a range of backing musicians including Rico Rodriguez on trombone. A year later, Smith was stoned to death by unnamed JLP supporters angry at his heckling of Mavis Gilmour, the JLP minister of education, at a political meeting in Stony Hill, just outside of Kingston.

With 'Five Nights of Bleeding (for Leroy Harris)' on *Dread Beat an' Blood*, Johnson busts open the British reggae scene with an exploration of the occasional violence surrounding reggae sound systems, setting out his stall as a chronicler of life within Brixton's Black community. Other poems and recordings explored race relations in Britain more generally, often with a focus on racist policing. 'Sonny's Lettah (Anti-Sus Poem)' on *Forces of Victory* deals with the role of the 'sus' laws in the life of Black men in Britain, where the police were able to arrest and detain on the mere suspicion that an individual was about to break the law, rather than the more usual suspicion that an individual had actually committed an offence. Johnson explains his motives for penning the poem:

'Sonny's Lettah' was written as a contribution to a campaign that was being waged in our communities against the infamous sus law – a Vagrancy Act from 1824 which had been dormant for many years and was reinvoked – in which a significant number of black youth were criminalized by racist police officers. A policeman could just simply say that they had reasonable suspicion that you were thinking about putting your hand into somebody's bag or pocket. It was as vague as that. The black communities were up in arms about it . . . I had been arrested by the police and brutalized and assaulted and charged with assault and GBH [grievous bodily harm], so 'Sonny's Lettah' drew on that experience plus the experience of many other people I knew who had been unjustly persecuted by the police.[25]

Unsurprisingly for anyone familiar with policing in the English inner cities at the time, young Black men were massively over-represented in 'sus' arrests, and such was the disproportionality of the reported numbers that the police practice could easily be seen as internment by arrest. Later, 'Reggae fi Peach' on *Bass Culture* dealt with the murder of Clement Blair Peach, a teacher killed during protests against the NF in Southall in April 1979. A subsequent report compiled after the event by Commander John Cass of the Metropolitan Police stated that it was 'almost certain' that Peach was killed by an officer in the now disbanded Special Patrol Group, an infamous anti-riot unit of the Met.[26]

By the start of the 1980s, dub poetry was proving to be an essential commentary on the racial politics of Britain at the time, while also contesting established linguistic norms and hierarchies, placing patois alongside the Queen's English and placing dub poetry on a par with poetry per se. With a growing reputation as a serious figure within both English literature and British reggae, Johnson's reputation was only enhanced by his ability to take the temperature of Britain's Black community, which by 1981 had reached boiling point.

At the time of the general election in May 1979, unemployment figures stood at 5.4 per cent of the working-age population, whereas by January 1981, it was at 10.1 per cent and rising.[27] Within Brixton, unemployment among young Black men was said to be as high as 55 per cent,[28] higher than in Kingston, Jamaica, despite the fact that the UK was at the time the world's fifth largest economy while Jamaica was the 89th.[29]

January 1981 also saw a devastating house fire at a sixteen-year-old's birthday party in New Cross, around 8 kilometres (5 mi.) east of Brixton, which left thirteen Black teenagers dead. The cause of the fire was never officially established, largely due to a bungled and racist police investigation that sought to pin the blame for the fire on the partygoers. In response, Linton Kwesi Johnson and others formed the New Cross Massacre Action Committee, which sought justice for the dead and injured. Six weeks after the fire, 10,000 marched against police racism and incompetence. In 'New Craas Massahkah', Johnson articulates the widely held view that the New Cross fire was the result of a racist petrol bombing.[30] A month after the march, Brixton exploded in events that Johnson referred to as 'Di Great Insohreckshan'.[31] A public inquiry chaired by Lord Scarman found that the rioting was a near spontaneous response by Black youths in Brixton to their lack of educational opportunities, poor housing, unemployment and racist policing.

This then was the setting for the Specials' 'Ghost Town', a state of the nation address that captured the changing times and which evokes the fear and dread of British society through the long, hot summer of 1981. The song itself was recorded at the end of a period of sustained tension within the band. Following its release, the Specials split two ways, with lead singer Terry Hall, vocalist Neville Staple and guitarist Lynval Golding leaving the band while the single was at number one. Band leader Dammers persevered, recruiting the Bodysnatchers' Rhoda Dakar as vocalist for their next single. Released under the moniker of Rhoda with the Special AKA, 'The Boiler' is a spoken-word account by Dakar of an assault and rape in which Dakar breaks down screaming at the end of the recording on one of the most uncompromising and unlikely top-forty hits in the history of the UK charts. The remnants of the band released three further singles without commercial success, but there would be one last hit with a single that captured the world's attention. The Special AKA's 'Free Nelson Mandela' (1984) called for the release of South Africa's most prominent political prisoner and reached number nine in the UK charts, although its cultural and political impact was far greater than its sales figures suggest. The track, produced by Elvis Costello, was such a success that it was adopted within South Africa as a liberation anthem and was performed in front of Mandela in Hyde Park in London on his ninetieth birthday, in June 2008.

The ska revival of the late 1970s and early 1980s was a brief youth movement that saw young British ska fans attend matinee shows and spend their pocket money on cheap seven-inch singles. As both the bands and their audiences matured, the scene came to what was perhaps an inevitable end. Explaining the legacy of 2 Tone, Rick Rogers, the Specials' former manager, is quoted as saying:

> 2 Tone spoke directly to a young, disaffected generation. It was massively political. The power of the message in the songs, in the artwork, visually; just the fact that there were young black and white kids together in a band making music: that the audience could relate to and understand and share. It had an enormous effect.[32]

Formed at the same moment as the Specials, UB40 were no less political but differed in having a far more reverential relationship to reggae. For UB40, reggae was serious business, and whereas the

Specials wished to innovate after their early ska-fuelled success, UB40 eschewed experimentation in their desire to perfect the reggae form. The band's make-up reflected the multiracial and multi-national mix of their home city of Birmingham, and in tune with the times, the band were explicitly political during their foundational years. With a moniker and iconography based on the registration card issued to the unemployed by the Department of Employment, debut album *Signing Off* signalled the band's intent – to get off the dole and commence a career as a reggae band in the traditional mould. Conscious and political, dramatic yet steadily paced, the album sold well. The album's opener, 'Tyler', deals with the case of Gary Tyler, a seventeen-year-old Black boy convicted by an all-white Louisiana jury of the 1974 murder of a younger boy and the wounding of another. Elsewhere on the album, 'Burden of Shame' was a reggae ballad that focused on the band's discomfort with their British citizenship. The more musically upbeat 'Food for Thought' also dealt with the legacy of empire, with an examination of the role of neo-colonial politics in modern developing-world famine. As a solidly working-class band, the depth of UB40's debut gave the lie to the notion of unemployment being a result of laziness or educational underachievement.

Signing Off eventually formed the first act in a trilogy of polit-ically charged reggae albums worthy of any self-respecting Jamaican band. *Present Arms*, the band's second album, contained the single 'One in Ten', an attack on the labour policy of the Conservative gov-ernment elected in 1979, who saw unemployment as a price worth paying for low inflation. The single was a top-ten hit, but the band had no such luck with their follow-up, 'I Won't Close My Eyes' (1982), unsurprising when considering that it was recorded at a par-ticularly slow tempo when its audience was more used to hearing ska, recorded at almost twice the speed. With 'I Won't Close My Eyes', the casual listener could be forgiven for thinking that the band were all Rastas, for here was a reggae ballad for the sufferahs, whose cries for justice are unheard shots in the dark. UB40 did such a good job of replicating the ethos of traditional roots reggae that it was easy to forget that this was an English band with a message for their own countryfolk. The flipside of 'I Won't Close My Eyes' was 'Folitician', picking up in England where others had left off in Jamaica, with an attack on a vote-hungry politician set to roots reggae. Best heard on the extended twelve-inch mix, the toasting vocal covers the same themes as the band's Jamaican contemporaries, portraying a deep distrust of all politicians. In the end, the 'box' of the chorus turns out to be the coffin of a constituent rather than a ballot box. Elsewhere on *Present Arms*, the band felt confident enough to record not one but two weed anthems, 'Lamb's Bread' and 'Don't Walk on the Grass'. The third in the trilogy of albums, 1982's *UB44*, followed in a similar vein. Here protest songs focus on the iniquities of the English justice system, with more than a hint of dread at the Cold War rhetoric being exchanged by the newly elected U.S. leader Ronald Reagan and the Soviet veteran Leonid Brezhnev and his 1982 successor Yuri Andropov.

UB44's dubbed-out politicism eventually gave way to a mellifluousness that drew on a more mainstream reggae tradition that the band would refine and develop, allowing them to become global stars and the biggest reggae band since Bob Marley and the Wailers. As the 1980s progressed, lead singer Ali Campbell's golden voice, honeyed but with just enough smoker's gravel, fronted a succession of pop reggae albums, interspersed with a series of compilations entitled *Labour of Love*, where the band drew on their inner fantasies and recorded authentic enough sounding covers of Jamaican classics by the Pioneers, the Slickers, the Ethiopians, the Melodians, Jimmy Cliff, Ken Boothe and Bob Marley. Ironically, though, the biggest single from the first *Labour of Love* was not quite the reverential rerub of an authentic Jamaican original that the band had initially envisaged. UB40's cover of 'Red Red Wine' (1983) was certainly very much in the style of the Tony Tribe recording that was Trojan's first big hit in 1969, but it was only after recording the track that the band became aware of the song's true origins. After its release, singer Ali Campbell claimed: 'nobody was as shocked as we were to find out that Neil Diamond wrote "Red Red Wine". To me, it was always a Tony Tribe song.'[33] It would not be long before the uninitiated British public saw 'Red Red Wine' as neither a Neil Diamond nor a Tony Tribe song, but as a UB40 one.

UB40's journey to superstardom eventually saw them leave their Birmingham home for a series of worldwide stadium tours. Although the band never fully shook off their politicized roots, their heyday was characterized by a musical mellowing before financial problems and an acrimonious rift saw the band split two ways. In 2008, original lead singer Ali Campbell and two other band members left to form 'UB40 with Ali, Astro and Mickey', while Campbell's brother Robin persevered under the unadorned UB40 moniker, recruiting older brother Duncan for vocal duties. Before the split, the band had around fifty UK hit singles, and sold albums by the million worldwide, yet by 2008 both bands were practically penniless. UB40 was one of the best-selling reggae acts of all time and were it not for a series of disastrous business decisions made at key points in their career, the band would now be rich beyond their wildest dreams. While the band missed out on what was rightfully theirs, there are other musicians who found wealth due to receiving royalty payments resulting from UB40 cover versions, including Lord Creator, who purchased several properties with royalty payments for 'Kingston Town', a global hit for in UB40 in 1990.[34] While you cannot accuse either of the two contemporary versions of UB40 of going through the motions, earning an income from live performances clearly remains a priority. In recent years, both versions of the band have seemed keen to return to political themes. In 2017, UB40 with Ali, Astro and Mickey headlined *Féile an Phobail*, the West Belfast community festival that has its origins in Irish republicanism, while the other UB40 christened their most recent album *For the Many* (2019), after the slogan used during the 2017 general election campaign by Labour leader Jeremy Corbyn, who in turn had borrowed the phrase from Percy Bysshe Shelley's *The Masque of Anarchy*.

UB40's chart-friendly sound brought reggae into the mainstream and appealed to a section of the musical audience much neglected by reggae in the past – namely, women. The same can be said of lovers rock, another reggae scene that developed in England in the 1980s and which featured a melodic style of reggae championed by Dennis Bovell. As he explains:

> Lovers Rock ... was the first British-made reggae that made it onto the sound systems. Reggae seemed to be a bit macho. If it was a sound system the audience would certainly be 80 per cent men and if it was just a blues dance or a reggae show girls would be there. So I spotted a space in the reggae sphere where there was a shortage of female vocalists taking the lead.[35]

Rooted in the softer vocals of rocksteady, lovers rock saw a return to the fore of melody and harmony after the punishing bass experiments of the 1970s. Rasta righteousness seemed in decline, and love and romance were now back in charge. Girl- and woman-friendly reggae wasn't entirely unknown in the UK at this point. Louisa Mark, a fifteen-year-old guest vocalist on Dennis Bovell's Sufferer sound system, had already had a hit with 'Caught You in a Lie' (1975), while Jamaican teenagers Althea and Donna had reached number one in the UK with 'Uptown Top Ranking' (1977), sung over the rhythm of Alton Ellis's 'I'm Still in Love with You'.

While these may have been hits, many reggae aficionados – perhaps chauvinistically – saw both releases as inferior to the work of the Rasta men coming out of Jamaica. Lovers rock turned the tables, privileging the female voice and the concerns of a female audience after many years effectively in a wilderness.

Where lovers rock differed from the vocal reggae of the 1960s was that it saw UK-based musicians at the forefront, although a feedback loop eventually formed between England and Jamaica, with Jamaican artists such as Gregory Isaacs and Sugar Minott jumping on board the new trend. This transatlantic working became obvious when Dennis Brown recorded a smooth new version of 'Money in My Pocket', giving him his first UK top-forty hit in 1979. But while Jamaican lovers-rock artists were popular, perhaps the best-known singer working in the style was the English-born Carroll Thompson, whose 'I'm So Sorry' single and *Hopelessly in Love* album were particularly successful. Suddenly, the righteousness of roots reggae that had appealed to the punks was under threat from a new sound, while the male dominance of the reggae scene became the subject of further critique. The Selecter's Pauline Black, who had grown up listening to Bob and Marcia's 'Young, Gifted and Black', had seen the promise of reggae as a unifying force broken by what she viewed as the retrogressive gender relations of the Rastafari:

> I admired that Aswad existed but I'm afraid I didn't go too much for the English variety of it. We had a bit of a run-in much later on the television programme I hosted, *Black on Black*, about women and the Rasta religion. That didn't go down real well. Rastas were outsiders from Jamaican life so they were to be admired for that but if you start breaking down how they felt about women then that wasn't too good. But you could say that about men in this country who probably felt equally bad about women and they weren't Rastas.[36]

A chunk of Aswad's best-known output was recorded for Island Records, which, despite being independent of the increasingly globalized major labels, had the scale and reach to sign both Jamaican and UK artists and turn them into global stars, releasing albums by Black Uhuru, Inner Circle, Bob Marley, Toots Hibbert and Sly and Robbie. When Bob Marley died in May 1981 of cancer, which had spread from a malignant melanoma in a toe that he refused to have amputated, this proved to be a turning point in Chris Blackwell's relationship with reggae as the label boss turned his attention back to rock music. At the time, Virgin Records were Island's big competitor, and they too had moved away from reggae, allowing a series of smaller insurgents to rise to prominence. Alan Davidson's Lightning Records had shown the way with hits in the single charts including 'Uptown Top Ranking' and 'Money in My Pocket', alongside full-length releases such as Culture's *Two Sevens Clash*, Joe Gibbs and the Professionals' *African Dub All-Mighty* and Prince Far I's *Under Heavy Manners*. In 1979 and 1980, the label Sufferers Heights also burned bright with a series of releases by Sugar Minott, Horace Andy and Mikey Dread.

Meanwhile the label Greensleeves, born out of a record shop in west London, would go on to become a global leader. In 1981 alone, the label released seventeen albums along with a plethora of releases on a new format that would become increasingly influential as the decade continued: the twelve-inch single. The Greensleeves back catalogue from this era reads like a long list of the most influential reggae acts of the time, including Dr Alimantado, Keith Hudson, Johnny Clarke, Black Uhuru, Barrington Levy, Clint Eastwood, Junior Delgado, Eek-a-Mouse, the Mighty Diamonds, General Echo, Yellowman and Scientist. Releases by these acts would soundtrack a UK reggae scene that faithfully served first- and second-generation Jamaican migrants and their black and white allies, listening to reggae on English sound systems that emerged in the 1970s, such as those by Jah Shaka, Lloyd Coxsone and Saxon, playing the latest releases coming out of Jamaica.

Jah Shaka had arrived in the UK from Jamaica in the early 1960s and built a loyal following through the 1970s with a fierce sound drenched in Rasta imagery, before releasing a series of albums on his own label, Jah Shaka King of the Zulu Tribe. Lloyd 'Coxsone' Blackwood's story was similar: emigrating from Jamaica to London before setting up a sound system in 1969 named after Coxsone Dodd and gaining prominence through a residency at the Roaring Twenties club on Carnaby Street in Soho, central London, before moving into production with his own Tribesman label. By the 1980s, Blackwood had gradually relinquished control of his sound system to a team of younger apprentices known as the Sir Coxsone Outernational.

With buoyant sound systems and an unquenchable appetite for new releases, the UK reggae scene was in rude health. Perhaps the biggest player was Saxon, who attracted a succession of deejays riding fierce Jamaican rhythms and who developed a form of toasting referred to as 'fast chat'. A significant number of Saxon deejays went on to have successful recording careers, including Maxi Priest (Max Elliott), Tippa Irie (Anthony Henry) and, best-known of all, Smiley Culture (David Emmanuel), who gained chart success and national fame while employing a fast-chat style of delivery on his debut 'Cockney Translation' and a series of follow-ups.

Although initially appearing to some to be a comedy single, 'Cockney Translation' (1984) was concerned with how working-class culture in London often valorized white gangsters yet remained irrationally fearful of the spread of so-called 'Yardie' criminals of Jamaican descent. Later in the 1980s, Paul Gilroy wrote of the duality found within 'Cockney Translation', pointing out how Smiley Culture was comparing stereotypical representations of East End culture with equally stereotypical representations of Black British culture. In particular, Gilroy observed that East End Cockney culture was inextricably linked in the popular imagination to criminality through popular television programmes such as *Minder* and *The Sweeney*, yet while a blind eye was turned to the activities of 'traditional' British villains, crime involving Jamaicans was demonized.[37] Within 'Cockney Translation', the first order of meaning is denotative, with 'shoota' translated into 'bus gun', 'tea leaf' (thief) into 'sticks man', 'wedge' into 'corn', 'grass' into 'informer' and 'Old Bill' into 'dutty Babylon'. Yet beyond these simple translations, a second order of meaning is quickly formed, with listeners offered a position from which they can judge the two contrasting representations of criminality as being equally stereotypical.

'Cockney Translation' was satirical in its contrasting of the linguistic tradition of an older white working class with the new multiracial language of a younger generation of Londoners. For Gilroy, 'Cockney Translation' pointed towards a future where young people would embrace Jamaican linguistic forms, with the song providing 'the basic framework for a potential black Britishness'.[38] Building on this analysis, Simon Reynolds has suggested that at the time of its release, 'Cockney Translation' led white youth to adopt the patois of their black friends, and in doing so helped shape the language of subsequent musical developments on the eastern seaboard of the Black Atlantic, including rave, jungle and grime.[39] Gilroy was certainly on the button when he wrote that:

> The patois into which the record translates white working-class dialect is shown to be more than a merely defensive argot, more even than a vehicle for the collective identity and solidarity of the blacks who have created it. It is the oppositional core of a black culture based no longer in a wholehearted rejection of Englishness that answered the exclusionary effects of racism, but on an idea of its overcoming and redefinition

in the association of black and white urban subcultures and their characteristically encoded communications which the toast makes mutually intelligible.[40]

With an equally witty yet political follow-up, Smiley Culture's 'Police Officer' (1984) saw the deejay discussing his own fame, claiming that he had managed to talk his way out of being found in possession of cannabis by offering a police officer his signature. The single was a top-twenty hit and following its release Smiley Culture signed for Polydor, but further chart success eluded him, and he slowly faded from view until July 2010, when he was arrested for conspiracy to supply cocaine. One week prior to his scheduled trial, the Metropolitan Police raided the artist's house in Surrey. An hour and a half after the police entered the property, David Emmanuel died of a single stab wound to the heart, an alleged act of self-harm that took place while he was supposedly being guarded by a police officer who was also completing paperwork concerning the search. An inquest jury verdict of suicide did nothing to stem suggestions of police complicity in Emmanuel's death. After an investigation, the Independent Police Complaints Commission criticized the Metropolitan Police, stating that: 'Four experienced officers felt it appropriate to detain a suspect in the kitchen, potentially the most dangerous room in the house, and afforded him a level of freedom not normally associated with an operation of this kind.'[41]

PART II

5

'RING THE ALARM': THE 1980S AND THE DECADE OF DANCEHALL

Wayne Smith, *Under Mi Sleng Teng* (1985)

Dem is the one that start it ... wid dem smutty mind ... dem
tek it serious.

YELLOWMAN[1]

In the run-up to the general election of October 1980, much
of Jamaica held its breath as predictions of electoral bloodshed
multiplied. As in the 1970s, both the PNP and JLP continued to
use imagery drawn loosely from both the Rastafari and reggae, but
with much less conviction. In opposition since 1972, the JLP adopted
'Deliverance' as a theme, a handy term that could mean a number
of things to both Rastas and Christians, with 'Stand Up for Your

Rights' another slogan. The PNP countered with 'Stand Firm for the Third Term', 'Foundations for the Future' and 'Stepping', the last a nod to the 'steppers' style of reggae popular towards the end of the 1970s, which featured a kick drum on each beat of the bar. As part of their campaign, the PNP used on an election leaflet the silhouetted figure of a Rasta with a guitar, and with Bob Marley at the height of his fame, both parties used 'Bad Card' and 'Coming in from the Cold' from Marley's final studio album in their campaigning. One of Anita Waters's respondents, who were all musicians, campaigners or party officials, claims that the JLP approached Marley for official endorsement, but were rebuffed, and another informed Waters that the PNP had approached Marcia Griffiths for permission to use her 'Steppin' Out a Babylon', with the same response.[2]

Echoing the PNP's earlier 'caravan of stars', the JLP organized a series of music festivals in the run-up to the election, featuring, among others, Byron Lee, a member of the JLP faithful and a friend of Edward Seaga. The biggest JLP tune of the day was the specially commissioned mento number 'Deliverance Is Near' by the Tivoli Garden Singers,[3] although the JLP also used Anita Ward's 'Ring My Bell', largely due to a bell being the party's main symbol.[4] Whereas in 1972 the PNP had used the Ethiopians' 'Look Deh Now' refrain from 'Everything Crash' to highlight what they saw as the JLP's poor stewardship of the economy, this would come back to haunt the party, as the JLP began to use the song to emphasize the state of a crashed Jamaican economy in 1980. For the PNP, Neville Martin returned with 'Stand Firm' while the same singer's 'No Mr IMF' was used as a straight-up defence of the PNP's position of breaking with the IMF. Meanwhile Seaga's JLP was ever-more focused on economic liberalism and anti-communism, with the latter element of their emerging new-right ideology taken up a notch when the PNP began to use 'The Red Flag', the anthem of the British Labour Party.[5]

Although both the PNP and JLP traded political blows regarding economic and political issues, both parties shied away from referring to the development of garrison politics. Both parties were equally culpable, and reggae had long noticed that the gun was now firmly entrenched in Jamaican politics. When the rude boys of the 1960s gained access to handguns, their newly armed status was heralded on Baba Brooks's 'Guns Fever' (1965), where the sound of a single gunshot ricochet rings out through the track. By 1980, this sounded almost quaint when compared to the staccato rhythm of the MI6 assault rifles that were now heard on the streets of Jamaica. Michael Manley described the 'rapid-fire chatter' of the MI6 as being heard so frequently that it was 'like a theme song of the campaign'.[6] Throughout the year, gun tunes proliferated, including Lone Ranger's 'MI6', Barrington Levy's 'MI6', Neville Valentine's 'MI6 Gunman' and Little John's 'Bushmaster Connection'.

In retrospect, 1980 marked the nadir of a particular form of political gangsterism. Prior to the election, Seaga was quoted as saying, 'on that day I will dip mi finger in PNP blood to mark mi x.'[7] The result of the election was a JLP landslide, with the PNP reduced to only nine MPs compared to the JLP's 51. If the election of Margaret Thatcher in the UK in 1979 and that of Ronald Reagan in the USA in the following year heralded the end of an era, the same can be said of the JLP victory of 30 October 1980 in Jamaica. The country was moving with the global times as Seaga adopted the same emphasis on supply-side economics as Thatcher and Reagan. In the UK, this new-right economic philosophy was called monetarism by some and Thatcherism by others, and in the United States the term Reaganomics was popular. In Jamaica, the portmanteau term 'Seaganomics' stuck, as the country's new prime minister became a passionate spokesman for what was referred to in Jamaica as 'structural adjustment': privatization, deregulation, deficit reduction and unfettered market forces. By the 1990s, an old term was co-opted to describe this new world order, with neo-liberalism now used to define a new conjuncture not merely in the Western hemisphere, but throughout the globe.

The PNP governments of the 1970s saw an enlargement of the public sector, but after 1980 it began to shrivel as Jamaica adjusted to the free-market logic of a smaller state. Throughout the 1980s, Seaga set about economic reform, reducing state subsidies, loosening control over investment and exchange states, lowering import tariffs and reducing funding for social security and healthcare. Most controversial of all were the Export Processing Zones (EPZS), or 'Free Zones', in Kingston and Montego Bay: free of much taxation, and free of trade unions too. Jamaica was becoming the supplier of cheap labour to the forces of globalization. Also controversial was Seaga's formation of a 'Special Operations Squad', quickly dubbed the 'Eradication Squad', to rid Jamaica of subversive political violence. The squad was much feared, and reggae responded with Yellowman's *Operation Radication* album and Eek-a-Mouse's 'Operation Eradication' single, decrying the killing of innocent citizens. Overseas, Jamaica's new policy of extrajudicial killings was also controversial, and by the mid-1980s, the campaigning organization Americas Watch was claiming that such killings accounted for half of Jamaica's murders.[8]

Despite the change in national leadership and the formation of Seaga's new squad, garrison politics continued in Jamaica, with gang members continuing to perform security functions for their respective parties, while maintaining support and suppressing dissent. Within each garrison, the gangs were given a large degree of autonomy, particularly when the police and military forces withdrew from no-go areas, granting each warring party the licence to operate their own forms of street justice and welfare delivery.[9]

By the time of the next general election in December 1983, the euphoric independence campaign of 1962 was a distant memory. Both the PNP and JLP thought that independence would allow Jamaica to flower as a post-colonial nation, but both were wrong, as the dream of independence was broken on the rocks of continuing economic turmoil. Across the developed world, globalization was beginning to be seen as both welcome and inevitable, although in Jamaica and other developing regions, views were more mixed. One of the results of Seaganomics was that Jamaica was shifting from a largely mining and production-based economy to a consumer and service-oriented one, despite the great mineral wealth contained in its substantial bauxite reserves. The EPZs, along with a greater reliance on tourism, meant that America's relationship with Jamaica was also growing in importance. For many, there came a dawning realization that colonial rule by the United Kingdom was being replaced by a subservient neo-colonial relationship with the United States.

But did Seaganomics work? By 1983, unemployment had risen, the trade deficit had tripled and drug-related crime remained rampant. The only bright economic spot was an increase in tourism, but this was at the cost of a decline in Jamaica's industrial base. With industrial production falling, the 'informal economy' of small-scale vendors, including drug dealers, ballooned. The rolling back of the frontiers of the state also allowed PNP- and JLP-dominated ghettoes to function as mini-states. Gangs now resembled paramilitary forces that had one foot in domestic politics and the other foot in a global drugs trade, with Jamaica a staging post between cocaine-producing countries such as Colombia and the consumer markets of the United States. In the 1970s, both the PNP and JLP used gunmen to maintain their respective grips on power within each of their garrisons. Once a global cocaine economy had become established with Jamaica as one of its nexuses, the power balance shifted from politicians to gangsters. The result was that the cocaine Dons became more powerful than either the PNP or JLP and broke free from the control of their patrons.

According to Laurie Gunst, cocaine first appeared in any great quantity in the lead-up to the 1980 election, 'in the pockets and noses of JLP gunmen'.[10] By 1983, it was everywhere, and the effect was devastating – on individuals, society and the body politic. Cocaine changed much of Jamaica in the 1980s, although one of the determinants for the rise of the new cocaine economy was the Cold-War politics being fought elsewhere. From 1979 until the early 1990s, the United States surreptitiously backed the Contras – armed right-wing gangs whose *raison d'être* was destabilizing the left-wing Sandinista government of Nicaragua. The Reagan administration went as far as admitting that the Contras smuggled cocaine to fund their cause but claimed that the leaders of the Contras were not themselves involved.[11] Whether there had been an earlier CIA project to destabilize Jamaica remains open to debate. What is unquestionable is that Tivoli Gardens and other garrisons found themselves to be key locations in a global cocaine distribution business, importing cocaine from Colombia and sending it out to U.S. and European consumer markets, with rude boys doing the shipping by hand and with corruption in the docks adjacent to Tivoli Gardens ensuring that the drug could be moved in bulk.

In the 1960s and '70s, Jamaica's garrison communities were characterized by a form of clientelism, involving the exchange of goods and services for political support. This shifted subtly in the 1980s. In the 1970s, the politicians had constituted the executive, with a rude-boy middle management oiling the wheels of the clientelist structure and corralling the voters within their garrisons. But once cocaine arrived, the rude-boy dealers gradually became more powerful than the politicians. Who was the patron now? With mutinous talk in Seaga's Western Kingston constituency, the prime minister reasserted his symbolic authority as the Don of Dons.

At the time of Edward Seaga's assertion of Don supremacy, much of his constituency was controlled by his former bodyguard and chief enforcer, Lester 'Jim Brown' Coke, Claudie Massop's successor at the head of the Shower Posse and the man that Bob Marley told confidants had led the attempt on his life at Hope Road in December 1976.[12] Named after the physically intimidating American football player and movie star Jim Brown, by the 1980s Coke was so powerful that it was his writ that ran in Tivoli Gardens rather than that of the police, the army or the government. In one alleged incident in 1988, a minibus driver had a disagreement with Coke without realizing whom he was talking to. When he discovered that he was arguing with the local Don, the driver fled to the local police station. But the cops were having none of it, and promptly handed the bus driver over to Coke and his gang, who beat him to death directly outside the station. Coke was charged with murder but acquitted due to a lack of witnesses.[13] Marlon James lightly fictionalized these events in his novel *A Brief History of Seven Killings*. Though the events were reimagined by the author, many in Jamaica are keenly aware of the reality of what went on.

In addition to his growing cocaine empire and partly as a way of maintaining his popularity in West Kingston, Coke wished to replicate Claudie Massop's success in the music industry. Starting in the late 1980s, 'Jim Brown' inaugurated and funded an annual concert at Fort Clarence Beach in Portmore, to the west of Kingston. Called 'Champions in Action', the event catered for 15,000 attendees and gun salutes were common from the audience, many of whom wore the JLP party colour of green.[14] Meanwhile, over in Tivoli Gardens, whenever 'One Man against the World' by Gregory Isaacs was played at dances, it would be accompanied by a gun salute in tribute to Coke. In the PNP's Arnett Gardens stronghold, it would be Bob Marley's old friend 'Red Tony' Welsh who ran the local dancehall with his Papa Roots record label and Socialist Roots sound system, featuring Ranking Trevor on the mic.[15] In each rival area, deejays would be expected to pay tribute to the local Don, whether they wanted to or not.

Edward Seaga's victory in the 1980 general election and Jamaica's descent into becoming close to a narco-state was the context for the most significant musical development since roots reggae in the 1970s: the rise of what became known as dancehall. But there would be one more event that would come to symbolize the closing of one era and the inauguration of another – namely the death of Bob Marley on 11 May 1981 from cancer, seven months after Seaga's election victory. Afforded a state funeral that led to a delay in the announcement of the government's budget, 100,000 visited Marley's coffin as it lay in a specially constructed mausoleum at the National Arena. The service was presided over by His Eminence Abuna Yesehaq of the Ethiopian Orthodox Church, who had baptized Marley as Berhane Selassie ('Light of the Trinity') in November of the previous year. When Michael Manley entered the arena, it is said that he was met with considerable applause, whereas the entrance of Seaga was more muted as the prime minister was guided to his seat by uniformed guards.[16]

Bob Marley's passing led many to suggest that the roots reggae that he played had died with him, to be replaced by dancehall, a new sound for a new era. Dancehall's origins are to be found in the development of the deejay style of talk-over vocals first heard on a handful of sound systems in the late 1950s. At this point, the most popular way of listening to music in Jamaica was via a selector playing records on a street-based sound system, with the best known being Duke Reid's Trojan and Coxsone Dodd's Downbeat. By the mid-1950s Dodd was employing Winston Cooper, under the stage name of Count Machuki, to introduce the selections, and Cooper began to develop a distinctively percussive close-microphone technique.[17] Machuki was later joined by an apprentice named Winston Sparkes, using the stage name King Stitt, who both played and introduced records.[18] Others followed and, slowly but surely, there began a shift from introducing records to talking over them. Using both memorized and improvised lyrics, the deejays drew upon the rhythmic structure of rocksteady and emerging reggae but added a new dynamic vocal layer over the top of the selectors' chosen records. As this style of delivery was developed, advances in sound-reproduction technology enabled selectors to emphasize or reduce bass and treble frequencies, carving out further aural space on which the deejay could place their vocals.

With the deejay style becoming popular in Jamaican dancehalls, recording engineers such as King Tubby (Osbourne Ruddock) and Lee 'Scratch' Perry began to produce customized 'specials': limited-edition seven-inch singles pressed onto acetate rather than the more expensive vinyl. These dubplates were most often instrumental tracks with the vocals removed and with the drum and bass patterns of the original accentuated. This would be the raw material with which a deejay could work. Michael Veal quotes Jamaican producer Bunny 'Striker' Lee on the origins of both 'dub' and what became known as 'the riddim':

> When dub started it wasn't really 'dub.' Tubbys and myself was at Duke Reid's studio one evening, and [a sound system operator] by the name of Ruddy [Redwood] from Spanish Town was cutting some riddims, with vocal. And the engin-eer made a mistake and him was going stop and Ruddy said, 'No man, make it run!' And then the pure riddim run because him didn't put in the voice. Ruddy said, 'Now take another cut with the voice.' And then, him take the cut with the voice.
>
> [Ruddy] was playing the next Saturday and I happened to be in the dance. And they play this tune, they play the riddim and the dance get so excited that them start to sing the lyrics over the riddim part and them have to play it for

about half an hour to an hour! The Monday morning when I come back into town I say, 'Tubbs, boy, that little mistake we made, the people them love it!' So Tubby say, 'All right, we'll try it.' We try it with some Slim Smith riddim like 'Ain't Too Proud To Beg.' And Tubbys start it with the voice and [then] bring in the riddim. Then him play the singing, and then him play the complete riddim without voice. We start a call the thing 'version.'[19]

To the English sensibility, there can appear to be a difference between a rhythm and a 'riddim'. While the former term denotes a sense of time, motion and accent, the term riddim seems to do more than this. Notable riddims feel like they are more than mere patterns of sound, with specific riddims incorporating distinctive keyboard riffs and horn melodies in addition to an interplay of guitars and drums. In rock and pop, rhythms are often borrowed, but not like they are in reggae. In particular, the forthcoming dancehall decade of the 1980s would see different versions of 1960s riddims proliferate, with Coxsone riddims coming to dominate. One example of a riddim that has remained popular in dancehalls from the 1960s to the present day is Real Rock, heard on the Coxsone-Dodd production of the 1967 single of the same name by Sound Dimension. In subsequent decades, the Real Rock riddim has featured on hundreds of recordings. Papa Michigan and General Smiley's 'Nice Up the Dance' (1979) is the best known, with the song also covered by Kabaka Pyramid on a big hit in the summer of 2020.

With the pairing of instrumental dubplate and toasting deejay increasingly popular in Jamaican dancehalls, it was inevitable that the deejays would begin to appear on vinyl themselves. In 1970 John Holt, then lead singer of the Paragons, recommended to Duke Reid that he ask Ewart Beckford, later known as Hugh Roy and then U-Roy, to visit Reid's studio to recreate the impact that Beckford was then having on Reid's Trojan sound system as he toasted over Treasure Isle classics by the Melodians, the Silvertones and Holt's own band the Paragons. The result was a string of releases that bust open rocksteady's melodies to reveal their underlying riddims, with deejay chatter high in the mix. 'Wake the Town' (1970) was Hugh Roy's first hit, a deejay version of Alton Ellis and the Flames' 'Girl I've Got a Date' (1966) that pushed the organ of the earlier track into the musical foreground, accompanied by the simple but effective bassline and drum pattern from Ellis's original hit. 'Wake the Town' was quickly followed by 'Rule the Nation', a version of the Techniques' 'Love Is Not a Gamble' (1967), and 'Wear You to the Ball', a reworking of the Paragons' track of the same name that contained just enough of the vocal harmonies of the original to be marketed by Reid as a duet. Released in quick succession, these three singles occupied the top three places in the Jamaican single charts for six weeks during 1970. Never one to look a gift horse in the mouth, Duke Reid put U-Roy in the studio to record around thirty further tracks, resulting in him toasting over much of the Treasure Isle back catalogue.

While U-Roy would eventually leave Duke Reid's studio for the life of a freelance deejay, the impact of his early work with Reid has remained undimmed, along with the work of other pioneers of the deejay style. By turns profound and profane, King Stitt began a successful global career as a deejay in the late 1960s, recording 'Fire Corner', a smash hit in 1969, followed in later years by 'Lee Van Cleef', 'King of Kings' and 'Herbsman Shuffle'. The latter track, released in 1980, became a smokers' anthem, featuring a distinctive and fierce bassline laid underneath Stitt's paean to ganja, with 'take a draw', 'tickle draw' and 'tickle it' delivered in King Stitt's distinctive percussive vocal style.

In contrast to U-Roy and King Stitt, Dennis Alcapone (Dennis Smith) often focused on a lyrical response to the vocals of the track he was toasting over, with his best-known work being 'Shades of Hudson' and 'Spanish Omego'. Getting in on the rude-boy trend, Alcapone also recorded a well-known gun tune with 'Guns Don't Argue' in 1971, toasting over snippets of Eric Donaldson's cover of the Everly Brothers' 'Love of the Common People'. After recording for Bunny Lee, among others, Alcapone eventually hit the big time, releasing more than a hundred singles, including 'Wake Up Jamaica', a vocal spar with Joya Landis's 'Moonlight Lover' and a big hit in 1973. Lyrically, Alcapone retained a rude-boy focus through a typical splash of Hollywood gangsterism, prefacing the popularity of 'gun tunes' in dancehall music in the following decade.

Originally, the lyrical content of the deejays was relatively apolitical, but as the 1970s progressed, there developed a new 'cultural' style of toasting, influenced by Rastafarian themes. U-Roy led the way with his 'Righteous Ruler' single, a Lee Perry production that saw the deejay toast over Nyabinghi drumming and a deep bassline drawn from the Reggae Boys' 'Selassie'. Others followed. The early work of I-Roy (Roy Reid) had drawn on nursery rhymes and a range of pop-culture references, but, gradually, he would take a lyrical turn towards the Rastafari, using the toasting style to explore those themes also in development within roots reggae. A prolific recording artist, I-Roy released sixteen albums in the 1970s alone, including a series of releases on Virgin Records' Front Line reggae imprint. Meanwhile, the breakthrough of fellow cultural deejay Big Youth (Manley Buchanan) came with his album *Screaming Target* (1972), a hit in both Jamaica and the UK. The album began with the title track, one of three mixes of K. C. White's version of Dawn Penn's 'You Don't Love Me' to feature on the album. As the album's opener, 'Screaming Target' had the outrageously simple innovation of featuring Big Youth's vocals on one of the track's two stereo channels, with the musical soundtrack, provided by his friend Augustus

'Gussie' Clarke, on the other. Increasingly conscious and political, latter albums by Big Youth would be more hard hitting, fusing contemporary social commentary with typical Rastafarian themes.

As the booming bass of stripped-down dubplates became more and more popular on Jamaican dance floors, either with or without a deejay, many reggae producers began to realize that they could harness this popularity by releasing singles with a deejay-led A-side and a vocal-free instrumental mix on the reverse. To begin with, these B-side versions were relatively straightforward – the producer mixed out the vocals, leaving snatches of horns and organ and perhaps occasionally reducing the mix to drum and bass. As four-track and then eight-track mixing desks became available to Jamaican recording engineers, electronic effects would be added to the music, and the B-side dub version began to morph into something quite different from the vocal-led A-side. Of all the effects used, the most important would be delay, echo and reverb, with the last enabling an engineer to take a sound from an acoustically 'dead' studio and transform it as if it were recorded in a space with a natural echo.

Instrumental B-sides gradually changed into what would become known as dub reggae. As the style developed, dub versions became ever sparser, with yet more accentuation of the bass and drums, aided and abetted by better recording technology that was able to enhance and deepen the recorded sound. A ghost of a melody might remain, snatches of singing perhaps, but with the vocal harmonizing of the 1960s left behind. As dub reggae developed, non-musical sounds would be added, including doorbells, telephones, gunshots and on some recordings the sounds of various animals. As studio engineers refined their craft, they would also become adept at tape splicing, in effect a rudimentary form of sampling that would enable separate recordings to be combined into a musical collage.

By the mid-1970s, dub proliferated, both on instrumental B-sides and full-length dub mixes of original albums, often with the same sequencing of tracks and released a few months after the original vocal recordings. The move towards the dub album began with three separate releases, although there is some debate as to which came first. Lee Perry's *Upsetters 14 Dub* was released in 1973 before being retitled as *Blackboard Jungle Dub*. At around the same time, Keith Hudson and Family Man recorded *Pick a Dub* while Herman Chin Loy released *Aquarius Dub*. These latter two albums are particularly austere and minimal, with several tracks broken down to their essence of rhythm and bass.

In 1974, King Tubby released his first long player, *Dub from the Roots*, the success of which prompted the quick release of a follow-up, *The Roots of Dub*, in the following year. Both albums feature a so-called 'flying cymbals' sound, actually a misnomer, for the hissing percussion heard throughout both recordings is a hi-hat, providing both albums with a distinctive sound. In 1976 another release involving Tubby, Augustus Pablo's *King Tubbys Meets Rockers Uptown*, brought the trend for dub albums to global attention, with Carlton Barrett on drums and Aston Barrett and Robbie Shakespeare sharing bass duties. Pablo's recording career began in 1969 with a series of cover versions of Studio One instrumentals which incorporated Pablo's use of the melodica, a small plastic keyboard operated by blowing through a tube which allows air to pass across a reed, leading to a melody perhaps reminiscent of an organ but distinctive enough to become his signature sound, and one seemingly made for dub reggae.

King Tubby remains the most enigmatic and influential of the 1970s dub artists, although his reputation was derived from humble origins, as Tubby's Kingston-based studio was too small for recording a full band, but ideal for perfecting the art of the dub mix, not least due to Tubby's ability to construct his own studio equipment. A twelve-channel mixing desk built by Tubby was the conduit for numerous analogue recording effects, including delay, echo, reverb, phasing and a parametric high-pass filter that enabled the engineer to add a distinctive sweeping sound to his output.

King Tubby's reputation as Jamaica's finest dub engineer was consolidated by the passing on of his skills to a new generation of dub remixers, most notably to protégés Scientist (Hopeton Brown) and Prince Jammy (Lloyd James), the latter of whom had shared production duties on *King Tubbys Meets Rockers Uptown*. In the 1980s, Scientist moved out from Tubby's shadow with a series of dub albums of his own, while *Kamikazi Dub* by Prince Jammy was taken from a set of recordings at the increasingly prominent Channel One studios and then mixed by Jammy in King Tubby's studio. The late 1970s and early 1980s was also a good time for dub albums from the UK, where Linton Kwesi Johnson's *LKJ in Dub* (1980) was a notable success. Later, a new wave of British dub came through with Aswad's *A New Chapter of Dub* (1982) and a series of albums by Guyana-born Neil Fraser, released under the name Mad Professor, beginning with 1982's *Dub Me Crazy!!*, recorded at Fraser's studio in south London and released on his own Ariwa record label.

Eddie Chambers, a cultural historian of Black Britain, posits the argument that the sum totality of dub was a 'decidedly counter-cultural type of music', defying the conventions of commercial music and refusing to engage with the star system in which so much popular music was invested.[20] At the forefront of this counter-culture in the UK was Adrian Sherwood and his On-U Sound record label and production house. Starting out as a teenage selector in a local reggae club in High Wycombe, Buckinghamshire, Sherwood soon became a junior partner in a record distribution business, selling Jamaican reggae to specialist shops around the country. When punk hit, Sherwood found himself in the right place at the right time, touring with the Clash and the Slits before forming his own label, which, four decades later, he still runs as an independent.

By the early 1980s, gathered around Adrian Sherwood were a group of artists who shared a post-punk sensibility and a deep love of reggae, and who, as an everchanging collective of English and Jamaican musicians, released a stream of envelope-pushing music that was never too far away from reggae and dub but which at points mutated into something unique to the label. Flitting between dub and a more avant-garde hybrid sound that was part post-punk and part Afrocentric collage, the label gradually built up a loyal fanbase. The creative tension between dub purism and experimental electronica first appeared during the recording of Creation Rebel's *Dub from Creation*, where Sherwood instructed Dennis Bovell to add ever more delay, echo and reverb, while experimenting successfully with mixing backwards, where effects that were played backwards would be added to recordings. Sherwood explains:

> If you take something that's playing forwards and then you turn it over so it's playing backwards – if you add a like a reverb to it [*sic*] and go 'kowww kowww' on the snare, if you play it back it would go 'shhhhok shhhhok', so the effects will play backwards. So that's putting delays on everything, and just randomly bringing things in and out, dubbing them out – bassline out, in, drums out, chops, jang jang jang juang jang, but played backwards. Then we'd put it onto a tape and play it forwards, but the effects were sucking and playing backwards.[21]

Sherwood continued on production duties with three albums by the New Age Steppers, a post-punk reggae supergroup formed by Ari Up and Viv Albertine of the Slits, Mark Stewart of the Pop Group, Keith Levine from Public Image Limited, Vicky Aspinall from the Raincoats, and John Waddington and Bruce Smith of Rip Rig + Panic.

Further away from reggae but clearly influenced by it were Tackhead, the result of a meeting in New York between Sherwood and guitarist Skip McDonald, bassist Doug Wimbish and drummer Keith LeBlanc, who were the rhythm section for Sugarhill Records and who had performed on the Sugarhill Gang's old-school rap classic 'Apache', as well as on Grandmaster Flash and Melle Mel's 'White Lines' and Grandmaster Flash and the Furious Five's 'The Message'. Relocating to London in 1984, McDonald, Wimbish and LeBlanc began work with Sherwood just at the point when his On-U Sound label was going through its most politicized period. Soon, Tackhead were recording with Mark Stewart, former lead singer of the Pop Group, on his solo album *As the Veneer of Democracy Starts to Fade* (1985), a collision of beats and percussion, sound effects and news footage, accompanied by Stewart's ranting vocals. Here also is the characteristic psychedelic edge of many of Sherwood's productions, also noticeable on releases by African Head Charge, with whom the label honcho had some success. The Sherwood sound was definitely dub but was clearly different from the earthy minimalism of King Tubby and others, with the On-U Sound template incorporating chants, spoken word and 'found sounds', all drenched in studio effects and on occasion straying beyond the furthest reaches of reggae into what were then unexplored musical terrains. Later in the 1980s, Tackhead would record a series of albums with Sherwood as part of a larger collective, touring as the On-U Sound System and fronted by DJ Gary Clail, who went on to have chart success with a series of hit singles in the early 1990s. Tackhead released three studio albums to critical acclaim, while also contributing to *The English Disease*, a reggae-influenced album with Sherwood at the controls and issued under the moniker of the Barmy Army. On the album, each track features audio snippets from football commentary, often focusing on one team within each recording, and with the sounds of miscellaneous crowds at English football games giving the album an anthropological feel.

If Sherwood's collaborations with the On-U Sound System ensemble occasionally veered from a reggae template, Sherwood's own heart clearly lay in dub, and it is here that his legacy was built, through an attention to detail during dub explorations in the studio. By the end of the 1980s, Sherwood had released a series of albums working with Lincoln 'Style' Scott of the Roots Radics in an ensemble called Dub Syndicate whose first few albums were dub at its finest. On *North of the River Thames* (1984), the melodica of Dr Pablo (Pete Stroud) is prominent, played in clear tribute to Augustus Pablo and giving the album a Jamaican feel. Meanwhile, the name Singers & Players was given to Sherwood's work with performers such as Prince Far I, Bim Sherman and Congo Ashanti Roy, but beneath the vocals sat the rich, cavernous dub that defined the Sherwood sound. Style Scott was found dead at his home in Jamaica in October 2014 in yet another murder that remains unsolved.

Describing himself as a mixologist, Sherwood has also spent much of his career as a remixer for hire, stripping back the music of the likes of Cabaret Voltaire, Nine Inch Nails and Ministry and then adding rich dub textures:

> With the dubs, you're working with a rhythm that's hanging on the verge of collapse all the time. You're pulling it to pieces, holding it together with delays and adding and spinning the rhythm . . . one bar blurs into another or distorts into the end of the four-bar figure, and then you pull it back, just when you think it's gonna collapse. You soothe people by bringing back the bass when you've taken it out. There's more space than anything.[22]

If, as Chambers suggests, dub's politics were countercultural in the UK, in Jamaica, the situation was complicated by garrison politics. Visitors to Prince Jammy's Studio in Waterhouse, to the west of Kingston, were soon made aware that they were in a PNP enclave, while visitors to King Tubby's studio in Tower Hill, to the east of Kingston, would pass gunmen on the door who would demand to know whether they were PNP or JLP. To gain entry, most would answer 'musician',[23] with singer Don Carlos stating that it was his dreadlocks that protected him: 'they saved my life because once you wore them, nobody would ask which party you voted for . . . You ah-Rasta, and people know say you nah vote.'[24]

With the likes of King Tubby, Scientist, Mad Professor and Adrian Sherwood positioned as the auteurs of dub reggae, there soon arose conflicts about the ownership of the intellectual property rights of the music. In particular, Scientist has been consistent in putting forward the argument that record companies frequently claim to own the rights of compositions and recordings that are not rightfully theirs, accusing the UK-based label Greensleeves of fraudulently claiming to have purchased from Henry 'Junjo' Lawes the rights to recordings that Scientist had supervised.[25] Conversely, Scientist also suggests that many of the recordings that he claims as his own have been pirated by record labels and released under the name of King Tubby to ensure that he, Scientist, does not receive any recompense, with labels also withholding any payment that might be due to King Tubby.[26] Scientist claims that Tubby only recorded three full albums, *Dub from the Roots*, *The Roots of Dub* and *Brass Rockers* by Tommy McCook and the Aggrovators, and had largely given up mixing by the end of the 1970s.[27] With 'Junjo' Lawes having been killed in London in 1999, Scientist states: 'it's highly convenient for Greensleeves to say they own the product when the producer is dead.'[28]

The controversy regarding who owns what within reggae is largely due to the centrality of Jamaican producers who retain ownership of the master tapes of recordings and use them as they see fit, irrespective of any intellectual property rights that a song's composer or a band who had performed on a recording might have. As Scientist points out, even though producers like Henry 'Junjo' Lawes may have had sole ownership of master tapes, they did not necessarily own the rights to the musical elements of the recordings captured within their studios. In Scientist's view, if a songwriter records for a producer or a label, the publishing rights to the song remains with the writer, unless he or she chooses to sign those rights away as part of a publishing contract:

> in order for Junjo to own the product, Junjo first have to have a contract with the artist, and the artist first have to sign away all their copyright to Junjo and then Junjo can sign it away to whoever they want. There is no such document trail ... I have relatives in London going all the way back from 1940. When I first started my career in Jamaica, they were the ones who started telling about all these records that were coming out in my name – *Scientist versus Prince Jammy, Scientist Rids the World of the Evil Vampires* ... When I contacted Greensleeves they tried to tell me that they had the permission from Junjo. I tried to explain to them I didn't give Junjo the permission ... When you talk to Freddie McGregor, Michigan and Smiley, all of them. They'll all tell you the same thing – they never signed any contract, any copyright, any publishing away to Junjo so that Junjo can take it and sign it away.[29]

The history of Scientist's struggles to obtain ownership of the intellectual property rights to recordings that he supervised and mixed can be seen within the changing covers of the releases that he is most often associated with. The year 1981 saw Greensleeves release *Scientist Meets the Space Invaders* and *Scientist Rids the World of the Evil Curse of the Vampires*, followed a year later by *Scientist Wins the World Cup*. Scientist is credited as the artist on all three releases, but the engineer has said that he was unaware of the release of these albums at the time. When the time came for Greensleeves to reissue these albums in digital formats in the twenty-first century, a subtle change meant that, this time around, it was the producer and not the studio engineer who was badged as the artist, with the album titles changed to *Linval Presents Space Invaders*, *Junjo Presents: Wins the World Cup*, and *Junjo Presents: The Evil Curse of the Vampires*. Recent releases of these albums also feature much of the distinctive artwork by Tony McDermott found on the first Greensleeves releases, but the particularly eagle-eyed will notice some slight differences, including a calculated insult to Scientist, erasing him from his position behind a mixing desk on the cover of the re-release of the *Space Invaders* recording.

Scientist's argument that it is he and not Henry 'Junjo' Lawes or Linval Thompson (or their heirs) who owns the rights to these albums is weakened by the fact that the music within the recordings was written by neither producer nor studio engineer but by the Roots Radics. As the house band at the Channel One Studios, the Roots Radics are finally credited as the recording artist on the back covers of the most recent releases of the albums listed above. However, with so much of their work being based on reworked riddims from the 1960s, the original composers are almost certainly lost in time.

The Dancehall Decade

The rise of both the riddim and the deejay set the scene for the rise of dancehall. Central to the development of the new style were the aforementioned Roots Radics, a collective of studio musicians who began to develop and work on Studio One riddims, stripping them back to their rhythmic essence and seemingly hardening them and slowing them down, giving a new generation of vocalists such as Sammy Dread and Little John further musical space on which to perform. Handily, the emerging fashion for the reuse of classic rock-steady riddims was also cheap, as minimal studio time was required by the band, who were well aware of the rhythmic structures of the original Studio One productions and who could replicate them quickly. Luckily for the studio producers employing the band, the new style was also popular in the dancehall. Reggae historians Steve Barrow and Peter Dalton make the point that the reuse of Studio One riddims was particularly suited to the financial circumstances of consumers in straightened times, offering the view that: 'cost-conscious consumers were more likely to spend any cash on what was already familiar, as long as it was combined with sufficient elements of the new, whether in the performer's style or a topical lyric.'[30]

Although dancehall originators Sammy Dread and Little John were popular in Jamaica, they were relatively unheard of outside of Jamaica. This was not the case with Sugar Minott and Barrington Levy, two other early exponents of the dancehall sound who began to pick up international attention, singing on classic Studio One riddims laid down in fresh recordings by either the Roots Radics or the Revolutionaries. The latter were another house band at Channel One Studios, featuring Robbie Shakespeare on piano and guitar and Sly Dunbar on drums, a duo who went on to feature on hundreds of recordings and whose influence on the development of the dancehall sound cannot be overestimated.

Sugar Minott's career began at Coxsone's Studio One as a jack of all trades: writing songs, singing and playing guitar and drums on whatever recordings he was asked to contribute to. After releasing his debut long player *Live Loving* (1977), the follow-ups of *Black Roots* (1978) and *Ghetto-ology* (1979) sealed his appeal and brought him instant international success, particularly in the UK, where he relocated, becoming a bigger star in Europe than he had been in Jamaica.

Beginning a career in music at the same time, Barrington Levy was another artist recording at Channel One with the Roots Radics. Levy's vinyl debut was 'Moonlight Lover', a relatively traditional vocal cut on the Treasure Isle classic of the same name, using a riddim that had been used earlier by Dennis Alcapone on 'Wake Up Jamaica' (1973). However, whereas Dennis Alcapone's version of the riddim was recorded at a rocksteady speed, Barrington Levy's singing was set to a far more languid tempo, revealing a stripped-back riddim, deep and dubby, with a heavy dose of reverb and 'flange' applied. Later, Levy would record 'Collie Weed' (1979) on the My Conversation riddim that originated on the 1968 single of the same name by Slim Smith and the Uniques. Again, the tempo of 'Collie Weed' is noticeably slower than the original rocksteady classic, with percussion and bass to the fore and with only the six-note piano line of the original forming any kind of melody. The style would remain the same for Levy's follow-up 'Looking for Love', set to the Real Rock riddim.

If the soundtrack of early releases by Sugar Minott and Barrington Levy pointed towards the direction of musical travel, two further developments would be required before dancehall could be said to have fully emerged from reggae. The first was a move away from melodic sung vocals by the likes of Minott and Levy to a rhythmic and partly spoken style far more reminiscent of deejays working in the live dancehall setting; and the second was an ideological shift away from lyrical themes of love and romance towards unadulterated sex. Both would be found on *Slackest LP*, an album by Ranking Slackness (Earl Robinson) released in late 1979 that looked and sounded markedly different from the better-known reggae releases of that year.

There had, of course, been innuendo and explicitness in earlier Jamaican releases, with double entendre featuring heavily in mento and some calypso. Written in 1952, 'Night Food' by Alerth Bedasse and Chin's Calypso Quintet was concerned with an older woman's frustration at the sexual naivety of her younger lover. The track went on to become the fastest-selling record in Jamaican history, proving that sex definitely sells. In the 1960s, Lord Creator's 'Big Bamboo' was also well known. Released in the same year, 'I Want My Cock' by Owen and Leon Silvera was an early release on Island Records that left little to the imagination. To hammer the title home, the song begins with the gossamer-thin double entendre of the sound of a cockerel. In 1966, recording for Coxsone Dodd, Lee Perry released 'Doctor Dick' and 'Rub and Squeeze' while also recording 'Pussy Galore' with the Wailers, a song that referenced the character of Pussy Galore in the 1964 film *Goldfinger* as well as its double meaning. Later in the rocksteady era, Max Romeo's 'Wet Dream' (1968), recorded for Bunny 'Striker' Lee, was a UK chart hit, despite being banned from radio. Somewhat disingenuously Max Romeo claimed the track was concerned with a leaky roof. Speaking to *Melody Maker* in the UK, Romeo said:

> It's not a dirty song at all . . . It's only immoral people who think it's dirty . . . I never had any bad ideas when I wrote the song. In Jamaica, what I said doesn't mean what people here think. I just had a dream and wrote the song afterwards. I dreamt that I was asleep, lying with my girlfriend and it was raining and the roof leaked and I got wet. That was what I meant by 'wet dream'. And then I asked my girl to move over so I could get a stick and push something up into the roof to keep that rain out. That's all it was to be. But people here took it to mean other things.[31]

The success of 'Wet Dream' led to Romeo recording a series of follow-ups including 'Wine Her Goosie', 'Belly Woman' and 'Mini Skirt Vision' before he heard the call of the Rastafari.

A year after 'Wet Dream', Prince Buster's 'Wreck a Pum Pum' was also a portent of future dancehall concerns, set to the melody of 'The Little Drummer Boy'. While 'wrecking' was said to refer to intercourse rather than any violent act, a line in the first verse of the track, 'tear a pum pum', was more ambiguous. An album by Prince Buster placed 'Wreck a Pum Pum' alongside other tracks including 'Rough Rider', 'Whine and Grine', 'Beg You Little More', 'Pussy Cat Bite Me', 'Train to Girls Town' and 'Stir the Pot'. Female artists responded accordingly, with 'Wreck a Buddy' by the Soul Sisters and 'Barbwire' by Nora Dean, on which she recounts how her partner 'got barbwire in his underpants', resulting in him being hit on the head with a brick ('barbwire' is Jamaican slang for a sexually transmitted disease).

The lyrical concerns of the *Slackest LP* picked up where the likes of Max Romeo and Prince Buster left off, beginning with the album's opener 'Bath Room Sex' and ending with 'Lift Up Your Dress Fat Gal'. Throughout the album, sexual explicitness is paired with the new slowed-down grooves of the Roots Radics, with vocals delivered in a part-sung, part-spoken deejay style.

For his follow-up single, Earl Robinson would be rechristened General Echo, releasing 'Arleen' as a deejay cut on the famous Stalag riddim that had originally appeared in 1973 on the Winston Riley-produced 'Stalag 17' single by Ansell Collins. 'Stalag 17' also sat beneath Barrington Levy's earlier single 'Rock and Come In'. Levy's single was concerned with whether 'the best dressed girl' is 'under sixteen or over sixteen', and the listener required no further information to work out the Jamaican age of consent. On 'Arlene', General Echo picks up on the theme, with the opening line 'under seventeen, are you over sixteen?' set to a deep bassline. Here there is little in the way of any other percussion bar a little hi-hat and some light snare drum, with General Echo's vocals as loud and as central to the mix as was possible.

In a signal that a new musical era had now begun, General Echo's 'Arleen' went straight to number one in the Jamaican singles chart. Operating his own Echo Tone sound system and having huge hits meant that General Echo should have had a successful career in front of him, but on 22 November 1980, a car in which he was travelling with his selector Flux and their compatriot Big John was stopped by the Jamaican Police and all three were shot dead in an action that remains unexplained. Although a new generation of dancehall deejays were shifting attention away from party politics and towards sex, garrison politics remained rife, and the police were still shooting people in the street in the wake of the general election of the previous month. Briefly, dancehall would return to political concerns with Clint Eastwood & General Saint's 'Tribute to General Echo' and 'Echo Get Shot' by Tippa Ranking.

With dancehall producers now crowbarring open Studio One riddims to reveal deep basslines and danceable drum patterns, and with slack dancehall's first star taken in disputed circumstances, a void opened, only for it to be quickly filled by a series of successors. The deejay Trinity (Wade Brammer) was an early contender, having already recorded 'Three Piece Suit' for Joe Gibbs in 1977, a deejay talk-over version of Marcia Aitken's 'I'm Still in Love' (itself a cover version of the rocksteady classic by Alton Ellis). On 'Three Piece Suit', Trinity informs the listener that he has taken his amour to bed while wearing 'diamond socks and ting' and 'earth-man shoes and ting'. The track became so well known that it warranted an answer record, Althea and Donna's 'Uptown Top Ranking', recorded by the same producer on the same riddim. Despite a promising start, 'Three Piece Suit' marked the highpoint of Trinity's career as a deejay and it would be Anthony Waldron, recording under the name Lone Ranger, who would eventually take General Echo's crown. After releasing deejay-led reggae singles for both Studio One and Channel One, the Lone Ranger moved studios and recorded 'Barnabus Collins' for Alvin 'GG' Ranglin. Like Barrington Levy's 'Collie Weed', the Lone Ranger's single was voiced on the 'My Conversation' riddim. Unlike Barrington Levy's traditional defence of ganja, the theme of 'Barnabus Collins' is a vampire cavorting with his girlfriend, with the track containing an immortal line where the vampire narrator promises to his lover that he will 'chew ya neck like a Wrigley's'.

If General Echo and the Lone Ranger pointed in the direction of lewdness, there was a host of dancehall deejays who were prepared to up the ante. Most popular of them all was Yellowman (Winston Foster). As prolific in the studio as he was in the dancehall, Jamaica's biggest star of the 1980s released some 37 known singles between 1980 and 1983 and became the first dancehall star to gain a major-label record deal. The appeal of dancehall to CBS Records was obvious – major labels had always looked enviously at the sales volumes of Bob Marley but were wary of signing another independently minded political militant. Shorn of much of roots reggae's political militancy and signalling a return of 'good time' themes, the new sound of dancehall was ripe for major label exploitation.

Yellowman has been perhaps unfairly labelled as the king of slack; his early work was not always sexual in focus, with 1981's 'Eventide Fire' being a coruscating critique of the scandalous deaths of 155 elderly women in a fire at the Eventide residential care home in Kingston in October 1980. Whereas Barrington Levy and General Echo's earlier track, 'Eventide Fire a Disaster', was a melancholic number mourning the sheer number of deaths, by the time of the Yellowman release anger had set in around the state of the home at the time of the fire and the poor response of the emergency services.

Following Yellowman's flirtation with politics, a focus on bawdiness took over, with the deejay's own romantic prowess featuring prominently on subsequent releases. On the face of it, the notion of a male dancehall star informing listeners of his own attractiveness and success with women might be so normal as to pass without comment, but in Yellowman's case, the albinism from which he took his stage name makes this more notable. Here was a man with a lack of skin pigmentation, working in a music scene noted for its celebration of Blackness and releasing records in a society where albinos were shunned and persecuted. The audience's response to the audaciousness of Yellowman's claims saw his popularity increase, and the artist went on to have a long and successful career in both Jamaica and overseas.

In retrospect, it is easy to forget how big a star Yellowman was by the time he appeared on CBS's radar, having already released a plethora of albums and completed a sold-out tour of the UK prior to his unveiling as the major label's latest star. For his debut long player for CBS, Yellowman was persuaded to incorporate a range of different sounds drawn from R&B and disco, but despite the populist stylings, the album was a commercial failure for CBS and an artistic failure for Yellowman. International dancehall fans wanted authentic Jamaican energy, not a major-label mishmash of genres that messed with the dancehall blueprint. In the end, CBS jettisoned Yellowman, who returned to what he did best, riding classic riddims with unredacted slackness, and his career quickly recovered. In 1982, Yellowman was diagnosed with cancer, and an operation in 1986 left his face permanently disfigured, but this did little to hamper his appeal.

Never particularly comfortable with slackness, early dancehall star Barrington Levy continued to release recordings with a cultural theme before going on to have an international hit with the evergreen 'Under Mi Sensi' (1985), a Junjo Lawes production and a paean to sinsemilla, unfertilized female ganja plants prized for their potency. After this traditional plea to free the weed, the following release, 'Here I Come', tells the tale of a couple who have a baby prior to the mother absenting herself of her responsibilities. In press interviews at the time, Levy was keen to emphasize his difference from the new generation of slack deejays, putting forward the view that mothers should be allowed equal recreational time as men: 'It's nice if the father can take some of the pressure off the mother, so she can go and have fun too. Make it half and half, so neither miss out on anything.'[32]

If the first quantum leap in the development of dancehall was the development of slack lyrics delivered over a minimal riddim laid down by a house band, with deejay vocals high in the mix, the next step saw dancehall enter the digital age. In 1985 King Jammy, formerly known as Prince Jammy but coronated in acknowledgement of his advanced studio skills, used a Casiotone MT-40 keyboard in the studio to form the basis of a brand new riddim. The keyboard itself was little more than a toy, and certainly not designed for use in a recording studio. Like many of the consumer-oriented electronic synthesizers of the era, the MT-40 had several pre-set rhythms that could be used to accompany a melody played on the keyboard. Legend has it that the rock pre-set was supposed to mimic Eddie Cochran's 'Somethin' Else', but to dancehall initiates, the pattern of the sound is instantly recognizable as the Sleng Teng riddim, first heard on the King Jammy-engineered 'Under Me Sleng Teng' (1985) by Wayne Smith.

The designer of the MT-40 was Hiroko Okuda, who at the time was a young graduate of musicology at Tokyo's Kunitachi College of Music.[33] Interestingly, Okudo was also a reggae fan, and it is easy to imagine how her love of Jamaican music found its way into the rhythmic structure of the Sleng Teng riddim, if not into its sound, which is sharp and edgy – a world apart from the gentle heartbeat of roots reggae. Within a few weeks of the release of Wayne Smith's single, several Sleng Teng variants were in production, with Tenor Saw's 'Pumpkin Belly' hitting the charts in the United States and Europe. Innumerable deejay versions on the Sleng Teng riddim were to follow, as the new sound picked up speed and began to take over Jamaican music.

With the digital dancehall genie out of the bottle, roots reggae seemed like a distant memory in Jamaica, even if it continued to be popular abroad. Drum machines had been heard before on reggae, for example on Marley's 'So Jah Say', the first track on side two of *Natty Dread*, but nothing had prepared listeners for Sleng Teng's aural onslaught. Soon, drum machines would come to dominate dancehall as part of a broader shift from analogue to digital, with dancehall featuring the first significant time-signature change in Jamaican music for decades.

Up until this point, most reggae featured a 'one-drop' riddim. While there is much debate within reggae as to the meaning of the term 'one drop', many point towards what happens on the third beat of each bar within a 4:4 time signature, where 'the drop' refers to simultaneous hits of the kick and snare drums with the snare often struck on its metal tuning edge in reggae's distinctive rim shot. Other drummers, including Cleveland 'Clevie' Brown, define one-drop reggae as featuring a kick drum and rim-shot snare on beats two and four. The only real difference between these two definitions is how you count each beat, with one drummer explaining it to me as the difference between counting 'one, two, three, four' versus 'a one and two and three and four', with both ways of counting having the same impact. A third possibility in any definition of one-drop reggae involves what happens on the first beat of each bar, where the beat is often omitted, and it is this feature that is most prominent on Bob Marley and the Wailers' 'One Drop' on *Survival*, where the upstroke of an electric guitar, but no drum, is found on the first beat of each bar.

Irrespective of origins and definitions, by the 1980s, reggae's distinctive one-drop sound was complemented by 'steppers' and 'rockers' styles that featured a bass-drum emphasis on all four beats of the bar, leading to a heavier, more pounding sound. This latter stylistic shift was overseen by Joseph 'Joe Joe' Hookim at his Channel One studios, where Sly Dunbar adapted funk and rock drumming for reggae. Although there had been some controversy regarding one drop versus steppers and rockers, the differences between these styles paled into insignificance when compared to the new digital dancehall. In particular, the new digital sound often featured a time-signature change, using a syncopated two-bar pattern said to be derived from the clave found in Afro-Cuban music.[34] Within much dancehall from 1985 onwards, these two-bar patterns came to dominate in all their brutal simplicity, with the form derided as such by roots-reggae aficionados.

By the end of 1985, dancehall was now fully formed, rhythmically, stylistically and ideologically. Slowly, the new digital sound began to have serious repercussions for those roots-reggae musicians still plying their trade. With digital sounds sweeping through Jamaican dancehalls, why would a producer pay musicians to perform in a full-sized recording studio when more popular releases could be produced in much smaller facilities using relatively cheap digital technology such as the MT-40? The popularity of digital dancehall saw many of the larger studios shut down, and the whole ecosystem of the Jamaican music industry shifted as a result.[35] Such was the popularity of the Sleng Teng riddim that individual releases began to be collected together on albums, beginning with *Under Me Sleng Teng Extravaganza* (1985), which contained ten versions on the Sleng Teng riddim, including Wayne Smith's original, with a follow-up, *Sleng Teng Extravaganza: 1985 Master Mega Hits, Volume 2*, released later in the year.

From this point onwards, dancehall eclipsed roots reggae in terms of both sales and popularity, with Greensleeves and VP Records particularly influential in spreading the dancehall gospel outside of Jamaica. Greensleeves' reputation had originally been built with roots reggae, but dancehall dominated the label following a deal struck with Henry 'Junjo' Lawes to release work he produced in the Channel One studio in Kingston.[36] Throughout the 1980s, Greensleeves would release dancehall recordings by General Echo, Eek-a-Mouse, Yellowman, Lone Ranger, Yabby You and Frankie Paul, in addition to double-header albums by Clint Eastwood & General Saint and Nicodemus & Toyan, as well as also releasing some of the finest dub by Prince Jammy and Scientist. Although the perception was of Greensleeves as a dancehall and dub label, this ignored a slew of roots reggae and lovers rock releases by the cream of the 1980s' crop, including albums by Burning Spear, the Wailing Souls, Linval Thompson, Sugar Minott and Gregory Isaacs. The strength of Greensleeves sales in the UK was enough to make many Jamaican artists begin to see the UK rather than Jamaica as their primary source of income. By this point, Henry 'Junjo' Lawes had faded from view after he moved to New York in 1985, although he was eventually deported back to Jamaica due to his involvement in drug crime. Lawes was killed in London in a drive-by shooting in 1999, with some suggesting that garrison politics may have been behind his murder.[37] In 2006 Zest Group PLC, a holding company formed to purchase music recording and publishing companies, purchased Greensleeves for £3.25 million, and set about repackaging the label's back catalogue for a new generation.[38]

During the period of Greensleeves' dominance in the UK, over in New York another independent reggae empire was being built. VP Records was founded by Vincent 'Randy' Chin and his wife Patricia in Kingston, Jamaica, in the 1960s, and like Virgin and Greensleeves, this was a label with humble origins. Vincent Chin's father originated in China and arrived in Jamaica via Cuba, while Patricia Chin is of Chinese and Indian ancestry. Vincent had worked, managing jukeboxes in bars and restaurants since 1958. Once the patrons of his employer had tired of the choices available in each jukebox, Chin removed the seven-inch singles, took them away and sold them as used in a shop that the couple shared with a vitamin-supplement vendor. Patricia Chin then began to run the store, allowing her husband to scour the island for more used vinyl to sell to his customers. Remembering this time, Patricia Chin told *Billboard*:

> Music is the only thing that really keeps people alive . . .
> I remember when I had my record store, even if someone had
> only two dollars to buy bread, they'd prefer to buy a record.
> They would take it home and play it over and over and over,
> and they'd sing along, and they'd dream.[39]

The store, Randy's Record Mart, was a great success. With the profits from the shop, the couple developed their own recording facility and began to produce their own records. An early success was 'Independent Jamaica' by Lord Creator, the Trinidadian calypso singer, which the Chins then licensed to Chris Blackwell for Island Records' first ever UK release, with the catalogue number 'Island 001'.

With a studio, label and record store, the obvious next step within the Chin strategy of vertical integration was to develop a record-pressing facility and distribution network. Once they had established a studio-to-store business model, the Chins then began to involve Vincent's son Clive in the family business, and he eventually took on production duties, using the name Randy's All Stars for a house band that included Aston Barrett, Sly Dunbar and Augustus Pablo. Other notable producers also used the Chin studio, with Lee Perry recording the Wailers there in 1970–71.

Once their emerging empire was in place, the Chins began to draw their other sons, Christopher and Randy Junior, and daughter Angela into the family business and started to look abroad for expansion opportunities. In 1979 the family closed their store in Kingston and slowly relocated to New York. Vincent and Chris moved first, opening a VP Records store on Jamaica Avenue in Queens in 1979. Having seen the benefits of diversification back in Jamaica, the Chins soon realized that they could use their store as a national distribution storage hub and began selling reggae to other retailers. vp Records was then formed as a label to ride the dancehall boom. In the 1980s, all the majors wanted the next Bob Marley, but none found him. What the major labels did not realize was that Bob Marley was not 'found' by Lee Perry or Chris Blackwell but developed by them. vp Records showed that with an in-depth knowledge of both reggae and dancehall, artists picked by the label would eventually break through into the charts, long after a major label would have given up. With Chris Chin in charge of A&R, vp Records were in for the long haul, whereas the major labels' attentions were fleeting: 'they ended up dropping most of the artists after a year or two. So we picked them up, and stuck it out.'[40]

If Greensleeves and vp Records had their fingers on the pulse of dancehall and showed the major labels how to have hits without watering down the product, the most famous independent of them all, Island Records, was sitting things out, waiting for the tide to turn back to roots reggae. They would be waiting some time, but in the meanwhile, there was the small matter of Bob Marley's estate. As Marley had died intestate, a series of court cases was required to determine who would own what. In October 1984, New Jersey-based music publisher Danny Sims, who had served as producer and publisher to the Wailers before they signed to Island Records, began legal action against Marley's estate. Sims claimed that Marley had avoided contractual obligations to him by withholding some songs and publishing others under pseudonyms, citing breach of contract, misrepresentation, intentional interference with contractual obligations and conspiracy to defraud.

In July 1986, Marley's manager Don Taylor, who Marley had sacked in 1980 after he discovered that Taylor had expropriated funds, alleged that documents held by Rita Marley, which ensured that her late husband's chief assets were passed to her, were fraudulent and signed retrospectively by Rita Marley after her husband's death.[41] In the end, Rita Marley admitted this, but claimed that she did so after legal advice.[42] As a result of this revelation, the Jamaican Supreme Court dismissed Rita Marley as an administrator of Bob Marley's estate. After a hiatus of three years, the Supreme Court of New York then declared that under a six-year statute of limitations, Danny Sims was too late in bringing aspects of his legal case, but the dispute rumbled on with claim and counter-claim.[43] Outside the court, Sims claimed to have discouraged Marley from singing revolutionary hymns to the sufferahs of Jamaica: 'I'm a commercial guy. I want to sell songs to thirteen-year-old girls, not to guys throwing spears.'[44] In the end, the jury found in favour of Marley's estate, and Danny Sims lost his case.

By 1989, Chris Blackwell was in the process of purchasing the assets of Bob Marley's estate for a subsidiary of his called Island Logic Inc., despite opposition from the Marley clan. Eventually, the Supreme Court of Jamaica laid down a ruling that Blackwell's bid for Marley's estate should be accepted. In a separate case, the administrators for Marley's estate sued Rita Marley and Marley's mother Cedella Booker for illegal withdrawals of JA$16 million and JA$500,000 respectively.[45] Blackwell's successful purchase of the Marley estate ensured that Island owned the publishing rights to the most important Marley compositions, along with Marley's trademark and his biographical rights. Other bidders, including A&M, Virgin Records and Island Life, a Japanese company, only bid for the publishing rights to the Marley song catalogue, whereas Blackwell was prepared to take all of Marley's assets. The Marley family appealed to the Privy Council in London to overturn the purchase and to grant the family the right to buy much of Marley's back catalogue. At the time, Blackwell stated that he remained close to the Marleys and was disturbed by what he considered to be a private matter becoming public.[46] In another twist, it became apparent that Blackwell had lent money to the family so that they could be joint beneficiaries of the publishing rights, and that the terms of the deal meant that the newly formed Marley Foundation would receive royalty payments once the debt to Blackwell was repaid.

With Marley's estate finally settled, merchandizing operations were brought under the umbrella of the Marley Foundation, as was the Tuff Gong label and recording facility (the former Federal Records studio bought off Ken Khouri) and the Bob Marley Museum, although there remained confusion regarding the songs that the Wailers wrote and performed prior to their signing for Island Records.[47] An investigation by *Billboard* revealed that Coxsone Dodd had registered much of the songwriting output of the pre-Island Wailers with the Performing Rights Society (PRS) in the UK and Broadcast Music Inc. (BMI) in the United States, claiming to have been the sole songwriter of the compositions sung by the Wailers during the 1960s. However, the situation was confused by the fact that others had also registered different versions of the same songs. By way of an example, a spokesperson for the PRS stated that they had seven different versions of 'Simmer Down' on their books, including one dated 1978 that was credited to Bob Marley and another, from 1981, credited to Coxsone Dodd under a songwriting alias of Scorcher. Bunny Wailer called this 'bullshit, Coxsone Dodd is not a writer'.[48] In a counter-claim, Danny Sims argued that he had acquired the rights to these songs through his 1967 agreement with the band, saying that he had collected millions in royalties from them before he sold his catalogue to Island Logic. Following this deal, Sims noted that the songs are now 'owned by Rita and the kids'.[49]

Shortly after his deal with the Marleys, Chris Blackwell sold Island Records to the PolyGram conglomerate for an estimated $300 million in a deal that raised eyebrows concerning the valuation of Island. David Geffen of Geffen Records, one of the few remaining independent labels with any global reach, said at the time:

[the valuation] is a lot of money, and it indicates how important the record business is becoming ... Record companies
are becoming as rare as hen's teeth, and by the end of the
decade there probably won't be anybody left except the five
international distributors (Warner, CBS Records, PolyGram,
Thorn-EMI PLC and the Bertelsmann Music Group) and one
domestic distributor (MCA Inc's MCA Records).[50]

Blackwell explained that the rationale behind the deal was to
ensure that he had the financial firepower to sign global artists: 'we
were too big to be small, and too small to be big.'[51] Blackwell was
reported to have personally received 30 per cent of the purchase
price paid by PolyGram, with the remainder going to undisclosed
investor groups.[52] At the time, the deal with Island meant that
PolyGram had around 9 per cent of the U.S. market share for album
sales of all genres of music, dwarfed by Warner's U.S. share of around
44 per cent and smaller than CBS's share of around 14 per cent
and that of Bertelsmann at just under 11 per cent.[53] Following the
deal, Blackwell took a high-profile job at PolyGram and formed a
subsidiary within it entitled Island/Jamaica.

If VP Records and Greensleeves were having success with
riddim-driven dancehall while Island Records sat things out and
avoided the new genre, the major labels did not wish to be left out
regarding the latest development in Jamaica, although CBS's experience with Yellowman was a salutary lesson for them all. The next
out of the blocks was Atlantic Records, part of the Warner-Elektra-
Atlantic (WEA) conglomerate, who were building a considerable
market share by incorporating add-ons, such as Seymour Stein's
Sire Records, while also acting as distributor for various independents. In 1988, Atlantic signed the Spanish-Town deejay Lieutenant
Stitchie (Cleveland Laing), whose own profile had been boosted by
his 'Natty Dread' single, which topped the Jamaican singles chart for

fourteen weeks earlier in the year. Stitchie's own career had taken off when he began working with King Jammy in 1987; however, his major-label career would be similar to that of Yellowman, with WEA encouraging the deejay to develop a mainstream sound that drew him away from the dancehall community that had made him popular. Lt Stitchie recorded three albums for Atlantic over a five-year period, but as with Yellowman, Jamaican hits only returned once he was released by the major label and began recording again for Jamaican independents, including Jammy's, Bobby Dixon's Digital-B label and Donovan Germain's Penthouse Records.

The development of slack dancehall during the 1980s saw Jamaican music turn away from commenting on political matters, but within a few years, some dancehall deejays and a range of reggae musicians were returning to the theme. This was perhaps unsurprising considering the political turmoil of the decade, with unemployment in Jamaica being above 20 per cent for much of it. This time, though, the partisan politics of the 1970s was avoided as reggae and dancehall called a plague on both houses of JLP and PNP, arguing that all politicians were as duplicitous as each other. A good example of this form of political dancehall is the King Tubby-produced 'Politician' (1984) by Barry Brown, backed by the Aggrovators. Here, the singer informs 'Mr Politician' that he could be seen clearly from the garrisons, stoking a war from which only the politician would profit, squirrelling away profits into a Swiss bank account. Brown advised the Rastafari that, should Mr Politician come to them to 'talk 'bout election', he should be turned away and only then would there be peace in Tivoli and Jungle. 'We nuh want no politics' says Brown, with all kings, queens, presidents and prime ministers merely oppressing God's people (presumably Selassie was not included in this list).

Two years later, Al Campbell picked up the theme on his reggae single 'Politicians'. On Campbell's track, absentee politicians are evil men and only ever seen at election times. In the same year, Admiral

Bailey released the first of a diptych of singles on the subject of party politics. The first, 'Ballot Box', was voiced in combination with Josey Wales, where both deejays deny any involvement in party politics on a digital version of Larry Marshall's Through Me Corn riddim. In the follow-up, 'Politician', Admiral Bailey rails against the 'shit-stem', placing the politics of the day in the context of slavery and the plantation, the root of all sufferation in Jamaica. Bailey would be one of many reggae and dancehall artists to make the connection between the armed garrison politics of Jamaica and the ongoing conflict in the Middle East, referencing Lebanon specifically, then in the throes of its long civil war.

'Ballot Box' and 'Politician' were relative anomalies, with most deejays turning their backs on politics and several lining up for the title of king of slackness. At the front of the queue was Shabba Ranks (Rexton Gordon), one of the few dancehall deejays to become a household name in the UK, at least partly due to his deal with Epic Records, which by this time was part of the giant Sony cor-poration. However, it is with a single that preceded his major-label career that 'Shabba' was at his most influential.

'Dem Bow' is the seventh track on *Just Reality*, Shabba Ranks's fifth studio album and his first for Bobby Dixon's Digital B studio. On the track, a narrator criticises those who perform fellatio and cunnilin-gus. Sensing that dancehall was about to become ever cruder, a small army of dancehall deejays followed on the same theme, including Danny Dread, Shad Du and Bounty Killer, who all released singles with the same title of 'Dem Bow'. However, although the lyrics were influential, it was Bobby Dixon's soundtrack that set much of Latin America on fire. Some have gone as far as to suggest that the Dem Bow riddim is the sole defining feature of reggaeton, a half-dancehall and half-rap hybrid that rose to popularity in the early 1990s.

The riddim itself, known as Dem Bow or occasionally the Pocco riddim, was influenced by the drumming used within Pocomania, a Kumina ceremony where rhythms that are African in origin are incorporated into ceremonies that mix Afrocentric ancestor worship with aspects of Protestantism. Clevie Browne of the duo Steely & Clevie explains:

> Steely came to studio one morning and said he could not sleep all night long because there was this revival taking place, a tent was set up near his house, and all night this music was playing so he said 'if you cannot beat it, join it', so he came to the studio and said Clevie: 'I want make a Pocco riddim'. He started including some tambourine in the riddims but at the same time I was being inspired by what I was hearing at church ... At that time, the One Drop was what was running the place in Jamaica ... Reggae one drop with the third beat accent but Steely and I wanted to do something different. We needed something new. What can we do new? So, we stopped listening to everything that was out there, we stopped listening to radio, we just took time out to just try find something from our roots ... We just worked with what we were feeling and we took time out to listen to people ... To listen to the rhythm of life and just observe the people. We used to leave the studio at times, drive, go to Trench Town, go to Tivoli, just drive through Jamaica, and just listen to how people spoke, the rhythm of speech, the body language.[54]

On the Steely & Clevie riddim, a snare roll introduces a kick drum playing crotchets, with the snare continuing in and around each beat of the bar. Steely & Clevie's use of *timbales*, a pair of single-headed metal drums that are Cuban in origin, gives the riddim a Latin feel. Following the release of Shabba Ranks's 'Dem Bow', the riddim was almost immediately picked up by the Panamanian musician Nando Boom, who adapted it during a recording session in New

York, working with both Jamaican and Panamanian musicians on a track entitled 'Ellos Benia'. This track was aimed at the city's Spanish-speaking community, but it incorporates the rhythm from the Shabba Ranks original, along with its 'dem bow' chorus line. Musically, some of Clevie's improvised drum rolls were replaced with further *timbale* beats that feel more programmed than live, although the recurring drum roll at the end of every measure is retained.

Lyrically, Shabba Ranks's 'Dem Bow' equated fellatio and cunnilingus ('bowing') with colonial servility (also 'bowing'), seeing both as alien to the Jamaican temperament, with the song reflecting the popular misconception that such acts are a decadent Western import. Jamaicans should not bow before each other or before those foreigners who are their oppressors. 'A gunshot for them' is Shabba Ranks's prescription for both. In 'Ellos Benia', the term 'bow' is recontextualized, but it retains much of its original malign intent, with Nando Boom drawing upon similar levels of innuendo and accusing men who 'swallow microphones' (*'tragas un microfono'*) of bowing. The list of those accused is then extended to any man who wears a skirt and any man who carries a cane; they are all 'a bow', turning Shabba's malevolent verb into a homophobic noun. The anti-colonial refusal to bow is also found in 'Ellos Benia', where Nando Boom states confidently that Panama is definitely not 'un bow'.[55]

'Ellos Benia' was followed by 'Son Bow' by fellow Panamanian El General, further establishing the popularity of the riddim. Both 'Ellos Benia' and 'Son Bow' were released in the same year as Shabba Ranks's original, merely emphasizing the speed with which the original riddim travelled from Jamaica to Panama via New York, where Nando Boom and El General found themselves following their flight from the military regime of General Manuel Noriega. Like 'Ellos Benia' there is is an element of homophobia in 'Son Bow', and in a contribution designed to increase its pan-Latin appeal, Puerto Rico and Colombia are added to the list of countries that are 'not bow'.

Women in the Dancehall

With narratives of sex almost entirely told from the perspective of male deejays, it was perhaps unsurprising that very few women broke through into the new musical form of dancehall, at least initially. Jamaican music had never been exactly overrun with female performers, although there were some particularly successful singers in the 1960s. As noted earlier, Millie Small sung on one of the biggest-selling records of the 1960s, and by the end of the decade Joya Landis, Dawn Penn and Phyllis Dillon were also having hits, with the last singing for Duke Reid on 'Don't Stay Away' (1966) and the risqué 'Don't Touch Me Tomato' (1968). However, as reggae emerged from rocksteady and the Rastafari began to dominate the new style, female singers were edged out of the picture, although the dearth of female artists through the 1970s was partially hidden by the prominence of a handful of international stars. Most notable of these were the I Threes – Marcia Griffiths, Judy Mowatt and Rita Marley – all of whom had successful solo careers prior to their incorporation in Bob Marley's band following the departure of Peter Tosh and Bunny Wailer.

Prior to her involvement with Marley, Marcia Griffiths was reggae's highest-profile female performer, having starred on Studio One releases in the rocksteady era, including her first hit with 'Feel Like Jumping' (1968). Despite a busy international tour schedule with Marley and his band, Griffiths released three albums in the 1970s, *Sweet and Nice*, *Naturally* and *At Studio One*, a compilation of her early work. With these, Griffiths developed an accessible style of reggae that was rewarded with significant record sales, demonstrating that while Rasta roots reggae dominated the 1970s, this was not to the total exclusion of other styles. Judy Mowatt began her career as lead vocalist for the Gaylettes in 1967 and while still performing with the I Threes released *Black Woman* in 1979, which reggae historians Kevin O'Brien Chang and Wayne Chen refer to as being 'generally acclaimed [to be] the best reggae album ever made by a woman'.[56] Finally, Rita Marley, perhaps the best known of the I Threes, began her recording career in 1964 at Studio One, where she sung duets with both Bunny Wailer and Peter Tosh before performing in the Soulettes with Nora Dean. Following the Wailers' split, Rita Marley focused on her work with the I Threes, although for much of the 1970s, when Griffiths and Mowatt were recording in Jamaica, she was raising six children, four of whom were Bob's, who for some of this period was living in London with Cindy Breakspeare.

There were other female artists, but they were few and far between. In the UK, and less connected to reggae royalty than the I Threes, was Janet Kay, the first British-born Black woman to have a reggae song at the top of the British charts with the lovers rock classic 'Silly Games', written and produced by Dennis Bovell. And in a significant contribution to unadulterated roots reggae, by 1981 Black Uhuru featured the talents of Sandra 'Puma' Jones working alongside Michael Rose, Sly Dunbar and Robbie Shakespeare.

Having mentioned some notable exceptions, it is fair to say that by the 1980s, Jamaican music was dominated by male musicians and vocalists, and the gender relations of both Jamaica and roots reggae was then replicated within the dancehall decade, where there were few significant female deejays – the best known being the incomparable Sister Nancy (Ophlin Russell). Introduced to dancehall by her brother Brigadier Jerry (Robert Russell), Sister Nancy began performing on the microphone at the age of fifteen, appearing first on the Chalice sound system before moving to Black Star to work alongside her brother, and eventually ending up with General Echo on the Stereosonic sound system. Nancy describes General Echo as 'the first slack DJ; slack mean them talk about men parts and woman parts, how people do in the bedroom. He was a very

X-rated deejay but he was loved and he was nice, and people love him. Him just talk it raw.'[57]

General Echo took a shine to a particular toast that Nancy had originally titled 'Papa Dean Want to Give Me Sardine' and he eventually persuaded Winston Riley to record the single in the Channel One studio. Riley's own career began with the Techniques before he eventually formed his own record label with the same name, which became well known for a series of international hits that included 'Double Barrel', the UK number one performed by Dave and Ansell Collins that Riley had licensed to Trojan Records.

'Papa Dean' was a Jamaican hit for Sister Nancy, leading to the Winston Riley-produced album *One Two* (1982) – which remains her only original long-player release – from which 'One Two' and 'Bam Bam' were released as singles. While 'Bam Bam' referenced the 1966 Toots and the Maytals single of the same name, the riddim was Stalag 17, previously used by Big Youth, General Echo, Barrington Levy and Prince Far I, and which would feature again later at the dawn of the digital age on Tenor Saw's 'Ring the Alarm' (1985). Tenor Saw was the deejay name for Clive Bright, originally an acolyte of George Phang, a PNP activist who used his connections in politics to become both a reggae producer and an 'area leader'.[58] Bright had been introduced to Phang by the deejay Nitty Gritty, who some implicated in Bright's death in Houston, Texas, in August 1988.[59] Despite the whispers regarding his involvement, Nitty Gritty eventually recorded the tribute 'Who Killed Tenor Saw?'.

While Sister Nancy released several seven-inch follow-ups, none had the impact of 'One Two' or 'Bam Bam', and when digital dancehall broke big in 1985, she stepped back from performing and recording 'to give other people a chance to experience the glory'.[60] In more recent years, Nancy has reflected on the international success of 'Bam Bam', stating that its popularity was hidden from her by her producer, so as to discourage her from requesting payment for her services: 'Back in the days, they don't pay you. You just want your voice to be heard, you just want to hear your record play on the radio, and you feel good.'[61]

Sister Nancy only became conscious of her global success when she moved from Jamaica to New Jersey in 1996, and since then she has decried the extent to which elements of 'Bam Bam' have been taken by other artists who have profited more from the track than herself, including the use of a sample on tracks by Kanye West ('Famous' feat. Rihanna), Chris Brown, Pete Rock, Lauryn Hill and Alicia Keys. For Nancy, the process of recovering payments for her songwriting and deejay work began when she became aware of the appearance of 'Bam Bam' on a Reebok commercial, tracing the track's use to Westbury Music in the UK, who stated that they had purchased the rights from Winston Riley. With some suggesting that 'Bam Bam' is the most sampled and remixed reggae track of all time,[62] Nancy eventually recovered some of those rights and now owns 50 per cent of the songwriting and publishing royalties, with ten years of back payments enabling her to give up her work as an accountant. In a series of interviews to mark a return to live deejaying in 2017, Nancy also spoke of how, as the sole female deejay in Jamaica at the time, she was discouraged from performing by her father and only gained control of the microphone at dancehall events due to the respect that other deejays had for her brother, who she would turn to for protection when harassed by men: 'when them get hot 'pon me, me just turn Brigadier 'pon them and mash them up.'[63]

Sister Nancy's isolation during the 1980s was symptomatic of both the lack of women's roles in Jamaican music production and an effective male prohibition on women stepping up to the mic in the dancehall. This marginalization was at least partly reflective of a society where most women were excluded from the best-paid employment; Jamaican patriarchy ensured that women remained ideologically and physically bound to the traditional roles of homemaker and provider of childcare. Up until the 1980s, this suited the needs of Jamaican capitalism, which had few formal uses for female labour beyond a handful of white-collar occupations for 'respectable' lighter-skinned women. It was not until the decline of old occupational certainties within the new economic order of the 1980s that gender relations would change.

'Structural adjustment' led to a decline in white-collar and blue-collar employment and the expansion of a semi-regulated, small-scale, informal entrepreneurial economy. This saw the rapid expansion of a new form of female entrepreneurship among 'higglers': women engaged in international trade within the Caribbean and beyond through the small-scale export of rum and other Jamaican commodities, with the resulting revenue then used to import manufactured goods from overseas. Eventually dubbed 'informal commercial importers' (ICIs) and regulated and taxed as such, higglers were most often women who had previously been excluded from formal employment.[64] Within the racial gradations of Jamaican ethnicity, higglers were black rather than brown. Professor Donna Hope of the University of the West Indies describes the higgler as 'a dark-skinned, overweight or mampy-size Afro-Jamaican woman dressed in tight, revealing, garish costumes with both large amounts of gold jewellery and one of many elaborate hairstyles that negate the traditional conventions of Eurocentric beauty'.[65]

The higgler style of the 1980s carved out a cultural space for Jamaican women in the brave new world of global supply-side economics. This came at a time when traditional male roles in the economy were declining and Jamaican men were finding work opportunities much harder to come by as they too negotiated their way through a tightly gendered order.

Having considered the changing relationship of women to the Jamaican economy, it comes as less of a surprise, although it may have felt like a shock, that slack dancehall exploded in the 1980s. Perhaps we should see the forcefulness of slack dancehall as being the dying throes of a very specific patriarchal ideology rooted in the economy of the previous era and part of a broader backlash on the part of masculinity. 'Backlash' is of course a concept well known within feminism, at least partly due to Susan Faludi's book *Backlash: The Undeclared War Against Women*.[66] Just as the turbulence of changing gender relations in Jamaica was felt at large, the good-time riddims of the Studio One era returned, ousting the earnestness of roots reggae. The new queens of the dancehall had money to spend on higgler style, and as male deejays began to crank up the slackness, women's dance styles and clothing became ever more sexualized.

As the 1980s progressed, the slack male deejay backlash grew stronger and more vicious as male artists portrayed themselves as both courting and conquering women, in what became known as 'punanny' lyrics. This lyrical form is described by Donna Hope as 'an instance of patriarchy's operation at its most elemental, basest and sexual level, where the most extreme manifestations of this behaviour are often perceived as misogynistic'.[67]

From 1985 onwards, slack male deejays competed with each other to voice the most brutal and denigrative celebrations of female genitalia and the power of their own penises. Deejay versions recorded on the Punanny riddim are testament to this, with the term used to describe both female genitalia and women themselves, reducing half of the Jamaican adult population to their sexualized essence. The riddim itself was produced by King Jammy and first appeared on 'Punaany' (1986), a number-one dancehall smash by Admiral Bailey that topped the JBC radio chart for several weeks. Within subsequent versions, male deejays profess both a love for the punanny and an ability to master it: 'mi a punanny guineagog' extols Shabba Ranks in 'Love Punnany Bad' (1987), which after Admiral Bailey's version was the best-known deejay voicing on the riddim. For Shabba Ranks, the punanny was to be worshipped, but for lesser mortals it should be feared for its power. The Greensleeves riddim album *Punanny* collects together twelve versions on the original King Jammy riddim and ten versions on a later reworking of the riddim by Ward 21.

Within a few years, the notion of punanny lyrics had taken hold and by 1989 almost all the deejays featured at Reggae Sunsplash and Sting, Jamaica's biggest musical events, focused at some point on praising the punanny or criticizing its shape, size or colour. In what seemed like an important moment, the following year saw Bunny Wailer and his band the Solomonics abused and bottled off the stage at Sting by a restless crowd keen to hear slack head-liners Ninjaman and Shabba Ranks.[68] So, the dancehall decade finished as it had begun, with X-rated lyrics set to dance floor-friendly riddims and delivered in a deejay style, only by this point much of the language of dancehall had lost its power to shock as each new deejay attempted to outdo their predecessors by record-ing ever more explicit lyrics. In addition to punanny, Donna Hope lists a number of other equally unflattering synonyms in circulation within dancehall, including 'glammity, punash, pump um, punny, good hole, rekin meat, tight underneath, vaggi and ukubit'.[69] Some thought the change was permanent and dancehall would con-tinue through the 1990s in the same vein, while others sensed that punanny dancehall would not last long. Changes were certainly round the corner, as the women of the Jamaican dancehall, never quiet for too long, began to bite back and respond to their male peers, many of whom started to swallow their own words as they turned their backs on punanny and gunplay and began to return to the lure of old friends Marcus Garvey and Haile Selassie.

6

'YUH NUH READY FI DIS YET': WOMEN AND THE POLITICS OF DANCEHALL AND REGGAE, 1990–2010

Tanya Stephens, *Gangsta Blues* (2004)

I remember the mayor in Montego Bay was calling me the queen of slackness. So I was showing him, telling the government – another side of slackness that needs to be addressed. What the word really means. 'Cause I can control my slackness, you know? But there's so many other things – guns being issued out to youths in the ghettoes, killing each other; sufferation and hardship; people can't get a job when they finish school. That's *slack,* that's the meaning of the word.

LADY SAW[1]

The only female artist to appear on the *Punanny* riddim album was Lady Saw (Marion Hall) and it is this artist, the 'First Lady of the Dancehall', who led a backlash against the backlash, puncturing the male deejays' pictures of themselves and matching their sexual aggression in no uncertain terms. Not only did Lady Saw break nearly all Judeo-Christian sexual taboos, she asserted an Afrocentric eroticism that was largely absent from the work of the male deejays. In this, she fought a gender war on multiple fronts, against the derogatory male deejays, but also against Eurocentric views of acceptable femininity and against social taboos and societal expectations of Jamaican women. At points, Lady Saw would also have to battle with the law to be allowed to perform her work.

Starting out in the late 1980s, Lady Saw first took to the mic at the age of fifteen at local dances in the parish of St Mary on the north coast of Jamaica, with little success initially. Her debut single, 1992's 'Stone', sank without a trace, but attention increased two years later with *Lover Girl* for VP Records, where the deejay sets out her stall as an aggressive sexual conqueror. To promote the album, 'Hardcore' was released as a single, where the melody from the nursery rhyme 'It's Raining, It's Pouring' sits in stark contrast to lyrics that profess the narrator's ability and willing-ness to perform sexual gymnastics and acrobatics in 'any style yuh want'. The move from unremarkable dancehall to X-rated slackness was confirmed by 'Stab Out Mi Meat', the final single taken from the album. There is very little that can prepare the uninitiated listener for the 'joy and pain' that a 'stiff and hard' fuck brings. The only concession that Lady Saw makes to her lover's masculinity is the promise that if 'mi get breed' she would not inform the world of the father's name. On 'Dem Bow', Shabba Ranks had pushed the envelope with his attack on what he saw as the contemporary sexual deviance of oral and anal sex. With 'Stab Out Mi Meat', Lady Saw took this one step further and shocked Jamaica by demanding her own sexual satisfaction, while also issuing broadsides against those deejays who had belittled their sexual partners. As she was to say later, 'I never got much recognition when I went about it the proper way, so I had to put my foot down and kick it like a man.'[2]

Sensing that there was a popularity to be gained from lurid tales of the inadequacies of former lovers, Lady Saw recorded 'Peanut Punch Mek Man Shit Up Gal Bed', only to be accused of hypocrisy for claiming that her work was being censored. The criticisms were somewhat ill-judged though, for while Lady Saw may have been able to continue releasing slack recordings, they were banned from Jamaican radio and she soon found herself under heavy police pressure and prevented from taking to the stage in specific Jamaican jurisdictions, while the slack male deejays continued to perform widely.

Seemingly tiring of straight-up dancehall relatively quickly, Lady Saw began to experiment with a range of styles on her third album *Give Me the Reason* (1996), including on a country ballad on the title track, while the gospel-tinged 'Glory Be to God' prefaced her later turn towards Christianity. 'Life without Dick' was another ballad with little in common with dancehall reggae barring its subject-matter and Lady Saw's deejay-style vocals. Other tracks continued with Lady Saw's characteristic playfulness, but there was also a harder-edged politics on the peerless track 'What Is Slackness'. With no distance between narrator and deejay, Lady Saw contrasts her supposed slackness with the far greater sins of the Jamaican state, which are swept over in popular ideology as the press whip up a controversy around sexually explicit lyrics. For Lady

Saw, slackness is not a dancehall phenomenon; rather slackness is when the roads need fixing, when governments break promises, and when the politicians of the PNP and JLP ('di two party') import guns so that their respective street warriors can shoot each other dead.

In the years that followed the release of 'What Is Slackness', Lady Saw gave a good impression of being the hardest-working performer in Jamaica, releasing over two hundred singles in total, including tracks where she features as a guest vocalist, such as on No Doubt's 2002 single 'Underneath It All', which went platinum and for which she won a Grammy under the category Best Performance by a Duo or Group with a Vocal. A particularly strong period in Lady Saw's career was around 2004's *Strip Tease*, which reached the *Billboard* U.S. reggae charts and which many saw as her most accomplished work. The album was accompanied by the eminently cheeky 'I've Got Your Man' single, where the deejay claimed that her new lover had left his previous girlfriend due to her 'tush' being 'a little slack', before retorting that the anonymous former girlfriend should not complain, for Lady Saw was 'only stating facts'. Elsewhere on the album, 'Pretty Pussy' was a high-pitched autotuned fast-chat vocal on Donovan Bennett's Trifecta riddim, which outlined all the beautiful aspects of the pretty pussy of the title, 'black and beautiful', 'pink and fruitiful'. Lady Saw had travelled from recording on the Punanny riddim to issuing her own declaration of sisterhood, encouraging self-love on the part of women.

By 2010 Lady Saw had her own production company, Hall Productions, and was producing digital riddims herself for use by Capleton, Spragga Benz, Sizzla, Bounty Killer and Beenie Man. However, by the time of her final album, *Alter Ego*, in 2014, Lady Saw's increasing unease with her adopted persona was becoming apparent, and the album contained a roughly equal number of ballads and dancehall numbers, alongside a brief foray into house music with 'Pretty Fingers'. Following a baptism in her new home in the United States in December 2015, the artist formerly known as Lady Saw abandoned both her moniker and dancehall reggae in preference for a career in gospel under the name Minister Marion Hall. Having made a decision to cancel all scheduled performances, Hall was then denigrated for rejecting slack dancehall in much the same way she was attacked for taking it up in the first place:

> After my baptism, I found that a lot of people in Jamaica were persecuting me, criticising me, condemning me for making my decision – talking a lot of mess. You'd think people would be praying me up when many were talking against me . . . I've gone through so much.[3]

In beating men at their own game, Lady Saw opened the gates of the dancehall for other female deejays, and it was Tanya Stephens (Vivienne Tanya Stephenson), a contemporary of Lady Saw, who had the most success. With ten full-length albums following her first single 'One Touch' (1994), Stephens has had a career as rounded as that of any male deejay, although it could be suggested that none of her contemporaries, male or female, have been quite as effective at melding cutting-edge lyrical content with a diverse range of reggae and dancehall styles, and it is this that marks her out as one of Jamaica's leading artists of the twenty-first century. Throughout her career, Stephens has successfully blended good-time dancehall vibes with a keen political consciousness. She is perhaps at her most successful when combining the political consciousness of roots reggae with the production techniques of modern dancehall, deftly switching between different vocal registers including deejaying, singing and all points between, with Stephens as comfortable riding a riddim in a dancehall style as she is when singing a capella.

After a series of singles for Shelly Power and 'No More Lies' for Xterminator, one of the big labels of the 1990s, Stephens's first statement regarding dancehall slackness was the single 'Yuh Nuh Ready fi Dis Yet' (1996). Here she addresses 'Mr Mention', riffing off the title of the second album by rising star Buju Banton, asking the otherwise generic dancehall male whether he had ever wondered why his women cheat on him. Having portrayed her potential suitor as not up to the standards of any decent woman, Stephens then ponders whether he has ever wondered what makes a woman reach orgasm, before destroying her suitor with a further rendition of the track's title, appending the diminutive 'bwoy' by way of a coda. 'Yuh Nuh Ready fi Dis Yet' was sung on Madhouse's Joyride riddim, on which Lady Saw also voiced 'Sycamore Tree' in the same year. Both tracks are comparable, but although Stephens's version is arresting and has a great pay-off line, Lady Saw's is denser, lyrically and narratively. The subject-matter remains the same, where a boy asks a female narrator for fellatio but is told to flee. In her first verse, Lady Saw's narrator explains that she didn't know how; she was a church-going girl and no boy would turn her into a freak. A final chorus sees Lady Saw's character explain that food alone would go in her mouth. This is very different from Stephens's knowing narrator, whose sexual experience is used as a weapon against men. While dissimilar, both narratives were critiques from one side of a gender war, on the other side were Mr Easy & Baby Cham, whose voicing on the same Joyride riddim was entitled 'Funny Man', a lacklustre homophobic track that was no match to the singles by Lady Saw and Stephens.

Coming to the attention of VP Records, 'Yuh Nuh Ready fi Dis Yet' then featured on *Too Hype* (1997), Tanya Stephens's debut for the label. On the album, Stephens hops between deejay-style vocals and singing on a range of riddims from different producers, including 'Too Hype' and 'Mi and Mi God' on the Farajan and

Swing Easy riddims for Delroy 'Callo' Collins, and on the Cloak & Dagger riddim for Patrick Roberts on 'Goggle'. The latter track is a critique of the sexual inadequacies of the average Jamaican man, who takes on the 'big heavy wuck' of being Stephens's narrator's lover, but whose sexual inexperience leads to 'him flop' and request fellatio, with Stephens's narrator responding to the request with the line 'gal never gaggle'.

Two full-length albums followed: *Work Out* (1997) for Joe Gibbs and *Ruff Rider* (1998) for VP. Both are fine releases and see Stephens voicing on the best riddims of the period, with notable examples including 'Handle the Ride' on Bobby Digital's Lecturer riddim, which was ubiquitous at the time with over twenty versions released. By this time, Tanya Stephens and Lady Saw were the best-selling and best-known female artists from Jamaica, and a pair who were now used to standing on their own feet without help from others. Unlike contemporaries, there were few combinations from either artist.

As Tanya Stephens's career developed and expanded, so did the aural palette from which she painted her vocals, voicing on one-drop riddims and moving beyond reggae to other hybridized Black Atlantic sounds, reaching out from Jamaican reggae to American soul and R&B. The best example of her ability to ride a one-drop reggae riddim is her international hit 'It's a Pity' (2002), set to the Doctor's Darling riddim and originally released on Germaican Records, an unlikely but significant outpost of dancehall based in Leipzig, Germany. 'It's a Pity' contains distinctively rich vocals delivered with aplomb while the song's lyrics differ significantly from the braggadocio of Stephens's male counterparts. While the *Doctor's Darling* (2004) riddim album collected together sixteen versions from dancehall and reggae heavyweights such as Sizzla, Michael Rose, Luciano, Capleton and Turbulence, it is Stephens's track that is the standout.

'It's a Pity' would eventually appear on *Gangsta Blues* (2004), something of a breakthrough album and one that demonstrated Stephens's musical breadth and depth. Recorded in Jamaica and the United States between 2001 and 2004, the album contains a neat balance of dancehall and reggae, with some tracks defying categorization – most notably 'Way Back', a song situated somewhere between soul and reggae. On it, Stephens rails against a number of ills within the modern music industry, including sexualized gender stereotypes, MTV, 'recycling shit' and out-of-key singers, before harking back to the era of Smokey Robinson and Nina Simone, where meaningful lyrics were set to engaging music by artists who had a respectful rather than antagonistic relationship with their fans. Although not voiced over what any dancehall fan would recognize as a riddim, vocal delivery remains set to a precise metre, with a rhyme to accompany the rhythm and with vocals switching between spoken word, deejaying and singing.

Ultimately, 'Way Back' was a call to arms that Stephens responded to herself on the rest of her album, delivering that which she cited as being missing from within the music of her contemporaries, on a release that does not involve the listener being forced to purchase what she calls 'a whole bullshit album' just to get the only decent track on it. Having set out her stall, with *Gangsta Blues* Stephens continues with gender-war ballads 'Little White Lie' and 'This Is Love' (with Wyclef Jean), gangster dancehall on 'Gangsta Gal' (a combination with Spragga Benz) and straight-up reggae numbers 'Tek Him Back', 'What's Your Story' and 'Can't Breathe'. These are all fictional narratives from the front line of the interpersonal gender war in Jamaica, with tales of men who are simultaneously absent and suffocating. On 'Boom Wuk', a classic slice of riddim-driven slackness, the tables are turned, and the woman is the sexual aggressor and dominant partner, while 'Sound of My Tears' is a ghetto ballad focusing on the role that both the

JLP and PNP have in keeping the garrisons poor: 'this one bag of orange turn green'. The album ends with the return of a dancehall riddim, but with no corresponding return to slackness. 'We a Lead' is a continuation of the theme of infidelity, only in the first person this time, where Stephens and her narrator merge, with the deejay promising to bury her love rival, and if the woman concerned would select a suitable coffin, 'Tanya will pay for it'.

Following the international success of *Gangsta Blues*, the artist followed up with *Rebelution* for VP Records. By this stage in her career, Stephens was being compared to Bob Marley in terms of critical acclaim, although poor luck with major labels meant that she would never achieve Marley's sales figures. While such a comparison might be overblown when considering the cultural importance and ubiquity of Marley, if judged solely on recorded output there is as consistent a level of artistic development in Stephens's ten studio albums as in Marley's dozen. Throughout her work, one notable phenomenon is Stephens's bravery in approaching topics that are not only taboo within the dancehall but within Jamaica at large, allowing her output to move beyond what she calls 'the same old four topics' dancehall. There have been experimentations with form too, with her 2010 album *Infallible* released as a free download. Here, the track on which Stephens really pushes the envelope is 'Still Alive', a ballad where a promiscuous wife reveals to her faithful husband that she is HIV-positive. Once the news spreads through their community, the husband loses his job. As the vocal register changes from speaking to singing, the narrative point of view reverses, and the track is now sung from Johnny's perspective as he loses his job due to his wife's illness. The song finishes with a coda sung from Johnny's perspective: 'I'm still alive.' In addition to appearing on *Infallible*, the song was also performed live in Jamaica, to much controversy.

If Lady Saw and Tanya Stephens were standout performers in terms of their ability to turn the tables on male deejays and carve out careers riding the best riddims and singing songs told from a woman's point of view, there were others. Patra is a contemporary of both – all three artists were born within twelve months of each other. After a clutch of singles for Steely & Clevie, Jammy's Records and Greensleeves, Patra (Dorothy Smith) came to international attention thanks to her vocals on Shabba Ranks's 'Family Affair' (1993). Building on this success, she signed to Epic Records (by then part of Sony Music) for her debut long-player *Queen of the Pack* (1993). The album sold well and contained a number of hit singles that had their roots in dancehall, but with an R&B sensibility that enabled the deejay and singer to cross over into the mainstream pop world. The follow-up album, *Scent of Attraction* (1995), also on Epic, was less successful, but still sold in respectable numbers internationally, as did the singles contained within it, particularly the album's opener, a cover version of fellow Jamaican Grace Jones's 'Pull Up to the Bumper'. Here was a vocal partly delivered in a deejay style, but with a riddim that had far more in common with breakbeat-driven rap than reggae dancehall.

It would be eight years before Patra's follow-up to *Scent of Attraction*, during which time dancehall had moved on, as had Patra, having gained a bachelor's degree in history and political science during her extended career break. By this point, Lady Saw had left the business, and Tanya Stephens had moved on from being seen solely as a dancehall artist. Therefore, the stage was relatively clear for Patra, who stated that it was the absence of politics in her work that enabled her to return to dancehall after a break in recording and performing:

> It's always going to be about sex with me, nothing political. I'm just focusing on being sexy all the time. That's all I'm doing right now. Just being sexy, chopping up the charts and everything ... When you have old school artists like me, you

can evolve and change. I haven't evolved, but I've evolved in terms of my company, but I'm not changing anything. I haven't seen a change really. I think everybody is doing what they're doing. I'm just blessed to be doing what I'm doing and taking reggae music to a whole other level. There's nothing for me to compare myself to. There's nobody doing what I'm doing right now as a woman.[4]

Despite her optimism, Patra's career soon stalled. This only highlighted the sexism of Jamaican dancehall, where men are allowed long and illustrious recording careers and who are able to retain their 'lover-man' status well into middle age, whereas there is an unofficial retirement age for female deejays, who are encouraged to move away from sexual themes once they hit their forties. Patra has not released any new music since 2014's *Patra: The Continuation* album.

Macka Diamond (Charmaine Munroe) was born within a year of Lady Saw, Tanya Stephens and Patra, but began her deejay career first, with Sister Nancy an influence during her formative years. In 1987, Major Mackrel recorded 'Don Bon', prompting Munroe to record 'Don Girl', a response record released under the name Lady 'Mackrel' Worries, a moniker forced upon her by her label. Stuck with the name, Munroe performed as Lady Mackerel throughout the 1990s, specializing in narratives told from a woman's point of view with an increasingly feminist bent, often in combination with Queen Paula – such as on 'Done Tek Man' (1995) and 'Hot Girls Like We' (1996). Switching to the name Macka Diamond in 2003, she immediately took on Vybz Kartel with 'Tekk Con', another response record. Unlike with her debut, this time Munroe was replying to one of the biggest names in dancehall, who had recorded 'Tek Buggy Gyal' as a tale of a money-grabbing girlfriend. On his track, Vybz Kartel's narrator demands a blowjob before he is prepared to finance his girlfriend's lifestyle. In response, Macka Diamond puts Vybz Kartel very much in his place, humiliating him for his naivety in assuming that he could purchase sexual favours from this particular deejay.

After 'Tekk Con' had raised her profile, the rechristened deejay had her first Jamaican number one with 'Done Already', an explicit report of the sexual inadequacies and premature ejaculations of the average Jamaican male. High-profile combinations followed, including 'Money-Washing Machine' with Mad Cobra, 'Mi Ready' with Capleton and 'Bun Him' with Black-er. The last is a classic dancehall tale, accompanied by an engaging video that recounts a first-person first-name narrative between Macka and Black-er. Having had his advice sought regarding a cheating man, Black-er replies that Macka Diamond should pack up her clothes and 'bun him', and then take his car, van, house and land and sell them all; Macka duly obliges.

By 2006, Macka Diamond had released over seventy singles, yet she had not been offered an album deal, which was rectified with *Money-O* (2006) on Greensleeves, although this remains her only long player. Like Tanya Stephens, Macka Diamond continues to perform, but unlike Stephens, she has very rarely deviated from straight-up dancehall and continues to trade in raunchy videos, as with 'Birthday S3x' (2019) and 'Cucumber' (2019), the latter influenced by her veganism as well as traditional dancehall concerns. Nonetheless, the longevity of the careers of the likes of Tanya Stephens and Macka Diamond merely highlights the relative dearth of other well-established female deejays. While there are plenty of onstage opportunities for those male deejays who have been recording since the 1980s, there remains an unofficial retirement age for female deejays, with few bucking the trend. It is strange for an artist to receive opprobrium for career longevity, but this frequently occurs with women deejays who, like Macka

Diamond, are told to retire with dignity. Commenting on this, the deejay suggests:

> When me look pon di man dem, dem a perform till dem old and people still accepting them. Me look good same way; mi no see nuttn wrong wid mi. When me look inna my mirror mi no si no old lady wid no stick and mi no si no problem. Mi still sound good. Mi voice no sound cracky-cracky. Di older mi get, mi a sound sweeter.[5]

In predicting the end of her career as a dancehall performer, Diamond began to focus on ensuring that she had online product to sell:

> Even if mi sing music and mi no get no show, music is selling and dat's where I earn my money. A lot a dem don't understand dat part suh dem just tink seh 'shi a try fi compete wid di young people dem'. Noooo. I am doing my job; I am selling products. If mi even sing 10 song and put it up online on iTunes, I make money. That's how I make my money and pay my bills.[6]

There were other women deejays of note during the first decades of dancehall. Another protégé of Brigadier Jerry, Sister Carol (Carol East) was a contemporary of Sister Nancy and began riding rhythms with conscious lyrics after returning to Jamaica from New York, where her family had moved when she was fourteen and where she gained a BSC in education at the City College of New York while also performing as a deejay. Suffused with reggae history (her father had been an engineer at RJR and had a role in several Studio One releases) and influenced by the I Threes along with Cynthia Richards (who had recorded for Coxsone Dodd and Clancy Eccles in the 1960s and '70s), Sister Carol dropped her earlier singing style and began to enter deejaying competitions in both Kingston and Brooklyn. Unlike Sister Nancy, Sister Carol has had a lengthy recording career, releasing ten albums between 1983 and 2006, along with a host of singles. After the limited release of her long-playing debut *Liberation for Africa* (1983), it would be the follow-up *Black Cinderella* (1984) that would bring her to international attention. Sister Carol also had a successful acting career, featuring in two Jonathan Demme films in the 1980s before releasing the follow-up to *Black Cinderella*, *Jah Disciple* (1989), on the Island Records off-shoot Mango. In the same year, she formed her Black Cinderella record label, primarily as a vehicle for her own singles. Sister Carol continues to tour and record today, as a conscious reggae artiste performing in a dancehall style.

In contrast to the career of Sister Carol, the work of Ce'cile (Cecile Charlton) focused largely on traditional dancehall themes. Starting work as a studio manager for Steven Ventura of Celestial Sound Records, Ce'cile was encouraged to record a series of demo tapes, with a subsequent recording career based upon the release of singles rather than albums. A few years younger than Lady Saw and Tanya Stephens, she had a relatively slow start to her career, although by 2001 her combination with Sean Paul entitled 'Can You Do the Work' brought her considerable international fame. The track's subsequent appearance on Sean Paul's multi-million-selling album *Dutty Rock*, on Atlantic Records, further raised her profile. At this point, Ce'cile was very much under the wing of Lady Saw and was seen as her artistic progeny. But despite growing fame, there would be fifteen years between her first single, 'Kill You with It' (1992), and her debut album, 2008's *Bad Gyal*, although she released over a hundred singles during this period, either solo or in combination with the likes of Beenie Man, Elephant Man, Barrington Levy and Delly Ranks. That it took sixteen years before

Ce'cile was offered an album deal, by Sweden's Kingstone Records, merely highlights the reticence of Jamaican labels to offer female deejays the same opportunities that are afforded their male compatriots, although more recently VP Records has consciously turned its focus towards signing and promoting female artists.

Like Lady Saw and Tanya Stephens, Ce'cile shocked Jamaican society not merely with explicit language but also with a lyrical insistence on her own sexual gratification, a concept seemingly alien to male dancehall performers if not female dancehall attendees. On 'Do It to Me' (2003), on the Coolie Dance riddim, Ce'cile points out that while male dancehall deejays might be explicit in their slackness and promise all sorts of sexual options for their chosen partners, they all seem to fall short when it came to cunnilingus, as she berates her lyrical suitors for their inadequacies before insisting that they should 'bow' down and 'gwaan, use yuh tongue'. It was not for nothing that Ce'cile was referred to by herself and others as the original 'bad gal', but as with Patra, dancehall's unofficial retirement age for women deejays has struck again. At the time of writing, Ce'cile has stepped back from dancehall performances but remains within the dancehall industry, signing a new generation of female deejays to her own label. As label boss, Ce'cile now signs and breaks new female artists, as with her promotion of Lvna, her own deejay mentee.

Ce'cile's role as an entrepreneur highlights the often-hidden roles that leading Jamaican women have had within reggae and dancehall beyond the stage. Perhaps surprisingly, a number of women have occupied significant roles in a music industry renowned for being dominated by men. This is at least partly due to the increasing role of major conglomerates in the Jamaican music industry, but there were similar moves within the sphere of local independents, too. In 1993, Mercury Records' Vice President Lisa Cortes took personal responsibility for signing Buju Banton, while Vivian Scott, director of A&R at Epic Records, worked with the JLP's Olivia Grange to break Shabba Ranks and Patra internationally. Grange had been a JLP activist who was interned without trial for seven months during the state of emergency of 1976 before going on to become a senator and Minister of State during Edward Seaga's premiership. Outside of dancehall but within reggae, Trish Farrell was president of Island/Jamaica, Chris Blackwell's major-label subsidiary. Within the independent sphere, the largest reggae independent is VP Records, where Patricia Chin oversaw the operation of the label following her husband's death in 2003, although the couple's sons Chris and Randy Junior are now CEO and president respectively. Over in the Marley empire, Cedella Marley is the long-standing CEO of Tuff Gong International, which is almost entirely staffed by women. Explaining the organization's women-only philosophy, Marley states: 'At Tuff Gong, women do everything from pressing records to selling records, as well as producing. They may not be at the forefront, but they are, in a lot of ways, a crucial part of the industry's backbone.'[7]

Outside of record labels, the late Louise Frazier Bennett was an artist manager, booking agent and in the 1990s the founder and President of the Sound System Organization of Jamaica. By the time of her death, Bennett had expressed regrets about her early role in dancehall:

> I was performing a negative role in music . . . Me and my set of artistes was giving the people weh we think dem want – sex and violence . . . This is a warped society, where we indulge in self-degradation. We keep blaming others instead of looking inside ourselves.[8]

In reflecting on her subsequent career, Bennett attributed her success to her ability to be more macho and money-grabbing than her male counterparts: 'I'm in this for the money. As a woman, that's the way you have to deal with them. If you're too soft and too humble, they walk on your femininity.'[9]

Like Louise Bennett, Sharon Burke was the CEO of another relatively unsung organization, even though the roster of her Solid Agency, formed in 1991, included such A-list stars as Bounty Killer, Half Pint, Marcia Griffiths and Shaggy, although it was her work with Lady Saw that she was most proud of. In 1996, Burke said: 'I'm trying to get more women front and centre. They haven't done so before because they've been too reserved. The men are much bolder, and in the highly competitive Jamaican music business you have to be very aggressive.'[10]

Despite the leading role of some women within the industry, there remains in Jamaican reggae and dancehall areas that are bastions of maleness. One example is studio engineering, which continues to largely exclude women, and a lack of female engineers and producers has repercussions for who is allowed to step up to the mic in a recording studio. Diana King was a singer and dancehall deejay best known for her 1995 single 'Shy Guy' and her cover version of Burt Bacharach and Hal David's 'I Say a Little Prayer', which featured in the Hollywood film *My Best Friend's Wedding*. Citing sexual harassment in Jamaican recording studios, King eventually moved to the United States to develop a career as a studio executive rather than as a singer: 'It's really rough, so rough that at one point all the female singers had affairs with the producers. They don't want you to move outside of what they're doing. They always want to hold you back.'[11] More seriously, in late 2021 Jamaican dancehall had its own #MeToo moment, as a number of female deejays came forward to say that they were survivors of sexual violence perpetrated by male producers and performers from the 1980s onwards.

At Columbia Records, King worked with the label's A&R director Maxine Stowe, a fellow Jamaican, and it was here that she had her greatest success, which King attributed to the access she had to senior executives in America, in contrast to her exclusion from the male-owned studios and labels of Jamaica. The figures back up King's point, with 'Shy Guy' eventually selling more than 500,000 units globally, a number that any Jamaican independent would surely be envious of.

Keeping a watchful eye over the gender relations of reggae and dancehall throughout the period covered by this chapter was former youth worker, artist manager and founding member and director of the Jamaican Association of Composers, Artistes and Producers (JACAP) Olivia Grange, the JLP MP for the constituency of St Catherine Central since 1997 and cabinet minister from 2007 to 2011. Grange frequently speaks of the positive impact of reggae and dancehall on the economy and culture of Jamaica and has shown herself to be an astute observer of gender relations in Jamaican music. Currently Minister of Culture, Gender, Entertainment and Sport, Grange recently commented on the relative paucity of female performers at the 2020 staging of Rebel Salute, Jamaica's premier roots reggae and cultural dancehall festival, stating that:

> It is actually a concern to me why at this time we do not have enough female artistes; the well-established, they are few in numbers and primarily leave for tours and are not available for a lot of these events and I am concerned about that . . . It is a mission that we [are] going have to be on and it's an important one; I made the decision to search for the artistes, work with them, help them develop and get exposure for the purpose of seeing the numbers change. We have to get more female artistes out there, in the streets, on charts and essentially on stage and a greater variety, and it cannot be reduced to dancehall only but about all the genres that have over the years helped to produce Jamaica's music. I am going to produce that.[12]

While the gender relations of reggae and dancehall was changed by the new cadre of women deejays that rose to prominence in the 1990s and 2000s, life in Jamaica remains tightly gendered, constricting the opportunities for women working within Jamaica's music industry and dictating to men what their roles should be too. Men and women remain at war on Jamaica, in what one theorist refers to as a 'gender antagonism', with both sides bemoaning the attitudes and behaviour of the other.[13] As long as this is the case, reggae and dancehall will both reflect that fact and contribute to its continuation.

7

'NOBODY CAN SING "BOOM BYE BYE" FOR ME': MEN AND THE POLITICS OF DANCEHALL AND REGGAE, 1990-2010

Buju Banton, *'Til Shiloh* (1995)

Nobody can sing 'Boom Bye Bye' for me.

EDWARD SEAGA[1]

With some notable exceptions, the 1980s belonged to dance-hall and roots reggae took a back seat, and this looked set to continue in the 1990s, as the major record labels all searched for a new Jamaican star. By 1990, Shabba Ranks had signed to Epic Records. Here he would release a slew of singles and full-length albums, beginning with *As Raw as Ever* (1991), an album title designed to reassure dancehall fans that the major-label route would not lead to a watering down of Shabba's style. If anything, though, this album title looked like appeasement, for while *As Raw as Ever* began with the track 'Trailer Load of Girls', there was a noticeable dialling down of any slackness. This was no punanny album. Although Shabba Ranks might have been lyrically neutered, it is undeniable that *As Raw as Ever* put dancehall on the international music map, while the follow-up album *Rough & Ready, Vol. 1* (1992) was equally popular. Showing the power of a major label, *Rough & Ready* begins with the single 'Mr Loverman', which had originally been released four years prior to Shabba signing to Epic but which the major label took on and flogged mercilessly across a range of formats and with a selection of new remixes, leading to a massive international hit.

Buoyed by their success with Shabba Ranks, other parts of the Sony music empire looked to get in on the act. Next out of the blocks was Maxine Stowe at Columbia (which Sony had acquired in 1988), who signed Super Cat (William Maragh), an early protégé of Winston Riley and a self-professed PNP supporter.[2] In signing Super Cat, Stowe was prising the deejay away from his own Wild Apache label, with Columbia seemingly unphased by the dee-jay's prison sentence in 1980,[3] or by the controversy regarding his involvement in the death of deejay Nitty Gritty (Glen Holness), who was shot dead in New York in 1991 (Maragh was eventually exonerated).[4] The end result of Super Cat's Columbia deal was *Don Dada* (1992), which saw him bound on a course that would eventually lead to a number of dancehall/hip-hop collaborations, including recordings with Kriss Kross and the Notorious B.I.G.

At the heart of *Don Dada* sat Super Cat's ongoing beef with Ninjaman (Desmond Ballentine), who had worked with Super Cat in the early 1980s but who, despite being one of the ruling expon-ents of slack dancehall at the turn of the decade, had not picked up a major-label deal. At Sting 1990, Ninjaman had outperformed Shabba Ranks, with the latter said to have been reduced to tears while on stage.[5] This gave Ninjaman the licence to return to Sting in 1991 claiming the title of ruling deejay, although Super Cat was determined to bring him down a peg or two. With Super Cat insulting Ninjaman on the mic, Ninjaman fans began to throw glass bottles at the stage and one hit Super Cat, who promptly threw one bottle whence it came and informed the audience that he was armed, and they had all better watch out.

For two years straight, Ninjaman crowned himself king of the dancehall, but he would quickly fade into the background for a decade, save for a reappearance in 1997 as Brother Desmond, a born-again gospel artist. Meanwhile, Shabba Ranks would conquer the world, and Super Cat would release three more albums for Columbia, with *Don Dada* followed by *The Good, the Bad, the Ugly & the Crazy* and *The Struggle Continues*. Following a departure from Sony, Super Cat returned to his own Wild Apache label, releasing a handful of singles each year until 2003, but there would be no further albums. On these later singles, fans would see the more spiritual side of the deejay, with 'Jah Run Things' (2000) capturing attention. This is Super Cat at his best, declaring that neither he nor politicians 'run things', only Jah Jah run things, all delivered in a mature singjay style. Building on their success with Super Cat, Columbia also signed Mad Cobra (Ewart Brown), releasing *Hard to Wet, Easy to Dry* in 1992, which, while containing the Temptations-influenced hit single 'Flex', failed to set the world alight. There would be one more major-label album, 1996's *Milkman*, before Mad Cobra moved to Greensleeves and VP Records, where he seemed to fare better.

Not wishing to miss out on the dancehall party, Mercury Records, a subsidiary of Polygram, signed Buju Banton (Mark Myrie) through a partnership deal with Penthouse Records, run by the producer and engineer Donovan Germain, who by the 1990s had usurped King Jammy and Winston Riley as dancehall's leading riddim creator. Building an unrivalled roster of acts for Penthouse, Germain recorded and released music by veterans such as Sugar Minott, Marcia Griffiths and Beres Hammond (a lovers-rock stalwart who had turned to dancehall) alongside a new breed of younger deejays. The label's first hit was Chaka Demus's 'Chaka on the Move' (1989), the proceeds of which allowed Germain to invest in technology that would give his recordings an aural edge in the 1990s. This led other producers to seek out the same pristine digital sound as heard on Germain's productions by booking their own acts into the Penthouse studio in Kingston.[6] At Penthouse, Germain specialized in employing different studio engineers to rework classic Studio One and Bob Marley riddims, while also devising original loops for his roster of more than 280 artists, including Bounty Killer, Buju Banton (who Germain managed as well as produced), Capleton, Jah Cure, Elephant Man, Freddie McGregor, Morgan Heritage, Frankie Paul, Queen Ifrica, Lady Saw, Tony Rebel, Tarrus Riley, Sanchez, Richie Spice, Tanya Stephens and Wayne Wonder. While Penthouse Records had a wide stable of artists, rarely did you find more than half a dozen deejays voicing on any one Penthouse riddim. Observers have suggested that this was to limit the amount of 'riddim juggling' by selectors, who were thus encouraged to play tracks from beginning to end, or at least to play most of the recording, rather than segue snatches from several recordings into a megamix.

Buju Banton had first appeared on Penthouse Records at the tender age of eighteen on a track with Ed Robinson entitled 'Watch How You Flex' (1991), which was a good example of the trend for combination singles. The track begins with Robinson's rich and sweet vocals, which then sit in contrast to the instantly recognizable vocal style of Banton, all baritone gruffness and gravel. Banton followed the track with a series of singles for a range of Jamaican indies, including 'Petty Thief fi Dead' and 'Informer fi Dead' for Rude Boy Kelly Records, and 'Yardie' for Xterminator, all released in 1991.

Working in the by now familiar deejay territory of 'guns 'n' gals', there was also a brief glimpse of a possible move away from dancehall's celebration of all things sexual with another release on Penthouse Records, 1992's 'Batty Rider', a single on which Banton derided the dancehall fashion of ultra-short hotpants for women. In the track, the deejay seems conflicted. Sure, he likes the 'fruits ripe' of the girls in the dancehall, and like much of the African diaspora, he celebrates the voluptuousness of women, but what particularly exercised Banton was battyriders 'exposing the property' of plus-sized women who were 'like a coke bottle without the top'. More controversially, and largely missed at the time, was the suggestion within his lyrics that Banton's aversion to the battyrider was because it exposed the black 'batty jaw' of Jamaican women, who, according to the song, should employ a skin-whitening cream sold under the brand name of Nadinola to bleach that part of their anatomy.

The controversial themes of sex and race continued on Buju Banton's follow-up, 'Love Mi Browning' (1992). As on much dancehall of the era, the deejay celebrates wealth and personal possessions, however he rapidly departs from the usual script in expressing a preference for lighter-skinned Jamaican women (the 'browning' of the title) over and above the darker-skinned Jamaicans further down the racialized hierarchy of Jamaica. Here we see a hint that Jamaican women might bleach their skin in an attempt to rise up the island's pigmentocracy. This prompted the lesser known Nardo Ranks to release 'Dem a Bleach' in response, in which he attributes an increase in the popularity of skin bleaching to the earlier release by Buju Banton. While the rise of dancehall had seen the Rastafarian promotion of Black pride move into the background, this did not mean that Banton's valorization of brownness was able to pass without an outcry. The dancehall backlash was so fierce that Banton was forced to pen a follow-up in 'Love Black Woman' (1992), where he announces that he is 'black and proud' and has a love for girls with a dark complexion.

While 'Love Mi Browning' caused a hullabaloo in dancehall, Buju Banton's follow-up single had a far greater impact, with repercussions continuing to be felt some thirty years later. Originally titled 'Boom By By' for its inaugural outing on Shang Records and retitled 'Boom Bye Bye' on subsequent releases, here was a deejay espousing an unashamedly homophobic opinion that was shared by many in Jamaica, but which was beyond the pale in the global North.

The storm was slow to start and began with immediate condemnation of the track by the English gay-rights activist Peter Tatchell, who in August 1992 reported the deejay to the director of public prosecutions in England and Wales for incitement to violence.[7] Two months later, Banton's lyrics appeared on the front page of the *New York Post*, and in the ensuing outcry, the mayor of New York condemned the track, forcing the deejay's new label to pressure Banton into making what sounded like a half-hearted apology.[8]

'Boom Bye Bye' was soon excised from radio playlists in New York amid grumblings of discontent from the city's authorities. There is a possibility that the controversy might have faded had Buju Banton not been interviewed on Channel 4's *The Word* in the UK shortly afterwards. Ironically, it was a live interview with Shabba Ranks rather than the pre-recorded interview with Banton that would spark a wider debate. While *The Word* often flirted with controversy, this was usually fleeting and forgotten shortly afterwards, but the feature on Buju Banton was the real deal, a genuine television 'moment' that crackled with tension and which set rolling a train that would see leading reggae and dancehall acts banned from entering the UK and other jurisdictions and gigs cancelled after widespread protests.

The programme's sequence began with news that the music festival WOMAD had pulled a scheduled performance by a nineteen-year-old Banton due to concerns that his lyrics might, in studio presenter Mark Lamarr's words, 'cause offence'. In the pre-recorded interview with Banton in Jamaica, Lamarr's co-presenter Terry Christian gives the deejay an easy ride, allowing Banton to get his defence in early, alleging double standards through citing Guns N' Roses largely ignored 1988 track 'One in a Million', which contained both racist and homophobic epithets. The interview concluded with Banton apologizing for 'causing controversy'. Cutting back to the Channel 4 studio, Shabba Ranks then spoke in stalwart defence of both 'Boom Bye Bye' and homophobia in general, adding 'from you [sic] forfeit the law of God Almighty, you deserve, crucifixion, most definitely.'[9]

Although Shabba Ranks's homophobia would have come as no surprise to watchers of Jamaican dancehall, Channel 4's studio audience was left in an obvious state of disquiet as Ranks was censured by Lamarr, while The Word's liberal and cosmopolitan viewers watched with horror. Such was the strength of the controversy surrounding Shabba Ranks's words that he was forced to deliver an expansive apology three months later, saying in a press release that

> I now realise my comments were a mistake, because they advocated violence against gay men and lesbians. I regret having made such statements ... I do not approve of any act of violence against gay men or lesbians or any other human beings ... Gay bashing is wrong.[10]

While Shabba would eventually be forgiven for his outburst, the same was not true for Buju Banton, whose career has been dogged by the controversy regarding 'Boom Bye Bye' ever since.

Listening to 'Boom Bye Bye' now, the combination of both the riddim and the clarity of Banton's diction still has the power to shock. Voiced over a stripped-down version of Clifton 'Specialist' Dillon's Flex riddim and said to be recorded several years before its release, the track's sedate tempo of 78 bpm and sparse backing allow the lyrics to come to the fore. Now, as then, even those entirely unfamiliar with Jamaican patois can understand the gist of the song, if not each individual word. The key question that would be asked at numerous points from that moment on was whether this was merely a grossly offensive homophobic recording or something more sinister, a literal incitement to the murder of gay men. But just as this controversy really got going, Buju Banton went to ground and disappeared for a couple of years, recording a follow-up to his *Voice of Jamaica* album.

When Banton returned to the limelight, he cut a very different figure from the one who had recorded 'Boom Bye Bye', and for the rest of the decade, gay-rights campaigners in the global North seemed to be prepared to let bygones be bygones. With dancehall slackness now seen as very much behind him, Banton's 'Murderer', released in 1993, saw the artist reborn. There had been earlier conscious deejays in the dancehall, but none were backed with the clout of Sony Music. Garnett Silk (Garnett Smith) was the most significant early example. Silk's first single, 'Problem Everywhere' (released under the name Little Bimbo) hinted at a conscious theme, but it would not be until he joined Sugar Minott's label Youth Promotion and worked with producer and musician Tony Rebel (himself a Rasta) that his work would become more devout. Yasus Afari, the Jamaican dub poet, was said to be an influence.[11] In 1989 Silk switched from deejaying to singing at the instigation of

Derrick Morgan, recording a version of Roberta Flack's 'Killing Me Softly' under his new name. Newly rechristened, Garnett Silk then recorded a famous version of Horace Andy's 'Skylarking' before the release of 1992's *It's Growing*. Two years later, Silk signed a distribution deal with Atlantic Records, effectively placing him in the hands of the Warners conglomerate. The end result was sessions engineered by Errol Brown, a nephew of Duke Reid, in the Tuff Gong Studios, employing an all-star cast of Aston Barrett, Sly & Robbie, Tyrone Downie, Earl 'Chinna' Smith and Uziah 'Sticky' Thompson.

Garnett Silk might have gone on to have as significant a career as Buju Banton, but it would be gunplay that would be his downfall. Silk was at his mother's house in Mandeville, Jamaica, in December 1994, when he showed weapons (which he had obtained to protect himself from burglary) to visiting friends. One of the visitors discharged a gun, puncturing a propane tank and causing an explosion. Silk and his friends left the house, but fearing for his mother's life, he re-entered the property to save her, but they became trapped inside and both died in the fire.[12]

Buju Banton's 'Murderer' had perhaps the greatest impact of any single released in the 1990s. The track is concerned with the death of Pan Head, the deejay alter ego of Anthony Johnson, a rude boy from the parish of St Mary whose early singles, especially 'Gun Man Tune' (1990), were classic slackness, and who was killed as he left a dance in Spanish Town in October 1993.[13] Prior to his death, Pan Head had himself turned away from slackness and lyrical gunplay, with 1991's 'Too Much Gun' being a turning point. No longer would there be 'respect to all di gunman dem'; in contrast, Pan Head now preached 'roots and reality'.

For a while, only the trope of the gunman would be removed from Pan Head's rude-boy consciousness. 'Rude Boy Face' (1992) for King Jammy was a homophobic recording where the deejay contrasts the 'rude-boy face' of an opponent with their 'batty-boy heart'. Equally, traditional slackness was retained for a while. 'Punny Printer' was a combination with Pennie Irie on a King Jammy reworking of the Bam Bam riddim, previously heard on Pliers's cover version of the Toots and the Maytals' classic 'Bam Bam' and a feature of Chaka Demus and Pliers's global hit 'Murder She Wrote' in 1992. Gradually, though, sexual slackness would also be jettisoned along with the gunplay, and by 1993 Pan Head's conversion was complete, with a series of seven-inch single releases for a range of Jamaican labels including 'Proud', 'Bun It Down' and 'Under Bondage', all sharing a traditional Rasta theme.

Pan Head's death had an immediate impact. Capleton recorded 'Cold Blooded Murderer' in response, and Beenie Man went to number one in the Jamaican charts with the Sly & Robbie-produced tribute 'No Mama No Cry'. Buju Banton would follow with 'Murderer'. Despite the fact that Donovan Germain was reversioning the Far East Riddim previously heard on Capleton's earlier tribute, 'Murderer' was a tune so big that it would change dancehall both sonically and ideologically. Using Clive Hunt, Danny Bassie, Handel Tucker and Sly Dunbar to rework the riddim in the studio, giving it extra sub-bass, the musical bedrock of 'Murderer' is as deep and coruscating as Banton's vocal attack on Pan Head's unknown assailant. Lyrically, the track is full of biblical righteousness, with Banton asking the unknown killer of Pan Head why he disobeyed the first commandment and warning him that he will not escape God's judgement. While Beenie Man and Bounty Killer clashed at Sting 1993 and garnered headlines as a result, it was Banton's performance of 'Murderer' that would have the biggest impact. Soon, everyone from Beenie Man to Capleton, Bounty Killer and Pinchers would come with the same anti-gun ideology.

'Murderer' preceded the album *'Til Shiloh*, which completed Buju Banton's transformation from rude boy to Rasta, signalling

223

both an ideological and a musical rupture. Here was an album that looked back to the depth and resonance of roots reggae's golden age, but with the sound of roots given a crisp update using the latest digital technology, which by the mid-1990s had progressed significantly. Following an a capella version of the Lord's Prayer as the album's opener, the album begins with 'Til I'm Laid to Rest', which contains some fine Nyabinghi drumming and a warm bassline, and the rest of the album unfolds thus, a musical journey that combines both sweetness and toughness. Following the release of *'Til Shiloh* came the international hit single 'Champion', full of gruff machismo and proving that while Banton had embraced righteousness, he could retain the swagger of a dancehall deejay. Although Banton had left Donovan Germain's Penthouse stable for Polygram, he retained Germain as both manager and producer. The result was an album that showcased what major-label distribution could do in terms of global reach, with Penthouse selling the album in Jamaica and Polygram badging it as an Island Records release internationally.

Considering the success of *'Til Shiloh*, it is notable that Polygram dropped Banton shortly after the album's release. For the follow-up, *Inna Heights* in 1997, Banton signed deals with a range of independents including Germain Records and VP. By now the work of the major conglomerate was done, Banton was on the world stage and the new Rasta genie would not go back in the bottle. *Inna Heights* picked up where *'Til Shiloh* left off, lyrically, musically and philosophically, although there were perhaps more lighter notes. In particular, 'Love Sponge' is a witty dancehall/lovers hybrid, 'Small Axe' a jaunty ska number introduced by original 1960s deejay King Stitt, and '54/46' is a combination with Toots Hibbert and an update on the latter's autobiographical prison story from 1970. For the Rastas, though, it would be the sumptuous 'Hills and Valleys' that would take on epochal significance, containing a perfect balance of nature and nurture with lyrics set to a one-drop riddim composed by Banton himself. Also available on some digital releases of *Inna Heights* was the track 'Politics Time Again'. Here Banton employs the familiar lyrical figure of the absentee politician who only frequents the neighbourhood at election times. Sung powerfully in Banton's characteristic register, the track continues with threats to 'fire bun' the constitution, and with a chorus, of sorts, encouraging the listener to make love, not war.

Both *'Til Shiloh* and *Inna Heights* represented a significant break from the past. Over the following two decades, Banton's stature and significance would grow within both Jamaica and the global Rasta reggae community, even if subsequent releases would not have the same impact, although 1999's *Unchained Spirit* and 2003's *Friends for Life* represent another fine duet of albums. During this period of his career, Banton was one of the most dedicated to the use of the book of Psalms within lyrics. With 'Destiny', on *Inna Heights*, Banton returns to a theme from 'Murderer' but reverses the warning in Psalms 91:6 of 'pestilence *that* walketh in darkness' by asking for protection from the pestilence that also 'walketh at daylight'. Elsewhere in the track, the binding cords that appear in Psalms 2:3 are cast away by Jah, while the third verse of the song uses the Psalmic imagery of heathens being restrained with a rod of iron. On *Unchained Spirit*, '23rd Psalm' is a double header with Gramps from Morgan Heritage, using 'THE LORD *is* my shepherd; I shall not want' (Psalms 21:1) as its opening lyric. The following track, 'Voice of Jah', is an acoustic gospel ballad suffused with biblical imagery, where 'the voice of the LORD' of Psalms 29 becomes the voice of Jah and where the 'loving kindness' of the 'King of glory' (Psalms 24:8) protects the Rastafari like 'the wings of a dove' (Psalms 68:13).

'Til Shiloh and *Inna Heights* changed things, and in their wake sailed a generation of world-conquering Rastafari who eschewed the slackness of their predecessors. First and foremost would come

Sizzla (Miguel Collins), whose *Black Woman and Child* album, produced by King Jammy protégé Bobby 'Digital' Dixon and released in the same year as Banton's *Inna Heights*, was particularly influential, very much announcing the artist as a musical and lyrical force to be reckoned with. Following *Black Woman and Child*, Sizzla would release seven albums in the following two years alone, cementing his reputation as one of reggae's most prolific recording artists, even if the quality control on some releases was less than that exercised by Donovan Germain as he guided Buju Banton's career. Eventually, Sizzla would move his main business dealings away from the likes of vp Records and Greensleeves to his own label based at Judgement Yard, his community centre and recording studio in August Town, East Kingston.

Mirroring the careers of Buju Banton and Sizzla, Capleton also moved from slack dancehall chatter to firebrand Rasta consciousness as the 1990s progressed. By 1996 he had signed to Def Jam, then part of Polygram, with the label's A&R director Drew Dixon explaining why she had signed Capleton rather than any of the other deejays on offer: 'one reason I signed Capleton is because he doesn't preach slackness. He's interested in righteousness and eradicating, not glorifying, oppression.'[14] Gay rights campaigners might have begged to differ, as unlike Buju Banton, Capleton continued to record homophobic tracks throughout much of the decade, demonstrating that, in Jamaica, certain elements of offensiveness could survive the transition from slackness to righteousness.

The careers of Anthony B (Keith Blair) and Luciano (Jepther McClymont) followed different trajectories to those of Banton, Sizzla and Capleton, but they all ended up at the same destination. When Capleton was recording slackness and Banton was recording 'Boom Bye Bye', both Anthony B and Luciano had already begun to preach Rasta consciousness. Anthony B had joined the Rastafari in his teenage years, prior to releasing a number of tracks for different producers and labels, but it would be his partnership with producer Richard Bell, who also produced Capleton's *Prophecy* in 1995, that would lead to a series of hit singles in Jamaica and a dozen or so albums on a range of labels in the following decade. Meanwhile, Luciano was the oldest of the crop, releasing several conscious dancehall singles and albums before his major-label debut *Where There Is Life* (1995) on Chris Blackwell's Island/Jamaica. Island/Jamaica would eventually team up with VP Records in a distribution arrangement that saw VP release the likes of Luciano in Jamaica, and if the resultant radio play and retail sales were to the liking of Chris Blackwell, the artist would then be moved to the PolyGram Group Distribution system and promoted by the major label internationally.[15] Initially, Island/Jamaica was a success, releasing tracks by the likes of Beenie Man, Chaka Demus and Pliers, and Spanner Banner. However, the results seemed to disappoint both Polygram and Chris Blackwell, and they parted on disgruntled terms in 1997. Blackwell was quoted at the time as saying: 'I never really had a job until I sold Island to PolyGram in 1989. It had gotten too corporate.'[16]

While some of the new crop of deejays became bigger figures than others, what they all had in common was that they were as comfortable riding a dancehall riddim as they were singing roots reggae, with a hybridity of vocal styles the order of the day, often within the same track. What these artists also had in common during the 1990s and 2000s was that they all recorded virulently homophobic tracks, leading to considerable international unease.

OutRage! The UK's Reaction to Dancehall Homophobia

Although there had been a controversy regarding the appearance of Buju Banton and Shabba Ranks on *The Word* in 1992, the issue of dancehall homophobia went away for a while, even though deejays continued to use homophobic slurs within their live performances in Jamaica. During this period, and away from the glare of the Western media, the supposedly righteous fires of the deejays were also being stoked by Jamaica's political leaders. The 1989 general election saw the return of Michael Manley as the nation's leader, only for him to retire three years later due to ill health, with P. J. Patterson replacing him as party leader and prime minister. JLP activists had long whispered about the sexuality of Patterson, for while he had two children, he was not married, and this set tongues wagging. At a JLP rally in 1997, Edward Seaga told the crowd that 'nobody can sing "Boom Bye Bye" for me', implying that while *he* was heterosexual, his chief opponent, the Jamaican prime minister, might not be.[17] By 2001, the JLP were using T.O.K.'s 'Chi Chi Man' as a campaign anthem in a local election in North East St Ann, the best-known homophobic recording since 'Boom Bye Bye' a decade earlier. Seaga denied all homophobic intent:[18]

> I heard a song being played one night while on the platform. The melody was catchy and, most of all, the rhythm was exciting. I asked Desmond McKenzie about it. He told me it was called Chi Chi Man. The lyrics were not clear to me. I don't usually listen much to lyrics as, with the exception of Bob Marley, the words are usually trite . . . I only found out more than halfway through the campaign that the lyrics of the song were referring to homosexuals. Worse than that, people were using it to refer to a specific politician.[19]

With the drip drip of innuendo and rumour beginning to swirl around P. J. Patterson, the Jamaican prime minister soon felt compelled to respond, stating that his government did not propose to decriminalize homosexuality and that 'my credentials as a lifelong heterosexual person are impeccable.'[20] By then, though, Patterson's long tenure at the head of government was coming to a natural end and Portia Simpson-Miller took over as both party leader and prime minister. At around the same time, Edward Seaga retired as leader of the JLP, to be replaced by Bruce Golding, who had only recently returned to the party after a failed attempt to form a new venture in 1995. On his retirement as JLP leader, Seaga also stood down from his West Kingston seat, which Golding won at a by-election two months later, with 87 per cent of the vote.

Over in the UK, a decade after 'Boom Bye Bye' had shocked viewers of Channel 4, a new controversy was brewing concerning homophobic dancehall. By 2002 the sheer volume of homophobic deejay releases suggested that this new aberrant form of dancehall was becoming increasingly popular, much to the alarm of gay-rights campaigners. There was particular controversy surrounding the forthcoming MOBO (Music of Black Origin) Awards in London, with T.O.K., Capleton and Elephant Man all nominated for the Best Reggae Act category. Whether by accident or design, a crisis was narrowly averted when the award went to the relatively safe figure of Sean Paul. The same could not be said for the following year, when OutRage!, a gay-rights group formed a decade earlier by Peter Tatchell, began a 'Stop Murder Music' campaign, alleging that tracks by 2003 MOBO Award nominees Elephant Man, Bounty Killer and Beenie Man contravened sections 4 and 5 of the Public Order Act 1986 and Section 4 of the Offences against the Person Act 1861, while also alleging that they breached the common-law offence of incitement to murder.[21] In a number of press releases, OutRage! stated that they had been liaising with Detective Chief Inspector Clive Driscoll of the Diversity Directorate at New Scotland Yard and that the Metropolitan Police agreed with their analysis concerning the illegality of homophobic recordings by the MOBO nominees. Following a 'five-week police investigation', which included the translation of lyrics 'from Jamaican patois to standard English by an independent linguistic expert', OutRage! claimed that DCI Driscoll not only was seeking the agreement of the Crown Prosecution Service (CPS) to lay charges against the dee-jays but was investigating their record companies, along with music retailers and the BBC's Radio 1Xtra radio station, all for 'inciting homophobic violence and murder'.[22]

While awaiting what they saw as a series of inevitable prosecutions, OutRage! turned their focus to live events and campaigned successfully against two concerts by Bounty Killer in Birmingham and London. Nervous promoters pulled both gigs, with Peter Tatchell claiming that this was as a result of promoters and venues receiving warnings from the police that they might be guilty of aiding and abetting criminal offences were the concerts to go ahead. Although the cancellations were seen as a success, gay-rights campaigners were beginning to be concerned that there was still no news of any impending prosecutions. OutRage! began to put further pressure on Driscoll to act against Beenie Man, who was due to start a UK tour. But whereas OutRage! had previously presented a picture of Driscoll as being bullish at the possibility of prosecutions, this no longer seemed the case. In discussing Beenie Man's recordings, Driscoll announced that 'the advice of the Crown Prosecution Service is that it doesn't believe, on the evidence of the lyrics presented to them, that offences have been committed.'[23] This advice did not stop Driscoll from personally questioning Beenie Man on the latter's arrival at London Heathrow Airport on 24 June 2004, with Driscoll quoted as saying: 'our duty is to protect people. As a result of that, I spoke to Beenie Man asking him not to sing lyrics which were homophobic or promoted violence. He was extremely reasonable.'[24]

The controversy surrounding Beenie Man was no surprise to fans of the deejay. A decade earlier he had caused alarm with the release of 'Acid Attack'. Although he gets his defence in at the start of this track, informing the listener that the song was a light-hearted joke, the deejay then adds 'but what you know?' and launches into the chorus of 'Let the Power Fall on I', the Max Romeo release that lit up the 1972 general election. Following this, Beenie Man moves on to list many of the leading politicians of the 1990s, flinging metaphorical acid into their faces. Luckily for him, this was Jamaica, so this was not taken as a literal threat. A decade later, and in a different jurisdiction, Beenie Man's threats against gays were being taken seriously, and he was being accused, in the press at least, of incitement to murder.

Beenie Man was allowed to enter the country, but his scheduled concert at Ocean in Hackney was pulled by the promoters, who put out a press release stating that 'due to concerns for public safety and following discussions with the Metropolitan Police, Ocean has cancelled this Thursday's Beenie Man concert.' Clive Driscoll denied that he had offered advice to Ocean, stating that he had merely alerted the venue to the concerns of OutRage![25]

In a dramatic turn of events, June 2004 also saw OutRage! claim that Buju Banton's relationship with homophobia had gone beyond mere incitement, alleging that he was part of a gang responsible for physically attacking six men, all of whom were said to be gay, in their Jamaican home.[26] Banton's spokesperson denied the allegation ('it didn't happen – it's totally fabricated'[27]), but Amnesty International were convinced there was a prima facie case, as were prosecutors in Jamaica, where Myrie (Banton) was charged with assault but acquitted at the end of a controversial trial. In response to Myrie's acquittal, Amnesty International were dismissive of Jamaican justice, alleging that witnesses were deemed unreliable by the female magistrate purely because they were gay, while other witnesses were so intimidated that they did not show up in court.[28]

Despite announcing that they were not seeking to prosecute Beenie Man, in August 2004, the CPS reopened their earlier investigation into dancehall lyrics, stating that they were 'awaiting a translation as to the exact content of the lyrics'.[29] By this point, the 'Stop Murder Music' campaign involved not just OutRage! but also the UK's Black Gay Men's Advisory Group and the Jamaican Forum for Lesbians and Gays (JFLAG), who turned their collective attentions away from the deejays and their record companies towards sponsors and advertisers, pressuring global corporations to act if they had any association with deejays said to be homophobic. Under pressure, Puma, the official sponsor of the Jamaican Olympic team, announced that it would withdraw sponsorship from homophobic deejays.[30] Behind the headlines, though, it became apparent that Puma's press statement was a mere warning shot rather than a prelude to breaking all links with dancehall deejays. In a press release, the sportswear manufacturer informed interested parties that,

> upon Buju Banton's arrival in Athens, a senior PUMA staff member will brief him on our zero tolerance policy towards homophobia and other forms of prejudice. Buju Banton will be told that if he chooses to break this policy he will not be allowed to perform at the Athens show and will no longer be supported by the PUMA brand. Additionally, if Banton defies this agreement and performs a song using anti-gay lyrics – either at the Athens concert or at any future concert anywhere in the world – PUMA will not associate with him in the future. This also holds true for all performers with which PUMA works.[31]

As pressure mounted on Buju Banton, DCI Driscoll turned his attentions to Sizzla, with the officer quoted in the UK press as saying that the Metropolitan Police were looking into Sizzla's lyrics: 'we have obtained CDs and we are having them translated by an official from Jamaican patois to English, and then it will be up to the Crown Prosecution Service to decide whether any offence has been committed.'[32]

According to OutRage!, the Met had first purchased Sizzla CDs no later than October 2003, but here were Driscoll and the CPS, some twelve months later, still supposedly deciphering his music. This, though, was the last the public would hear from the authorities about the prosecution of dancehall deejays. By December 2004 Driscoll had moved on to other unconnected investigations and OutRage! had lost its key ally. But what was the eventual position of the state prosecutor? Ken Macdonald, director of public prosecutions, took personal responsibility for the case and eventually decided not to prosecute.[33] In 2018, I made a Freedom of Information request for details of the CPS's decision-making at the time. The CPS informed me that they were unable to locate any records on the case, and they had nothing in relation to the file that the Metropolitan Police had said was passed to them.

Although the prosecution of deejays for homophobic recordings was no longer on the agenda, OutRage! continued with their campaign, concentrating instead on live performances. The first scheduled date of Sizzla's 2004 tour was abandoned while he waited to receive a visa to enter the UK, but in the meanwhile the Stop Murder Music campaign was successful in persuading promoters at two venues that it would not be worth their while allowing the concerts to take place. This left one concert in Bradford and one in London as the only surviving tour dates. With hours to go before Sizzla was due on stage in Bradford, Home Secretary David Blunkett made his move, with the *Manchester Evening News* quoting an anonymous Home Office source as stating that 'the Home Secretary has always made clear his feelings about individuals who preach hatred, whether in speeches or song lyrics. We can confirm that a letter has been sent to Mr Collins regarding his immigration status.'[34]

The British press murmured support for the move, with the *Evening Standard* in London excoriating Sizzla for his role as 'part of the so called "Murder Music" movement, whose lyrics encourage violence against gays'.[35] *The Independent* added that it was not merely Sizzla's lyrics that led the Home Office to act, but his 'public incitements to violence'.[36] Sizzla was unrepentant: in his first major interview since being banned from the UK, he informed BBC Radio 1Xtra that 'They can't ask me to apologize . . . They've got to apologize to God because they break God's law.'[37]

In the following year, OutRage! announced that 'with the help of Scotland Yard' they had struck a deal with many of the Jamaican deejays, with the press reporting that they had also secured a commitment from record companies to ban future material. Like all such negotiated settlements, there were compromises on both sides – the artists would not be required to apologize for past actions, and gay-rights campaigners would suspend their campaign and no longer call for the withdrawal of recordings already on sale. The sigh of relief at Scotland Yard was almost audible when they realized that should the deal hold, they would no longer be required to harry Jamaican deejays performing in the UK. Reggae promoter Glen Yearwood, who had worked closely with the Met in brokering the deal, claimed 'the idea is to let the industry regulate itself.'[38] But the fragility of the arrangement was immediately apparent when it became known that key figures such as Capleton's manager Claudette Kemp had no knowledge of the discussions, and that Peter Tatchell had walked out of the negotiations.

The deal, brokered by the Black Gay Men's Advisory Group, soon fell apart, and Sizzla released the single 'Nah Apologize' (2005) in response. In a spoken-word introduction, the deejay informs his fans that he hasn't apologized to 'batty boy', before issuing the usual threats of shooting and burning in a lake of fire. Others also voiced their disquiet at the deal, with Capleton stating that his words were metaphorical when he spoke of 'burning': 'why when Capleton seh, "bun a fire", people interpret it to mean something literal? Check di energy, when Bob Marley, Peter Tosh an dem man deh seh "bun", is a metaphorical ting. Suh why when Capleton seh it, dem tek it literal?'[39]

Capleton's defence of the metaphor of fire was made in the context of the term being increasingly controversial in Jamaica and elsewhere in the Caribbean. For some, the deejays were not speaking of a metaphorical cleansing but were contributing to the promotion of a destructive urge. The debate continued to rage when on 31 December 2000 at the Cathedral of the Immaculate Conception on the island of St Lucia, a group of young men said to have been Rastafari covered a priest and others in petrol before applying a torch. An Irish nun bled to death at the scene and the priest died of his burns four months later. According to the island's police, the men claimed to have received a vision from Selassie.[40] In response, many felt compelled to defend the Rastafari as being peaceable amid overblown fears that a new generation of Bobo Dreads had developed a murderous version of the creed. Those charged with the murder by St Lucian police were eventually represented by Michael Lorne, a Jamaican attorney who suggested that his clients were influenced by deejay rhetoric. Here, Anthony B's 'Fire Pon Rome' was seen as being particularly provocative, with the song naming Edward Seaga, P. J. Patterson and Bruce Golding as all being worthy of being burned alongside 'Fi Pope Paul'. The song was eventually banned from Jamaican radio play, although the companion track 'Bun Down Sodom' was not. In an interview, Anthony B explained the meaning behind his lyrics:

> I see Rome as a system that we're living off right now in the Western hemisphere. Rome form the first senate. Rome go

in other people's countries, change their laws, change their way of living, change their minds. So I say fire on Rome and that system that create inequality, racial discrimination, downpression, slavery. All of these things.[41]

In being so closely associated with the Bobo Dreads, the 'fire burn' controversy also forced a wedge between an older generation of roots-reggae musicians and the new breed of deejays. Burning Spear was probably the leading member of the roots-reggae generation still recording and performing in the 1990s, and he expressed his horror at the new trend with his single 'Rasta No Fire Burn Rasta', while Peter Morgan of Morgan Heritage also expressed reservations: 'Things are just getting crazy with this whole fire-burning thing. It's like everyone in Jamaica is about burning fire. It's gotten to the state where kids are setting each other on fire. They're burning down houses.'[42]

The problem of 'fire bun' was also evident in Jamaican dance-halls. At the 2000 staging of Sumfest, Capleton's set had to be cut short amid fears that the stage would burn down, such was the heat coming off the improvised aerosol torches that were being used by so many in the crowd. Later, Capleton's *Still Blazin* heaped fuel onto the fires of controversy, and following its release, he was invited to meet Prime Minister Patterson. Press reports indicated that the pair discussed, among other incidents, the case of a girl who had set her own house alight before waking her mother with the words 'more fire'. Chillingly, *Still Blazin* contains the track 'Cooyah Cooyah', on which an obviously young girl chants 'more fire, more fire!' Meanwhile, Patterson's opposite number Edward Seaga had taken to using a cigarette lighter to accompany recordings of T.O.K.'s 'Chi Chi Man' when campaigning in the 2002 general election, with the track's chorus declaring 'fire make we burn them'. Again, Seaga claimed innocence of the meaning of the track.

Despite his earlier defence, and perhaps as a surprise to his fans, Capleton eventually took a step back and issued an apology regarding his homophobia. Sizzla also seemed to relent, at least publicly. While 'Nah Apologize' may have comforted his fans with a promise that he would not compromise, Sizzla issued a formal statement that adhered to at least one of the demands of the Stop Murder Music campaign, stating:

> I know that in the past some of my material may have seemed to incite violence towards others which was never my intention. However, I will not perform these materials on stage so as not to offend anyone anywhere. I will however reserve the right as a citizen of earth to express my art in any way I see fit and to say what I feel; this is the right of a free man afforded to me by the almighty. I do however understand that words and music are powerful tools and as such one should be careful in its use.[43]

Although Sizzla's statement was clear enough, it soon became apparent that he was facing two ways. In the direction of Europe and the United States, Sizzla would issue statements of contrition. But on his own turf in Jamaica, it was business as usual. On dancehall night at Sumfest in July 2005, he returned to the fray, issuing a series of 'bun battyman and run out pon dem' denunciations, reiterating that he had not apologized.[44] So far, so normal. But while there was little in the way of criticism from his Western detractors, presumably because his onstage pronouncements passed them by, the response of Sumfest was notable. Under heavy pressure from Jamaica's Coalition of Corporate Sponsors, representing Red Stripe, Cable & Wireless, Supreme Ventures, Digicel, Courts, Wray & Nephew and the Jamaican Tourist Board, the festival appeared to wobble in their support of

Sizzla, with some press outlets stating that he would be dropped from future festivals.[45]

Despite the negative publicity about his performance at Sumfest in 2005, Sizzla returned to perform at the festival in July the following year. However, T.O.K. were not so fortunate in their dealings with the Jamaican Coalition of Corporate Sponsors. At a 'Smirnoff Experience' concert in Jamaica in December 2005, the band welshed on a contractual commitment with Smirnoff to avoid discriminatory language during their set, and launched into 'Chi Chi Man', their biggest hit to date. Their microphones went dead, forcing the band to leave the stage. It seemed that corporate sponsors meant business and were prepared to alienate audiences, some of whom cried that 'battyman' had sabotaged T.O.K.'s set.[46]

October 2006 saw controversy following a performance by Buju Banton in Miami, with gay-rights campaigners claiming that he had broken the truce of 2005 with a performance of 'Boom Bye Bye'. Tracii McGregor, president of Gargamel Music, rejected the charge:

> juicy stuff . . . but alas, context is everything. Buju has not actually performed 'Boom Bye Bye' in years. He has, however, railed off the first couple of lines of the song as a springboard to discuss with fans the ongoing troubles he's been faced with. It's a pity the camera didn't catch all that in Miami.[47]

Having watched a video snippet of the performance at the time, it was obvious that Banton was shadow boxing with gay-rights campaigners, teasing both them and his devoted audiences with the intro to 'Boom Bye Bye', before pulling up just short of repeating any contentious lyrics. For this indiscretion, Buju Banton was to pay dearly. The tour fell apart as venue after venue cancelled bookings, despite Banton not having uttered a homophobic word. Viewing his live performance as sticking to the letter of an agreement that he did not sign in the first place, Banton pulled no punches in his response to the cancelled tour: 'Fuck them ... I have never bashed any gays before, and if I bashed gays, I bashed them 16 years ago ... There's no tolerance from [gay-rights campaigners]. I'm not a gay-basher. I'm not a homophobe.'[48]

The collapse of Buju Banton's tour kept the issue of dancehall homophobia in the news in the UK. In autumn 2006 the Conservative party's new leader David Cameron weighed into the debate at the party's annual conference, stating that 'record companies that profit from violent and homophobic lyrics are ... morally wrong and socially unacceptable.'[49]

With the 2005 truce beginning to look frayed at the edges, the Stop Murder Music coalition pulled off a major coup when in March 2007 they announced that they had persuaded Beenie Man to sign a 'Reggae Compassionate Act', a formal declaration suffused with sufficient Rasta language to appeal to the deejays, while also containing enough to satisfy Western campaigners:

> We, the artists of the Reggae community, hereby present this letter as a symbol of our dedication to the guiding principles of Reggae's enduring foundation ONE LOVE. Throughout time, Reggae has been recognized as a healing remedy and an agent of positive social change. We will continue this proud and righteous tradition.
>
> Reggae Artists and their music have fought against injustices, inequalities, poverty and violence even while enduring some of those same circumstances themselves. Over the years, reggae music has become popularized and enjoyed by an unprecedented audience all over the world. Artists of the Reggae Community respect and uphold the rights of all individuals to live without fear of hatred and violence due to their religion, sexual orientation, race, ethnicity or gender.

While we recognize that our artistic community comprises many different individuals who express themselves in different ways and hold a myriad of beliefs, we believe firmly that the way forward lies in tolerance. Everyone can keep his own conviction and we must receive respect for our freedom of speech as far as we respect the law, but it must be clear there's no space in the music community for hatred and prejudice, including no place for racism, violence, sexism or homophobia.

We do not encourage nor minister to HATE but rather uphold a philosophy of LOVE, RESPECT and UNDERSTANDING towards all human beings as the cornerstone of reggae music.

This Compassionate Act is hereby calling on a return to the following principles as the guiding vision for the future of a healthy Reggae music community:

- Positive Vibrations
- Consciousness raising
- Social and Civic Engagement
- Democracy and Freedom
- Peace and Non-Violence
- Mother Nature
- Equal Rights and Justice
- One Love
- Individual Rights
- Humanity
- Tolerance and Understanding

We, as artists, are committed to a holistic and healthy existence in the world, and to respect to the utmost the human and natural world. We pledge that our music will continue to contribute positively to the world dialogue on peace, respect and justice for all.

240

To this end, we agree to not make statements or perform songs that incite hatred or violence against anyone from any community.[50]

With Beenie Man's signature in pen and ink on a document dated 23 March 2007, Sizzla and Capleton followed suit. Peter Tatchell explained that the involvement of the dancehall deejays followed on from an approach from Eddie Brown of Pride Music UK (a concert promotions company), who offered to contact the artists directly to see if they would be prepared to put their names to a negotiated agreement. Following some to-ing and fro-ing of different drafts, both sets of parties agreed on a final text, with printed and signed copies of the 'Act' sent to the UK for safe keeping.[51]

OutRage! formally suspended their campaign, but no sooner had the deejays signed the Act than they began to test its mettle. Sizzla was the first to act, singing 'Nah Apologize' throughout a European tour, but omitting 'batty boy' from the first line of the chorus, leaving his audience to sing it for him. Strictly speaking, Sizzla was adhering to the letter of the agreement, but certainly not its spirit. If Sizzla's approach was to see how far he could stretch the agreement, Beenie Man's approach was even less subtle. Unable to deny that he had signed the Act as Tatchell had both a signed copy of the Act and confirmation of the authenticity of the signature, Beenie Man claimed to have been duped into adding his name:

A guy come fi my sign paper inna Spain and tell we say we must sign, and mi tell dem mi nah sing no song about them so mi nah sign it. Ah politics dem a deal wid, me know that, so dem caan trick me ... Why would I sign when I am going to continue to perform these songs I have? I know that if the vibes lick me, and me decide fi do a song, mi not going to be able to do it, because mi dun sign already so that is why me nah go sign. No compromise.[52]

With Buju Banton also denying that he had ever signed the Act, the result was an immediate and dramatic breakdown of the new truce. A concert by Sizzla in Toronto was pulled after protests by the Canadian branch of the Stop Murder Music franchise, before attention turned to a tour by Elephant Man (Oneal Bryan). A deal brokered by the Carlton University Students Association saw an offer by Elephant Man to sign the Act at a press conference rejected by campaigners. Akim Larcher of gay-rights campaigning organization Egale Canada was quoted as saying that Elephant Man's signature would 'not be worth the paper it's signed on' if the Act was not physically signed in Jamaica.[53] There was also an additional condition slipped in by Larcher, who stated that 'the most important thing would be a public apology.'[54]

Back in Jamaica, the JLP's new leader, Bruce Golding, was proving popular. At the next general election on 3 September 2007, the political pendulum swung away from the PNP and towards the JLP, with Golding's party receiving 50.3 per cent of the vote and a slim majority of four seats. Soundtracking Golding's campaign was Buju Banton's big hit 'Driver A', not a homophobic track but a controversial one nonetheless, with Golding seemingly unperturbed by the track's lyrical content, a tale of ganja smuggling and betrayal at the hands of an informer.[55] In any other nation, this would be controversial, but although there were some minor rumblings in the tabloid press, the JLP's use of 'Driver A' went largely without comment in Jamaica.[56] For Golding, there was an alternative meaning to the song: 'If you are not changing course, it means that few will continue to live with the rampant corruption that has characterized this government. But Jamaica has to change course. I have a team that is committed to changing that course, and I am the driver.'[57]

By this time, there were murmurings of a possible tourism boycott of Jamaica. Following this, tensions then appeared between gay-rights campaigners in the global North and those in Jamaica, who were far more attuned to how the message was being received in the Caribbean. Jaevion Nelson of JFLAG claimed the development 'really came across as white people beating down on the Jamaican name'.[58] In May 2008 the Egale Canada Human Rights Trust called for both a tourism boycott and a ban on Jamaican goods and services. Such was the size of the Canadian market, the Jamaican Hotel and Tourist Association expressed concerns. Sensing trouble, and wishing to nip the campaign in the bud, Jamaica's new prime minister intervened, stating that his government would not bow to demands from Canada, and that decriminalization of homosexuality was 'a road down which I'm not going to allow this country to go under my leadership'.[59]

In the end, Egale Canada backed down under pressure from JFLAG, but Bruce Golding took this as a sign of weakness and on 20 May 2008 went on the offensive on the BBC's *HARDtalk* programme.[60] The interview started as one might expect. Golding suggested that Jamaica was changing, and that there was a greater acceptance of homosexuality than in previous eras: 'People have different lifestyles and their privacy must be respected.' But when Golding was pressed on the possible inclusion of gays within his cabinet, the mask of liberalism soon slipped. Jamaican values might adapt over time, said Golding, but as prime minister he would not bow to pressure groups from overseas intent on 'assaulting' Jamaican values. The inclusion of gays within his cabinet was not a matter of human rights, it was a matter for the prime minister alone.

In Jamaica, Bruce Golding was seen to have rebuffed Western cultural colonialism and returned home to a hero's welcome. However, the press were less confident in their assessment of the wisdom of Golding's move, with *The Gleaner* accusing him of a failure of leadership. Golding responded angrily, saying: 'we are prejudiced against incest and prostitution. Should we now be required to recognize the rights of incestors and prostitutes and find accommodation for them in the Cabinet?'[61]

Come 2009, the campaign against homophobic dancehall was fully internationalized, with pressure mounting in North America, Europe and Australasia. The campaigners' biggest success was the cancellation of much of Buju Banton's 'Rasta Got Soul' U.S. tour, with only one date going ahead in San Francisco after a successful sit-down meeting between local activists and Buju Banton. Both parties acknowledged that they were making compromises, with lesbian activist Andrea Shorter stating 'I'm not gonna get a medal for talking to you.'[62] Shorter was perhaps moving faster than Buju Banton, who remained steadfast in his view that he was no longer homophobic, pointing to his promotion of safe sex through 'Operation Willy', an earlier single, before adding 'I don't advocate violence, Rastafari is not about that.'[63] Commenting from the UK, Peter Tatchell was furious: 'This meeting is a big propaganda victory for Banton. He can now use it to show that he has dialogue with the LGBT community. It will be ruthlessly exploited by his management to undermine the LGBT campaign and the concert cancellations.'[64]

Ignoring the fact that he already had in his possession a copy of the Reggae Compassionate Act accompanied by Mark Myrie's signature, Tatchell added: 'I am shocked that no one seems to have asked Banton to sign the Reggae Compassionate Act. This was the least that he should have been asked to do.'[65] When the concert went ahead the following day, there was a picket of around thirty campaigners. During the gig, some members of the audience were pepper-sprayed by unknown assailants, with Banton quick to blame gay-rights campaigners.[66]

In the end, the campaign against Buju Banton's 'Rasta Got Soul' tour was the last gasp of the Stop Murder Music campaign, and OutRage! quietly wound down their protests. Campaigners had achieved tactical goals in getting concerts and tours cancelled and several sponsors had withdrawn their support for the deejays, but their overall strategic aim, of transforming dancehall and preventing it from being used as a vehicle for homophobic views, was only partially fulfilled. In a state of obeyance, the campaign against homophobic dancehall had effectively ended by the time of the general election of December 2011, which saw the PNP return to power and Portia Simpson-Miller gain a second term as prime minister. During her campaign, Simpson-Miller declared that 'no one should be discriminated against because of their sexual orientation' and stated that, unlike her JLP predecessor, she would be willing to appoint a gay cabinet member.[67] This was certainly progress.

While it might be easy to attribute the original upsurge of homophobic releases to dancehall's embrace of Rastafarian themes, the fact is that not all of those who recorded homophobic dancehall were Rastas. The homophobic dancehall of the 1990s and 2000s united the profane with the devout, with Christians joining Rastas and the agnostic in lyrical gay bashing. Not that all of reggae and dancehall in the 2000s was resolutely homophobic or quasi-biblical, but support for gay rights was exceptionally rare. One artist prepared to espouse an unapologetically pro-rights perspective was Tanya Stephens. On *Rebelution*, the much touted follow-up to *Gangsta Blues*, the ballad 'Do You Still Care?' tells of Bigga, an archetypal rude boy, who is shot as a result of a 'beef' but whose life is saved by a passer-by whose car displays a gay-pride sign. Later, in 2011, came *Tolerance* by Mista Majah, the first pro-gay reggae album. Initially this might seem to be a milestone, but the fact that the Jamaican-born artist remains exiled in California after having been warned that his life was in danger should he return to Jamaica makes the point about how far reggae and dancehall must go before it can be said to be free of hatred.

When 'Boom Bye Bye' was originally released in 1992, homo-phobia was no stranger to reggae and dancehall but there was little available for sale barring a handful of earlier recordings. This did not stay like this for long, and the following is a summary of the most significant homophobic dancehall releases in the following fifteen years, organized in general order of release:

'As It Done Load It Back' (1993) – Jigsy King
'Dis the System' (1993) – Mega Banton
'Gay Man' (1993) – Papa San
'Shot a Batty Boy' (1993) – Top Cat
'Shot Batty Boy' (1993) – Mega Banton
'Bomb and Dynamite' (1994) – Beenie Man
'Buggering' (1994) – Capleton
'Number 2' (1994) – Terror Fabulous (feat. Brian & Tony Gold)
'Funny Guy' (1995) – Professor Nuts
'Bun Down Sodom' (1996) – Anthony B
'Funny Guy Thing' (1996) – Spragga Benz
'Funny Man' (1996) – Baby Cham & Mr Easy
'No Like Batty Boy' (1996) – Virgo Man
'Silent Violence' (1996) – Beenie Man
'Strange Thing' (1996) – Baby Cham & Mr Easy
'Funny Man' (1997) – Hawkeye
'Gallong Yah Gal / We No Sorry' (1997) – Baby Cham
'Stand Tall' (1997) – Capleton
'We Nuh Like' (1997) – Spragga Benz
'Who Am I (Sim Simma)' (1997) – Beenie Man
'A Nuh fi Wi Fault' (1998) – Elephant
'Azanido' (1998) – Sizzla
'Bad Man Nuh Dress Like Girl' (1998) – Harry Toddler
'Can I Get a . . .' (1998) – Baby Cham
'Cut Out That' (1998) – Anthony B

'Funny Man' (1998) – Galaxy P

'Gay Waan Rights' (1998) – Buju Banton

'Haters' (1998) – Ward 21

'Kill Dem' (1998) – Harry Toddler

'Mr Wanna Be' (1998) – Bounty Killer

'Pure Sodom' (1998) – Capleton

'Rupaul System' (1998) – Elephant Man

'Another Level' (1999) – Bounty Killer with Baby Cham

'Badman Knowledge' (1999) – Capleton

'Blood Stain' (1999) – Ward 21

'Bun Friend' (1999) – Capleton

'Damm!!' (1999) – Beenie Man

'Fire Pon a Man' (1999) – Harry Toddler

'Funny Man' (1999) – Kiprich & Elephant Man

'Hang Dem Up' (1999) – Capleton

'I Rather Die' (1999) – Lexxus

'In or Out' (1999) – Capleton

'Judgement Day' (1999) – Ward 21

'Haters and Fools' (1999) – Beenie Man & Mr Easy

'Mi Nuh Play Chess' (1999) – Madd Anju

'Mr Fassy' (1999) – Ward 21

'More Prophet' (1999) – Capleton

'Never Get Down' (1999) – Capleton

'Nuh Like' (1999) – Elephant Man

'Slew Dem' (1999) – Capleton

'Who Dem?' (1999) – Capleton

'Babylon Bwoy' (2000) – Baby Cham

'Battyman fi Get Boom' (2000) – Capleton

'Bun a Fag' (2000) – Demo Delgado

'Chi Chi' (2000) – Filco Ranks

'Chi Chi Crew' (2000) – Alozade

'Chi Chi Man fi Heng' (2000) – Kevin Evil

'Cut Him Off' (2000) – Kiprich

'Dun a Chi Chi Man' (2000) – Kiprich

'Elimination' (2000) – Ghetto Max

'Fake Man' (2000) – Elephant Man

'Groundsman' (2000) – Baby Cham

'Hands Up' (2000) – Capleton

'Heard of Dem' (2000) – Sizzla

'Hunt You' (2000) – Capleton

'Man a Man' (2000) – Baby Cham

'Mr Foggaty' (2000) – Bounty Killer

'Nah Promote' (2000) – Mr Vegas

'Nuh inna Dat' (2000) – Spragga Benz

'Tight Pants' (2000) – Mega Banton

'To the Point' (2000) – Sizzla

'Woman Caan Too Much' (2000) – Sizzla

'Your Bad Luck' (2000) – Beenie Man

'Bad Man Chi Chi Man' (2001) – Beenie Man

'Boom Boom' (2001) – Sizzla

'Buggerism' (2001) – Mega Banton

'Bun a Chi Chi Man' (2001) – Hot Shot Crew

'Bun Chi Chi Man' (2001) – Tappa Zukie & Family

'Bun Out di Chi Chi' (2001) – Capleton

'Bun Out Gay Guy' (2001) – Elephant Man

'Bun Dem' (2001) – Junior Demus

'Buss Your Gun' (2001) – Singer J

'Chi Chi Man' (2001) – T.O.K.

'Chi Chi Man and Chi Chi Gal' (2001) – Hammer Mouth

'Chi Chi Man fi Dead' (2001) – Beenie Man

'Dead' (2001) – Gringo & ARP

'Falla We' (2001) – T.O.K.

'Get Yourself a Gun' (2001) – Beenie Man & Gringo

'Gi Dem Gunshot' (2001) – Sizzla

'Girls Gungu Walk' (2001) – Wickerman

'Karate' (2001) – Sizzla

'Log On' (2001) – Elephant Man

'Man a Badman' (2001) – Bounty Killer & T.O.K.

'Man and Woman' (2001) – Bunny Wailer

'Mystery Is the Man' (2001) – Bounty Killer

'Nuh Chi Chi Man' (2001) – General B

'Oh What a Night' (2001) – Mr Vegas

'Straight as an Arrow' (Chi Chi Man Part 2) (2001) – T.O.K.

'Victory (Chi Chi Man fi Dead)' (2001) – Beenie Man

'Which One' (2001) – Mad Cobra

'Woah' (2001) – Capleton

'All Out War' (2002) – Bounty Killer

'Baddest Girl' (2002) – Lady Saw

'Batty Boy Dead' (2002) – Admiral T & Lovy Jam

'Bounty' (2002) – Bounty Killer

'Bun Batty Bwoy' (2002) – Baby Cham

'Couldn't Be Real' (2002) – Mega Banton

'Frenzy' (2002) – Sanchez

'Haunted' (2002) – Mad Cobra

'Just Dead' (2002) – Bounty Killer

'Killa Is a Killa' (2002) – Bounty Killer

'No Apology' (2002) – Anthony B

'Tek It Off' (2002) – Capleton

'That's Right' (2002) – Beenie Man

'World Nuh Need Dem' (2002) – YT

'Anything-A-Anything' (2003) – Elephant Man & Ward 21

'Badman Surprise' (2003) – Spragga Benz, Bounty Killer, Madd Cobra & Assassin

'Bedroom Slaughteration' (2003) – Vybz Kartel & Spragga Benz

'Bun Chi Chi Man' (2003) – Beenie Man

'Bun Bad Mind' (2003) – Beenie Man

'Funny Man Stay Far' (2003) – Delly Ranks & Mega Banton

'Dun Fassies' (2003) – Mega Banton

'Gunz Like Mine' (2003) – Vybz Kartel

'Han Up Deh' (2003) – Beenie Man

'Head Gone / Genie Dance' (2003) – Elephant Man

'Nah Gwan a Jamaica' (2003) – Elephant Man

'Nah Mix Up' (2003) – Elephant Man

'Nah No Head' (2003) – Predator

'Pussy Jaw' (2003) – Vybz Kartel

'Real Badman' (2003) – Mad Cobra

'Weh Yuh No fi Do' (2003) – Beenie Man

'Badman Nah Apologize' (2004) – Beenie Man

'Batty Boy' (2004) – Sayrus

'Batty Boy fi Dead' (2004) – Chicken

'Batty Bwoy Friend' (2004) – Ras Berry

'Batty Man fi Dead' (2004) – Beenie Man

'Bun a Sadomite' (2004) – Spragga Benz

'Bun Dem' (2004) – Daddy Mory

'Bun Dem Now' (2004) – Assassin

'Burn Pédofil' (2004) – Admiral T

'Chrome' (2004) – Bounty Killer

'Dat A True' (2004) – Bounty Killer

'Done See It' (2004) – Spragga Benz

'Dunn A Chi Chi Boy' (2004) – Mega Banton

'Faggot Correction' (Spragga Dis) (2004) – Vybz Kartel

'Fire Time' (2004) – Capleton

'Gunz A Rule' (2004) – Bounty Killer

'Haters' (2004) – Beenie Man

'Hypocrite Friend' (2004) – Beenie Man

'No Apology' (2004) – Vybz Kartel

'No Batty' (2004) – Vybz Kartel

'No Lean No Bend' (2004) – Rally Bop

'Not Afraid' (2004) – Elephant Man

'Run Out Pon Dem' (2004) – Sizzla

'Run Tings' (2004) – Spragga Benz

'Woman Mi Give Talk' (2004) – Hawkeye

'Yippy Yow' (2004) – Elephant Man & Busta Rhymes

'Batty Bwoy fi Dead' (2005) – Vybz Kartel feat. Beenie Man

'Don't Play with Me' (2005) – Baby Cham

'Free Up the Atmosphere' (2005) – Bounty Killer

'J. A. Don't Like Gay' (2005) – Dr Evil

'Judgement Day' (2005) – Warrior King

'Nah Apologize' (2005) – Sizzla

'No Apology' (2005) – Beenie Man

'Spy on Me' (2005) – Sizzla

'Head Out' (2006) – Sizzla

'Lu Lu Lu' (2006) – Busy Signal

'Osama' (2006) – Dr Evil

'Shot a Fire' (2006) – Shabba Ranks

'Stay Far from We (Batty Bwoy)' (2006) – Dr Evil

'Funny Man' (2007) – Junior Reid

'Hit Them Hard' (2007) – Stapler

'Lef Dem to Time' (2007) – Elephant Man feat. Jigsy

'Man a Bad Man' (2007) – Bounty Killer

'Move Like Sissy' (2007) – Assassin

'Nuh Friend Fish' (2007) – Bounty Killer

'Battyman' (2008) – Mavado

'Bullet Proof Skin' (2008) – Bounty Killer

'Dem a Fag' (2008) – Mavado

'Nuh Par Wid (Batty Bwoy)' (2008) – Busy Signal

'Brokeback Rodeo' (2009) – Lovindeer

In addition to noting the puerile nature of many of the song titles, the effect of placing the most significant homophobic releases in chronological order is to note a bell curve effect as time passed. In one sense, the trajectory of the whole controversy regarding dancehall homophobia mirrors that of a moral panic. The term is best understood through reference to the work of criminologist Stanley Cohen, who developed an analytical model to describe media reporting of a series of beach-side disturbances between 'mods' and 'rockers' in England in the summer of 1964. To be a moral panic, a social controversy must have an explicitly moral dimension, with there being a perceived threat to cherished values and a social reaction to events that is out of all proportion to their true significance. Cohen's model of a modern mediatized moral panic is both circular and amplificatory, as media reporting of earlier clashes between mods and rockers set the stage for future, more serious events. Here, Cohen notes that media reporting sensitized the public to future events. The mods and rockers disturbances had started in Easter 1964. But by August of that year, many young people had become so fascinated with the media's confident prediction of a forthcoming riot in Brighton on the August bank holiday of that year that they flocked to the seaside resort hopeful of witnessing the events unfold. Unbeknown to these new protagonists, earlier media reporting was, according to Cohen, 'scene setting' and those young people who travelled to Brighton hoping to witness rioting by others found that they themselves had been cast in the role of rioters, with the police responding as such.[68]

The bell curve of the slow rise and gradual fall and decline of dancehall homophobia can be mapped onto Cohen's circular model. Following each cycle of Jamaican action and British reaction, there was an amplificatory feedback loop. Each denunciation by gay-rights campaigners spurred on the dancehall protagonists to record ever more offensive material, leading to greater condemnation in the global North. Within a few years, the debate was at fever pitch, with the UK state drawn into the fray, leading to changes in the way gigs are regulated by local authorities and changes to the law and the way it is applied. What started off as a controversy about a single recording led to the banning of Sizzla from entering the UK, a relatively rare occurrence placing him on a par with more familiar hate preachers such as Omar Bakri Muhammad, the Syrian Islamist militant.

At the height of the controversy regarding homophobic dancehall, Elena Oumano of the *Village Voice* in New York argued that the 'dancehall eight' were facing competing commercial pressures and were caught between the rock of OutRage! and the much harder place of their constituency. If dancehall artists conceded to OutRage!, the promise was one of an international success untroubled by the attentions of first-world police forces. However, if the deejays did relent, their reputations in Jamaica as anti-authority rebels would lie in tatters along with their careers. As Oumano puts it:

> Dancehall's eight will not – cannot – apologize, despite a collective income loss, according to OutRage!, of over $9 million, and the agreement isn't asking them to. In a country that boasts of more churches per capita than any other, few artists can do more than reflect their culture.[69]

But Oumano was wrong to suggest there was no way out of the double bind in which the deejays found themselves and that they could do no more than reflect their culture. The homophobia of the dancehall eight did not merely reflect views found within Jamaican culture; it reaffirmed and reinvigorated them. Furthermore, the dancehall eight did eventually find a way out of the situation, through not only falling silent on homophobia but also by maintaining a silence on why they had given up recording homophobic tracks.

The decline of the moral panic started with the opposite of amplification, a quietening, which crept in just at the point when campaigners in the global North started to take the pressure off. With a creeping perception that they were no longer under heavy manners, the deejays could then quietly drop their homophobia from recordings without ever having to admit to Jamaican audiences that they had done so. The pressure would remain off, ensuring that those dancehall deejays still allowed visas were able to continue to perform in the global North. OutRage!'s website suggests that their campaign ended in 2009, but without any official announcement. But, as with Stanley Cohen's analysis of the mods and rockers, nothing would ever be the same afterwards. 'Boom Bye Bye' remains a problem, for global society and for dancehall. Should a similar controversy start again, British gay-rights campaigners, along with the UK's police force and the state prosecutor, will find that they have a new weapon in their legislative armoury. A 2008 amendment to Section 29b of the Public Order Act of 1986 now makes it an offence to distribute, perform, broadcast or possess material that stirs up hatred against someone because of their sexuality. For better or for worse, the law in the UK has changed, and Jamaican deejays keen on performing in the UK would be wise to pay attention to this new legislation should they ever consider reviving the trend for homophobic dancehall.

PART III

8

'DON'T TOUCH THE PRESIDENT': DANCEHALL AND THE TIVOLI GARDENS MASSACRE

I-Octane, 'Lose a Friend' (2012)

The country's ethnic minorities largely control the material resources and means of production of the nation. Many of their number are cut from the same cloth as the 'absentee landlord' of a bygone colonial era. And there are amongst them latent pockets of holdover racism. Those minorities must embrace the mantra of 'One Love', not just mindlessly sing along or dance to the mesmeric lines and tempo of the namesake 'Song of the (20th) Century' popularised by the Right Honourable Robert Nesta Marley, OM.

Interim Report to Parliament concerning
Investigations into the Conduct of the Security Forces
during the State of Emergency Declared May, 2010 –
West Kingston/Tivoli Gardens 'Incursion' –
The Killing of Mr. Keith Oxford Clarke
and Related Matters.[1]

T he death of Bob Marley in May 1981 seemed to symbolize the end of the era of roots reggae as dancehall became the main driving force within Jamaican music. Just short of thirty years later, it would be the deaths of over a hundred members of the public at the hands of the Jamaican state that would be the tragic spark for a change in the direction of both reggae and dancehall, with what became known as the Tivoli Gardens massacre of 2010 being a huge turning point in the history of Jamaica.

The events of 2010 were the culmination of forty years of garrison politics, with the familiar family name of Coke again at the centre of events. After taking over the reins of the Shower Posse following Claudie Massop's murder in 1979, Lester 'Jim Brown' Coke seemed unassailable in Tivoli Gardens, running a cocaine-smuggling empire that stretched from the Caribbean to the global North. In America, Shower Posse business was managed by Coke's partner Vivian Blake, who had moved to the States in 1973 and who by the early 1980s was responsible for flooding New York with imported cocaine before branching out to other major u.s. cities, leaving a trail of destruction in his wake. In 1988 u.s. police issued a warrant for Blake's arrest on murder charges related to the killing of five at a crack house in Miami in 1984, but he evaded capture and returned to Jamaica.[2] Meanwhile, Lester Coke, on one of his regular sojourns in the States, found himself under arrest and deported to Jamaica to face trial for the murder of twelve people in Rema, the new name for Wilton Gardens to the north of Tivoli

Gardens, a housing project built by the JLP in 1963 using U.S. state aid. With Edward Seaga providing political cover, the case never made it to trial. The judge freed Coke, with his release heralded by his henchmen, who fired a gun salute outside the courthouse.[3]

The protection offered to Coke by Edward Seaga would not last forever, and the return of Michael Manley to Jamaica House in February 1989 would be the beginning of the end of the Don's reign. During the nine years of his premiership, Seaga had been a great friend to the USA, whose government was reticent to confront him regarding the role the JLP might have played in the rise of cocaine smuggling into the States. However, Seaga's defeat at the general election of 1989 meant that the American authorities were now free to pursue their objectives in extraditing Coke. The Jamaican authorities were also searching for Coke and attempted to arrest him in July 1990 with a force of eighty men, only for four police officers to be shot dead and for Coke to make his escape. Following this, U.S. authorities heard rumours that should any extradition proceedings lead to Coke's arrest, Shower Posse gang members would travel from Tivoli Gardens to Montego Bay and start shooting American tourists. The USA paused its efforts as a result. Once they were confident that their actions would not lead to a bloodbath, the U.S. authorities made their move, and in 1992 issued an extradition request for Coke, who was arrested shortly afterwards.[4]

Prior to the arrest of Lester Coke, his eldest son Mark Anthony (known as Jah T) was in the process of organizing a tribute concert for his father's old mentor Claudie Massop when he was ambushed on his motorcycle and shot dead by what were said to be PNP-aligned gunmen. In retaliation, Shower Posse members stormed into the PNP neighbourhood of Hannah Town and killed thirty civilians.[5] Edward Seaga led a crowd of 20,000 at the funeral of Jah T, but during the service, shocked mourners were informed that Lester Coke had just died in an unexplained fire in his cell at the General

Penitentiary in Kingston. Prior to his death in custody, Coke was reported to have informed a fellow inmate that, were he to stand trial in the United States, he would reveal all about the relationship between Seaga and the Shower Posse, and rumours of either JLP or/and police involvement in Lester Coke's death were rife.[6] Coke's lawyer, the JLP senator Tom Tavares-Finson, commented: 'If you believe Jim Brown just burned to death, by accident, in his jail cell, you'll believe in the tooth fairy. The only thing I can tell you for sure is I saw the body, and Jim Brown is dead.'[7]

Again, it would be Edward Seaga who would lead the mourners at Lester Coke's funeral, this time accompanied by Olivia Grange. Seaga was at the graveside as one faction of the Shower Posse showed their respect for their departed leader with a volley of 21 shots of automatic gunfire, only for a rival faction to let off a salvo of shots in mimicry of the tribute. The original 21-gun salute had been organized by Christopher 'Dudus' Coke, Lester's youngest son, who saw his rivals' mocking as a grotesque show of disrespect. As a result, the interment of Lester Coke ended in bloodshed and chaos with at least two dead and dozens injured, with some mourners seeking refuge by climbing into the burial plot that awaited Coke's remains. When it was put to Edward Seaga that he had played a prominent role in the funeral of a man alleged to have been involved in numerous murders, his response was as pithy as it was telling: 'I look at the man in terms of how the community respects and treats him as a protector from their community.'[8]

After the funerals of Jah T and Lester Coke, Christopher Coke, then aged 22, took over his father's empire. During an initial period of establishing control over both the Shower Posse and the Tivoli Gardens neighbourhood, Coke clashed with Ziggy Marley over the building of a studio on the border of Coke's territory. It was expected that Marley would award the construction contract to Coke, but he handed the work to outside contractors instead. With his nose put out of joint, Coke is said to have ordered a series of 'message killings' to inform the singer of his grievance, and Marley eventually relented.[9]

Within two years of the death of his father, Christopher Coke had consolidated his grip on the reins of the Shower Posse and was becoming more powerful in West Kingston than even Edward Seaga. This was acknowledged by the former prime minister, who in 1994 handed over to the Jamaican Police the names of thirteen individuals who he stated were responsible for terrorizing his constituents, saying that he had asked them to cease their violence but they had ignored him, so he had little choice other than to seek their arrest.[10] At the top of Seaga's list was the name of Christopher Coke. In the past, Seaga's power and reputation would have been enough for him to get his way, but on this occasion, the police refused to act. The symbolism was not lost on ordinary Jamaicans – the Shower Posse no longer required the protection of Edward Seaga, they were now more powerful than any single politician.

Despite the controversy over Edward Seaga's role at Lester Coke's funeral in 1992, and despite Michael Manley's admission that his attendance at the funeral of Burry Boy in 1975 was the biggest error of his career, others in the PNP would make the same mistake at the May 2001 funeral of William 'Haggart' Moore, the leading Don in the PNP's Arnett Gardens stronghold. Moore, along with fellow Black Roses Crew gang members Ned 'Big Bunny' Hinds and Albert 'Blacka Douche' Bonner, were killed in a hail of bullets discharged by an unknown assassin, with rumours that the trio had crossed some Colombian drug barons.[11]

At the time of the murder of Moore, Hinds and Bonner, the Black Roses Crew were well known for their dance floor prowess. In particular, 'Haggart' had been namechecked in numerous recordings and had appeared in music videos performing alongside Beenie Man and Barrington Levy, so it was to be expected that his funeral would be a lavish affair. As a result, William Moore was given a hero's send-off in what was called the first dancehall funeral, with his body lying in state in Kingston's National Arena. In attendance was Dr Omar Davies, minister of finance with the PNP, and two other ministers, along with Moses Davis, aka Beenie Man.[12] In delivering the eulogy to Moore, Davies seemed to anticipate the inevitable criticism he would receive by saying: 'I am here to pay my last respect to a man I met seven and a half years ago when I came to represent the constituency of South St Andrew. He assisted me to achieve some of my objectives in the constituency. We never had a meeting which lasted more than ten minutes.'[13]

At least one source claims that Moore's funeral was attended by more people than that of Bob Marley.[14] One pall-bearer was George Phang, the producer behind the Powerhouse label who used Sly and Robbie as an in-house rhythm section and who favoured the acoustics of Dynamic Sounds for his recordings. Phang had developed a strong roster of artists over the years, including Brigadier Jerry, Admiral Bailey, Al Campbell, Cutty Ranks, Freddie McGregor, General Echo, Frankie Paul, Yellowman, Super Cat and Josey Wales. A long-standing friend of Omar Davies and Milton 'Red Tony' Welsh, Phang was a well-known figure in Arnett Gardens as the manager of the local football club, and if the Jamaican press are to be believed, as 'area leader'.[15] In 2003, Phang was shot in Jones Town, Kingston, suffering multiple injuries. At the time, the Jamaican Police were forced to deny that Phang was originally a suspect in the murder of Willie 'Haggart' Moore two years earlier, while seeming unsure as to whether the attempted assassination of Phang was because of conflict between Tivoli Gardens and Arnett Gardens, or the repercussions of a power struggle from within Arnett Gardens as Phang's influence began to wane.[16]

The killing of William Moore, Ned Hinds and Albert Bonner shocked dancehall and left Gerald Levy, better known as Bogle, as the best-known member of Jamaica's most famous dancehall troop. Taking his stage name from Paul Bogle, the leader of the Morant Bay Rebellion of 1865, Bogle was a dancehall star and choreographer who first came to Jamaica's attention in the 1970s on the Saturday morning TV show *Ring Ding* before rising to fame through the 1980s. Immortalized in Buju Banton's 'Bogle' (1992), Beenie Man's 'Row Like a Boat' (2004) and Elephant Man's 'Gully Creeper' (2008), Bogle was widely acknowledged as a dancehall legend and the creator of more named dance moves than any other figure.[17] With the motto of 'dance or die', Bogle frequently claimed that deejays did not have hits until he had created a new dance to accompany their recording. While this might have been an exaggeration, it is certainly the case that Bogle's fame rose with the dancehall deejays that surrounded him and there was a symbiotic relationship between them.

After William Moore's extravagant funeral, Beenie Man immortalized the Don in song with his single 'We Set di Trend' (2006), in which Haggart is credited with various fashions including 'burgundy Benz', briefly the favoured car of all the leading Dons, along with 'setting the trend' for Jah T, Dudus ('the youngest legend') and 'Skeng'. The last was a reference to PNP ally Kenneth 'Skeng Don' Black, who arrived at Moore's funeral in a bullet-proofed cavalcade flanked by motorcycle outriders, with Moore's sealed coffin reopened for him once he had arrived in the arena.[18]

Originally the PNP Don of Mandeville in the parish of Manchester, Kenneth Black was also a sound-system operator and dancehall producer whose roster often sung tributes to their employer and label boss. Examples include Junior Cat's 1987 release 'Skengdon Bring Reggae Music' along with 'Skengdon Crew' by Al Campbell & Tabby Diamond in the same year. Both were issued on the Skengdon label that also released recordings by Nicodemus, Johnny Osbourne & Junior Delgado, Cocoa Tea, Cutty Ranking,

Sugar Minott, Frankie Paul, Gregory Isaac, John Holt and Super Cat. In total, Skengdon would release 120 singles from 1985 to 1988, with Black combining politics and dancehall, appearing at political rallies that started to look like dancehall events, and at dancehall nights that started to look like political rallies. In 1986, Black contributed some JA$100,000 to the PNP's coffers at their September conference. Later that year, Jeremy Palmer, JLP parliamentary secretary and minister of agriculture, used parliamentary privilege to quote an article published in Venezuela's *La Religion* magazine that accused Black of being in charge of a ganja distribution network that stretched from Jamaica to Miami, Mexico and the Bahamas.[19] By 1988 the *Orlando Sentinel* was reporting that Black was residing in Miami, running a cocaine-smuggling empire.[20] With the PNP coming back to power in 1989, Black returned to Jamaica, building a career as a businessman in receipt of big-budget government construction contracts. In 2002, Black settled out of court in a legal case in which he accused Edward Seaga of slander for stating that Black was a gangster. The former prime minister was forced to issue a televised apology before paying Black's legal costs of JA$500,000.[21] When the political tide turned against the PNP and the JLP returned to government, Black found himself frozen out of lucrative government contracts by the new administration, leading to a series of successful lawsuits in which Black recouped lost earnings.[22]

If Michael Manley and Edward Seaga were compromised by their connections to gangsters such as Winston 'Burry Boy' Blake and Lester 'Jim Brown' Coke, it would fall to Manley's successor P. J. Patterson to take on the drug barons. In September 2000, Patterson formed an elite Crime Management Unit (CMU) to be led by Reneto Adams, a particularly controversial police superintendent. A year later, Reneto's unit was accused of acting as a paramilitary force during a search of Tivoli Gardens for drugs and guns that left at least 27 dead, with Adams himself accused of firing at civilians at random.[23] When members of the CMU found themselves pinned down by automatic gunfire from unknown would-be assassins, Edward Seaga turned up and the firing ceased. Seaga offered to provide Adams and his officers with safe passage out of the area, but Adams and his men refused to leave. The subsequent gun battle killed 27 people.[24] Two years later, Amnesty International accused the state inquiry into the events of being a whitewash, with an allegation that it did not even manage to identify the dead by name, never mind get to the bottom of the state killings involved.[25]

A year after the raid on Tivoli Gardens, Reneto Adams moved into the dancehall limelight at the popular Sting event in Portmore, which was associated in the popular imagination with Isaiah Laing, co-founder of Supreme Promotions and a former detective sergeant. Laing first came to prominence in the 1980s, and prior to his role as a music promoter had been lionized on record by the dancehall artist Tiger, whose hit 'When' described Laing as the most feared 'bad man' officer in Jamaica.[26] At Sting 2002, Reneto Adams took to the stage at the very moment when Ninjaman was leaving, with the deejay then returning with a Glock pistol, which he handed to Adams. With television cameras rolling, Ninjaman faced Adams and said:

> Me a di original gold teeth front teeth gunman deejay and you ah di original gunman police. I give you this gun because gunman fi stop shoot people and you fi stop shoot ghetto bwoy. All de yout wheh a carry gun yuh fe tek dem an train dem an tun dem inna police.[27]

Adams responded with similar sentiments, announcing an on-the-spot gun amnesty before joining Ninjaman in a rendition of the popular spiritual song 'It Soon Be Done'. Within three years, Reneto Adams would take it one step further with the recording of his own dancehall number, 'To Protect and Serve', released shortly after a jury acquitted him of murdering two men and two women and planting guns on their bodies.[28] Carolyn Gomes of the campaigning organization Jamaicans for Justice called the track 'irresponsible, frightening and distasteful'.[29]

The raid on Tivoli Gardens in 2001 was portrayed in the international press as Dirty Harry-style justice, although to do so risked ignoring the fact that so many innocent bystanders were killed. Adams's response to criticism of his methods was blunt: 'you're always talking about the police killing people. What about the criminals killing people? What about my men getting killed?'[30] Edward Seaga referred to the raid as an atrocity and called for Adams to be removed from his post, while Derrick Smith, the JLP spokesman for National Security, accused the security forces of trying to assassinate Seaga.[31]

One of the more unpredictable outcomes of the violence in Tivoli Gardens was the inauguration of Passa Passa, which would go on to become Jamaica's biggest dancehall event, drawing in thousands of dancehall fans from across the island alongside many international visitors. The event had humble origins in a sound-system test each Wednesday afternoon in preparation for weekend events that were sparsely attended due to much of Tivoli Gardens being under police lockdown. Passa Passa promoter Dylan Powe explains:

What happened was, after the first Reneto Adams raid in 2001, Tivoli people stopped going out. There was war and political friction going on and West Kingston became a more insular community. A lot of people weren't coming there to party and people weren't leaving to go party. My family has a business down there from the early 1950s, a drug store. Wednesdays downtown closes half day and the roads become less busy. So O'Neil used to set up the sound system in front of the store to test it for dates over the weekend, and he would take a couple of hours or so playing new records. When he'd play, people from the immediate area who wouldn't normally come out of their homes would come out. Maestro, who is one of the major selectors, actually coined the name Passa Passa because what he saw was people from different areas in West Kingston partying together by default since there was nothing else to go out to. So, Passa Passa really means, 'mix up'.[32]

Within a few years of the Tivoli Gardens raid, Passa Passa was attracting upwards of 20,000 attendees. Dylan Powe claims the event 'helped decriminalize Tivoli Gardens'.[33] On the ground and in the press, it was stated that the event was run by Presidential Click, the firm founded and run by Christopher Coke.[34] *The Gleaner* got into hot water when they made this allegation, with the newspaper forced to make an apology to cousins Dylan Powe and O'Neil Miles for the 'unfavourable association' the newspaper made when it accused Passa Passa of being connected to the Shower Posse. Powe and Miles pointed out that their business was properly registered with the authorities,[35] and while this may have been true, it was clear that Christopher Coke's soldiers policed the event, ensuring the safety of all participants in a move that would only heighten the aura of mystique around 'Dudus'. The BBC's Jamaica correspondent noted that due to Coke's involvement in Passa Passa, West Kingston had become 'quite glam for uptown people and it was safe. They could go and revel in that ghetto life for a night. And to be fair, those downtown dances are great fun, they are vibrant, they are what Jamaica is all about.'[36]

It was not just an anonymous elite that would attend Passa Passa; the deputy leader of the opposition, the JLP's James Robertson, was photographed there, as was Superintendent Harry Daley, the man in charge of the local police station at Denham Town.[37] Opposition leader and local MP Bruce Golding said that 'the peace and tranquillity the area has enjoyed has made life so much better for the people there.'[38] As the event only really got started at around 1 a.m. and usually ran for around eight hours, Golding's statement made a mockery of the country's strict licensing laws and the Jamaican Noise Abatement Act of 1997, legislation that was widely ignored by both dancehall promoters and the authorities. At the time, adherence to licensing laws was the last thing on the minds of the Jamaican authorities, although this would not always be the case.

One dancehall figure initially absent from Passa Passa was Bogle. Born in Trench Town and residing in Arnett Gardens, Bogle was seen as a PNP supporter, particularly due to his connections with Stone Love, seen as a PNP sound system. It was this that would have made his presence at Passa Passa dangerous, although by 2004, the event was so large and well run that he began to appear and made an immediate impact.[39] Within a year, though, Bogle was dead, shot by two motorcycle-riding assassins after an altercation with Beenie Man, while four other passengers were taken to hospital with bullet wounds. Beenie Man put up a JA$1 million bounty for the capture of those responsible, but they remain unknown and unpunished.[40]

At the time of his death, Bogle was turning his attention to how, as a Jamaican choreographer, he had no protection for what he saw as his intellectual property rights, even though he had performed all over the Caribbean and North America and was the star of many music videos. Since his death, Bogle's stature has only grown. The likes of Rihanna and Sean Paul have used his moves in various music videos and the athlete Usain Bolt popularized

Bogle's dancing style when celebrating victories at the 2008 Summer Olympics in Beijing.

While Powe and Miles were running Passa Passa, over in the neighbouring PNP stronghold of Matthews Lane, the big annual event was Spanglers Dance, organized by area leader Donald 'Zeeks' Phipps. Christopher A. D. Charles of the department of government at the University of the West Indies sets the scene of the Spanglers Dance in its heyday:

> During the dances, Matthews Lane is a tightly regulated countersociety. Zeeks's bar is the only commercial entity that is allowed to operate at the dances. The absence of vendors from within and outside the community is a situation unique to the dances held by the Spanglers Crew. The many dance-hall taste publics who attend dances in Jamaica constitute a survival market for some vendors. The vendors within and outside of the Matthews Lane countersociety recognize and respect the authority of the celebrity crew because they do not conduct business at Spanglers' dances.
>
> In the tightly regulated countersociety, Zeeks as the leader of the crew and as the biggest celebrity in the dance receives priority treatment from the line staff in the Spanglers' security structure. The don is closely guarded by the 'shottas' when he walks through the throng. Although Zeeks receives priority security, the 'shottas' also protect the taste publics by ensuring that peace and order prevail at the dances.[41]

The rein of Donald Phipps came to an end when in 2006 he was sentenced to life imprisonment for the murders of Rodney Leroy Farquharson and Dayton Williams in an argument over the sale of ganja.[42]

'Which Dudus?'

By 2007, with his Shower Posse now seemingly unassailable, Dudus Coke was being referred to as 'the President' in Kingston and beyond.[43] In Tivoli Gardens, such was the gang's influence that the area was unpoliced, or at least not policed by state forces. Electricity was supplied to residents for free and rent to the government was going unpaid without repercussions. When roads or government buildings needed repairing, it was the Shower Posse that won the contract, albeit under a cover name such as Incomparable Enterprises Ltd, the organization's construction company. Coke was now all-powerful, sitting at the epicentre of what became known as 'the system', with the Don ensuring that the electorate in West Kingston voted for the JLP. In return, it was said that Coke had a say on the JLP's electoral strategy.

At a later parliamentary inquiry, Bruce Golding would refer to Coke as 'a benefactor', but it seemed as if all of Jamaica knew the real relationship between the country's new prime minister and his best-known constituent.[44] The U.S. authorities certainly held the view that Coke was a malign influence, as within two years of Golding's victory at the general election of 2007, they issued an extradition warrant for Christopher Coke, accusing him of being among 'the world's most dangerous narcotics kingpins'.[45] The initial response of Golding was to hire the American lobbying firm Manatt, Phelps & Phillips to persuade the U.S. authorities to drop the extradition.[46] Golding eventually admitted that the £50,000 payment for the firm's services came from 'a contributor to the party', although he denied that it came from Christopher Coke 'or anyone of his ilk'.[47] Golding told the Jamaican Parliament that it was the JLP who engaged the services of Manatt, Phelps & Phillips, although the firm itself believed they were working for the Jamaican government.[48] Either way, Golding would resist the

extradition request for nine months, arguing, with some justification, that it was based on illegal phone taps. The United States
responded, accusing the JLP government of a 'lack of cooperation
in stopping drug trafficking'.[49]

By this time in his career, Christopher Coke was organizing
some of the largest entertainment events in Jamaica. In addition to
delivering Passa Passa, Jamaica's biggest dancehall night, Coke also
organized a 'Champions in Action' event in August of each year,
using the same name that his father had used for a 15,000-capacity
dancehall event in the late 1980s. Dudus also organized the West
Kingston Jamboree, a free pre-Christmas event that was focused on
entertainment for children during the day and dancehall music for
adults in the evening, featuring a roll-call of the biggest names in
Jamaica, including Shaggy, Beenie Man, Bounty Killer, Elephant
Man, Queen Ifrica and Tarrus Riley.[50] At Passa Passa, Coke invited
various politicians to attend, many of whom duly obliged. All of this
was organized from the Presidential Click offices in Tivoli Gardens,
with the name of his organization painted on the outside of his
HQ.[51] Media reports suggest that the deejays performed at Coke's
events for free, while those who refused to do so were threatened
or beaten.[52] Whether true or not, it did seem that a considerable
number of Jamaica's top deejays were on the side of 'the President'.
For a brief while, Presidential Click also operated a record label,
releasing a handful of singles by Fearless Crew, Frisco Kid, Beenie
Man and Mr Vegas.

In 2009, on the day after that year's West Kingston Jamboree,
Bruce Golding met two of the biggest figures in Jamaican music
to quell a feud that had its origins in dancehall, but which was
threatening to destabilize Jamaican politics. The conflict between
the chart-topping Vybz Kartel (Adidja Palmer) and the relatively
new kid on the block Mavado (David Brooks) had its origin in a
series of dancehall performances and recordings in the mid-2000s.

Although both artists were initially protégés of Bounty Killer, by 2006 Vybz Kartel was referring to Mavado as 'Mafraudo', claiming that beneath the lyrical bravado he was a phoney gangster. On stage at Sting in late 2008, the lyrical battle was fought at close quarters. With Vybz Kartel performing in full military attire and Mavado wearing a black mask, the two deejays traded the usual verbal blows. When Vybz Kartel carried onto the stage a coffin with 'R.I.P. Mavado' printed on it, his opponent became incensed and stormed off-stage. Afterwards, fights broke out in the audience as fans of both deejays clashed.

Within six months, the feud had spread throughout Jamaica and had taken on a distinct garrison flavour. On one side of the feud was the Gaza area of Vybz Kartel's town of Portmore, to the west of Kingston. On the other side was Mavado's Cassava Piece shantytown neighbourhood, a JLP stronghold that lines the Constant Spring gully in uptown Kingston in the north of the city. Soon, dancehall fans would be expected to take one side or the other while the feud was reported in lurid detail in Jamaica's tabloid press. Some dancehall fans were more enthusiastic participants in the feud than others, and there were those with a particularly high profile. At Usain Bolt's welcome-home party after the 2008 Olympics, it is said that the sprinter jumped into the selector's booth and decreed that only Gaza tunes should be played, 'and anybody nuh like dat ... can jump inna gully'.[53] Other dancehall deejays and performers also involved themselves in the feud, with Bounty Killer and Elephant Man taking the side of Mavado, while Beenie Man and Spice lined up behind Vybz Kartel.[54] Meanwhile, New York's *Village Voice* noted that the feud had spread to other islands in the Caribbean and beyond, including to the nightclubs of Brooklyn and Queens in New York, both districts with large Jamaican communities.[55]

By November 2009, the Gaza/Gully feud had escalated to such an extent as to warrant the intervention of Prime Minister

Golding, who issued a statement to condemn it, declaring that the feud was 'one example of the negative influences that destabilize us as a people'.[56] The PM requested a meeting with the two artists so he could negotiate a truce. On 7 December 2009, Christopher Coke would get there first, with Vybz Kartel and Mavado performing together at the West Kingston Jamboree and embracing each other on stage, signalling an end to their feud. In attendance at the event and providing political cover for the Shower Posse's 'state within a state' was the JLP Information Minister Daryl Vaz.[57] After the event, Mavado's manager said: 'Getting warring gangs in Jamaica to sign peace treaties is something Dudus did regularly . . . so Mavado and Kartel looked at it like, "If he can stop men out there from killing each other, then what is our lyrical feud to squash?"'[58]

The day after the West Kingston Jamboree, the two performers met with Prime Minister Golding, along with Information Minister Daryl Vaz, Minister of Education Andrew Holness, Culture Minister Olivia Grange, and Dwight Nelson, the National Security Minister.[59] Although Golding would try to gain credit for ending the feud, those on the ground knew that it was Dudus who really ended the violence.

Despite being a fugitive from U.S. justice, Christopher Coke had proved that on the ground of Bruce Golding's own constituency, he held more sway than Jamaica's prime minister. However, globally, the USA was a far greater power than any of the Jamaican players, and it was almost inevitable that Golding would eventually relent to U.S. pressure. Late on a Sunday night on 23 May 2010, in a dramatic television address, Bruce Golding announced a state of emergency, declaring that 'the criminal element who have placed the society under siege will not be allowed to triumph.'[60] In appearing on live television, it was said that this was Golding's signal to the residents of his constituency that his hand had been forced and that West Kingston should rise up in support of their Don. Many of Golding's constituents duly obliged.

Days later, hundreds of soldiers in a fleet of armoured vehicles and with support from helicopter gunships began the search for Christopher Coke. By this point, it was said that the entrances to Tivoli Gardens had been mined with improvised explosive devices, although whether this was true is debatable considering the eventual outcome of events. After days of aerial bombardment and heavy artillery fire, the Jamaica Defence Force broke through into the area, encountering little resistance as they did so as it became apparent that most gunmen had left the area. Once through the barricades, the Army fired indiscriminately, massacring at least 74 citizens, with multiple allegations of summary executions and rapes, and with bodies lying in the streets for days.[61] Four soldiers were shot dead, and a number of police stations burned down by way of reprisal.[62] Unofficial sources put the death toll as much higher than the Jamaican authorities would ever admit. The operation was a failure; four hundred men were under arrest, but Coke had escaped, and despite this being a raid on what was supposedly the most highly armed garrison in a country awash with weapons, only five guns were found in the first days of the action,[63] although there were press reports of further seizures in the following months.[64]

A week after the extended raid on Tivoli Gardens and with Jamaica reeling at the sheer level of force used by the state, the Jamaican Police would meekly call for Coke and twelve other men to surrender. Included in the police's list of wanted gang leaders was Powerhouse producer George Phang.[65] After handing himself in, Phang spent a week in custody, but was eventually released without charge.[66]

The Jamaican Parliament would eventually commission the public defender Earl Witter to complete a preliminary investigation into the events of May 2010. Witter had first visited Tivoli Gardens in the week after the raid and had been so shocked by what he saw that he opened an office in the area immediately. In what he called an interim report, Witter devotes a section to a comparison between the events in Tivoli Gardens, the British colonial response to the Morant Bay Rebellion and the British Army killings on Bloody Sunday in Derry, Northern Ireland, in January 1972. In concluding his report, Witter called for a full public inquiry along the lines of the Bloody Sunday Inquiry chaired by Lord Saville. This was the Inquiry established by British prime minister Tony Blair in 1998 and which published its findings on 15 June 2010, in the immediate period after the killings in Tivoli Gardens, while Christopher Coke was still at large. Earl Witter's report is a remarkable document, with an epilogue that quotes Haile Selassie, Marcus Garvey, Mahatma Gandhi, Martin Luther King and Bob Marley, and which calls for Love to be the defining feature of the conduct of the Jamaican security forces.[67]

In response to Witter's report, the Jamaican government formed a Commission of Enquiry headed by Sir David Simmons, former Attorney General of Barbados, who reported in 2016 and concluded that the Jamaican government should 'apologize in Parliament to the people of West Kingston and Jamaica as a whole *for the excesses* of the security forces during the operation'.[68]

After Bruce Golding's controversial on-air address of 23 May 2010, Dudus became the most celebrated outlaw in Jamaica since Rhyging, remaining free for a month before he was eventually arrested on the outskirts of Kingston and extradited four days later. The American journalist Ioan Grillo alleges that Coke was only found with the help of the British security service MI6, while u.s. spy planes had also been seen over Tivoli Gardens.[69]

Two days into the state of emergency, Vybz Kartel went on the offensive to decry both the JLP and PNP's role in the crisis:

Politics created these uncontrollable monsters called 'Garrisons' to exploit poor people. Tens of thousands of poor people have died in the name of politics, while the politicians themselves have lived to amass enormous wealth at the expense of the less fortunate. Both the JLP and the PNP are harvesting the seeds they sewed [sic] in the 60s/70s, and this is the cause of all of the ills in Jamaica, land we love.[70]

In response to the state massacre of its citizens, Vybz Kartel's former foe Mavado released the elegiac 'Change Right Now', expressing his disbelief that 'the government' would 'just delete people'.

Throughout the period of his reign, several dancehall deejays were prepared to extol the virtues of Dudus, with many lauding him on record and hailing him at dancehalls in JLP garrisons. Perhaps surprisingly when considering his turn towards Rasta consciousness in the 1990s, Buju Banton was an early contender; his 2001 number 'Top a di Top' (2001) namechecked both Dudus Coke and Jim Brown, stating that 'dem a gun specialist'. Later, pro-Dudus tunes would be recorded by Alley Cat ('Don's Anthem'), Cutty Corn ('Dudus a Hero'), Elephant Man ('President'), Soltex 3000 ('Killa Walk, Prezzi Bounce'), Wayne Marshall ('It's Evident'), Alozade ('Nuh Tall Talking' and 'Dads All of the Time') and Twin of Twins ('Which Dudus'), among others.

In his book on drug crime in Latin America, Ioan Grillo interviews Ce'cile, and asks her about the times she performed at dances organized by Coke, with the deejay admitting that she had been pressurized into supporting Dudus. Describing an appearance at a Presidential Click event, Ce'cile was open in saying: 'I was scared shitless. I didn't really get to enjoy the atmosphere and enjoy the people. You hear so much about Tivoli, you are scared. I am a young girl from the country, come on. But looking back, the atmosphere is really wonderful.'[71] When questioned by Grillo about her vocals on a version of Twin of Twins' 'Which Dudus', Ce'cile admitted to both naivety and bad-girl bravado: 'I just sang it in the name of bad girlness . . . Am I sorry I did it? No . . . I only heard stories from what people say. If they are hungry, he gives them food. He protected the community . . . I only heard good things. I never heard anything bad.'[72] Ce'cile's recording partner, Patrick Gaynor of Twin of Twins, was dismissive of any notion that he might be supporting a cocaine Don: 'it's just social commentary, about the respect he commands from people. It's not political.'[73]

Support for Dudus was not just coming from profane dancehall artists. Bunny Wailer, that great elder statesman of roots reggae, portrayed Coke as a benevolent Robin Hood character in 'Don't Touch the President' (2010), which was released after the USA's extradition request but with Coke still at large. On the recording, Bunny Wailer says that he is confident that 'the President' is innocent. Expanding further in interview, Wailer claimed: 'Dudus is a man of peace who makes sure people in his Tivoli Gardens community don't commit crimes.'[74] In another interview, Wailer topped this by saying: 'he's taking bad and turning it into good, like Jesus Christ.'[75] Maintaining more of a distance from its subject-matter was 'Lose a Friend', a number-one hit for I-Octane that was adapted to become a tribute to those who were killed in the hunt for Coke.

One inevitable casualty of the violence in Tivoli Gardens was Passa Passa, as Wednesday nights fell silent barring the sound of gunfire. The end of the reign of Christopher Coke also meant the end of the career of Bruce Golding, who initially survived a vote of no confidence after MPs voted along party lines, but whose grip on power was permanently weakened by the state's massacring of its own citizens, as well as by his obviously close connections to Christopher Coke. Dubbed by the press 'the crime minister', and with the U.S. authorities declaring that Golding was a 'known criminal affiliate' of Christopher Coke, the PM resigned in disgrace, paving the way for Andrew Holness to take the helm.[76] Holness was relatively untouched by earlier controversies, and when it came to be his turn to consider the Jamaican state's position on gay rights, Jamaica's new prime minister would present a very different position to that of his predecessor, stating that the sexuality of his cabinet was none of his business and that:

> whatever is in my interest to distribute politically, a person's sexuality, sexual orientation is not a criterion for the use of my discretion. It's not an issue that we are afraid to address. The truth is that in the past, like many developed countries, there was a very conservative view on the matter.[77]

A month before Golding resigned, Christopher Coke had struck a bargain with the U.S. authorities and pleaded guilty, 'because I am'.[78] Although prosecutors had obtained witness testimony of Coke's involvement in numerous murders in the Don's own private jail in Tivoli Gardens, where he killed and dismembered 'offenders' with a chainsaw or hatchet, he was eventually sentenced to 23 years in a federal U.S. prison for the lesser offences of trafficking more than 3 tonnes of marijuana and 30 kilograms (66 lb) of cocaine.[79] This was seen as a victory for Coke, whose guilty plea led to an almost audible sigh of relief by the Jamaican political establishment, who feared that an open trial would lay bare the sorry tale of Jamaica's garrison politics. After his conviction, *The Gleaner* reported that Horace Andy had recorded a tribute to Dudus. While Andy acknowledged that he was a friend of Coke, he would say of his support for him: 'the song is just a song about the man. Is no political thing.'[80]

9

'NICE UP THE DANCE': THE REGGAE REVIVAL

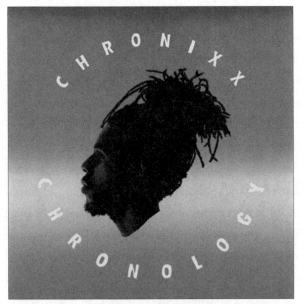

Chronixx, *Chronology* (2017)

I'm not a politician, but I suffer the consequences.

PETER TOSH AT THE ONE LOVE PEACE CONCERT,

22 APRIL 1978[1]

In my experience, and my study, and my practice of self-governance, I don't need politics . . . I don't even participate in the practice, but I do study it . . . I see what it is supposed to represent, and I see its failings, so I have acted to make my own way, and I promote people making their own way and relying upon themselves because you cannot look to a politician to save your life.

JAH9[2]

During the first decade of the twenty-first century, there came a point when the different genres found within Black Atlantic music began to move closer towards each other, with the boundaries between genres becoming blurred. In the USA, the rhythmic bedrock of much R&B and hip-hop began to bear a resemblance to contemporary Jamaican dancehall, while in the UK, a variety of post-rave and post-grime styles were adding dancehall riddims to their sonic armoury. In Jamaica, much of the newer dancehall was taking on hip-hop and R&B stylings in vocal delivery and timbre, while several Jamaican acts collaborated with North American soul, R&B and rap artists. As mainstream global pop took on the sounds and textures of dancehall, and as Jamaican dancehall edged closer to music from the USA and the UK, all three continued to draw influence from Africa, particularly the newer electronic forms coming from the continent.

By the 2000s, it was not unusual for dancehall riddims to feature at the top of both the U.S. and the UK charts with, for example, Sean Paul's 'Get Busy' in 2003 and Rihanna's 'Pon de Replay' in 2006. A decade later, the work of Popcaan (Andre Sutherland) could be seen to symbolize the trend. In 2014, the Vybz Kartel protégé teamed up with British singer Melissa Steel on 'Kisses for Breakfast', a top-ten hit in the UK. Following this, Popcaan signed to OVO Sound, the Warner Music Group subsidiary formed by Canada's multi-million-selling rapper Drake. At the time, Drake was no stranger to dancehall himself, with Vybz Kartel said to be an influence.

It might seem perplexing then that just at the point when the concept of genre was becoming less significant within both dancehall and global pop, there came a contrary trend from Jamaica,

with a twenty-first-century focus on what had become a remark-
ably stable genre itself, namely roots reggae. The trend was quickly
named Reggae Revival as a new generation of artists drew upon
the sound and rhythms of the 1970s while using the latest digital technology to capture reggae's traditional instrumentation of
guitar, bass, drums, keyboards and horns. On top of this pristinely
recorded musical bedrock were the preachings of a new generation of Rasta ideologues who were as comfortable with riding
one-drop rhythms in a deejay style as they were singing sweet
melodies, but who were explicitly rejecting the dark ideology of
much dancehall.

The name Reggae Revival was coined in 2011 by the Jamaican
cultural worker and author Dutty Bookman, who used two self-
published memoirs and a blog to reflect upon changes in Jamaica's
politics, culture and music. The new moniker is used to describe
both a style of music and a broader cultural and political project
that consciously rejects the perceived negativity and darkness of
dancehall and seeks a return to the idealism and righteousness of
roots reggae. Bookman was influenced by the Harlem Renaissance,
but rather than using the latter term, he settled on 'Revival' instead.
Protoje, a leading figure within the movement, explained further:

> If there was any Renaissance in reggae music, it was that era
> of Bob Marley and all of them. You can't revive something
> that's dead. It's always people from outside of Jamaica that
> come and name stuff. So when he [Bookman] took control
> of that as a Jamaican writer, I have to respect that.[3]

Describing the relationship between a new generation of
roots-reggae artists and an older dancehall generation that had
come to dominate the Jamaican charts, Bookman stated:

with dancehall, people were singing about demons, like that was something desirable to attain. It had really gone to the depths of where it could go. At that point, people were just not feeling the demon thing anymore – so they started looking around for other options.[4]

While the new name of Reggae Revival is used willingly by a fresh generation of Jamaican musicians, the name remains contentious. In particular, there are criticisms from within an earlier generation of musicians for whom roots reggae has never gone away. A whole generation of 1970s survivors have continued to tour and have kept the reggae flame burning through the dancehall years, with perhaps the oldest of the bunch, Lee 'Scratch' Perry, performing throughout all subsequent decades and continuing to record until his passing in August 2021 at the age of 85. There are also those who argue that Reggae Revival is an uptown marketing concept, hinting at a class divide between the dancehall of Jamaica's working class and the Reggae Revival of an elite who have access to education and to the levers of cultural power in Jamaica.[5] This, though, is contrary to the experiences of Bookman, whose writing is concerned with the way a new generation of cultural workers have had to negotiate their way across a challenging economic terrain, including dealing with new behemoths like the Tuff Gong empire as well as the old-school Babylon of an overseas music industry that extracts wealth from Jamaica and puts little back. For the Reggae Revival generation, the same old problems of Babylon are encountered, but from within a new world, and Bookman argues that his generation are no less hard done by than previous ones.

The time frame of the gestation of the Reggae Revival was from 2010 onwards, during the period after what the Jamaican state continues to refer to as the 'incursion' in Tivoli Gardens. This timing is no coincidence, with a revulsion at the events of that year reflected in the music of a righteous new generation. A month after the massacre, Dylan Powe, the former promotor of Passa Passa, sensed the changing mood, suggesting that 'the unrest may cause a shift in lyrical content, forcing artists to look at the messages they send.'[6] A month later, at the Reggae Sumfest festival in late July 2010, Bounty Killer denounced violent lyrics, saying in the press that: 'My nation is going backwards. So instead of prostituting my fans by singing foolishness, it's time to enlighten and educate. I think they will embrace my transition.'[7]

At around the same time, Dutty Bookman convened a series of 'reasonings' and weekly jams at Jamnesia, a performing space 16 kilometres (10 mi.) east of Kingston, while Bookman's radio show on Kingston's Roots FM began to feature those who would go on to become the leading figures of the Reggae Revival generation, including Bob and Rita Marley's granddaughter Donisha Prendergast, Protoje, Jah9 and Kabaka Pyramid.

By August 2010 even the American news agency Reuters had noted a change in the direction of Jamaican music, correctly attributing a decline of violent lyrics in dancehall to the nation's response to the events in Tivoli Gardens. Due to an earlier moral panic and clampdown on explicit lyrics, Jamaican broadcasters were already working within new parameters, so it was easy for them to reflect the shift towards conscious themes. Three months after the massacre, Ainsworth Higgins, senior presenter on Irie FM, was quoted as saying: 'there is clearly an outcry. We need a break from the violence.'[8] Although not all Jamaican deejays fully embraced the development, there were still signs of change in unlikely quarters, with Vybz Kartel recording a cover version of the Beatles' 'Let It Be' along with Mavado's 'Change Right Now' receiving rotation play during the second half of 2010. Over at the Rebel Salute festival, promoter Tony Rebel acknowledged that things had changed, stating that he was now prepared to book dancehall artists whom he had not approached in the past, providing that the deejays concerned were sincere in their promises to change their lyrics, adding: 'there's pressure throughout society for artists to clean up their music, so I hope their changes are genuine.'[9] Since this moment, dancehall acts performing at Rebel Salute have done so under their birth names, with Mavado billed as David Brooks for the 2011 staging of the festival.

While change was almost immediate, it would take a couple of years for the Reggae Revival to fully develop, although by 2012 most of the artists now collected under the moniker were releasing tracks that, when taken as a piece, clearly signalled the development of a new musical movement. In 2012, Jah9 appeared at Rebel Salute as a relatively unknown performer surrounded by established reggae luminaries such as Max Romeo and Luciano, but by 2013 the Reggae Revival generation were more fully represented with Chronixx, Kabaka Pyramid and Protoje appearing. In the same year, Dutty Bookman's friend Protoje, the most prominent and influential figure in the Reggae Revival, released his track 'Kingston Be Wise'. Based on a short story written in the immediate aftermath of the raid on Tivoli Gardens, the idea for the song arose while Protoje was attending the Kingston Dub Club in the hills of St Andrew, with the artist looking on as smoke rose ominously from West Kingston. Despite the subject-matter and the inclusion of politicians such as Edward Seaga and current PM Andrew Holness in the video accompanying the track, 'Kingston Be Wise' is surprisingly free of vitriol – but then provocative lyrics are not quite in the style of the Reggae Revival. Protoje's track arises out of a desire for remembrance for the dead rather than being a direct attack on those responsible.

'Four hundred years': The Antecedents of the Reggae Revival

While the Reggae Revival emerged out of the crisis of 2010, there were antecedents in roots reggae's eventual rejection of the politics of the 1970s, and these are worth exploring. For if there is a single event that continues to guide reggae's relationship with politics, it is Peter Tosh's appearance at the One Love Peace Concert of 22 April 1978, which preceded the better-known appearance of Michael Manley and Edward Seaga at Bob Marley's side at the event's denouement. With his stage in almost complete darkness, at Tosh's request to frustrate those who were filming the event, the former Wailer railed at a colonial and imperialist 'shitsem', bemoaning Jamaica's race relations in what was dubbed a 'live-a-tribe' (as opposed to a diatribe). 'Look how long. Four hundred years, and it's the same old-time *bucky-massa* philosophy,' proclaimed Tosh, evoking the ghost of the *backra-massa*, the white slave owner whose ideology of racial supremacism continues to the present day. In his introduction to the song 'Burial', Tosh argued that

> right now yu ave a system or a shitstem whey gwaan inna dis country ya fe a long ages a imes. Four hundred years, and de same *bucky massa* bizniz. An black inferiority, and brown superiority and white superiority rule dis lickle black country here fe a long imes.[10]

Looking on nervously from the second-to-front row were Seaga and Manley. As pale-skinned members of Jamaica's elite holding postgraduate qualifications from globally leading institutions (Seaga at Harvard and Manley at McGill University in Canada and the London School of Economics), both bore a responsibility for the position in which Jamaica found itself, teetering on the edge of an all-out war between the garrisons. Tosh promised: 'Well,

I-an-I come wid earthquake, lightnin and tunda to break down dese barriers of oppression, drive away transgression and rule equality between humble black people.'[11]

Later, in an extended speech in the middle of his hour-long set, Tosh articulated a view that saw Jamaica's supposed independence as an irrelevancy. Jamaica was ruled by the same elite as before within a country that had conducted a hidden burial of the collective trauma of slavery rather than confront it head-on. For Tosh, the Jamaican Rastafari were Israelites, exiled in Babylon and still seeking liberation a century and a half after the so-called emancipation of 1834. Taunting both Seaga and Manley in front of him, and those police officers eager to arrest him for smoking ganja, Tosh accused both politicians and the police of maintaining a system in which the poor were penalized for their poverty, while Rastas were brutalized for their herb.

Within ten years, Peter Tosh would be dead, killed in his home by a gunman that he had previously befriended. Along with two others, Dennis 'Leppo' Lobban had entered Tosh's house on the evening of 11 September 1987 to rob him, but instead shot Tosh, along with both Jeff Dixon, a well-known Jamaican radio broadcaster, and Wilton Brown, a local herbalist. Michael Manley referred to the murder of Peter Tosh as 'a blot of shame on all Jamaicans', a view with which few dissented.[12]

From the One Love Peace Concert onwards, chanting against Babylon became intertwined with chanting against 'politricks'. This continued into the twenty-first century following the arrival of the new breed of Rasta deejays and singers, who were very much the forerunners of the Reggae Revival in using the latest technology to combine old-school roots reggae with the newer forms of vocal delivery derived from dancehall.

A key example of an influence upon this new generation is Anthony B, whose album *Real Revolutionary* formed an intriguing

musical foundation on which he could expound his vision, seeing a
return of old-school reggae, but this time reinvented for the digital
age. While there was significant controversy regarding 'Fire Pon
Rome', this detracted from tracks such as 'Cold Feet', a down-tempo
anti-gun tune based on Marley's 'No Woman, No Cry'. In addition
to influencing the sound of the Reggae Revival, Anthony B was
also clearly an influence on its ideology. A year after his incendi-
ary 'Fire Pon Rome' came the single 'Nah Vote Again' (1997). In
encouraging electoral disengagement, Anthony B was only one step
ahead of the Jamaican population at large. In the two decades after
independence, there had been a steady increase in voter turnout
at general elections, reaching a peak of 86.1 per cent at the bloody
1980 election when politics was at its most polarized and deadly.
Turnout fell back to 28.94 per cent at the 1983 election, which was
boycotted by the PNP, and while it bounced back to 77.59 per cent
in 1989, it fell again in the next two elections. Coincidentally, or
perhaps not, the 1997 election was almost entirely free of violence.
Anthony B put this down to the role of reggae:

> Reggae prevented the bloodbath, not the politicians. In the
> '70s, the singers them used to speak bout politics but them
> never quote no name. We call P. J. Patterson, Edward Seaga or
> Michael Manley. Before, them say: 'politicians are a problem'
> when we say: 'P. J. Patterson is a problem.' People from the
> ghetto won't tell you that 'cause them fear the consequences.
> Them know say the gunman work for the politicians.[13]

Also pre-figuring the Reggae Revival's return to one-drop
reggae was Buju Banton. *'Til Shiloh*, *Inna Heights* and *Unchained
Spirit* saw Banton singing on dancehall riddims and riding one-
drop reggae in a deejay style, blurring the distinctions between
the two and incorporating lyrics that focused on traditional Rasta

themes. Asked in May 1995 whether *'Til Shiloh* was a dancehall record, Banton responded with:

> I would consider this a reggae record, cause this whole thing is reggae, you know, despite whatever fusion. Too much fusion bring about too much confusion and everyone want to carry the music into a different channel. Hence people will either determine that this is dancehall or reggae or calypso or whatever. But as far as I am concern, this is reggae music. Don't abuse it.[14]

Regarding the links between Banton's trio of 1990s albums and the Reggae Revival, a feature on the 25th anniversary of *'Til Shiloh*'s release would make the point explicit, stating that the Reggae Revival could not have taken off without Buju Banton's work bridging the gap between hardcore dancehall and conscious reggae.[15] This view is corroborated by many of the Reggae Revival musicians themselves, with, for example, Jesse Royal quoted as saying: 'The seeds were already sown. Buju paved the way for us and we carried on. He is an example to us. He displayed how to cross over from dancehall to reggae and we appreciate and look up to him.'[16]

In addition to the influence of Anthony B and Buju Banton on the Reggae Revival, it is hard to overstate the importance of both the late Bobby 'Digital' Dixon's stable at Digital B Records, which contained at one point Morgan Heritage, Tony Rebel, Buju Banton and Sizzla, and Xterminator Records, the label formed in 1993 by Philip 'Fatis' Burrell, whose roster stuck with him once they had made their name. Both Digital B and Xterminator were labels founded on reggae, but which used a dancehall approach in booking different vocalists to ride one-drop riddims in a deejay style, with the artists incorporating their own distinctive phrases and lyrical themes on each recording. Burrell, who died in 2011, was a veteran of the garrison conflicts of the 1970s. His obituary in *The Guardian* in the UK referred to Burrell and George Phang as being 'briefly involved' in internecine struggles in the 1970s and credited Burrell as being the leading figure behind a 'Rasta renaissance'.[17] Five years later, the author S. Thomas Liston would not use such euphemistic terms when considering Phang and Burrell's activities in the 1970s, referring to both as 'PNP terrorists'.[18] Here Liston was making the allegation that Burrell, along with Anthony Brown and George Flash, were responsible for the murder of Edward O'Gilvie, a leading civil servant who was killed after making headway in investigating corruption in Jamaica's Ministry of Works.[19] At the time, Burrell was arrested and charged with the murder, but he was freed in December 1978 due to insufficient evidence. Brown and Flash were also charged, but a 'missing file' meant that they went free. The pair fled to Cuba, confident that the Castro-led regime would refuse to extradite them to Jamaica, and they only returned once the PNP regained power in 1989.[20]

The Reggae Revival of 2010 onwards built on the legacy of the likes of Digital B Records and Xterminator, allowing a new generation of vocalists to combine the delivery styles of the deejay with those of the reggae singer. This emphasizes that it is not dancehall per se that the Reggae Revival rejects, merely its slackness, either in the form of punanny or lyrical gunplay. Artists such as Protoje and Chronixx are emblematic of a scene where singjays incorporate both deejaying and singing within their oeuvre, often on the same track. With 'Kingston Be Wise', Protoje took on the riddim of Ini Kamoze's 'England Be Nice' (1984), adapting the band's opening lyric to fit his theme, while 'Criminal' on his debut album for RCA makes the influence of Peter Tosh explicit, comparing the criminalization of Marcus Garvey and Leonard Howell with those who killed Tosh on 11 September 1987.

Also drawing influence from Ini Kamoze was Chronixx, who sampled the band's big hit 'Here Comes the Hot Stepper' for his breakthrough single 'Here Comes Trouble'. Four years later, Chronixx's 'Spanish Town Rockin' opened his debut album *Chronology* (2017). The track is notable for the switch between singing and deejaying that Chronixx delivers mid-track, with a wonderful pay-off line at the end of the song with the lyric 'you cyaan dance with no M16', an obvious rejection of the gun and gang violence of previous generations. Elsewhere on the album, 'Country Boy' sees Chronixx update the narrative from *The Harder They Come*, advising the song's generic rude boy to go in peace and sin no more. On 'Smile Jamaica', he stretches even further back in the history of Jamaican music to use the same lyrical device as that of Jimmy Cliff on 'Miss Jamaica', where Chronixx meets a girl called Jamaica who is tired of exploitation and lies, but who gives the people reggae music to make them smile.

Bridging the gap between the Rasta deejays of the 1990s and the Reggae Revivalists of 2010 onwards was both Damian Marley and Tarrus Riley, two global stars whose biggest singles can be seen to define the musical interregnum between the two generations. Marley, the only son of Bob Marley and Cindy Breakspeare, took the name Junior Gong in tribute to his late father, and his third studio album, 2005's *Welcome to Jamrock*, became one of the best-selling reggae albums of the century. The title track samples a Sly and Robbie riddim originally recorded for Ini Kamoze's 'World-a-Music' twenty years earlier, with lyrics focusing on poverty and political violence in Jamaica. At roughly the same time, Tarrus Riley also rose to international prominence with 'She's Royal' (2006), a traditional roots-reggae hymn to the ladies, explaining that:

> Buju and Sizzla were before me in the 1990s and Chronixx
> is after me so I understand the roots and I understand the

youths ... It's a new decade now, new things are happening
so while the people from before want to hold on to music that
had its time, the youths want to give you something new.[21]

As the sound of the Reggae Revival was being built on the
musical legacy of Digital B Records and Xterminator, the new ideologues at the centre of the movement were developing the lyrical
themes of Buju Banton, Anthony B, Sizzla, Damian Marley and
Tarrus Riley, offering traditional Rasta praises and steering their
music well away from the clutches of politicians – encouraging a
new generation to avoid getting their fingers burned by standing too
close to either the JLP or the PNP. The result was a Reggae Revival
keen to distance itself from politics, however that was defined.
When I interviewed Jah9 in England in 2019, she seemed genuinely
annoyed when I suggested to her that her music might constitute
a form of political engagement. For her, all politics is 'politricks':

> When I was growing up, politics was always something that
> seemed very divisive. It seemed like the thing to turn to for
> comfort, but it caused a lot of division not just in the inner-
> city communities, just in general, it would split the nation.
> And you would see the people who would align themselves
> with politicians, who would become like celebrities. You
> didn't really see the expectation of what a leader could be,
> or what, in my experience, a leader is supposed to be. I saw
> more leadership in my father as a pastor or community lead-
> ers who were not aligned to politics. I saw where politics was
> a source of violence ... where the political leader was seen
> as this kind of God figure, who came and gave handouts to
> people at a particular time of year. So, I don't have a lot of
> faith in politics, especially in Jamaica where politicians are
> really puppets ... We make some decisions, but the really

powerful life-changing decisions that could really shape the country are handed down to us by a figurehead, a governor-general who serves no purpose and who represents a queen who we are supposed to be emancipated from, so there is a lot of disillusion surrounding politics.[22]

Jah9 is quite typical in this regard, with some of the most radical of the Reggae Revival acts disengaging from formal political systems to make their own way in the twenty-first-century world. Hempress Sativa (Kerida Johnson), another prominent female Revivalist, is similar, seeming to reject any engagement with politics yet wrapping her music in explicitly revolutionary lyrics, saying: 'as Rastafarians we go against the system and whenever you do that you need to be rebellious.'[23]

If the Reggae Revival retains the revolutionary force for emancipation of earlier roots reggae, the way these modern artists go about achieving their aims has changed dramatically since the days when so many reggae artists chose to line up behind either the JLP or PNP. Since the 1970s, new political divisions have arisen within reggae. Contemporary political battles are as likely to be fought on the terrains of gender and sexuality as on the old ground of economics and civil rights, while new forms of anti-imperialism sit alongside a continued veneration of Haile Selassie. As with Jah9, the music of Hempress Sativa has both a Rastafarian and feminist twist, reconciling two ideological strands that are seen by many as being in conflict. Jah9 explores further how feminists can now embrace the Rastafari, and vice versa:

the truth of His Imperial Majesty is made beautifully obvious when we observe Empress Menen and the uninterrupted union they shared . . . Being the revolutionary leader he was, Haile Selassie broke tradition by putting off his coronation so that he and his Queen, Empress Menen, could be crowned on the same day, setting a great example for the world at a time when women's rights were not valued. Empress Menen was married once prior to marrying His Imperial Majesty and they remained in an uninterrupted union.[24]

Up 2 di Time: The Troubling Case of Vybz Kartel

If one of the determining features in the development of the Reggae Revival was its objection to the excesses of dancehall, it must be said that there was an awful lot for it to object to. At the time of the state of emergency of May 2010, there was no bigger dancehall star than Vybz Kartel. Both a friend of Bruce Golding and a vocal supporter of Christopher Coke, Vybz Kartel had spoken up for Dudus at dancehall events organized by Presidential Click and released a couple of singles for Liv Up Records, the West Kingston label run by Leighton 'Livity' Coke, the younger half-brother of Christopher. Shortly after the beginning of Christopher Coke's trial in New York in September 2011, the Jamaican Police announced that Adidja Palmer had been arrested and was being held for murder. Alongside the events in Tivoli Gardens, the arrest of Vybz Kartel gave the Reggae Revival movement further impetus to pull their music away from the darkness of dancehall, with clear blue water separating the two genres for much of the following decade.

Born in January 1976, Adidja Azim Palmer began working in the dancehall as a teenager, with his debut 'Love Fat Woman' (1993) released under the name Adi Banton, a tribute to Buju Banton, three years his senior. After a series of solo singles, Palmer went on to form Vybz Kartel as a group, with the name said to be influenced by Pablo Escobar's infamous Medellín cocaine cartel. As a group, Vybz Kartel had little success, and Palmer returned to solo working shortly after, using the same moniker. Entering a particularly prolific period, Vybz Kartel released over thirty singles in 2001 and 2002, including the popular 'Girls Like Mine', a combination with his mentor Bounty Killer for VP Records. On an upward trajectory, the deejay went on to release over fifty singles in Jamaica in 2003 alone, along with an album *Up 2 di Time* selling well overseas. On these releases, Vybz Kartel combines slack lyrics and gun talk with aplomb, but as a rising star, he was always going to come into conflict with other artists working the same themes, at least partly due to the keen sense of competition between deejays. At the 2003 staging of Sting, the premier dancehall event in Jamaica at the time, rivalry between Vybz Kartel and Ninjaman spilled over into violence when the former was seen to punch the latter during an onstage brawl that was then echoed by violent clashes between the entourages of the two parties. Both deejays were arrested after the event and charged, but the two made it up within days, announcing to the press that their beef was finally over.[25]

The year 2004 saw no let-up in Vybz Kartel's prolific production line of Jamaican hits. By this time, homophobia was added to the mix, with 'Faggot Correction' for Donovan Bennett's Don Corleon label. A survey of other song titles gives a general indication of their content, From 'Tekk Gun Shot', 'Badda Than Dem', 'Top Rankin' and 'Real Bad Man', to 'More Pussy', 'Bag a Gal' and 'Girl Link Up', this was a slack deejay who combined lyrical gunmanship with the image of the loverman, moving effortlessly between the two, and ping-ponging between labels, often recording for different producers on the same day. Vybz Kartel's vocals were all delivered on top of a bewildering array of dancehall riddims, as the warp and weft of musical development criss-crossed different studios, while the deejay flitted between producers in search of the latest killer sound. The years 2005 and 2006 continued in the same vein, during a period when much of Jamaica's dancehall elite wanted to record with Vybz Kartel, including the up-and-coming slack women of the dancehall such as Miss Thing, Macka Diamond and Marlene, along with the older male mainstays of Beenie Man, Buccaneer, Richie Spice, Shabba Ranks, Mega Banton and Buju Banton.

Supplementing his role as a recording artist, Palmer formed his own production stable, the Portmore Empire, before branching out into his own branded Street Vybz Rum and a controversial line in prophylactics called 'Daggering Condoms'. Using the Portmore Empire as a launching pad, the artist would make an assault on the global fame that had so far eluded him, notwithstanding the respectable sales figures for three albums released overseas in a partnership with the UK's Greensleeves Records.

The song that catapulted Vybz Kartel to international attention was a combination with the female deejay Spice, whose own career took off with the same record. Heavy on the autotune (as was much dancehall from this period onwards), 'Romping Shop' (2009) was a hip-hop/dancehall ballad, over-produced to within an inch of its life, and while Spice was initially reticent to voice on such a down-tempo tune, the contrast between hardcore lyrics and a musically mellow and mainstream sound delighted dancehall fans. The track was massive in Jamaica and elsewhere, but not before it was banned by the Broadcasting Commission for its explicit content, although it would take lurid tabloid reports of five-year-olds singing the song before the regulator acted.[26] Partially hidden by the boastful sexual explicitness on the part of the song's two protagonists was the same old homophobia, with 'man to man' and 'gyal to gyal' attacked. As ever, though, the JBC were less concerned with homophobia than with sexual explicitness. Following the release of further copycat 'daggering' tunes, the JBC acted further, issuing the following directive to their licensees:

There shall not be transmitted through radio or television or cable services, any recording, live song or music video which promotes the act of 'daggering', or which makes reference to, or is otherwise suggestive of 'daggering'.

There shall not be transmitted through radio or television or cable services, any audio recording, song or music video which employs editing techniques of 'bleeping' or 'beeping' of its original lyrical content.

Programme managers and station owners or operators are hereby required to take immediate steps to prevent transmission of any recorded material relating to 'daggering' or which fall into the category of edited musical content using techniques of 'bleeping' or 'beeping'.[27]

Following the success of 'Romping Shop', for his follow-up Vybz Kartel homed in on the relatively safe topic of Jamaica's esoteric love affair with a much-loved consumer staple, the Clarks 'Wallabee' shoe. Although Kartel was not the first to record in tribute to the shoe brand (he was beaten to the post by several others, including Barrington Levy, Errol Scorcher, Ranking Joe and Little John), he was the most successful, and in the end 'Clarks' (2009) by Vybz Kartel feat. Popcaan and Gaza Slim was so popular that it increased sales of Clarks shoes in Jamaica and elsewhere, leading to sharp price rises in the shops as the English firm cashed in on their new-found popularity.[28] Sensing further victory, 'Clarks 2 (Clarks Again)' and 'Clarks 3 (Wear Weh Yuh Have)' followed in quick succession.

Following 'Romping Shop' and his Clarks singles, Vybz Kartel was the biggest star in Jamaica, and any controversial action by him was likely to cause waves in both Jamaica and abroad. This is what came to pass when he started to address long-standing rumours that he was using a skin-whitening agent to lighten his complexion.

Mavado had been one of the first to notice this when three years earlier he released his single 'Nuh Bleach wid Cream', accusing Kartel
of being a disgrace. Adding to the growing public opprobrium, Vybz
Kartel released 'Straight Jeans and Fitted (feat. Russian)' in which
he admitted to the practice, followed by the more obvious 'Cake
Soap'. In his defence, the deejay told the Jamaican press that his
actions were 'tantamount to white people getting a sun tan', before
announcing that he was using his own proprietary brand, 'Vybz
cake soap' and 'it shaped like Viagra because it's just as potent'.[29]

The controversy over cake soap paled into insignificance when
on 29 September 2011 Palmer was arrested for marijuana possession,
but charged days later with the illegal possession of a handgun and
the murder of Barrington 'Bossy' Burton, whose remains were found
by the police when they raided one of Palmer's homes. Although
Palmer was to be acquitted of Burton's murder two years later, he
remained in jail pending trial for the separate murder of Clive
'Lizard' Williams, a dancer in his entourage, in an argument over
two missing handguns.[30]

While remanded in custody, Palmer co-wrote and published
The Voice of the Jamaican Ghetto: Incarcerated but Not Silenced, further
adding to the controversy regarding the murders of both Burton
and Williams. The book itself is of interest in that it encourages
the reader to separate the actions of Adidja Palmer from those of
his Vybz Kartel alter ego. In the book's preface, co-author Michael
Dawson argues for an essential difference between the two: 'the
news keeps reporting that Vybz Kartel is in jail but I disagree with
that . . . The public, the police and the media have tried and convicted the controversial deejay Vybz Kartel that they love to hate
and have Adidja Palmer serving Kartel's sentence.'[31] Elsewhere,
the book's blurb claims that Palmer/Kartel 'challenged the political status quo by encouraging his fans to express allegiance to his
Gaza crew instead of the PNP or JLP'.[32]

In addition to his self-serving tome, and adding yet more to the swirling controversies surrounding him, Vybz Kartel continued to release a slew of singles. While the official line was that all these releases were recorded prior to his arrest, there remained suggestions that some were recorded on a mobile phone smuggled into his cell. On one of these tracks, 'Poor People Land', the deejay expands on the futility of aligning himself to either the PNP or JLP, delivering a heavily autotuned vocal that takes for its opening line the title of the poem 'Me Cyaan Believe It' by Michael Smith, the Jamaican dub poet murdered after heckling a JLP minister of education at a rally in Stony Hill in August 1983.[33] Following his introduction, Vybz Kartel launches into incredulous rage, claiming to be a refugee in his own country, and promising that he would never vote again 'cah di MP don't give a damn'. Over a one-drop reggae riddim, blasting Babylon's bulldozers, you would never know this was anything other than an authentic Rasta sufferah, and you would also never know that the deejay was on remand for murder.

Having been in custody since September 2011, Adidja Palmer went on trial on 20 November 2013. The press reported that it was the longest trial in Jamaica's history, finally concluding on 3 April 2014, and whether true or not, it was certainly the most sensational. Crucially, there was only circumstantial evidence of Palmer's involvement in the murder of Williams, with the prosecution employing the legal principle of 'common design', often used to convict gang members for murders that they did not physically take part in but at which they were present. Palmer and all four co-accused (including fellow deejay Shawn Storm) were found guilty of the murder of Clive Williams by a majority verdict of ten-to-one. In summing up, the judge said that there was 'a great deal of premeditation' in Williams's death as well as in the concealment of the body. A key piece of evidence was an SMS text message found on Palmer's phone, implicating him in the murder. The message read: 'Between me and you a chop wi chop up di bwoy Lizard fine fine and dash him weh nuh. As long as wi a live dem can never find him.'[34] This was controversial as there were allegations that the mobile phone on which the message was said to have been received had been tampered with by the police.[35] Williams's body has never been found. Within hours of Palmer's conviction, the Twitter account @iamthekartel, previously used by Palmer, issued the following tweet: 'GazaArmy. we nuh deh pon nuh mourning ting. Addi said "Justice however long it takes will prevail, a so Haile Selassie sey." so we a move fwd.'[36]

Despite being a sentenced prisoner, Vybz Kartel continued to maintain a respectable output of singles and albums in the years after his conviction, and in 2016 he released his most successful album to date, the 22-track *King of the Dancehall*, which peaked at number two in the *Billboard* reggae charts. In the following year, there was an outcry among his fans when Lisa Hanna, the MP for St Ann South East, weighed into the various debates concerning the artist. Hanna claimed that the reason why Vybz Kartel was releasing so many recordings was because of corruption at the maximum-security prison in which he was held, amid suggestions that warders were turning a blind eye while Palmer used a mobile phone to record verses for release. Calling for 'less of a democracy' in Jamaica, Hanna put forward the view that all of Vybz Kartel's output should be banned from broadcast due to its negative impact on Jamaican society as a whole. The MP was said to have received death threats for this.[37] Later, Hanna expanded her view by comparing Vybz Kartel to a character in the film *The Godfather*, stating that Palmer 'is the Godfather to the Gaza Empire one built on musical talent, fear, violence and vulgarity. Gaza loyalists threaten death to anyone who dares contradict their Godfather's authenticity, relevance or authority.'[38]

While accusing Palmer of criminality, Hanna suggested that while other Jamaican politicians might be corrupt, she was not, and she stood by her view that Vybz Kartel was a bad influence on Jamaican society and that his music should be banned as a result:

> I'm an unapologetic lover of music, including dancehall. But there's no necessity for some artistes to use music as a medium for promoting violence and abuse of women. The data confirms that violent and sexually explicit lyrics have negatively influenced many Jamaican youth's thought processes through increased feelings of hostility and aggression. These negative influences are exacerbated when we turn a blind eye to radio airplay of new productions by persons we know are incarcerated and so may have been abetted by corruption in our prison system. This reality necessitates us being urgently honest with ourselves. We should be prepared to have a national discussion about messages glorifying criminality being conveyed to our children that'll ultimately bring deleterious consequences. These messages have been pushing us towards a different society from the one in which we all say we want to live.[39]

In 2017, the Jamaican commissioner of corrections argued that any suggestion that Palmer was recording in prison without authorization was 'only speculation'.[40] Two years later, with growing incredulity regarding the suggestion that all of the tracks released by Vybz Kartel since September 2011 had been recorded prior to his arrest, there were calls from scholars including Sonjah Stanley Niaah and Donna Hope for him to be given the right to record in jail legally.[41] As is common in such prison-based rehabilitation initiatives, the use of recording facilities in Jamaican prisons is limited to those inmates who have admitted their guilt and begun to show remorse for their crimes. As Palmer has consistently maintained his innocence he is not entitled to such a privilege. Vybz Kartel fans have countered with the suggestion that the government are persecuting Palmer in retaliation for his promotion of a Jamaican lotto slam on 'Reparation' (2012), where the deejay puts forward the argument that the fleecing of largely elderly u.s. pensioners was just compensation for slavery.

All of this occurred while what has become a soap opera of an appeal has continued, with legal proceedings running in parallel with the trial of Livingston Cain. Cain was the only juror in Palmer's original trial to return a verdict of not guilty, and he was arrested on the day that Palmer was found guilty and accused of bribing the rest of the jury. Other jurors in the original trial have also been in the news, with one overseas in a witness-protection programme and another in hiding.[42]

Throughout the period of his arrest and trial, Adidja Palmer's lawyer was the long-standing JLP senator Tom Tavares-Finson, who also represented Christopher Coke until his extradition to the United States and, before that, Lester Coke during the extradition proceedings of 1992. At various points, Tavares-Finson has also represented Grace Jones, Bounty Killer, Mavado, Sean Paul and Shabba Ranks.[43] Tavares-Finson is well known throughout Jamaican society, having been married to Bob Marley's muse Cindy Breakspeare. In response to newspaper reports concerning how a juror in Palmer's trial was in hiding and feared for her life, Tavares-Finson hit back, questioning how the press had come to approach a juror who was supposed to be untraceable and living in a witness-protection programme abroad. Tavares-Finson also questioned the timing of the controversy, claiming that it was designed to imperil the ongoing appeal of Palmer and his co-accused.[44]

Aditja Palmer is currently awaiting his opportunity to plea to the Judicial Committee of the Privy Council in London, having gained leave to do so by the Jamaican Court of Appeal in 2020. In August 2021 Vybz Kartel gave a live interview with the New York television station Fox5, sparking a crisis at the Horizon Remand Centre in downtown Kingston, where he had been moved due to the supposedly improved mobile-phone-blocking facility there.

Ghetto Life: Dancehall in the Dock

The arrest and conviction of Adidja Palmer for murder shocked Jamaica and was surely a factor in the artists of the Reggae Revival turning their back on dancehall ideology. But Vybz Kartel was not the only deejay where slackness and lyrical gunplay preceded a conviction for a violent offence, and it is worthwhile noting the sheer number of deejays incarcerated for serious crime in the past two decades. Not only did these deejays perpetuate a dancehall ideology that the Reggae Revival would react against, but their enforced absence from music making opened up a space through which a new generation could come through.

Jah Cure (Siccature Alcock) had first appeared in 1997 on a Beres-Hammond-produced duet with Sizzla entitled 'King in the Jungle', leading to almost instant fame, a follow-up single for Xterminator and an international tour. In November 1998, Alcock was arrested in Montego Bay and charged with gun possession, robbery and rape. He was granted bail and continued touring until he was sentenced in April 1999 on two accounts of rape, robbery with aggravation and illegal possession of a firearm. Shortly after incarceration, Alcock was transferred to the Tower Street Adult Correctional Centre, which had recording facilities, leading to three albums: *Free Jah's Cure: The Album the Truth* (2000), which funded an unsuccessful appeal, followed by *Ghetto Life* (2003) and *Freedom Blues* (2005), after which *The Guardian* newspaper in the UK referred to him as 'The Reggae Star Rapist'.[45] Alcock was released in 2007 and started performing straight away, although like Sizzla, he found himself banned from entering the UK on the eve of a national tour.[46] In 2011 his victim gave an interview in which she described in detail how Alcock had been in a car that had forcibly stopped the vehicle in which she was travelling, and how she was robbed, abused and taken away at gunpoint and raped by Alcock.[47] In 2011 Jah Cure was removed from the shortlist for Best Reggae Act for the annual MOBO Awards. Somewhat bizarrely, news outlets suggested that the artist's conviction had only recently come to the attention of the organizers.[48]

In 2009, Ninjaman and his son Janiel were arrested for the murder of Ricardo Johnson, but multiple delays in commencing the trial meant that it would be eight years before the deejay was convicted and sentenced. In the years before his arrest, Desmond Ballentine/Ninjaman had turned against dancehall and become a born-again Christian, before rejecting his conversion and returning to the stage under his old moniker. Despite being charged with murder, the courts issued a JA$2 million bail notice, allowing him to continue to perform. While on bail for murder, the deejay was invited by the National Security Minister to speak to members of the police force on ways to combat crime.[49] Some eight years after his initial arrest, Ballentine and two co-accused, including his son, were found guilty of the murder of Richard Johnson and given life sentences.[50] Whereas with Jah Cure, incarceration came early in his development as an artist and did not stop it, with Ninjaman, a 25-year tariff surely means the end of his musical career.

Another figure who was absent during the gestation and birth of the Reggae Revival was Buju Banton (Mark Myrie); however, unlike Vybz Kartel, Jah Cure and Ninjaman, Banton was a huge influence on the new movement and an artist who would have been expected to have had a role in a musical development that bore his imprint. But it was not to be. In December 2009, four days after receiving a Grammy nomination for Best Reggae Album for his *Rasta Got Soul*, Banton was arrested in Miami and charged with conspiracy to possess and distribute more than 5 kilograms (11 lb) of cocaine. An initial trial resulted in a hung jury, and following this, Banton was granted bail but kept under house arrest, although he was allowed to perform one concert in Miami in January 2011. After a four-month retrial, Mark Myrie was sentenced to ten years in prison.

Being in prison in the United States meant that, unlike Jah Cure in Jamaica, Buju Banton was not entitled to use a recording studio, so it would not be until after his release that his supporters would hear him perform again. Freed in December 2018, Myrie was scheduled for deportation back to Jamaica, where there was a question as to whether the state would be organizing a homecoming event. Unlike the crimes for which Jah Cure, Ninjaman and Vybz Kartel were imprisoned, the Jamaican public did not view Mark Myrie's conviction as representing a slur on his character, particularly as prosecutors had conceded that he did not stand to benefit personally from the cocaine deal.[51] The government, though, were wary, but such was the significance of the moment that Olivia Grange was forced to issue a statement on the matter, telling the LoopJamaica website that:

> The government will not be organising an event to mark the return of Buju Banton to Jamaica . . . Buju Banton is one of those who we recognise as a young veteran in the world of entertainment. Yes, he had a few problems but we welcome home all our citizens whatever the time and the circumstances. Buju Banton has been through a lot . . . We are aware that Buju Banton and his management team will be having a concert, and the Ministry of Culture may have a presence, but it is nothing that the government will

be actively organising. Buju Banton has done his time. It is not the place of any government to believe in incarceration and not rehabilitation. Buju Banton is rehabilitated and he has the right to come home . . . He showed the world that dancehall music is not about violence and homophobia, he even regretted singing some of the negative songs he sang; through his music, he helped to transform thousands of lives. How can you castigate someone like that?[52]

In the end, Banton was more than capable of organizing his own homecoming, with a concert at the National Stadium on 16 March 2019 drawing an estimated 40,000 attendees to see what the BBC called 'the biggest music event in Jamaica since Bob Marley's Smile Jamaica concert'.[53]

Buju Banton's musical homecoming was the first concert on a nine-date tour of the Caribbean before dates in Cologne, the Netherlands, Switzerland, France and Belgium. With some *chutz-pah*, Banton would name it the 'Long Walk to Freedom' tour, as if Nelson Mandela's 27 years in Robben Island for a series of explicitly political acts was comparable to his own eight years in jail for cocaine smuggling. Banton has always professed his innocence of the charge, even after the release of covertly recorded police footage of him licking cocaine off the end of a knife and saying, 'I like it.'[54] In particular, he has always claimed that the Jamaican and American authorities colluded in his entrapment in revenge for his controversial 2006 acquittal. A decade and a half after the initial incident, Banton revived the controversy by denying that what he referred to as an 'altercation' was homophobic, adding that after the event, the Jamaican and U.S. governments sought to 'neutralize' him.[55]

While Banton's tour was considered a success, in that most scheduled dates were fulfilled, the perennial problem of 'Boom Bye

Bye' continued to raise its head. In an attempt to head off trouble, Banton issued a further apology on the matter:

> In recent days there has been a great deal of press coverage about the song 'Boom Bye Bye' from my past which I long ago stopped performing and removed from any platform that I control or have influence over. I recognize that the song has caused much pain to listeners, as well as to my fans, my family and myself. After all the adversity we've been through I am determined to put this song in the past and continue moving forward as an artist and as a man. I affirm once and for all that everyone has the right to live as they so choose. In the words of the great Dennis Brown, 'Love and hate can never be friends'. I welcome everyone to my shows in a spirit of peace and love. Please come join me in that same spirit.[56]

Perhaps this would put the matter to bed for a generation. In late 2020, Buju Banton won Best Reggae Act at the UK MOBO Awards without a whisper of dissent. In what felt like a concluding statement to the whole 'Boom Bye Bye' affair, *The Guardian*, impeccable in its liberal credentials, published an interview with Banton where the focus of attention was on the artist's music, rather than the issue of homophobia.[57] Some thirty years after he recorded it, 'Boom Bye Bye' would no longer be seen by the British press as the single defining moment of Buju Banton's career. Untroubled by the forces of law and order, Banton is now perhaps reggae's biggest player, astride the world's stage and the father of a Reggae Revival that had to grow up without having him around.

Also having drug-related problems in the 2000s was rising dancehall star Busy Signal (Reanno Devon Gordon), who released one album for Greensleeves and three for VP Records before he was arrested in 2012 at Norman Manley International Airport in

Kingston and extradited to the United States on a ten-year-old charge of conspiracy to distribute no less than 5 kilograms (11 lb) of cocaine. Having pleaded guilty, Gordon served four months of a six-month prison sentence before he was deported back to Jamaica, putting paid to any notion that he may have had about perform-ing again in the United States.[58] In order to reach his American fans, Busy Signal ended up joining Popcaan, Jah Cure and Bounty Killer on a five-day 'Jamrock Reggae Cruise' organized by Damian Marley, allowing American fans to see a host of dancehall deejays who had been refused U.S. work visas.

While untouched by allegations of criminality, at least in Jamaica, other artists who might have been expected to fill the gap left by Buju Banton while he was in an American prison were also suffering career wise, and this opened up further space for the Reggae Revival generation. A good example would be Sizzla, prevented from building on his global popularity due to the allega-tions of homophobia that have dogged him for decades, and with the performer remaining *persona non grata* in the UK and other jurisdictions. In an interview conducted in 2019, DJ 745 noted that Sizzla had not been played in Europe or the UK for many years. 'Are we going to see you in the UK one day in the future?', asked the selector and radio host. 'Certainly, one day soon' was Sizzla's response.[59] The year 2004 might seem a long time ago, and a lot of political water has flowed under the bridge since David Blunkett was Home Secretary, but it remains unlikely that any present or future holder of that office will rescind the view that Sizzla cannot enter the UK, not unless Sizzla publicly recants his former views, which seems unlikely.

It is not just DJ 745 and Sizzla who have short memories; others have made the same mistake regarding a generation of deejays and singers whose careers have been stunted by allegations of hate speech and the more serious offences of rape and murder. In

2012, Island Records UK's General Manager Jon Turner noted that: 'there are some great modern artists out there – acts like Sizzla and Vybz Kartel, but unfortunately they're not breaching the barriers of Kingston Airport. There are a lot of people in Jamaica making music but it's just not travelling for one reason or another.'[60] At the point when this comment was made, Adidja Palmer was in prison, so it was perhaps unsurprising that Vybz Kartel was not available for international tours.

One of the artists expected to capitalize on Vybz Kartel's enforced absence was another one of Tom Tavares-Finson's clients, David Brooks, aka the deejay Mavado. Mavado did fill the gap left by Vybz Kartel for a while, but on the morning of Saturday 2 June 2018, he narrowly escaped with his life after becoming embroiled in a dispute that his son had with a local Don from his Cassava Piece neighbourhood. After being shot at several times, Mavado fled to the nearby Constant Spring Police Station.[61] A press photograph from the scene shows Mavado's front windscreen punctured by seven bullet holes.[62] Within hours of the incident, Mavado's associate Ian Robinson, aka Gaza Man, was shot and killed.[63]

Three days after the initial shooting, the police ordered Brooks to turn himself in for questioning 'in relation to a number of developments in the Cassava Piece area'.[64] Here the police were referring to the brutal murder of Lorenzo Thomas, aka Israel or Trulups, who had been partially beheaded and then shot and whose remains were found in Cassava Piece three days after the initial incident involving Mavado.[65] By this time, Brooks had fled to the United States, where he had permanent residency and where he remained while his brother, nephew, cousin and son were taken into custody.[66] On 14 June 2018 the Jamaican constabulary announced that they had jointly charged Andre Hinds and a sixteen-year-old male with conspiracy to murder, illegal gun possession, possession of ammunition and arson. Initially, the police did not name the sixteen-year-old, but it soon became clear that this was Mavado's son. An arrest warrant for Brooks remains outstanding and the Jamaican Police continue to threaten him with an extradition request that has never materialized.[67] By October 2018 Mavado had released the song 'Dancehall Prophecy', a tribute to his son, who the courts decided would stand trial as an adult. In May 2019, Mavado appeared alongside Buju Banton and Sizzla on DJ Khaled's single 'Lonely Mountain' and later that year performed in a series of dates in the States. It is unclear whether he will ever return to Jamaica. In January 2021, Dantay Brooks, Mavado's son, and co-accused Andre Hinds were convicted of the murder of Lorenzo Thomas.[68]

Even when they have kept their noses clean and remained out of jail, other deejays are prevented from touring the United States due to visa problems. Beenie Man, Bounty Killer, Aidonia and Ricky Trooper all had visas cancelled in 2010 as the USA sought to pressure the Jamaican government, via the deejays' fans, to extradite Christopher Coke, and this has never been reversed by the American authorities.[69] In a decade when these artists might have been expected to cross over into global success, all remain unable to travel to the United States, including Beenie Man, one of those most expected to break into the American mainstream.

For the Reggae Revival generation, the dancehall generation that preceded them was far too implicated in garrison politics for comfort, and there is clearly a desire within the Revivalists to steer a path away from dancehall's dark past. So in addition to reviving reggae, what this new generation also want to do is 'Nice Up the Dance'. This point is only emphasized by Kabaka Pyramid's big hit of 2020, a cover version of Papa Michigan and General Smiley's 'Nice Up the Dance' from 1979. Here we have a member of the Reggae Revival generation riding one of the original riddims of the first dancehall boom, before cocaine, punanny and gunplay took over. This might be called Reggae Revival, but it is important to also see it as a dancehall revival. On Kabaka Pyramid's track the Real Rock riddim is given a crisp digital update, but with a warm aesthetic, missing the jagged edges of post-Sleng Teng digital dancehall and with the vocals containing no hint of the auto-tune heard on so many contemporary dancehall hits. There is also a link to the very first reggae generation, with the use of a Coxsone Dodd riddim dating back to the 1967 release of the Sound Dimension single 'Real Rock'. On Kabaka Pyramid's hit, roots reggae and dancehall are reunited at last, after so many years of facing each other in opposition. Whatever your chosen theoretical model, be it circular, pendular or dialectical, what goes around eventually comes around in both reggae and dancehall, but the moment must be right, for this is a music that moves in sync with the times.

Chronology: The Political Economy of Reggae in the Era of Its Revival

With dancehall in the dock and its leading deejays either in jail or corralled in Jamaica, the stage was set for the Reggae Revival generation to break free from the confines imposed on the previous generation of Jamaican artists, and in doing so, to place reggae back on an international stage. When looking at signings and sales figures for the new generation of Reggae Revival artists, Jamaican music is clearly in rude health, with a range of internationally renowned stars releasing music on both major conglomerates and independent labels of various sizes. Of the big stars, Jamar McNaughton records under the name Chronixx for Virgin EMI (part of the Universal Music Group), with a debut album *Chronology* that topped the *Billboard* reggae chart in 2017 and with several high-profile global tours now under his belt. Chronixx initially signed a publishing deal with Chris Blackwell's

Blue Mountain Music, with his songs then transferred to Primary Wave Music when Blackwell sold his song catalogue in 2018.[70]

Chronixx's contemporary, the Grammy-winning teenager Koffee (Mikayla Simpson), had only one independently released single before she signed to Sony Music's Columbia label. Koffee now vies for the title of the most popular reggae artist inside and outside of Jamaica. In 2020, her COVID-19-themed single 'Lockdown' received 38 million views, beating dancehall stars Teejay and Shenseea to the top spot in a noticeable changing of the guard.

Recording since 2011, Protoje (Oje Ollivierre) has gained considerable international sales with Jamaican independent Don Corleon Records, run by songwriter, producer and mixer Donovan Bennett, before signing to RCA, another Sony subsidiary. Protoje's deal saw RCA sign the entire In.Digg.Nation Collective, a label and management company founded by the singer, with lesser-known artists Lila Iké, Jaz Elize and Sevana also included in the deal. Buju Banton signed a similar deal in 2019, placing his Gargamel Music Company in the hands of Roc Nation, founded by rapper Jay-Z. Roc Nation is one of a new generation of entertainment agencies signing artists on '360 deals' that incorporate traditional recording contracts alongside deals for music publishing, licensing, tour management and merchandizing.

While Protoje signed to RCA, both Jah9 (Janine Cunningham) and the band Raging Fyah have taken the VP Records route. On a different path is Kabaka Pyramid (Keron Salmon), who has remained on the Kingston-based indie Bebble Rock, which has a major-label distribution deal for overseas territories through a tie-up between the Universal Music Group and the Marley-owned Ghetto Youths International imprint. Also signed to several independents in different countries is Addis Pablo, son of Augustus Pablo, who plays the same instrument as his father, providing a neat link between the new generation and the old. As the largest independent record label in the reggae universe, VP Records drove through the dancehall boom of the 1990s but had their greatest period of success from 2000 onwards when Joel Chin signed Sean Paul prior to the release of his debut album *Stage One*. For his follow-up, VP developed what would become a long-term partnership with Atlantic Records and Warner Music International, releasing the album *Dutty Rock* in 2002. VP Records could now sign relatively unknown artists, and with Atlantic and Warner's international distribution reach, they could develop them and turn them into international stars. On sealing the deal with VP, Atlantic Records Vice President Craig Kallman signalled the joint ambition of the two labels:

> It's going to be an all-encompassing partnership to bring reggae to the mainstream in a way that we haven't seen since Chris Blackwell and Island Records . . . Our idea is to co-opt our strengths and make this a core, integral part of our urban music division, as well as crossing over to pop and the mainstream. We believe that we've signed the most important reggae artist in the world in Sean Paul.[71]

While VP Records has grown, its size and ability to hoover up back catalogues and new signings raises serious questions as to whether it is operating in a monopolistic manner, in Jamaica at least. In January 2008, in a move that would cause some unease, VP purchased Greensleeves from Zest Group for a reported £3.1 million. Dub maestro Scientist claims that the only reason Zest sold Greensleeves was due to his ongoing legal battles with the label, with Zest finding themselves in receipt of a lawsuit from Scientist relating to the use of music recorded by him that appears within the computer game *Grand Theft Auto*.[72] Zest deny this, stating that their justification for the sale was that an increase of digital sales was not sufficient to offset a fall in sales of physical product, as the bottom fell out of the CD market but before the advent of streaming would provide a financial fillip to the music industry as a whole.[73]

When the deal to purchase Greensleeves was announced, many within reggae voiced concerns. *The Gleaner* quoted publicist Ray Alexander as suggesting that the new company would come to dominate the industry: 'I don't think it's good for business. You can't have one company controlling reggae music. Monopoly can never be good.'[74] At the time, it seemed that Greensleeves had neglected to inform at least one of their artists of the deal, with Macka Diamond claiming 'I don't know where I stand.'[75] Randy Chin attempted to calm nerves by stating that 'Greensleeves will continue as a free-standing, fully operational label with its own A&R staff and release schedule.'[76]

The predominant attraction for VP Records in their purchase of Greensleeves was the latter's publishing arm, which at the time of purchase owned the rights to 30,000 songs.[77] The notion of music publishing and the copyrighting of songs had come late to the reggae party, as, although the British Copyright Act remained in law in Jamaica from 1913 until 1993, the legislation was almost entirely unenforced. David Betteridge, formerly of Trojan Records, explains further:

> The interesting thing about the ownership of a lot of the material from the late '50s and certainly the '60s and '70s is, in many cases, people just don't know who owns them. Because it really wasn't catalogues; it was somebody who just came along that had some tracks or songs – it might be a retailer in Jamaica, who would do some productions on the side. Apart from Duke Reid and Coxsone Dodd, there were about 20–30 people, perhaps two of which were regular, and the difficulty is [the way in which] a lot of those deals were done. I mean,

we've all heard the famous stories about a T-shirt and a bottle of coke [for payment of material]. Well, that's not dissimilar to what happened, because there were certainly times I can remember in the early days where proof of contract was the returned cheque, signed by the person who cashed it. A lot of the time there wasn't royalties; it was an outright purchase, which is of course absolutely unknown today, really. There was no copyrighting ownership, who owned what, in Jamaica for many years, so it wasn't ratified. There wasn't a contract, we didn't have renewals, options. You bought the music not off the artist but straight from the producer.[78]

Regarding publishing rights, a new player emerged in 2008 when Phoenix Music International began purchasing catalogues of reggae compositions. The firm now owns titles by Augustus Pablo, Capleton, Lee Perry, Buju Banton, Sizzla and Beenie Man, providing Phoenix with the opportunity to overturn what the firm's Business Development Director John Carnell sees as a reticence on the part of Jamaican musicians to promote their material abroad, possibly due to a collective memory of the bad business deals of the past:

There are lots of ownership issues, but generally the people are very nice to deal with and if you treat people decently then you do fine. We find that artists feel, whether it's true or not, that they've been ripped off, historically. They haven't been accounted to. That's why I think one of the biggest problems is the requirement of a better business structure as we move forward. It's partly the Jamaican industry's fault. The historical model is that the producers would pay artists some money to record some tracks and then they own them and go off and flog them. Obviously then, if they're successful, the artists don't get any royalties. It is a legal, legitimate model but it leads to a situation where the artists feel like they are being ripped off in some fashion.[79]

Although David Betteridge and John Carnell point the finger at the Jamaican model where producers are seen to own the rights to a song merely because they owned the studio in which it was first recorded, others see the main problem as being a global music industry that cuts fast and loose with the intellectual property of others. Errol Michael Henley represents Dave Barker in the UK, assisting him in seeking to gain control over the rights to 'Double Barrel', Trojan's first number-one hit in the UK and a track that the label relicensed for sale in the U.S. Barker claims to have written the song's melody and lyrics, but back in 1972 Lee Gopthal stated that Barker was merely a session singer who had been paid a single session fee as a result.[80] Barker states that his problems are not a result of the Jamaican business model, but due to the business practices of the likes of Trojan. Barker claims that the only payment he ever received from the label was £1,000, and that was only to offset touring costs, enabling Barker to continue on the road, promoting a single from which he did not benefit financially.[81]

With so much confusion regarding songwriting credits and the ownership of specific recordings, successive Jamaican governments promised to clean up the Jamaican model, but progress has been slow. The JLP governments of 1980–89 were the first to promise reform, but it was not until 1993 that a new Copyright Act came into law. More recently, the Copyright (Amendment) Act of 2015 brought in new and expanded rights for copyright owners and performers, with an extension of copyright protection for musical works, ensuring that a series of high-profile recordings in the 1950s, '60s and '70s were removed from the public domain and returned to their original rights-holders.

The updating of the legislative framework surrounding the Jamaican music industry has not prevented historic disputes from continuing to rumble on. Music by reggae's biggest-earning act, Bob Marley and the Wailers, continues to feature in legal cases around the world. The terms of the deal between Marley's family and Chris Blackwell in 1989 ensured that the publishing rights to Marley's work with Island Records were jointly owned by the Marley estate and Chris Blackwell's Blue Mountain Music before Blackwell sold his catalogue to Primary Wave. However, this has not stopped a series of court cases contesting the terms of this deal, including one in 2006 where Aston Barrett unsuccessfully sued Universal and the Marleys for royalties from six songs that he claimed to have co-written.[82]

In 2014, Danny Sims failed to persuade the High Court in London that a deal he cut with Blue Mountain in 1992 excluded thirteen specific songs, including 'No Woman, No Cry' and 'Positive Vibration',[83] with the judge saying that it was 'little short of ridiculous' that what should have been a watertight contract excluded explicit reference to the thirteen compositions in question.[84] In 2016 it would be the turn of Allan 'Skill' Cole in court, with Marley's former tour manager unsuccessful in persuading a federal court in Pennsylvania that he had co-written 'War' and 'Natty Dread' with Marley. On its original release, 'War' was credited to Allan 'Skill' Cole (idea) and Carlton Barrett (music), an act seen by many as an attempt by Marley to subvert the unfavourable publishing contract that he had with Danny Sims. In publicity around the case, Cole claimed to have been unaware that he held no copyright to 'War' until he attempted to transfer what he saw as his half of the song to the estate of Haile Selassie.[85]

If courts around the world have often struggled to determine who owned the songwriting and recording royalties of Bob Marley's most famous works, they were hopeless at ascertaining who might, and who might not, have a claim over the rights to the riddims that so often featured in the works of Marley and others. Luckily for reggae, if not for every reggae musician, these riddims have become close to public property, passed on from generation to generation. If in the pre-digital age, studio musicians had been prevented from borrowing each other's riddims, much reggae would not have existed in a form that could be sold via retail outlets, even if it might have survived on dubplates and a culture of informality. There would certainly have been no Island or Trojan record labels moving back and forth from Jamaica to the UK, signing deals with producers who had hired and fired musicians at will, and who did not care for any notion that the musicians might have a lasting ownership over either their compositions or the recordings on which they feature.

Had Jamaican popular music emerged in a society where intellectual property rights were taken more seriously, the riddim culture of much reggae and dancehall would have been strangled at birth. But no legislature can cheat history, even if recent reform has brought Jamaica into line with the Berne Convention for the Protection of Literary and Artistic Works of 1886, using the principle that copyright exists at the moment of creation and does not require any formal registration. Nowadays, the Jamaican music industry operates to the same international standards as elsewhere, with the Jamaica Association of Composers, Authors and Publishers (JACAP) managing the collective rights of songwriters and music publishers, not unlike the UK's Performing Rights Society (PRS) and the American Society of Composers, Authors and Publishers (ASCAP). Nowadays, when members of the Reggae Revival generation write a new song, they retain ownership of it, even if they are quietly borrowing musical licks and riddims from previous generations. However, just because a modern composition or recording is contractually protected, this does necessarily mean that the composer or musician will receive all of the royalties due to them, as JACAP's collection rate is noticeably lower than that found elsewhere.

Dancehall and the Dubplate Election of 2020

If the musicians of the Reggae Revival are studious in avoiding the lure of party politics, the same cannot be said of their compatriots in dancehall. While the likes of Jah9 attack politicians for their role in Jamaican society, many dancehall deejays looked to politicians for both support and a pay cheque in the so-called 'dubplate election' of 2020.

The origins of dancehall's re-engagement with party politics began in 2009 when the Jamaica Constabulary Force (JCF) announced that they were about to take a new approach to the Jamaican Noise Abatement Act of 1997, which was largely unenforced until Jamaica's tourism sector began to lobby for police action against both licensed and unlicensed dancehall events. In a document marked 'CONFIDENTIAL', the JCF outlined their new approach to 'noise nuisance', which they stated was not confined to what they referred to as 'the Corporate Area' but which 'permeated the entire country':

CURRENT SITUATION

- Dances are being held without approval.
- Music being played beyond the cut off time (12mn weekdays and 2:00am weekends).
- Music causing a nuisance to the public.
- Musical events held in the streets impeding vehicular and pedestrian traffic.
- Use of firearms at these events resulting in injury or death to patrons.
- Use of drugs at these musical events.

- Traffic concerns – improper parking which creates congestion.
- Breaches of the National Solid Waste Management Act – improper disposal of garbage.
- Abstraction of electricity.
- Expression of lewd lyrics by disc jockeys.
- Attendance of children at these musical events.

. . . ACTION

- Monitor geographic areas of command to prevent the unauthorized staging of musical events.
- Monitoring of approved musical events.
- Locking down of music systems being played beyond the cut off time.
- Prosecution of violators.
- Arrest where desirable.
- Seizure of equipment if necessary.
- Where members of the force, who are host of the events, impede the police in their execution of duties, strict disciplinary action will be taken.[86]

The document went on to state that officers would be accountable to their superiors if they deviated from the above, concluding that 'it is imperative that all members take steps to ensure the separation of good, honest and professional members from the small minority of corrupt individuals whose actions continue to tarnish the reputation of the Jamaica Constabulary Force and its membership.'[87]

While noise abatement is generally accepted as an uncontentious necessity in the developed North, it is more politically contentious in Jamaica, where it touches on concerns regarding globalization, urbanization and the rights of locals versus international guests.

Unlike in the UK, noise abatement in Jamaica rubs up against the notion of music and drumming as a cultural and religious right, cherished and held tight on a journey through slavery and since. In the developed North, new residents are attracted to inner cities for their popular culture, but when they move there, they find that not all is to their liking and that life in the inner city is noisy. A similar phenomenon occurs with hotel residents in Jamaica, attracted to the island for its music scene but, once there, upset when they find they cannot sleep at night due to the local dancehall.

After years of controversy regarding the shutting down of events, the JLP national security minister Robert Montague announced that he was consulting on a series of amendments to the Act. In 2011, Montague unveiled a proposal to set up 'entertainment zones' in which dancehall events could be held, while also liberalizing closing hours beyond the statutory 2 a.m. at the weekends and midnight during the week. Focusing on his crime-fighting remit, the minister also proposed that dancehall promoters should install closed-circuit television cameras and metal detectors.[88] A change in government in January 2012 ensured that the consultation would drag on. In November 2015, Damion Crawford, the PNP's minister of tourism and entertainment, announced that he was 'very close' to achieving a relaxation of the original Noise Abatement Act, although there was some confusion as to whether it was the Security or Tourism and Entertainment Ministry that was taking a lead on the ongoing consultation. Crawford told the press that 'the law is being drafted and I can show a copy of what the law is going to be . . . So by January 2016 we should be good.'[89]

January 2016 came and went, and a general election in March 2016 saw the pendulum swing back towards the JLP, with Andrew Holness returning as prime minister and with Olivia Grange given the post of Minister of Culture, Gender, Entertainment and Sport. After taking office, Grange announced that she too had been 'in consultation' with the Ministry of Security to see how the 1997 legislation could be amended to prevent incidents such as the forced shutdown of the weekly Dub Club on Skyline Drive in Kingston in April 2017, when the promoter Karlyle Lee was unable to produce a suitable permit and where the police closed down the event as a result, pepper spraying attendees to encourage them to disperse. Both Lee and his selector Gabre Selassie were arrested and taken into custody on the eve of a Carnival event due to take place in the resort area of Kingston. Hinting at some of the politics involved, Olivia Grange stated:

> I want to quickly express my concern and regret that an incident like this should have happened on a day when Carnival, a quite different cultural event, was taking place. It is really unfortunate that something like this happened at the same time as Carnival, as it sends the wrong message that there are 'two Jamaicas'.[90]

Two years later, the JLP government announced that their proposed legislation was now ready. The resulting newspaper headlines focused on a liberalization of licensing hours beyond the midnight and 2 a.m. limits within the 1997 Act.[91] Soon, Omar Robinson of the Jamaica Hotel and Tourism Association (JHTA) would express his alarm, saying that visitors were complaining about their inability to sleep due to a lack of enforcement of the existing law, and that any liberalization was unwanted, as the status quo 'at least gives the police the ability to intervene should we call them'.[92] Here, dancehall is seen as an inconvenience to local hotels, and with a class dimension to the debate as a powerful economic sector lines up against what tourism minister Edmund Bartlett called the 'small people' who make a livelihood around the dancehall, selling refreshments and the like.[93]

Later in 2019, the JCF met with promoters after receiving complaints regarding the constabulary's application of the law. This included concerns about the closure of a retro dancehall party entitled FootLoose at the Mas Camp event venue in Kingston, with the promoter claiming to have an official letter requesting that the JCF use discretion and allow a 4 a.m. closure time. Despite this, at precisely 1:59 a.m., the police stepped in and closed the event.[94]

Not only is noise abatement a class issue, but it has also become a party-political one. A localized application of legislation is a legacy of the garrison politics that has carved urban Jamaica up into competing political fiefdoms, with corruption rife. Dancehall figures state that the police have always used 'discretion' to allow events to go on for longer, with some promoters claiming to have official documentation requesting that the police allow their events to go beyond the statutorily allowed times.[95] But when the JCF do allow events to go on for longer, this is most often the decision of an individual officer rather than due to formal policy.

The debate had been rumbling on for a decade before it exploded in September 2019, when figures from dancehall's music-making community began a campaign entitled 'No Music, No Vote!', threatening to hit the JLP and PNP at the ballot box. Leading selector Ricky Trooper cut to what he saw as the heart of the debate:

> When it comes on to politics, the main weapon is music. No PNP or JLP rally happen without the music; dem [politicians] have to use it to inject the energy to rile up di people so when dem go on the stage dem have dem attention . . . None ah dem can go on a stage ah chat, chat, chat the whole day or night. Dem use the music to make dem speech inject certain songs to share a message. So why use the music when you need the vote and after that you spit pon it?[96]

Jumping on board the campaign, Bounty Killer issued a veiled threat on social media: 'Police, government, authorities etc, be careful of how you treat the common man, mid class or poor people; everybody's lives and their livelihood matters not just yours, Enough being said, poor people fed up from bout '95.'[97] Baby Cham (Damian Beckett) agreed: 'Too long dancehall and reggae music been fighting for our rights; they take our music and they use it, and use the artistes to promote Jamaica and the tourism.'[98]

With only 3,549 votes separating the two national parties at the 2016 general election, the PNP and JLP were bound to respond. Within days, Olivia Grange met with stakeholders to discuss the Act, arguing for

> a well-reasoned and fair approach that allows for good order and sustainable management of entertainment as an industry and an economic driver. Amending the legislation and the development of entertainment zones will make a difference in arriving at a solution.[99]

Two days later, the prime minister, Andrew Holness, weighed into the debate in terms that offered dancehall more hope: 'I believe that there is a way to allow the sound system operator, the musician, the entertainer, to have their party. If they want to party until 5 o'clock, then so let it be.'[100]

In the end, a compromise was struck during a trial period. A Noise Abatement (Temporary Amendment) Act allowed for a two-hour extension to the 2 a.m. limit during the 'festive season' from 13 December 2019 until 31 January 2020. However, when I bumped into Olivia Grange and Andrew Holness backstage at Rebel Salute in St Ann's Bay during the period in question, it was around 5 a.m., with the show not finishing for another four hours, despite there being a clear cut-off in legislation of 4 a.m.

for such an event. I eventually left the festival at around 9 a.m. as the final act, Anthony B, performed 'Fire pon Rome' in broad daylight, and I could hear the last few bars of his set from the nearby residential community of Richmond. Why Rebel Salute was allowed to continue into the late morning while other events are curtailed is moot. But whatever the reason, the differing treatment of dancehall and roots reggae has clearly impacted on the progress of both forms of music.

Following their campaign against tighter noise-abatement legislation, it might have been expected for dancehall deejays to follow Reggae Revival musicians in preaching a plague on both houses of JLP and PNP. However, the opposite occurred, and in the immediate run-up to the general election of 3 September 2020, a significant number of dancehall deejays released exclusive tracks in support of a range of candidates in what the Jamaican press referred to as a 'dubplate election'. The trend began with the campaign to re-elect the PNP's Lisa Hanna in the seat of South East St Ann. In support of the sitting MP, the Universal Music Group's Shenseea (Chinsea Lee), one of the bigger dancehall stars of recent years, re-recorded her 2019 hit 'Trending Gyal', with the deejay praising the politician as an 'independent gyal' with her own income. Despite being a so-called election special, the accompanying social-media video focused more on the MP's clothes than on her politics. Shenseea's support for Hanna was swiftly followed by that of her friend Spice (Grace Hamilton), who re-recorded a version of 'So Mi Like It' in support of the same candidate. The track and accompanying video includes a reference to Hanna's previous role as Miss World 1993, even though she has been an MP since 2007.

Joining Hanna on the musical campaign trail was the PNP's new leader Dr Peter Phillips. As candidate for the seat of East Central St Andrew, Phillips obtained the endorsement of Atlanta-based deejay Dovey Magnum (Simsky Harrison), who recorded a cleaned-up version of her biggest hit 'Bawl Out' for Phillips's exclusive use. Standing against Phillips was the JLP's Jodian Myrie, the daughter of Buju Banton, whose dubplate special was provided by Wayne Wonder. The Jamaican press suggested that it was Jodian's father who had ensured that she could obtain such a high-profile endorsement in a campaign that she was unlikely to win (the PNP had held the seat continuously since 1967). Banton refused to commit to either candidate, in contrast to Beenie Man, who had no qualms about re-recording his 'We Run Road' in support of his fiancé Krystal Tomlinson, a PNP candidate hoping to unseat the JLP's Juliet Cuthbert-Flynn in West Rural St Andrew. In an unusual twist, recording in support of Cuthbert-Flynn was D'Angel (Michelle Downer), Beenie Man's ex-wife, who stated that her motives for supporting the JLP were neither personal nor ideological but financial, confirming that she was paid for the job and that she would be willing to record for the PNP if the price was right.[101]

Another high-profile musical tie-up for the PNP was between Peter Bunting, the former national security minister and the sitting MP for Manchester Central, and Stylo G (Jason McDermott), the Anglo-Jamaican deejay best known for his UK single 'Soundbwoy'. Like the Lisa Hanna and Shenseea recordings, the Bunting/Stylo G collaboration was accompanied by a social-media video that ended with a spoken-word endorsement. Only this time, it was the politician endorsing the deejay, with Bunting issuing the line 'yow dis have a buzz still, ya know'. In a press interview, Bunting explained the appeal of working with a deejay:

> music is a key part of the campaign season and will play an even more important role this year given the COVID-related restrictions on mass gatherings. Political parties will have to re-invent themselves and find creative ways of communicating their message and energising their supporters.[102]

With the PNP having gained the support of Shenseea, Dovey Magnum and Stylo G, the JLP was quick to respond with finance minister Dr Nigel Clarke obtaining a musical endorsement by Jahvillani (Dujon Edwards), who re-recorded his 'Clarks pon Foot' in support of Clarke's candidacy in North West St Andrew, while Floyd Green, state minister of industry, commerce, agriculture and fisheries, procured the services of Teejay (Timoy Jones), who recorded a version of his 'Owna Lane' in support of the sitting MP in South West St Elizabeth. In a statement as bland as that of Bunting's, Floyd Green spoke admiringly of Teejay's original track:

> Teejay has really connected with the Jamaican people over the last few years and has consistently put out good work. Owna Lane connects with me because it's about focusing on the task at hand and not to be distracted which is what this election period requires . . . Music has always been essential to the Jamaicans. Music is our language and for politics it is no different. Music is still the most effective way to communicate, especially now with the COVID restrictions.[103]

Not that Teejay fully bought into the JLP's vision, as he contributed to Tarrus Riley's 'Babylon Warfare (feat. Teejay & Dean Fraser)' at the same time as releasing the 'Owna Lane' dubplate. 'Babylon Warfare' is a dancehall ballad that uses the melody and chorus of Max Romeo's 'War ina Babylon' to highlight racial injustice in the COVID-19 era.

Another JLP politician obtaining an exclusive musical endorsement was Robert Nesta Morgan, contesting the North Central Clarendon seat vacated following the retirement of Pearnel Charles. Morgan's campaign for election was soundtracked by Christopher Martin's 'Big Big' single, re-recorded to refer to 'Nesta ah General'. Following the perceived success of Morgan's dubplate special, Martin recorded a further version of the track for Alando Terrelonge, the JLP incumbent in St Catherine East Central. Meanwhile, Masicka recorded a dub in support of Charles's son, Pearnel Jr, for his campaign in the constituency of Clarendon South East.

Unsurprisingly, Olivia Grange was also able to obtain a high-profile dubplate special, by I-Octane (Byiome Muir), the Rasta deejay who had signed to Donovan Germain's Penthouse Records before starting his own Conquer the Globe Productions. Not to be outdone, by the end of the campaign Andrew Holness was able to commission no less than four separate dubplate specials. Shenseea re-recorded 'Sure, Sure' (balancing out her earlier endorsement of the PNP's Lisa Hanna), while Skillibeng re-recorded 'Mr Universe', Masicka re-recorded 'Just a Minute' and Ishwana re-recorded 'Equal Rights', all in support of the sitting PM, who hit the campaign trail in a fine pair of Clarks suede shoes in JLP green.

Such was the ubiquity of freshly recorded dubplate endorsements that some candidates began to feel left out. Contesting the seat of Portland Western, the PNP's Valerie Neita-Robertson QC suggested on Twitter that she was going through a list of artists that she had represented in court to obtain an endorsement. Perhaps Neita-Robertson was forgetting that out of the four artists she cited (Vybz Kartel, Dexta Daps, Aidonia and Ninjaman), two were in jail for murder. From his prison cell, Adidja Palmer responded to the general trend for dancehall endorsements with an attack on both the deejays and the politicians, stating on his socia-media feeds that 'Dancehall burn politics, now artistes doing dubs fi dem. smfh.. me stop do conscious song bout ya.. a bay gun lyrics !! cause unuh beyond learning tpc!'[104] Following this, Palmer then posted a clip from the video to his 2005 track 'Emergency', which contrasts the plight of Jamaica's poor with the lives of politicians' dogs and which places the blame for introducing the gun into Jamaican politics firmly at the door of the political class. It is an irony that the deejay most seen to have encapsulated dancehall's embrace of materialism should also have such explicitly political tracks as 'Emergency' in his back catalogue. During his meteoric rise, few would have singled out Vybz Kartel as likely to become a politically radical figure prepared to confront the JLP/PNP duopoly head on; but in jail, he has nothing to lose.

Adding a little vitriol to the dubplate election was Vybz Kartel's former mentor, Bounty Killer, who took a swipe at Peter Bunting's use of dancehall by drawing attention to a 2013 article in the *Jamaica Observer*. In this piece, Bunting had alleged that dancehall promoted criminality, criticizing Vybz Kartel's 'Reparation' specifically.[105] In a further social-media post, Bounty Killer claimed to have turned down requests for dubplate specials from various politicians, while also decrying the fact that the election was being fought through what he saw as a depoliticized musical sphere rather than through a debate concerning competing policies. Here, Bounty Killer had a good point. All of the dubplate specials were light on policies and heavy on bland and generalized endorsements of individual politicians. One of the policies that Bounty Killer wanted to see debated in the election was Jamaica's licensing laws and the recent curtailment of dancehall's traditional all-night-long ethos. Sensing hypocrisy in Bounty Killer's criticisms of politicians, one fan hit back, reminding the deejay that as recently as 2017 he had performed at a birthday party for the JLP's Daryl Vaz, during which he had lauded the politician's many achievements.

While it was dancehall rather than reggae that featured heavily in the 2020 general election, the question remained as to what was behind this contemporary revival of an old trend for musical electioneering, thought to have died a death after the bloody general election of 1980. The answers were plain to see. First, the coronavirus pandemic meant that the election was being fought away from its usual stomping ground of the street rally, and social-media videos of politicians on the campaign trail captured the COVID mood nicely.

Second, with the enforced closure of dancehalls and a consequent drop in income for deejays, most of those recording dubplates did so for a fee rather than for any overriding political preference for either the JLP or PNP. This is nothing new. From the days when Edward Seaga employed Duke Reid and Coxsone Dodd to promote a new sense of independence, through to the PNP paying JA$150 to each of the Wailers for them to appear on the party's travelling caravan of stars, there have always been Jamaican politicians looking to employ reggae musicians to promote their candidacies, and there have always been performers willing to take a politician's shilling.

Third, and irrespective of any direct payments by the politicians, the benefits of dubplate tie-ups between parliamentary candidates and deejays ended up benefitting both parties equally. Politicians grabbed the attention of dancehall fans, while some of the lesser-known deejays suddenly found that they had broken out of a working-class dancehall subculture and were performing on a national and international stage. The case of Paparatzzi (Akiem Bradbury) is instructive here, with the deejay acknowledging that his motives for recording a track in support of Dwayne Vaz, the PNP's candidate for Central Westmoreland, was the exposure that he would receive rather than being due to any steadfast political commitment to Vaz. The risk for dancehall deejays and politicians is weighted towards the latter though, with deejays expecting politicians to be supportive of dancehall should they be elected. Having said this, it is dangerous for any deejay to assume that a quid pro quo is at work in their dealings with politicians.

Watching on the sidelines of the dubplate election of 2020 were the Reggae Revival artists, wary of any involvement. Seen as one of the leading figures of the Reggae Revival, Protoje quickly aired his objection to the dubplates, recording 'No Politician Can't Beg

No Dubplate from Me' in response, in which a politician's concerns for the electorate ends on the morning after election day. In commenting on his track, Protoje was keen to point out that politicians were hypocritical for attacking dancehall criminality between elections, only for them to embrace the music when a few extra votes were needed.

Protoje had a point. Despite the fact that Vybz Kartel was imprisoned for murder, there were still politicians prepared to trade on his popularity. During a PNP rally in Old Harbour prior to the 2016 general election, Dwayne Vaz quoted lyrics from 'Wha' Dem Feel Like', a gun tune by Vybz Kartel. Such brazen appropriation brought censure from Vaz's cousin, Daryl, the MP for Portland Western.[106] From his perspective, Protoje saw the involvement of dancehall deejays in electoral politics as short-sighted, accusing politicians of shutting down dancehall events at inappropriate hours and denigrating the music through unfounded accusations of violence.[107] This vision was further fleshed out on his album *In Search of Lost Time*, released in the week before the general election, with lyrics from the song 'Self Defence' advising: 'youth be wise'. In the song, Protoje also references trap dancehall, a hybrid subgenre particularly popular in the southern states of America and another Black Atlantic form. In incorporating elements of this music within *In Search of Lost Time*, Protoje was beginning a journey away from the purity of roots reggae towards a variety of sounds, including American soul, R&B and laid-back rap. Formed to revitalize the roots sound, even the Reggae Revival never stays still for long.

Although the dubplate election of 2020 saw the return of party politics to dancehall, this was different from the 1970s in that very few of the election specials referenced the respective policies of either the JLP or PNP. Since the neo-liberalism of Seaga beat the non-aligned democratic socialism of Manley, the PNP have marched to much the same economic and political tune as the JLP and they now compete on the same territory. Both parties are keen to demonstrate that they are the most efficient controllers of the levers of economic and political power, and both parties like to emphasize that it is they who occupy a sensible middle ground.

In the run-up to the election, the PNP issued a new form of manifesto on a website that asked individual members of the electorate to rank the eight issues of most importance to them before allowing them to download their own bespoke document of election promises. Of the separate categories of agriculture, COVID-19 Management Plan, education, entertainment, environment and sustainability, healthcare, housing, justice, land use, security, technology, tourism and transportation, the obvious missing category was economics. Only the final category of 'wealth plan' hinted at the PNP's earlier promise of transformational rather than technocratic politics. Noticeable also within these categories was 'land use' rather than anything as radical as land ownership or reform. One of the key political issues in Jamaica from emancipation onwards is now seen to be beyond the spectrum of acceptable opinion found within the Jamaican political mainstream. The JLP and PNP's shared ideology of individualism also colours the relationship between politicians and deejays. Irie FM founder and dancehall producer Clyde McKenzie has noted that the key difference between the 1970s and the present day is that the dubplate specials of 2020 were largely apolitical endorsements of individual candidates rather than rallying cries for a specific ideology:

> I see it as a way for artistes to have it both ways supporting a particular candidate who might be their friend while being able to claim that they are not supporting a political party, they are backing an individual candidate. The dubplates I have heard seem only to be praising the preferred candidates

of the artistes and is not belittling of their opponents. In fact, there is little, if any reference, to the opponents of the artistes' preferred candidates in these specials.[108]

With both the JLP and PNP competing on similar ground, seeking to establish themselves as the more competent stewards of the Jamaican economy, it was unsurprising that the JLP should win the election in what was close to a landslide, increasing their majority and gaining 49 of the 63 seats in the Jamaican Parliament. In Jamaica at least, the JLP had invented neo-liberalism, so it might be expected that voters would assume that they were better at managing it than the PNP. However, the hype around the dubplate election of 2020 masked the continuation of a disengagement among voters. Turnout has continued to fall since its highpoint in the bloody election of 1980, slipping into dangerous territory with 47.72 per cent of the electorate voting in 2016, and only 37 per cent doing so in the COVID election of November 2020.[109] With numbers as low as these, democracy in Jamaica must be seen to be under threat. But did democracy ever exist in Jamaica in the first place? As already noted, the transition from colony to an independent state remains incomplete, and when Vybz Kartel's only hope of freedom lies with the Judicial Committee of the Privy Council in London, there is surely something wrong. Many politicians have promised to replace the Privy Council with a local Court of Justice, but all have failed to do so. Equally, many Jamaican politicians have promised land reform, yet peasant and plantation agriculture remain the largest sources of direct employment on an island where 4 per cent of the population controls 65 per cent of all agricultural land, including most of the fertile coastal plains.[110] And 2010 is not so long ago, when the Jamaican state was prepared to massacre the citizens that it was supposed to be protecting. 'Four hundred years, and de same *bucky massa* bizniz' indeed.

EPILOGUE

Bobi Wine

St Ann's Bay, Jamaica, 2020

It's 9 a.m. at Rebel Salute, and the headliner Beenie Man is on stage, wearing a gold lamé suit and looking every inch a star. Confident that my photographic work is done, I pack away my camera and look up to notice that security are taking a liberal approach to entry into the photographers' pit and an impromptu dance floor has formed. I then notice a familiar figure dancing in front of me, the silhouette of a man who is unique in being both a reggae musician and the leader of a 'People Power' movement that is rocking a major African nation to its core. I realize that I am in the presence of a man considered by his peers to be a reggae revolutionary, and the man who I had most hoped to speak to at the festival.

Combining conscious roots reggae with Afrobeat stylings, Bobi Wine (Robert Kyagulanyi Ssentamu) has recorded over seventy songs over a fifteen-year career, with the Fire Base Crew, the Ghetto Republic of Uganja and as a soloist. The artist's best-known recording is almost certainly the single 'Kiwani' (2016), which appeared on the soundtrack to the Disney movie *Queen of Katwe*, although other recordings are popular in Uganda. 'Kiwani' features a beautifully shuffling rhythm and the characteristic sound of East African rhythm guitar, accompanied by lyrics sung in the Bantu language of Luganda.

Musically, Bobi Wine's career might be characterized as slow burning, but politically, his activism has been explosive and the artist is now feted internationally as one of the greatest African thinkers of his generation. His political career began with humanitarian work among one of the poorest districts in the sprawling city of Kampala, building latrines and drainage channels in a district where most households lack toilets. In 2012 his keyboard-driven Afrobeat single 'Tugambire ku Jennifer' accused Jennifer Musisi, the Kampala Capital City Authority's newly appointed Executive Director, of brutality in the implementation of development plans, bulldozing street-vendor pitches from the city's streets.[1] Further political releases followed, including 'Obululu Tebutwawula' ('elections should not divide us'), the first of a series of singles concerned with electoral violence, while 'Carolina' was a tale of educational underachievement and an unwanted pregnancy.

In 2016, Kyagulanyi won a seat in the Ugandan Parliament by a landslide, wiping the floor with candidates from both the ruling National Resistance Movement (NRM) and the opposition Forum for Democratic Change (FDC), who had shunned Kyagulanyi's earlier overtures and who were humiliated at the poll for not giving him their support. Within months of winning his seat, Kyagulanyi found himself at the forefront of a campaign to prevent the increasingly autocratic president Yoweri Museveni from altering the country's constitution to allow him to stand again for the presidency. By the end of the year, in a sign of the government's increasing anxiety, a police order banned Bobi Wine from performing in Uganda.[2] In response, the artist released 'Freedom', a devastating and outspoken attack on the Ugandan state that sees the artist switch between singing and deejaying in Luganda, English and patois.

With three-quarters of Uganda's population aged under 35, a series of by-elections in 2018 saw three parliamentary seats fall to what was being called a 'youthquake', with Kyagulanyi at its head. Later that year, his driver was shot dead in what looked like a botched assassination attempt on Kyagulanyi himself, who was arrested and tortured. Speaking to *Rolling Stone*, the artist said: 'They tie a rope on your testicles, then [attach] a car battery and say, "Stand up".'[3] Although initially prevented from leaving Uganda, Kyagulanyi eventually travelled to the USA for medical treatment.

Throughout his political activism, Kyagulanyi has always remained close to roots-reggae values, and while he may now be shorn of his dreads, his distinctive red beret remains redolent with meaning and is described by him as a symbol of resistance. During his meteoric rise, the Ugandan establishment have remained wary of his support.

At a rally in January 2020, the state's response to Kyagulanyi's activism was to arrest him and tear gas his supporters. Only a few days after being released, he appeared in front of me in the photographers' pit at Rebel Salute, flushed with the success of headlining the previous night. I leaned forward and introduced myself, and we began a conversation on the relationship between reggae and politics. In discussing his plans to stand for the Ugandan presidency, Kyagulanyi insisted that I should not characterize him as a politician but as a leader instead. When I told him that he should not forget that he was also a musician, and that music could change the world, he smiled broadly and spoke of how it was a dream come true to perform at such a significant event in Jamaica. On stage, he introduced himself as Uganda's next president, and he said that he remained hopeful that there would be a road to a peaceful transition in his home country. In person, he seemed humble, and I was left with a deep impression of him as an extraordinary man, dedicated to progressive social and economic change, and with youth, beauty and charisma on his side.

At Rebel Salute, with Bobi Wine dancing in front of me, I am not ashamed to admit that I was awestruck. I am also happy to say that I remain so, particularly when considering the events that have occurred since we spoke. Kyagulanyi's campaigning for the presidency of Uganda was met with shocking levels of brutality. In November 2020 dozens of his supporters were killed after security forces opened fire on protestors who had taken to the streets after he was arrested for unauthorized assembly and violating anti-coronavirus measures.[4] From that moment and up until election day on 14 January 2021, the police continued to break up Kyagulanyi's open-air meetings, and one week prior to the election, almost all of his campaign team were arrested, while the singer was dragged out of his vehicle and tear gassed while he was conducting a hastily convened press conference at the side of a road in Kampala. Once he had been returned to his vehicle, the singer-cum-politician recorded a video message on his mobile phone, saying 'I expect a live bullet targeted at me any time. The biggest safety net we get is from having cameras around us.'[5]

By the week of the election, the Museveni regime had closed down much of the Internet, preventing any access to social media, which by then was the most effective way that Kyagulanyi had of reaching his electoral base. Amid numerous allegations of widespread electoral malpractice, and with concern expressed by the EU, the UN and various human-rights groups, Museveni was declared winner of the election with 57 per cent of the vote.[6] Since the poll, Kyagulanyi has claimed a moral victory. He now travels in an armoured car and always wears a bulletproof vest in public.

Nobody knows if Robert Kyagulanyi will lead Uganda, and if he does, nobody knows what sort of leader he will turn out to be. After all, Museveni was himself once a revolutionary national hero. Right now, though, Kyagulanyi is showing leadership by saying: 'I tell my people not to wait for the Government to educate their children and feed them, because I know they can do it themselves but just need to be shown how to do it.'[7] That, my readers, is the mark of a true reggae revolutionary, and one who works in the spirit of Marcus Garvey's injunction that Africans must look to themselves for upliftment, for nobody will do it for them. If much of this book has focused on the legacy of Marcus Garvey as found within Jamaican music, one must not forget that Garvey's legacy lives on in Africa too. 'Africa for the Africans, at home and abroad.'

Cape Coast Castle

Cape Coast, Ghana

'What am I doing here?,' I ask myself, standing outside Cape Coast Castle again. This time, I had an answer to the question that I was first asked all those years ago. I am in Ghana to research a book on reggae and to see if I can answer another, far more challenging, question. Putting Jamaica to one side for the moment, I am now asking myself, 'Is this where reggae is *really* from?'

On this trip, Rachel and I are with our children Lily and Seán, to show them a country that we have both fallen in love with. Prior to our visit, I had attended a 'Ghana Celebration and Homecoming Summit' in the UK. This was part of Ghana's 'Year of Return', a clever promotional device by the Ghanaian government that could mean a number of things, including the return of Ghanaian emigrants to live in the country. Doctors, nurses, engineers and other economic émigrés are now invited back to a nation categorized by the World Bank as a middle-income country, with the return of Ghana's professional class seen as essential for future economic growth. For others, it might mean a different type of return, the one envisaged by Marcus Garvey, both a physical and spiritual return, with a global Black diaspora visiting Ghana to experience its life and culture, perhaps with a view to permanent residency sometime in the future. The 'Year of Return' would also mean tourists spending valuable hard currencies in an under-developed economy, too. For Rachel and me, it would also be an opportunity for the two of us to return to the spot where we were married, on the beach in Ampenyi, to the west of the forts of Cape Coast and Elmina.

After settling into the beautiful beach resort of Ko-Sa, we decide on a trip to Cape Coast to do some shopping and to visit the castle. The day before we visited, Nancy Pelosi, the Speaker of the U.S. House of Representatives, had led a delegation of members of the Congressional Black Caucus there. This was an important time for Ghana, at the centre of the world's attention, even if for only one day.

During the formal tour of the castle, tourists are led to the 'door of no return' through which the kidnapped were pushed onto boats, where they were held captive during their journey west in the most terrible of conditions. We were here to learn again about mankind's inhumanity, but while my family went on the tour, I felt unable to enter the castle again. It would be too heartbreaking.

So, I scramble down to the beach to take some photographs, thinking that an image of the castle might be suitable for inclusion in this book. Looking through my viewfinder, I walk backwards, away from the castle, and stumble through an ocean of plastic. For as far as I can see along the beach, there are thousands of empty plastic sachets (the way most Ghanaians purchase drinking water) along with endless bottles, bin bags, clothes, toothbrushes and other detritus of African life. A storm drain emits a stinking sludge, dribbling down to the shore. When I finally sit down and look out to sea, away from Africa, at the huge waves as they crash onto the shore, I can think only of the contrast between the view of the sea, with nature at its most awe inspiring, and the sorry state of the beach, in what is a prestigious tourist location. I turn around to see a double-storey bamboo hut, occupied by a group of Rastas. I approach them and we exchange greetings, and I am welcomed onto the upper balcony of their property, with a beautiful view out to sea. Ghanaians are renowned for their friendliness, and this group were no exception to that. In the heat of midday, we discuss the state of the nation and the state of the beach. They had ceased to be shocked by it, while I was dismayed and could not help but contrast it to the relatively clean beaches I had seen only fifteen years previously.

Later, in Ampenyi, I meet another Rasta, Bobo Amuah, who welcomes me into the wooden hut that serves as both his home and as an art gallery for his paintings. I feel honoured to be invited, and tell him so, and we bond quickly. In his hut, I notice a small pile of books, on top of which, in pride of place, is a copy of *Message to the People: The Course of African Philosophy*, the closest thing that there is to a full-length book written by Marcus Garvey. This edition is shorn of its cover and well thumbed in the manner of an obviously much-loved companion.

Bobo and I became friends, and I returned to see him a couple of times a day for around a fortnight, and by the second week of our stay, we had discussed the possibility of a formal interview. So, on one sunny afternoon, I sat down to discuss Marcus Garvey's 'Back to Africa', a phrase and concept developed by a man who had never visited Africa, with a young man who had never left it. How did such a thing come to pass? How did a white middle manager from a mid-tier university in the North of England come to discuss a vision of Black pride with a young African living on the Ghanaian coast? The answer is, of course, reggae.

I ask Bobo what his favourite reggae recording is, and he quickly says Peter Tosh's *Bush Doctor*, the ex-Wailer's follow-up to the albums *Legalize It* and *Equal Rights*. Bobo scrambles for his mobile phone and puts the album on. Ironically, his favourite album is seen as Peter Tosh's most Westernized – ignoring the widespread notion that Jamaica is not in 'the West', even if it is due west from here in Ghana. If Peter Tosh's 'live-atribe' against the 'shitsem' at the One Love Peace Concert is a buried rhizome of the Reggae Revival movement, the other legacy of his performance is that it was witnessed by Mick Jagger, who was so enamoured with the figure of Tosh that he approached him to enquire whether he would like to sign to Rolling Stones Records, the band's new label. In his memoir, Don Taylor makes it clear that Marley himself wanted nothing to do with Mick Jagger, for homophobic reasons (so much for 'One Love'), while Tosh was more receptive.[8] *Bush Doctor* was the label's inaugural release and features Keith Richards on guitar on the album's title track and Mick Jagger on co-vocals on the opener, a cover version of the Temptations '(You Gotta Walk) Don't Look Back'. Initially, the partnership between the Stones and Tosh might have been seen to be a marriage made in heaven, where the Stones would regain some outlaw chic and continue their love affair with Black music, while Peter Tosh would acquire a sprinkling of the glitter of global celebrity, which might catapult him over his erstwhile bandmate Bob Marley. Although Tosh would go on to become tour support for the Stones in 1979, the roots of a disillusionment with the relationship were already showing by this stage. Vivien Goldman suggests that Tosh referred to Jagger and Richards as 'two little batty baameclaat'.[9] The partnership did not last long, and the Stones and Tosh soon went their separate ways.

But is this a digression? Perhaps not. The rhythms on Tosh's album had criss-crossed the Black Atlantic numerous times before alighting on the mobile phone in Bobo's outdoor painting studio at the side of his wooden hut, with the music shifting and morphing as it went on its long journey. This is a key part of the story of reggae. Even before the recording was laid down at Dynamic Sounds in Kingston, the music found on *Bush Doctor* had changed numerous times, as the rhythms of enslaved Africans clashed and merged with the sounds of their captors. Following emancipation came the rhythm's long journey down from the hills and valleys to the towns and cities of Jamaica, where it would bump into both the music of Kumina and mento, the latter itself a musical fusion of African and European styles. By the early 1960s, this music was known to some as 'upside down R&B', more than hinting at musical roots that went beyond Jamaica, connecting ska to another great musical legacy of the Black Atlantic. Lyrically, ska went on to articulate the hopes and dreams of a new nation that were to be broken on the rocks of disillusionment as the Rasta faith and the sound of roots reggae developed side-by-side through the 1970s.

If Marcus Garvey was the midwife of the Rastafari, and Selassie the father of the family, Bob Marley was its most faithful son and the man who popularized reggae around the globe. Marley made for a great ambassador for reggae, but Peter Tosh stayed in the role of the militant, and on *Legalize It* and *Equal Rights*, he was free from the constraints of being in a band with Marley as its high-profile figurehead. But far from being uncompromising, *Bush Doctor* represented a partial break from reggae rather than a return to its essence. The mix by Karl Pitterson that is heard on the album is clearly aimed at an international rather than a Jamaican audience. Thirty years after it was recorded, a digitized file of the album bypasses all the musical changes of the subsequent decades, skipping past dancehall, punanny and gunplay, past the Tivoli Gardens massacre and the Reggae Revival, before finally alighting on Bobo's mobile phone, blasting out a trebly mix in a wooden hut with no electricity.

Earlier that day, all the family had taken a drumming lesson with Asif, an old friend. Asif had performed the talking drums on the morning of our wedding in Ampenyi fifteen years earlier, calling the invited to a relatively unplanned service, where I refused to repeat the word God to a bemused Registrar, quickly substituting it with Gaia, and where my wife would promise to honour me, but not to obey me as the Registrar had instructed. The drumming lesson took place on the precise spot where we were married. Rachel, Lily and Seán took to it easily, but my distinctly arrhythmic efforts seemed amateurish in comparison, as I added an extra beat into each bar, disrupting the work of the ensemble. As well as being tone deaf, I also have little sense of rhythm, as anyone who has ever seen me in a reggae dance will confirm. Despite my lack of formal musicological training, even I could hear that the music that Asif was playing was a distant relation of one-drop reggae, when Jamaican music swallowed a whole beat in the bar. Since last in Ghana, I had listened to reggae non-stop, yet here I was, ignoring the absence on which much of reggae was built, drumming 'four to the floor' like a typical tourist.

After the lesson, with European hands sore from the *djembe* drums, Asif continued, while I sat back and listened to the rhythms interacting with the birds and cicadas at sunset. I hesitate to call this authentic African drumming, for who knows the influences that have played on Asif's drumming style during his life? But the rhythms certainly sounded African to my ears, as they drifted out towards the Black Atlantic a short distance away, merging with the waves as they crashed against the rocks that protected the bay in which we swam.

I could still hear Asif's drumming as I went to visit Bobo and sat down beside his home. Like those pushed through the door of no return at Cape Coast Castle, Bobo is a Fante-speaking Akan, but at one point in our discussion, he was keen to emphasize to me that his principal heritage is as a member of the Tribe of Judah rather than that of the Fante. Warming to his theme, Bobo said:

> Selassie I is the Almighty I King, he is my teacher, he gives me I-tation . . . He is giving me more confidence to do my work, he is a great man, a great African, Emperor Selassie I, King of Kings, Lord of Lords, Conquering Lion of the Tribe of Judah.

So with our minds now on Selassie, I guided the discussion towards Marcus Mosiah Garvey and his Back to Africa ideology. I put to Bobo a question that I was nervous of asking. Why did Bobo, an African man, need a copy of a book by someone who had never visited the continent, despite evidence suggesting that at many points in his life Garvey had the wherewithal to do so? In the nicest way possible, Bobo abmonished me for questioning Garvey, and rightly so. 'If you are black, you are an African,' said Bobo, before explaining that it was through this vision that Garvey was able to inspire an entire diaspora to consider themselves to be truly African. As Bobo explained, it was Garvey's life's work

> to fight for equal rights and justice, and self-independence ... He was a great man, who could let you know who you are. You can do something, you can create something, and creativity rules the world. But he did make a mistake. He should have come! But only he knows why!

When it was time for me and my family to leave, we gave Bobo some gifts and he presented me with a painting of a flag that riffed on both the colours found within the Ghanaian flag along with the red, green and black standard favoured by Garvey. Bobo and I had discussed the symbolism previously and talked of how the design of the Ghanaian flag by Theodosia Okoh incorporates a black star to evoke Garvey's Black Star Line.[10] In his life, Garvey would see Africa's only uncolonized country invaded by Italy but he would die before its liberation. Neither did Garvey see his black star grace the flag of Ghana, a post-colonial success story but one still deeply impoverished by its relationship to an exploitative West and a rapacious global capitalism. As in Jamaica, decolonization remains incomplete, for although Ghana may be a republic with few ties to the UK other than cultural ones, it remains yoked to Western economies that continue to extract wealth from it. The Rastas call this Babylon, and rightly so.

As Bobo and I said our goodbyes, I had not a revelation, but a realization. *Positive Vibrations* is not only about the politics of reggae, but it is also what Garvey himself called for, namely the repositioning of African culture to sit at the pinnacle of humanity. This is what I have tried to do with *Positive Vibrations*, to tell the story of how an Afrocentric musical form has come to sit at the centre of a mighty music industry, while telling the story of the days of slavery and saying 'never again, never forget'. There are surely no stories more important than this one, and in my view there is no form of music more beautiful than reggae.

Bush Doctor had long finished, and Bobo's mobile phone was now silent. But I could still hear that sound. I could see it too, as it washed up again on Ghana's shores. And I could feel its weight and its depth. Telling the story of a time gone by, not just of the days of slavery, but of the days before those. The days of beauty and splendour, of man and womankind living in harmony with themselves and their environment. This music also tells the story of a time in the future, of a return to a oneness with the world and its oceans. I look out to the Black Atlantic and then back to Africa and think, 'This is where reggae is really from.'

REFERENCES

INTRODUCTION

1 Michael de Koningh and Laurence Cane-Honeysett, *Young, Gifted and Black: The Story of Trojan Records* (London, 2003), p. 58.
2 Andrew Kopkind, 'Reggae: The Steady Rock of Black Jamaica', *Ramparts*, June 1973, p. 50.

1 'LOOK TO AFRICA': THE POLITICS OF THE RASTAFARI

1 See *The Jamaican New Testament* (*Di Jamiekan Nyuu Testiment*) (Jamaica, 2012), line 9.
2 Gad Heuman, *The Killing Time: The Morant Bay Rebellion in Jamaica* (London, 1994).
3 Rupert Lewis, *Marcus Garvey: Anti-Colonial Champion* (London, 1987), p. 45.
4 Colin Grant, *Negro with a Hat: The Rise and Fall of Marcus Garvey* (London, 2009), pp. 73–94.
5 Ibid., p. 164.
6 Marcus Garvey, *The Marcus Garvey and Universal Negro Improvement Association Papers*, ed. R. A. Hill (Los Angeles, CA, 1983), vol. I, p. 5.
7 Author's own transcription of the audio recording of Marcus Garvey in the G. Robert Vincent Voice Library, Michigan State University, catalogue record b5312190.
8 Grant, *Negro with a Hat*, pp. 388–412.
9 Kwame Nkrumah, *Ghana: The Autobiography of Kwame Nkrumah* (New York, 1976), p. 45.
10 M. G. Smith, R. Augier and R. Nettleford, *Report on the Rastafari Movement in Kingston, Jamaica* (Kingston, 1960), p. 8.
11 Robert Hill, *Dread History: Leonard P. Howell and Millenarian Visions in the Early Rastafarian Religion* (Chicago, IL, 2001), p. 14.
12 Amy J. Garvey, *The Philosophy and Opinions of Marcus Garvey: Or, Africa for the Africans* (New York, 2021), pp. 51–2.
13 Marcus Garvey, *The Marcus Garvey and Universal Negro Improvement Association Papers*, ed. R. A. Hill (Los Angeles, CA, 1983), vol. V, p. 565.
14 Leonard E. Barrett Sr, *The Rastafarians* (Boston, MA, 1997), p. 81.
15 Marcus Garvey, *The Marcus Garvey and Universal Negro Improvement Association Papers*, ed. R. A. Hill (Los Angeles, CA, 1983), vol. VII, p. 441.

16 Hill, *Dread History*, p. 25.

17 Marcus Garvey, 'The Work That Has Been Done', *Black Man*, July 1938, p. 10.

18 Garvey, *The Marcus Garvey . . . Papers*, vol. VII, p. 635.

19 Marcus Garvey, *Black Man*, January 1937, p. 8.

20 Grant, *Negro with a Hat*, p. 440.

21 Garvey, *The Marcus Garvey . . . Papers*, vol. VII, p. 739 and p. 741.

22 Paul Gilroy, 'Black Fascism', *Transition*, 81/82 (2000), pp. 70–91. The original source seems to be an interview with the American journalist Joel A. Rogers in his *World's Great Men of Color* (London, 1996), vol. II.

23 Amy J. Garvey, *Philosophy and Opinions of Marcus Garvey* (London, 1967), p. 37.

24 Alden Whitman, 'Haile Selassie of Ethiopia Dies at 83', *New York Times*, 28 August 1975.

25 Asfa-Wossen Asserate, *King of Kings: The Triumph and Tragedy of Emperor Haile Selassie I of Ethiopia* (London, 2015), pp. 348–50.

26 Kenneth Bilby and E. Leib, 'Kumina, the Howellite Church, and the Emergence of Rastafarian Traditional Music in Jamaica', in *Rastafari in the New Millennium*, ed. Michael Barnett (Syracuse, NY, 2012), pp. 255–69.

27 Robert A. Hill and B. Blair, *Marcus Garvey: Life and Lessons. A Centennial Companion to the Marcus Garvey and Universal Negro Improvement Association Papers* (Berkeley and Los Angeles, CA, 1987), p. xx.

28 Joseph Thompson, 'From Judah to Jamaica: The Psalms in Rastafari Reggae', *Religion and the Arts*, XVI (2012), p. 335.

29 Barrett Sr, *The Rastafarians*, p. 85.

30 Ibid., p. 104.

31 Marcus Garvey, *Message to the People: The Course of African Philosophy*, ed. Tony Martin (Fitchburg, MA, 1986), p. 25.

32 Ibid., p. 26.

33 Ibid., p. 25.

34 Hill, *Dread History*, p. 8.

35 Barrett Sr, *The Rastafarians*, p. 146.

36 Barry Chevannes, *Rastafari: Roots and Ideology* (Syracuse, NY, 1994), p. 43.

37 Ennis B. Edmonds, 'The Structure and Ethos of Rastafari', in *Chanting Down Babylon: The Rastafari Reader*, ed. N. S. Murrell, W. D. Spencer and A. A. McFarlane (Philadelphia, PA, 1998), p. 356.

38 Michael Barnett, 'The Many Faces of Rasta: Doctrinal Diversity within the Rastafari Movement', *Caribbean Quarterly*, VLI/2 (2005), p. 69.

39 Barrett Sr, *The Rastafarians*, pp. 229–30.

40 Monique Bedasse, 'Rasta Evolution: The Theology of the Twelve Tribes of Israel', *Journal of Black Studies*, XL/5 (2010), pp. 960–73.

41 Michael Barnett, 'From Wareika Hill to Zimbabwe: Exploring the Role of Rastafari Music', in *Rastafari in the New Millennium*, ed. M. Barnett (Syracuse, NY, 2012), p. 277.

42 Barrett Sr, *The Rastafarians*, p. 118.

43 Ibid., pp. 158–9.
44 Chris Summers, 'The Rastafarians' Flawed African "Promised Land"', www.bbc.co.uk, accessed 25 October 2018.
45 Darren J. N. Middleton, 'As It Is in Zion: Seeking the Rastafari in Ghana, West Africa', *Black Theology*, IV/2 (2006), p. 159.
46 Ibid., p. 169.

2 'MISS JAMAICA': MUSIC AND POLITICS, 1945–70

1 Andrew Kopkind, 'Reggae: The Steady Rock of Black Jamaica', *Ramparts*, June 1973, p. 50.
2 Perry Henzell (director), *The Harder They Come* [film] (Jamaica, International Films Inc., 1972).
3 Peter Mason, *Jamaica in Focus: A Guide to the People, Politics and Culture*, 2nd edn (New York, 2000), p. 29.
4 Harold Macmillan, *Pointing the Way, 1959–61* (London, 1972), p. 156.
5 Michael E. Veal, *Dub: Soundscapes and Shattered Songs in Jamaican Reggae* (Middletown, CT, 2007), p. 49.
6 See 'Stanley Motta – Motta's Recording Studio Kingston – MRS', www.bigmikeydread.wordpress.com, accessed 20 June 2019.
7 Chris Salewicz, *Keep On Running: The Story of Island Records* (London, 2009), p. 10.
8 Timothy White, *Catch a Fire: The Life of Bob Marley* (New York, 2006), p. 241.
9 Chris Salewicz, *Bob Marley: The Untold Story* (London, 2009), p. 206.
10 Michael Barnett, 'From Wareika Hill to Zimbabwe: Exploring the Role of Rastafari Music', in *Rastafari in the New Millennium*, ed. M. Barnett (Syracuse, NY, 2012), pp. 270–71.
11 David Katz, *Solid Foundation: An Oral History of Reggae* (London, 2003), p. 2.
12 Verena Reckord, 'From Burru Drums to Reggae Ridims: The Evolution of Rasta Music', in *Chanting Down Babylon: The Rastafari Reader*, ed. N. S. Murrell, W. D. Spencer and A. A. McFarlane (Philadelphia, PA, 1998), p. 235.
13 Ibid., p. 236.
14 Brian Bonitto, 'Sounds of Seaga', *Jamaica Observer*, 29 December 2019.
15 Katz, *Solid Foundation*, p. 19.
16 Veal, *Dub*, p. 48.
17 Lloyd Bradley, *Bass Culture: When Reggae Was King* (London, 2000), p. 210.
18 Edward Seaga, *My Life and Leadership*, vol. I: *Clash of Ideologies, 1930–1980* (Oxford, 2009), p. 123.
19 Balford Henry, 'Dancehall Politics', *The Gleaner*, 16 March 2001.
20 Katz, *Solid Foundation*, p. 36.
21 Dave Thompson, *Reggae and Caribbean Music* (San Francisco, CA, 2002), p. 13.
22 Seaga, *My Life and Leadership*: vol. I, pp. 113–14.

23 Ibid., p. 120.
24 Jim White, 'Where There's a Hit There's a Writ: A Rock Star's Guide to . . .', *The Independent*, 24 June 1994.
25 Chris Salewicz, 'Millie Small, Obituary', *The Guardian*, 6 May 2020.
26 Dennis O. Howard, *The Creative Echo Chamber: Contemporary Music Production in Kingston Jamaica* (Kingston, 2009), n.p.
27 Seaga, *My Life and Leadership*, vol. 1, p. 121.
28 Ibid., p. 123.
29 Kevin O'Brien Chang and Wayne Chen, *Reggae Routes: The Story of Jamaican Music* (Philadelphia, PA, 1998), p. 91.
30 Seaga, *My Life and Leadership*, vol. 1, p. 93.
31 Amanda Sives, 'Changing Patrons, from Politician to Drug Don: Clientelism in Downtown Kingston, Jamaica', *Latin American Perspectives*, XXIX/5 (2002), pp. 74–5. See also Anita M. Waters, *Race, Class and Political Symbols* (New Brunswick, NJ, 1985), pp. 64–5.
32 Darrell E. Levy, *Michael Manley: The Making of a Leader* (London, 1989), p. 138.
33 Colin Clarke, 'Politics, Violence and Drugs in Kingston, Jamaica', *Bulletin of Latin American Research*, XXV/3 (2006), p. 427.
34 Laurie Gunst, *Born fi' Dead: A Journey through the Yardie Underworld* (Edinburgh, 1995), p. 84.
35 Clinton Hutton, 'Oh Rudie: Jamaican Popular Music and the Narrative of Urban Badness in the Making of a Postcolonial Society', *Caribbean Quarterly: A Journal of Caribbean Culture*, LVI/4 (2010), pp. 23–4.
36 Katz, *Solid Foundation*, p. 81.
37 Erin Mackie, *Rakes, Highwaymen, and Pirates: The Making of the Modern Gentleman in the Eighteenth Century* (Baltimore, MD, 2009), p. 123.
38 Chang and Chen, *Reggae Routes*, p. 92.
39 West Indies Meteorological Service, *Jamaica Weather Report: Monthly Summary of Observations* (Kingston, 1966). See also previous year's reports from the same source.
40 Thibault Ehrengardt, *Reggae and Politics in the 1970s* (Paris, 2020), p. 62.
41 Michael de Koningh and Laurence Cane-Honeysett, *Young, Gifted and Black: The Story of Trojan Records* (London, 2003), pp. 27–8.
42 Norman Jopling, 'It's the Blue-Beat Craze', *Record Mirror*, 15 February 1964.
43 De Koningh and Cane-Honeysett, *Young, Gifted and Black*, pp. 27–34.
44 Ibid., pp. 35–44.

3 'BETTER MUST COME': ROOTS REGGAE AND THE POLITICS OF JAMAICA IN THE 1970S

1 Larry Katz, 'Bob Marley Raps It Up in Boston', *The Beat*, X/3 (1991), pp. 36–8.
2 Michael Smith, 'Me Cyaan Believe It', in *It A Come: Poems by Michael Smith*, ed. Michael Smith and Mervyn Morris (London, 1986), p. 13.
3 Quoted in Stephen David, *Reggae International* (London, 1983), p. 149.

4   Anita M. Waters, *Race, Class and Political Symbols: Rastafari and Reggae in Jamaican Politics* (New Brunswick, NJ, 1985), pp. 99–100.
5   Thibault Ehrengardt, *Reggae and Politics in the 1970s* (Paris, 2020), p. 13.
6   See radio interview with Prince Buster, www.rodigan.com, accessed 29 November 2018.
7   Waters, *Race, Class and Political Symbols*, pp. 133–4.
8   Dorian Lynskey, *33 Revolutions per Minute: A History of Protest Songs* (London, 2010), p. 315.
9   Ehrengardt, *Reggae and Politics in the 1970s*, p. 36.
10 Ibid., p. 44.
11 Andrew Ross, 'Mr Reggae DJ, Meet the International Monetary Fund', *Black Renaissance*, I/3 (1998), pp. 209–32.
12 Chris Salewicz, *Bob Marley: The Untold Story* (London, 2009), p. 188.
13 Colin Grant, *I & I. The Natural Mystics: Marley, Tosh and Wailer* (London, 2011), p. 198.
14 David Katz, *Solid Foundation: An Oral History of Reggae* (London, 2003), p. 171.
15 Lloyd Bradley, *Bass Culture: When Reggae Was King* (London, 2000), p. 285.
16 Heather Augustyn, *Ska: An Oral History* (Jefferson, NC, 2010), p. 69.
17 S. H. Fernando Jr, 'Murder Dem: The Turbulent Saga of Reggae Stars and Violent Crime', *Medium*, 10 December 2014.
18 Michael de Koningh and Laurence Cane-Honeysett, *Young, Gifted and Black: The Story of Trojan Records* (London, 2003), p. 74.
19 Bradley, *Bass Culture*, p. 398.
20 Salewicz, *Bob Marley*, p. 206.
21 Grant, *I & I. The Natural Mystics*, p. 210.
22 Waters, *Race, Class and Political Symbols*, p. 120.
23 Sybil E. Hibbert, 'Jamaica's First Treason/Felony Trial Featuring the Rev. Claudius Henry', *Jamaica Observer*, 10 December 2013.
24 Waters, *Race, Class and Political Symbols*, pp. 129–35.
25 Ibid., p. 112.
26 See 'I Have It Now! The Rod Rules in Central Kingston Tonight', *Daily Gleaner*, 28 February 1972, p. 29.
27 See 'Seaga Denies Carrying Violence to West Kingston', *Daily Gleaner*, 24 February 1972, p. 44.
28 Ibid., p. 44
29 Waters, *Race, Class and Political Symbols*, p. 112.
30 Ibid., p. 106.
31 Ibid.
32 Ibid., p. 176.
33 Edward Seaga, *My Life and Leadership*, vol. I: *Clash of Ideologies, 1930–1980* (Oxford, 2009), p. 209.
34 Ehrengardt, *Reggae and Politics in the 1970s*, p. 66.
35 Mike Alleyne, '"Babylon Makes the Rules": The Politics of the Reggae Crossover', *Social and Economic Studies*, XLVII, pt 1 (1998), p. 67.
36 Jo-Ann Greene, 'Burning Spear, Artist Biography', www.allmusic.com, accessed 11 July 2019.

37 Ehrengardt, *Reggae and Politics in the 1970s*, p. 46.
38 Stephen Cooper, '"How Do You Fight the Devil with a Lawyer?", An Interview with Reggae Legend Max Romeo', www.counterpunch.org, 5 April 2019.
39 See 'PM Says It Is Wrong to Cut Rastas' Hair', *Daily Gleaner*, 12 January 1976, p. 15.
40 Stephen A. King, 'The Co-optation of a "Revolution": Rastafari, Reggae and the Rhetoric of Social Control', *Howard Journal of Communication*, X/2 (1999), p. 84.
41 Neville G. Callam, 'Invitation to Docility: Defusing the Rastafarian Challenge', *Caribbean Journal of Religious Studies*, III (1980), pp. 28–48.
42 Lynskey, *33 Revolutions per Minute*, p. 323.
43 Dennis Howard, 'Dancehall Political Patronage and Gun Violence', *Jamaica Journal*, XXXIII (2010), p. 10.
44 Waters, *Race, Class and Political Symbols*, p. 126.
45 Michael Manley, 'Not for Sale', address to the 38th Annual Conference of the People's National Party, 19 September 1976.
46 Waters, *Race, Class and Political Symbols*, p. 136.
47 See 'Review of the State of Emergency' (1977), *Ministry Paper*, XXII (National Library of Jamaica).
48 See 'Arms Cache Found, Jamaica Declares State of Emergency', *New York Times*, 20 June 1976.
49 H. G. Helps, 'Charles: Give Basic Schools My Money', *Jamaica Observer*, 3 January 2021.
50 See 'Sympathy for Detainee', *Daily Gleaner*, 12 September 1976.
51 Michael Burke, 'State of Emergency, 1976', *Jamaica Observer*, 19 June 2014.
52 Evelyne Huber Stephens and John D. Stephens, *Democratic Socialism in Jamaica* (London, 1986), p. 136.
53 Seaga, *My Life and Leadership*, vol. I, pp. 249–64.
54 Michael Manley, *Jamaica: Struggle in the Periphery* (London, 1982), p. 142.
55 For claims that it was Marley's idea, see Grant, *I & I. The Natural Mystics*, p. 198 and Don Taylor, *So Much Things to Say* (London, 1995), pp. 131–48. For the alternative claim, see Timothy White, *Catch a Fire: The Life of Bob Marley* (New York, 2006), p. 287.
56 White, *Catch a Fire*, p. 287.
57 Rita Marley with H. Jones, *No Woman, No Cry: My Life with Bob Marley* (New York, 2004), p. 146.
58 Salewicz, *Bob Marley*, p. 296.
59 Ehrengardt, *Reggae and Politics in the 1970s*, p. 111.
60 Casey Gane-McCalla, *Inside the CIA's Secret War in Jamaica* (Los Angeles, CA, 2016), p. 42.
61 Laurie Gunst, *Born Fi' Dead: A Journey through the Yardie Underworld* (Edinburgh, 1995).
62 Gane-McCalla, *Inside the CIA's Secret War*, p. 42.
63 See 'Crack King Dudus Is Our Robin Hood', *The Express*, 27 May 2010.
64 Ioan Grillo, *Gangster Warlords: Drug Dollars, Killing Fields and the New Politics of Latin America* (London, 2016).

65 Taylor, *So Much Things to Say*, p. 140.

66 Vivien Goldman, 'Dread, Beat and Blood', *The Guardian*, 16 July 2006.

67 White, *Catch a Fire*, p. 287.

68 Ibid., p. 292.

69 Waters, *Race, Class and Political Symbols*, p. 190.

70 White, *Catch a Fire*, p. 370.

71 Taylor, *So Much Things to Say*, p. 168.

72 Don Taylor, *Guns and Ganja: The Secret Life of Bob Marley* (London, 2003), p. 158.

73 Roger Steffens, *So Much Things to Say: The Oral History of Bob Marley* (New York, 2017), p. 257.

74 White, *Catch a Fire*, p. 335.

75 Seaga, *My Life and Leadership*, vol. 1, p. 260.

76 Waters, *Race, Class and Political Symbols*, p. 162.

77 Garfield Higgins, '"Politics Songs" and Michael Manley's Message', *Jamaica Observer*, 1 June 2014; Mel Cooke, '"I Man Born Ya" Written in Pre-1976 Election Optimism', *The Gleaner*, 18 October 2009.

78 Howard, 'Dancehall Political Patronage and Gun Violence', p. 10.

79 See '"My Leader Born Yah" Singer Shocked, Not Upset over JLP's Use of Song', https://jamaica.loopnews.com, 25 October 2017.

80 See 'Man Ah Warrior: The Tappa Zukie Story', https://daily. redbullmusicacademy.com, accessed 18 March 2021.

81 Steffens, *So Much Things to Say*, p. 266.

82 Ibid., p. 346.

83 David Panton, *Jamaica's Michael Manley: The Great Transformation* (Kingston, 1993), p. 54.

84 Stephens and Stephens, *Democratic Socialism*, p. 116.

85 Amanda Sives, 'Changing Patrons, from Politician to Drug Don: Clientelism in Downtown Kingston, Jamaica', *Latin American Perspectives*, XXIX/5 (2002), pp. 74–5. See also Waters, *Race, Class and Political Symbols*, p. 77.

86 See 'Jamaica: Jah Kingdom Goes to Waste', *Time*, CVII/27 (1976).

87 Manley, *Jamaica*, p. 138.

88 Grillo, *Gangster Warlords*, p. 134.

89 Manley, *Jamaica*, p. 194.

90 Kevin Edmonds, 'Guns, Gangs and Garrison Communities in the Politics of Jamaica', *Race and Class*, LVII/4 (2016), p. 55.

91 Seaga, *My Life and Leadership*, vol. 1, p. 5.

92 Manley, *Jamaica*, p. 160.

93 Katz, *Solid Foundation*, p. 293.

94 Gane-McCalla, *Inside the CIA's Secret War*, p. 9.

95 Steffens, *So Much Things to Say*, p. 293.

96 Grillo, *Gangster Warlords*, p. 137.

97 Gunst, *Born Fi' Dead*, p. 196.

98 Howard Campbell, 'Tommy Cowan and the Claudie Massop Link', *Jamaica Observer*, 22 April 2018.

99 Seaga, *My Life and Leadership*, vol. 1, p. 291.

100 Gunst, *Born Fi' Dead*, p. 197.

101 Alan Eyre, 'Political Violence and Urban Geography in Kingston, Jamaica', *Geographical Review*, LXXIV/1 (1984), p. 30.

102 Sives, 'Changing Patrons', pp. 74–5. See also Waters, *Race, Class and Political Symbols*, pp. 64–5.

103 Amy J. Garvey, *Philosophy and Opinions of Marcus Garvey* (London, 1967), p. 10.

104 Barry Chevannes, *Rastafari Roots and Ideology* (Syracuse, NY, 1994), p. 104.

105 Lynskey, *33 Revolutions per Minute*, p. 330.

106 Haile Selassie, *Important Utterances of H.I.M. Emperor Haile Selassie I, 1963–1972* (Addis Ababa, 1972).

107 Leonard E. Barrett Sr, *The Rastafarians* (Boston, MA, 1997), pp. 254–6.

108 M. G. Smith, R. Augier and R. Nettleford, *The Rastafari Movement in Kingston, Jamaica* (Kingston, 1960), p. 9.

109 Horace Campbell, *Rasta and Resistance: From Marcus Garvey to Walter Rodney* (Trenton, NJ, 1987), p. 96.

110 Neil. J. Savishinsky, 'African Dimensions of the Jamaican Rastafarian Movement', in *Chanting Down Babylon: The Rastafari Reader*, ed. N. S. Murrell, W. D. Spencer and A. A. McFarlane (Philadelphia, PA, 1998), p. 133.

111 Michael Barnett, 'From Wareika Hill to Zimbabwe: Exploring the Role of Rastafari Music', in *Rastafari in the New Millennium*, ed. M. Barnett (Syracuse, NY, 2012), p. 276.

112 Sebastian Clarke, *Jah Music: The Evolution of the Popular Jamaican Song* (London, 1980), p. 53.

113 Kenneth Bilby and E. Leib, 'Kumina, the Howellite Church, and the Emergence of Rastafarian Traditional Music in Jamaica', in *Rastafari in the New Millennium*, ed. Michael Barnett (Syracuse, NY, 2012), pp. 255–69.

114 Verena Reckord, 'From Burru Drums to Reggae Ridims: The Evolution of Rasta Music', in *Chanting Down Babylon: The Rastafari Reader*, ed. N. S. Murrell, W. D. Spencer and A. A. McFarlane (Philadelphia, PA, 1998), p. 234.

115 Verena Reckord, 'Rastafarian Music: An Introductory Study', *Jamaica Journal*, XI/1–2 (1977), pp. 6–9.

116 Barrett Sr, *The Rastafarians*, p. 190.

117 Reckord, 'From Burru Drums to Reggae Ridims', p. 248.

4 'INGLAN IS A BITCH': REGGAE CROSSOVER IN THE UK

1 Linton Kwesi Johnson, *Inglan Is a Bitch* (London, 1980), p. 6.

2 Ernest Cashmore, *Rastaman: Rastafarian Movement in England* (London, 1979), p. 197.

3 Stuart Hall, C. Critcher, T. Jefferson, J. Clarke and B. Roberts, *Policing the Crisis: Mugging, the State and Law and Order* (London, 1978), p. 301.

4 See '1976: Notting Hill Carnival Ends in Riot', http://news.bbc.co.uk, accessed 11 April 2019.

5 Jon Savage, *England's Dreaming: Anarchy, Sex Pistols, Punk Rock, and Beyond* (New York, 1992), p. 238.

6 Vivien Goldman, 'Culture Clash: Bob Marley, Joe Strummer and the Punky Reggae Party', www.guardian.com, 19 September 2014.

7 Simon Reynolds, *Rip It Up and Start Again: Postpunk, 1978–1984* (London, 2005), p. 81.

8 Daniel Rachel, *Walls Come Tumbling Down: The Music and Politics of Rock against Racism, 2 Tone and Red Wedge* (London, 2016), p. xix.

9 Ibid., p. 51.

10 Dave Simpson, 'Roots Manoeuvre', *The Guardian*, 20 July 2007.

11 Rachel, *Walls Come Tumbling Down*, p. 58.

12 Ibid., p. 57.

13 Reynolds, *Rip It Up and Start Again*, p. 201.

14 See *Sounds*, 2 September 1978.

15 See 'S1 – The Specials', www.bandlogojukebox.com, accessed 1 November 2021.

16 Rachel, *Walls Come Tumbling Down*, p. 5.

17 Ibid., p. 277.

18 Ibid., p. 244.

19 J. Duffy, 'An Embarrassment No More', http://news.bbc.co.uk, 24 November 2005.

20 Rachel, *Walls Come Tumbling Down*, p. 264.

21 John Benyon 'The Riots: Perceptions and Distortions', in *Scarman and After: Essays Reflecting on Lord Scarman's Report, the Riots and Their Aftermath*, ed. J. Benyon (Oxford, 1984), pp. 38–9.

22 Jon Kelly, 'The Specials: How Ghost Town Defined an Era', www.bbc.co.uk, 17 June 2011.

23 Rachel, *Walls Come Tumbling Down*, p. 325.

24 Ibid., p. 72.

25 Ibid., p. 317.

26 Paul Lewis, 'Blair Peach: After 31 Years Met Police Say "Sorry" for Their Role in His Killing', *The Guardian*, 27 April 2010.

27 J. Denman and P. McDonald, 'Unemployment Statistics from 1881 to the Present Day', *Labour Market Trends*, civ/15–18 (1996), p. 10.

28 See 'On This Day August 29, 1981', *The Times*, 29 August 2007.

29 See World Bank annual rankings of GDP at http://en.classora.com, accessed 9 May 2019.

30 Dee Lahiri, 'I Don't Think I Can Die before I Find Out What Happened to My Son', *The Guardian*, 15 May 2001.

31 Linton Kwesi Johnson, *Selected Poems* (London, 1996).

32 Rachel, *Walls Come Tumbling Down*, p. 333.

33 Ethlie Ann Vare, 'UB40's "Labour" Paying Off', *Billboard*, 10 March 1984, p. 53.

34 See 'The Music Diaries – Lord Creator turns 81', *The Gleaner*, 2 September 2016.

35 Rachel, *Walls Come Tumbling Down*, p. 77.

36 Ibid., p. 82.

37 Paul Gilroy, *There Ain't No Black in the Union Jack* (London, 1987), pp. 260–65.

38 Ibid., p. 262.

39 Simon Reynolds, 'Old Bill Dutty Babylon', www.energyflashbysimonreynolds.com, 13 July 2019.

40 Gilroy, *There Ain't No Black in the Union Jack*, p. 262.

41 See 'Reggae Star Smiley Culture Stabbed Himself during Police Raid', www.bbc.co.uk, 2 July 2013.

5 'RING THE ALARM': THE 1980S AND THE DECADE OF DANCEHALL

1 Sonjah Stanley Niaah, '"Dis Slackness Ting": A Dichotomizing Master Narrative in Jamaican Dancehall', *Caribbean Quarterly*, LI/2 (2005), p. 59.

2 Anita M. Waters, *Race, Class and Political Symbols: Rastafari and Reggae in Jamaican Politics* (New Brunswick, NJ, 1985), p. 231.

3 Ibid., pp. 228–40.

4 Garfield Higgins, '"Politics Songs" and Michael Manley's Message', *Jamaica Observer*, 1 June 2014.

5 Waters, *Race, Class and Political Symbols*, pp. 240–44.

6 Michael Manley, *Jamaica: Struggle in the Periphery* (London, 1982), pp. 194–5.

7 Darrell E. Levy, *Michael Manley: The Making of a Leader* (London, 1989), p. 23.

8 Faye V. Harrison, 'Global Apartheid, Foreign Policy, and Human Rights', in *Transnational Blackness: Navigating the Global Color Line*, ed. M. Marable and V. Agard-Jones (New York, 2008), p. 20.

9 Kevin Edmonds, 'Guns, Gangs and Garrison Communities in the Politics of Jamaica', *Race and Class*, LVII/4 (2016), pp. 54–75.

10 Laurie Gunst, *Born Fi' Dead: A Journey through the Yardie Underworld* (Edinburgh, 1995), p. 117.

11 See 'U.S. Concedes Contras Linked to Drugs, but Denies Leadership Involved', *AP News*, 17 April 1986.

12 See 'Jamaica', www.globalsecurity.org, accessed 30 October 2020.

13 Edmonds, 'Guns, Gangs and Garrison Communities', p. 65.

14 K. C. Samuels, *Dudus, 1992–2010: His Rise – His Reign – His Demise. A Chronology of Lawlessness* (Kingston, 2011), n.p.

15 Dennis Howard, 'Dancehall Political Patronage and Gun Violence', *Jamaica Journal*, XXXIII (2010), p. 10.

16 Richard Williams, 'Bob Marley's Funeral, 21 May 1981: A Day of Jamaican History', *The Guardian*, 24 April 2011.

17 Steve Barrow and Peter Dalton, *Reggae: The Rough Guide* (London, 1997), pp. 15–19.

18 Ibid., p. 115.

19 Michael E. Veal, *Dub: Soundscapes and Shattered Songs in Jamaican Reggae* (Middletown, CT, 2007), p. 52.

20 Eddie Chambers, *Roots and Culture: Cultural Politics in the Making of Black Britain* (London, 2017), p. 112.
21 Melissa Bradshaw, 'Pay It All Back: Adrian Sherwood on 30 Years of On-U Sound', www.quietus.com, 19 April 2011.
22 Veal, *Dub*, p. 79.
23 Howard, 'Dancehall Political Patronage and Gun Violence', p. 12.
24 Thibault Ehrengardt, *Reggae and Politics in the 1970s* (Paris, 2020), p. 89.
25 Angus Taylor, 'Interview with Super Cat', www.reggaeville.com, accessed 18 September 2019.
26 Stephen Cooper, 'Scientist v. Cooper', www.counterpunch.org, 25 January 2019.
27 Ibid.
28 Angus Taylor, 'Interview: Scientist', www.unitedreggae.com, 24 September 2008.
29 Ibid.
30 Barrow and Dalton, *Reggae*, p. 233.
31 Alan Walsh, '"It's Not a Dirty Song At All," says Max Romeo', *Melody Maker*, 5 July 1969.
32 Deanne Pearson, 'Here Comes ... Barrington Levy', *No. 1*, 23 February 1985.
33 James Trew, 'How Casio Accidentally Started Reggae's Digital Revolution', www.endgadget.com, 12 April 2015.
34 Lloyd Stanbury, *Reggae Roadblocks: A Music Business Development Perspective* (Mississauga, 2015), p. 77.
35 Veal, *Dub*, p. 188.
36 Howard Campbell, 'Greensleeves Records Paves Way for Dancehall', *Jamaica Observer*, 4 July 2012.
37 Chris Salewicz, 'Obituary: Junjo Lawes', *The Independent*, 26 July 1999.
38 See 'Zest Group PLC Acquisition of Greensleeves', www.investegate.co.uk, 7 March 2006.
39 Wayne Robins, 'VP Celebrates 25 Years', *Billboard*, 8 May 2004, p. 21.
40 Ibid., p. 22.
41 Jason Toynbee, *Bob Marley: Herald of a Postcolonial World?* (Cambridge, 2007), p. 203.
42 Timothy White, *Catch a Fire: The Life of Bob Marley* (New York, 2006), p. 351.
43 Ibid., pp. 345–55.
44 Ibid., p. 378.
45 Ibid., p. 389.
46 Maureen Sheridan, 'Island Records Subsidiary Buys Marley's Assets, Despite Protests', *Billboard*, 21 January 1989, p. 95.
47 White, *Catch a Fire*, pp. 395–6.
48 Don Jeffrey, 'Copyrights "Scorch" Jamaican Artists', *Billboard*, 16 July 1994, p. 92.
49 Ibid.
50 Richard L. Hudson and L. Landro, 'Unit of Philips Agrees to Buy Island Records', *Wall Street Journal*, 2 August 1989, p. 1.
51 Ibid.

52 Ibid.

53 Ibid.

54 Stephen Delphin, 'Dancehall History: A Clevie Browne Interview from Steely and Clevie', www.academia.edu, January 2013.

55 Wayne Marshall, 'Dem Bow, Dembow, Dembo: Translation and Transnation in Reggaeton', *Song and Popular Culture*, LIII (2008), p. 140.

56 Kevin O'Brien Chang and Wayne Chen, *Reggae Routes: The Story of Jamaican Music* (Philadelphia, PA, 1998), p. 178.

57 See 'Beyond "Bam Bam": Dancehall Icon Sister Nancy on Her Improbable Career', http://daily.redbullmusicacademy.com, 21 March 2017.

58 Kimmo Matthews, 'George Phang in Police Hands', *Jamaica Observer*, 28 May 2010.

59 Rick Sawyer, 'The Tragedy of Tenor Saw', *JAMSBIO Magazine*, 4 September 2008.

60 Nazuk Kochhar, 'Ain't No Stopping Sister Nancy Now', www.thefader.com, 14 June 2017.

61 Ibid.

62 Cat Roberts, 'Sister Nancy', http://diplomatsofsound.com, accessed 28 February 2019.

63 See 'Beyond "Bam Bam"'.

64 Donna P. Hope, *Inna di Dancehall: Popular Culture and the Politics of Identity in Jamaica* (Kingston, 2006), p. 9.

65 Ibid., p. 46.

66 Susan Faludi, *Backlash: The Undeclared War Against Women* (New York, 1991).

67 Hope, *Inna di Dancehall*, p. 48.

68 See 'Wailer Feels the Sting', *Daily Gleaner*, 28 December 1990.

69 Hope, *Inna di Dancehall*, p. 48.

6 'YUH NUH READY FI DIS YET': WOMEN AND THE POLITICS OF DANCEHALL AND REGGAE, 1990–2010

1 Joshua Jelly-Schapiro, 'An Interview with Lady Saw [Queen of the Dancehall] "I'm Famous Because of My Slackness"', *Believer*, LXXXIII (2011).

2 See 'Lady Saw', www.reggaetimes.com, 29 April 2008.

3 Nadine White, 'Marion Hall: Life after Lady Saw', www.voice-online.co.uk, 21 October 2016.

4 Tyler K. McDermott, 'V Exclusive: Patra on Her Absence, New Music, and Female Sexuality in Reggae', www.vibe.com, 23 June 2012.

5 Claudia Gardner, 'Macka Diamond Says Her Dancehall Career Still Popping, Fans Urged Her to Retire', www.urbanislandz.com, 14 October 2019.

6 Ibid.

7 Elena Oumano, 'Women Increase Number, Scope of Roles in Reggae', *Billboard*, 27 January 1996, p. 37.

8 Jean Lowrie-Chin, 'Louise Speaks Out', www.jamaicans.com, accessed
    4 November 2020.
9 Oumano, 'Women Increase Number', p. 37.
10 Ibid.
11 Ibid.
12 Stephanie Lyew, 'Rebel Salute 2020: Lady G, Minister Grange Lobby
    for More Women on the Big Stage', *The Gleaner*, 19 January 2020.
13 Suzanne LaFont, 'Gender Wars in Jamaica', *Global Studies in Culture
    and Power*, VII/2 (2000), pp. 233–60.

7 'NOBODY CAN SING "BOOM BYE BYE" FOR ME': MEN AND THE POLITICS OF DANCEHALL AND REGGAE, 1990–2010

1 Noel M. Cowell, 'Public Discourse, Popular Culture and Attitudes
    towards Homosexuals in Jamaica', *Social and Economic Studies*, LX/1
    (2011), p. 35.
2 Dennis Howard, 'Dancehall Political Patronage and Gun Violence',
    Jamaica Journal, XXXIII (2010), p. 11.
3 Angus Taylor, 'Interview with Super Cat', www.reggaeville.com,
    accessed 18 September 2019.
4 Colin Larkin, *The Virgin Encyclopaedia of Reggae* (London, 1998),
    p. 286.
5 Donna Hope, 'Dons and Shottas: Performing Violent Masculinity in
    Dancehall Culture', *Social and Economic Studies*, LV/1–2 (2006), p. 120.
6 See 'Donovan Germain', http://penthouserecords.free.fr, accessed
    11 July 2019.
7 Tracey Skelton, '"Boom, Bye, Bye": Jamaican Ragga and Gay
    Resistance', in *Mapping Desire: Geographies of Sexuality*, ed. David Bell
    and G. Valentine (London, 1995), p. 246.
8 Ransdell Pierson, '"Kill Gays" Hit Song Stirs Fury', *New York Post*,
    24/5 October 1992, p. 5; Skelton, '"Boom, Bye, Bye"', p. 247.
9 Mike Hajimichael, 'Homophobia and Reggae: Shabba Ranks on *The
    Word* – Every Little Action Causes a Reaction', in *Revisiting Sexualities
    in the 21st Century*, ed. C. N. Phellas (Newcastle, 2015), p. 118.
10 Ibid., p. 121.
11 Dave Thompson, *Reggae and Caribbean Music* (San Francisco, CA, 2002),
    p. 256.
12 Ibid., p. 257.
13 King Sporty, 'Kill I Today You Cannot Kill I Tomorrow', www.genius.
    com, 18 July 2018.
14 Elena Oumano, 'Women Increase Number, Scope of Roles in Reggae',
    Billboard, 27 January 1996, p. 37.
15 Doug Reece, 'Popular Uprisings', *Billboard*, 22 February 1997, p. 17.
16 Pierre Perrone, 'Island: The Record Label That Changed the World',
    The Independent, 23 October 2011.
17 Cowell, 'Public Discourse', p. 35.
18 Balford Henry, 'Dancehall Politics', *The Gleaner*, 16 March 2001.

19 Thibault Ehrengardt, *Gangs of Jamaica: The Babylonian Wars* (Paris, 2014), p. 64.
20 See 'I'm No Chi Chi Man Says PJ', *Jamaica Observer*, 18 October 2005.
21 Peter Tatchell, 'Prosecution of Reggae Artists Who Incite Homophobic Assaults and Murder', www.outrage.org.uk, accessed 17 September 2018.
22 See 'Police Say Reggae Hate Is a Crime', www.soulrebels.org, 10 November 2013.
23 Tania Branigan, 'Beenie Man Concert Axed over Homophobia Fears', *The Guardian*, 25 June 2004.
24 Ibid.
25 Ibid.
26 Gary Younge, 'Police Seek Jamaican Singer After Armed Attack on Gay Men', *The Guardian*, 17 June 2004.
27 Kelefa Sanneh, 'Dancehall's Vicious Side: Antigay Attitudes', *New York Times*, 6 September 2004.
28 See 'Amnesty Confirms: Buju Banton Accused of Gay-Bashing', www.soulrebels.org, 20 August 2004.
29 See '"Anti-Gay" Lyrics Inquiry Starts', http://news.bbc.uk, 3 November 2004.
30 Sam Matthews, 'Puma Warns Jamaican Music Stars over Anti-Gay Songs', *Campaign*, 17 August 2004.
31 See 'Puma Issues Ultimatum: Drop Anti-Gay Songs or Lose Sponsorship', www.indymedia.org.uk, accessed 18 September 2018.
32 Jamie Doward and W. Lee, 'Police to Vet Lyrics of "Anti-Gay" Reggae Star on British Tour', *The Observer*, 31 October 2004.
33 Tania Branigan, 'Reggae Star Beenie Man Could Face Charges for "Homophobic" Lyrics', *The Guardian*, 17 August 2004.
34 See 'Reggae Star Banned from Britain', *Manchester Evening News*, 4 November 2004.
35 Andre Paine, 'Star Banned from Britain', *Evening Standard*, 13 April 2012.
36 Terry Kirby, 'Singer Banned from UK for Anti-Gay Lyrics', *The Independent*, 4 November 2004.
37 See 'No Apology from "Anti-Gay" Singer', news.bbc.co.uk, 25 November 2004.
38 Hugh Muir, 'Ceasefire Brokered in Reggae Lyrics War', *The Guardian*, 5 February 2005.
39 Teino Evans, 'More Fire! Capleton Defiant Despite Cancellations', *Jamaican Star*, 28 July 2005.
40 Rob Kenner, 'Catch a Fire', *Vibe*, October 2001, p. 120.
41 Ibid., p. 120.
42 Ibid., p. 118.
43 See 'Sizzla Apology', www.soulrebels.org, 10 June 2005.
44 Michael A. Edwards, 'Sumfest Likely to Drop Sizzla', *Jamaica Observer*, 27 July 2005.
45 Ibid.
46 Kandré McDonald, 'T.O.K. "Bun Up" Experience Concert', *Jamaican Star*, 29 December 2009.

47 Geoff Boucher, 'Reggae Stars Still Stir Up Activists', *LA Times*, 29 September 2006.

48 See 'Banton Presses On Despite Renewed Controversy', www.billboard.com, 29 September 2006.

49 Tony Grew, 'Cameron Attacks Homophobic Record Profits', *Pink News*, 3 October 2006.

50 See 'Reggae Compassionate Act', www.lgbthistorymonth.org.uk, accessed 20 September 2018.

51 See 'Another Reggae Superstar Comes Out against Anti-Gay Lyrics', www.ukgaynews.org.uk, 23 July 2007.

52 See 'Beenie Man: "I never signed the Reggae Compassionate Act"', www.soulrebels.org, accessed 20 September 2018.

53 See 'Elephant Man's Press Conference to Sign the RCA Is Cancelled', www.soulrebels.org, accessed 22 September 2018.

54 Krishna Rau, 'Jamaican Dancehall Performers Who Espouse Homophobia Should Be Prevented from Performing in Canada', in *Popular Culture*, ed. Noah Berlatsky (Farmington Hills, MI, 2011).

55 Gary Spaulding, 'Rough Ride, Driver!', *The Gleaner*, 21 March 2010.

56 Carolyn Cooper, 'I Have Outlived My Penis', *The Gleaner*, 3 June 2012.

57 Ioan Grillo, *Gangster Warlords: Drug Dollars, Killing Fields and the New Politics of Latin America* (London, 2016), p. 172.

58 Tom Faber, 'Bye Bye Bigotry – Does Dancehall Still Have a Homophobia Problem?', *Financial Times*, 18 January 2019.

59 Zadie Neufville, 'RIGHTS-JAMAICA: Spat Escalates Over Anti-Gay Lyrics', www.ipsnews.net, accessed 26 August 2021.

60 See 'Gays Won't Boycott Jamaica – Will Not Encourage Tourists to Shun the Island', *Jamaican Star*, 22 May 2008.

61 See 'Straight-Talking Golding Defends Stance on Gays', *The Gleaner*, 23 May 2008.

62 Eric Arnold, 'Exclusive: Buju Banton Sits Down with LGBT Activists', *SF Weekly*, 12 October 2009.

63 Ibid.

64 Ibid.

65 Ibid.

66 Eric Arnold, 'Fans Pepper Sprayed at Buju Banton Concert', *SF Weekly*, 13 October 2009.

67 Sarah Boseley, 'Jamaican Gay Rights Activists Hopeful of Repealing Anti-Homosexuality Law', *The Guardian*, 10 February 2012.

68 Stanley Cohen, *Folk Devils and Moral Panics* (London, 1972).

69 Elena Oumano, 'Homophobia in Jamaican Dancehall', *Village Voice*, 15 February 2005.

8 'DON'T TOUCH THE PRESIDENT': DANCEHALL AND THE TIVOLI GARDENS MASSACRE

1 Office of the Public Defender, *Interim Report to Parliament concerning Investigations into the Conduct of the Security Forces During the State of*

Emergency Declared May, 2010 – West Kingston/Tivoli Gardens, 'Incursion' – The Killing of Mr Keith Oxford Clarke and Related Matters (Kingston, 2013), p. 241.

2 Liz Robbins, 'Vivian Blake, 54, Founder of Jamaica Drug Gang, Dies', *New York Times*, 25 March 2010.

3 Ioan Grillo, *Gangster Warlords: Drug Dollars, Killing Fields and the New Politics of Latin America* (London, 2016), pp. 140–46.

4 Laurie Gunst, *Born Fi' Dead: A Journey through the Yardie Underworld* (Edinburgh, 1995), p. 212.

5 Dan Murphy, 'Jamaica Attacks: A Legacy of the Ties between Politicians and Gangs', *Christian Science Monitor*, 25 May 2010.

6 Gunst, *Born Fi' Dead*, pp. 238–40.

7 See '"Jim Brown" Is Still Dead, Isn't He?', *Newsweek*, 4 May 1992.

8 Jon Silverman 'Jamaica Violence "linked to u.s. drug market"', www.bbc.co.uk, accessed 15 January 2019.

9 K. C. Samuels, *Dudus, 1992–2010: His Rise – His Reign – His Demise. A Chronology of Lawlessness* (Kingston, 2011), n.p.

10 Amanda Sives, 'Changing Patrons, from Politician to Drug Don: Clientelism in Downtown Kingston, Jamaica', *Latin American Perspectives*, xxix/5 (2002), pp. 74–5.

11 Philip Delves Broughton, 'Through Drugs and Ingenuity, the Dons Are Now Independent of the Politicians', *Daily Telegraph*, 14 July 2001.

12 Ibid.

13 Glenroy Sinclair, 'Emotional Farewell for "Haggart"', *The Gleaner*, 9 May 2001.

14 S. Thomas Liston, *The Kingston Kingpins: How a Powerful Mobster Brought the Jamaican Government Down* (New York, 2016), p. 231.

15 See 'Tension in the Jungle', *The Star*, 16 April 2004.

16 Ibid.

17 Sonjah Stanley Niaah, *DanceHall: From Slave Ship to Ghetto* (Ottawa, 2010), pp. 125–6.

18 Broughton, 'Through Drugs and Ingenuity'.

19 See 'Magazine Alleges pnp Drug Links', *Daily Gleaner*, 3 December 1986, p. 8.

20 Gary Marx, 'Drug Trade Eats Away at Jamaica, Ruthless Gangs in the u.s. "Kill for Fun and Profit"', *Orlando Sentinel*, 5 June 1988.

21 See 'Seaga to Apologize to "Skeng Don"', *The Gleaner*, 17 December 2003.

22 See '"Skeng Don" Wins $200-m', *Jamaica Observer*, 24 October 2010.

23 Amnesty International, *JAMAICA: '. . . Until Their Voices Are Heard . . .': The West Kingston Commission of Inquiry* (Kingston, 2003).

24 Bernard Headley, 'Man on a Mission: Deconstructing Jamaica's Controversial Crime Management Head', *Social and Economic Studies*, li/1 (2002), pp. 179–91.

25 Amnesty International, *JAMAICA*.

26 Donna P. Hope, *Inna di Dancehall: Popular Culture and the Politics of Identity in Jamaica* (Kingston, 2006), pp. 109–10.

27 Donna Hope, 'Dons and Shottas: Performing Violent Masculinity in Dancehall Culture', *Social and Economic Studies*, LV/1–2 (2006), p. 123.

28 Ibid.

29 See 'Police-Chief Rapper Lays Down the Law on CD', *The Guardian*, 30 December 2005.

30 Julian Borger, 'Jamaican Justice, Dirty Harry Style', *The Guardian*, 17 July 2001.

31 David Williams, 'Seaga Wants Supr Adams out of West Kingston', *The Gleaner*, 9 July 2001.

32 See 'Dylan Powe Talks the Future of Passa Passa', www.thefader.com, June 2010.

33 Ibid.

34 See Tony Thompson, 'Kingston Residents Fear Police More Than Drug Dealer Michael [*sic*] "Dudus" Coke', *The Daily Telegraph*, 30 May 2010. See also Tony Allen-Mills, 'Family Feud Led to Jamaica Bloodbath', *The Times*, 30 May 2010.

35 See 'Apology to Organisers of Passa Passa', *The Gleaner*, 2 August 2010.

36 Grillo, *Gangster Warlords*, p. 160.

37 Henry Balford, 'The "Passa Passa" Phenomenon', *Jamaica Observer*, 21 November 2003.

38 Jacqueline Charles, 'Passa Passa Street Parties Sweep Jamaica', *Miami Herald*, 18 September 2006.

39 Niaah, *Dancehall*, pp. 124–9.

40 Karyl Walker, 'Beenie Man Offers $1M Bounty for Bogle's Killers', *Jamaica Observer*, 21 January 2005.

41 Christopher A. D. Charles, 'Violence, Musical Identity, and the Celebrity of the Spanglers Crew in Jamaica', *Wadabagei*, XII/2 (2009), p. 72.

42 See 'Zeeks Found Guilty', *The Gleaner*, 12 April 2006.

43 See 'Crack King Dudus Is Our Robin Hood', *The Express*, 27 May 2010.

44 Gary Spauding, '"Dudus Typically a Don" Says PM', *The Gleaner*, 18 March 2011.

45 See 'Jamaica Declares State of Emergency: Profile of Christopher "Dudus" Coke', *Daily Telegraph*, 24 May 2010.

46 Christopher Caldwell, 'Grown Wild in Tivoli Gardens', *Financial Times*, 28 May 2010.

47 Mattathias Schwartz, 'Jamaica's Former PM Opens Up about Coke Arrest, Extradition', *New Yorker*, 3 August 2012.

48 Caldwell, 'Grown Wild'.

49 See 'Jamaica Declares State of Emergency'.

50 Patricia Meschino, 'Jamaican Musicians Rally to Support Alleged Drug Kingpin "Dudus" Coke', *Billboard*, 18 June 2010.

51 Grillo, *Gangster Warlords*, pp. 161–2.

52 Samuels, *Dudus*, n.p.

53 Baz Dreisinger, 'Reggae's Civil War', *Village Voice*, 2 March 2010.

54 Caroline Wahome, 'Ragga Beef: Gully vs Gaza', *The Standard*, 21 August 2009.

55 Dreisinger, 'Reggae's Civil War'.
56 See 'PM Lists Gaza/Gully among Bad Influences on Society', www.jamaicalabourparty.com, 24 November 2019.
57 Kim Robinson-Walcott, 'Resistance, Legitimacy and a Different Reality', *International Journal of Postcolonial Studies*, XXII/1 (2020), p. 23.
58 Meschino, 'Jamaican Musicians Rally'.
59 See 'Growing Criticisms against PM's Gully/Gaza Meeting', *The Gleaner*, 8 December 2009.
60 See 'Jamaica Declares State of Emergency'.
61 Mattathias Schwartz, 'A Massacre in Jamaica', *New Yorker*, 4 December 2011.
62 Codine Williams, 'Massacre in Jamaica', www.vice.com, 7 May 2013.
63 Office of the Public Defender, *Interim Report to Parliament*, p. 39.
64 Kimmo Matthews, '"New" Guns Found in Tivoli Gardens', *Jamaica Observer*, 24 June 2010.
65 Arthur Hall, 'Deadly Dudus Raid', *The Gleaner*, 28 May 2010.
66 H. G. Helps, '"Clear My Name," Says George Phang. Arnett Gardens Area Leader Shuns Association with "Dudus"', *Jamaica Observer*, 13 June 2010.
67 Office of the Public Defender, *Interim Report to Parliament*.
68 Italics in original. See *Report of the Commission of Enquiry Appointed to Enquire into Events Which Occurred in Western Kingston and Related Areas in May 2010* (Kingston, 2016), p. 478.
69 See Grillo, *Gangster Warlords*, p. 171; Schwartz, 'Jamaica's Former PM'.
70 Mikey Fresh, 'Vybz Kartel: "Politics Created These Monsters Called 'Garrisons' to Exploit Poor People"', www.vibe.com, 25 May 2010.
71 Grillo, *Gangster Warlords*, p. 162.
72 Ibid., p. 163.
73 Meschino, 'Jamaican Musicians Rally'.
74 Ibid.
75 John Jeremiah Sullivan, 'The Last Wailer', *GQ*, 9 February 2011.
76 Allen-Mills, 'Family Feud Led to Jamaica Bloodbath'; Eliot C. McLaughlin, 'Affidavits: Witnesses Ran Cocaine, Guns for Jamaican Drug Lord', www.cnn.com, 27 May 2010. See 'Bruce Golding to Resign as Jamaican Prime Minister', *The Guardian*, 26 September 2011.
77 Erica Virtue, 'No Problem with Gays in My Cabinet', *The Gleaner*, 17 April 2018.
78 Chris McGreal, 'Christopher "Dudus" Coke Tells U.S. Court: I'm Pleading Guilty Because I Am', *The Guardian*, 1 September 2011.
79 Grillo, *Gangster Warlords*, pp. 148–53; Ed Pilkington, 'Christopher "Dudus" Coke Handed 23-Year U.S. Jail Term for Drug Trafficking', *The Guardian*, 8 June 2012.
80 Mel Cooke, 'Horace Andy at Home on Bond Street', *The Gleaner*, 4 March 2012.

9 'NICE UP THE DANCE': THE REGGAE REVIVAL

1 Mel Cooke, 'The Speech Jamaica Forgot – Tosh's One Love Peace Concert Overlooked', *The Gleaner*, 6 May 2012.

2 Interview with author, 23 June 2019.

3 Abby Aguirre, 'Reggae Revival: Meet the Millennial Musicians behind Jamaica's New Movement', *Vogue*, 28 October 2015.

4 Annie Day, 'Why You're Going to Love Jamaica's Reggae Revival Scene', www.afar.com, accessed 17 November 2020.

5 Kezia Page, 'Bongo Futures: The Reggae Revival and Its Genealogies', *Small Axe: A Caribbean Journal of Criticism*, 1/52 (2017), pp. 1–16.

6 Patricia Meschino, 'Jamaican Musicians Rally to Support Alleged Drug Kingpin "Dudus" Coke', *Billboard*, 18 June 2010.

7 Patricia Meschino, 'Jamaican Dancehall Stars Embrace "Conscious" Lyrics', www.reuters.com, 28 August 2010.

8 Ibid.

9 Ibid.

10 Rachel Mordecai, '"The Same Bucky-Massa Business": Peter Tosh and I-an-I at the One Love Peace Concert', *Kunapipi*, xxx/2 (2008), p. 34.

11 Ibid.

12 Quoted in Darrell E. Levy, *Michael Manley: The Making of a Leader* (London, 1989), p. 80.

13 Thibault Ehrengardt, *Reggae and Politics in the 1970s* (Paris, 2020), p. 187.

14 See 'Reasoning with Buju Banton: "My Life Is an Open Book"', www.boomshots.com, 15 July 2014.

15 King Sporty, 'Kill I Today You Cannot Kill I Tomorrow', www.genius.com, 18 July 2018.

16 See Loop News, 'Buju Banton's Journey: Incarceration; Reggae Revival', www.loopjamaica.com, 11 March 2019.

17 See 'Philip, "Fatis" Burrell', *The Guardian*, 6 December 2011.

18 S. Thomas Liston, *The Kingston Kingpins: How a Powerful Mobster Brought the Jamaican Government Down* (New York, 2016), p. 231.

19 Ibid., p. 219.

20 Sybil E. Hibbert, 'Permanent Secretary Gunned Down in Broad Daylight. After Alleged Hit on Ted O'Gilvie, George Flash, Tony Brown Fled to Cuba', *Jamaica Observer*, 8 January 2013.

21 Patricia Meschino, 'Are Jamaica's Biggest Stars Leaving Reggae Behind?', www.thedailybeast.com, 31 December 2020.

22 Interview with author, June 2019.

23 See 'Hempress Sativa – Reggae Geel', www.rebelbase.de, accessed 16 April 2020.

24 See '5 Things You Didn't Know about Rastafarianism', www.okayafrica.com, accessed 16 April 2020.

25 Glenroy Sinclair and G. Smith, '"We Were Wrong" – Ninja Man, Vybz Kartel Arrested and Charged following Sting "Slug-Fest"', *The Gleaner*, 31 December 2003.

26 See 'Kids Deep in "Rampin' Shop"', *Jamaica Star*, 6 February 2009.

27 Mel Cooke, '"Music and Lyrics" Assesses Impact of "Daggering" Ban', *The Gleaner*, 21 February 2010.
28 See 'Sales of Clarks Shoes Skyrocket in Jamaica Thanks to Vybz Kartel', www.repeatingislands.com, 9 July 2010.
29 Jorge Rivas, 'Jamaican Dancehall Star Vybz Kartel Bleached Skin', www.colorlines.com, 19 January 2011; Krista Henry, 'Kartel to Start Shoe Brand', *Jamaica Star*, 15 March 2011.
30 See 'Vybz Kartel Not Guilty . . . Acquitted after Prosecution Offers No Further Evidence', *The Gleaner*, 24 July 2013.
31 Adidja Palmer aka Vybz Kartel and M. Dawson, *The Voice of the Jamaican Ghetto: Incarcerated but Not Silenced* (Kingston, 2012), p. 60.
32 Ibid.
33 See 'LKJ Remembers Mikey Smith as One of the Caribbean's Most Original Voices', *Jamaica Observer*, 18 January 2002.
34 S. Leslie, 'Vybz Kartel Admitted to Murder in Damning Text Messages', www.urbanislandz.com, 24 July 2019.
35 Jesse Serwer, 'After Life Sentence, an Uncertain Fate for Vybz Kartel', *Rolling Stone*, 5 April 2014.
36 Annie Paul, 'Parsing Vybz Kartel's Sentence', www.anniepaul.net, 4 April 2014.
37 Soje Leslie, 'Lisa Hanna Stands Firm on Banning Vybz Kartel "Am Not Afraid of Death Threats"', www.urbanislandz.com, 21 February 2017.
38 See 'Lisa Hanna Compares Kartel to The Godfather; Offers to Work Together', www.loopjamaica.com, 23 April 2017.
39 Lisa Hanna, 'From My Life's Experiences I've Learned Courage Has No Limits', www.facebook.com, 27 February 2017.
40 See 'Speculation . . . Prison Boss Says No Evidence Kartel Recording behind Bars', *The Gleaner*, 2 March 2017.
41 Yasmine Peru, 'Don't Sentence the Music – Stakeholders Want Imprisoned Artistes to Record from behind Bars', *The Star*, 22 February 2019.
42 Soje Leslie, 'Vybz Kartel Murder Case Juror Say She Contemplates Suicide after Trial', www.urbanislandz.com, 20 August 2018.
43 Paul, 'Parsing Vybz Kartel's Sentence'.
44 Soje Leslie, 'Vybz Kartel Lawyer Tom Tavares-Finson Says Juror Trying to Prejudice Appeal', www.urbanislandz.com, 20 August 2018.
45 Dawn Knight, 'The Reggae Star Rapist', *The Guardian*, 8 April 2005.
46 See 'Reggae Star Barred from Britain after Serving 8 Years for Rape', *Daily Mail*, 8 October 2007.
47 See 'The Story That Almost Ended Jah Cure Career, Victim Relives Nightmare', www.urbanislandz.com, 12 August 2011.
48 Leonie Cooper, 'Rape Conviction Sees Reggae Artist Jah Cure Disqualified from MOBOS', www.nme.com, 7 September 2011.
49 Sade Gardner, 'Troubles and Trials of a Ninja', *Jamaica Observer*, 15 December 2017.
50 See 'Ninjaman Gets Life, 25 Years before Parole', *Jamaica Observer*, 18 December 2017.

51 See 'Buju Banton Sentenced to 10 Years in Prison', www.bbc.co.uk, 23 June 2011.

52 See 'No Government Event for Buju Banton's Return', www.loopjamaica.com, 29 November 2018.

53 Nesta McGregor, 'Buju Banton Comeback Labelled as "Legendary"', www.bbc.co.uk, 18 March 2019.

54 Mike Levine, 'Controversial Case of a Music Star Caught on Newly Unsealed Undercover Video', https://abcnews.go.com, 27 May 2018.

55 Sasha Lee, 'Buju Banton Addresses "Coke Head" Label, Links His Prison Sentence to Beating of Gay Man', www.urbanislandz.com, 26 July 2020.

56 Desire Thompson, 'Buju Banton Explains Why He Removed Controversial Song "Boom Bye Bye" from Catalog', www.vibe.com, 26 March 2019.

57 Lloyd Bradley, '"Every Black Man Have to Fight": Buju Banton on Prison and Liberation', *The Guardian*, 2 July 2020.

58 See 'Busy Signal Pleads Guilty', *The Gleaner*, 20 July 2012.

59 See interview with Sizzla, www.facebook.com, accessed 27 April 2021.

60 Tom Pakinkis, 'Territory Focus: Jamaica', *Music Week*, 27 July 2012, p. 15.

61 Soje Leslie, 'Mavado Shot at in Cassava Piece in Rain of Bullets', www.urbanislandz.com, 4 June 2018.

62 Soje Leslie, 'Mavado Shooting One Suspect Arrested', www.urbanislandz.com, 4 June 2018.

63 See 'Tensions High in Cassava Piece after Gun Attack on Mavado in the Area', www.loopjamaica, 3 June 2018.

64 See 'Jamaican Dancehall Artiste Wanted for Questioning', www.loopcayman.com, 5 June 2018.

65 See 'Second Suspect Charged in Cassava Piece Murder', *Jamaica Observer*, 18 June 2018.

66 See 'Jamaican Dancehall Artiste Wanted for Questioning', www.loopcayman.com, 5 June 2018.

67 Soje Leslie, 'Mavado's Son Bail Hearing Next Month While Singer Elude Cops', www.urbanislandz.com, 17 April 2019.

68 See 'Mavado's Son among Two Convicted for Murder on the "Gully Side"', *Jamaica Observer*, 28 January 2021.

69 Baz Dreisinger, 'Dancehall Artists Mavado and Beenie Man to Return to U.S. after Visa Snafu', *Rolling Stone*, 9 August 2011.

70 See 'Primary Wave Buys Chunk of Bob Marley Catalogue in $50M Deal', www.musicbusinessworldwide.com, 15 January 2018.

71 Rashun Hall, 'Indie Reggae Label VP Pacts with Atlantic', *Billboard*, 19 October 2002, p. 6.

72 Angus Taylor, 'Interview: Scientist', www.unitedreggae.com, 24 September 2008.

73 Krista Henry, 'Monopoly up VP's "Sleeves"', *Sunday Gleaner*, 17 February 2008, p. E2.

74 Ibid.

75 Ibid.

76 Patricia Meschino, 'Seeing Green: VP Records Acquires Greensleeves and Creates a Reggae Powerhouse', *Billboard*, 3 May 2008, p. 12.

77 See www.residentadvisor.net, accessed 26 June 2019.

78 Michael de Koningh and Laurence Cane-Honeysett, *Young, Gifted and Black: The Story of Trojan Records* (London, 2003), pp. 50–51.

79 Tom Pakinkis, 'Territory Focus: Jamaica', *Music Week*, 27 July 2012, p. 15.

80 De Koningh and Cane-Honeysett, *Young, Gifted and Black*, p. 51.

81 Ludovic Hunter-Tilney, 'Reggae's Reckoning: How 1970s Stars Were Deprived of Their Fair Share', *Financial Times*, 17 April 2021.

82 Paul Lewis, 'Wailer with 52 Children Waits in Vain for Marley's Millions', *The Guardian*, 16 May 2006.

83 See 'Bob Marley: Company Loses Bid to Win Back Rights', www.bbc.com, 4 June 2014.

84 See 'BSI Enterprises Ltd & Another v. Blue Mountain Music Ltd', EWCA Civ. 1151 (2015), www.bailii.org, accessed 1 November 2021.

85 Ashley Cullins, 'Bob Marley "War" Sparks Copyright Fight', *Billboard*, 16 September 2016.

86 See 'Jamaica Constabulary Force Orders', No. 3263, 17 December 2009, quoted in *The Gleaner*, 20 April 2013.

87 Ibid.

88 Marlon Tilling, 'Consultation Ongoing on Noise Abatement Act', https://jis.gov.jm, 22 July 2016.

89 Curtis Campbell, 'New Noise Abatement Act by January – Crawford', *The Star*, 7 November 2015.

90 See 'Jamaicans Outraged after Reggae Promoter Arrested over Event, on Same Day as Carnival!', www.loopjamaica.com, 24 April 2017.

91 See 'Consultations to Begin on Noise Abatement Act', *Jamaica Observer*, 18 April 2019.

92 Ibid.

93 Ibid.

94 Claudia Gardner, 'Skatta Burrell Calls for Unity to Protect Dancehall Events from Police', https://urbanislandz.com, 3 September 2019.

95 Yamsin Peru, 'Cops Pulling the Plug on Events – Footloose the Latest to Have "Early" Cut-Off', *The Star*, 2 September 2019.

96 Stephanie Lyew, 'No Music, No Vote! – Ricky Trooper Leads Lobby for Later Lock-Off Times for Events', *The Star*, 9 September 2019.

97 Ibid.

98 Ibid.

99 See 'Grange Meets Entertainment Industry Players on Noise Abatement Act', *Jamaica Observer*, 10 September 2019.

100 See 'Party All Day, All Night', *The Star*, 12 September 2019.

101 Dani Mallick and Shirvan Williams, 'D'Angel Does Election Dubplate for Krystal Tomlinson's Opponent', www.dancehallmag.com, 24 August 2020.

102 See 'Pull Up! – Bunting, Green Drop Dubplates', *The Star*, 14 August 2020.

103 Ibid.

104 Claudine Baugh, 'Vybz Kartel Not Pleased As Jamaican Politicians Roll Out More Dubplate-Styled Campaign Songs', www.dancehallmag.com, 14 August 2020.

105 Corey Robinson, 'Dancehall Pushing Crime – Bunting', *Jamaica Observer*, 13 January 2013.

106 See 'Daryl Vaz: I Would Have Been "Fired" for Using Gun Lyrics on Platform', *Jamaica Observer*, 15 December 2015.

107 Kady Anglin, 'Protoje Drops Anti-Political Dub as Dancehall Grips Jamaican Politic', https://urbanislandz.com, 19 August 2020.

108 Richard Johnson, 'Election Soundtrack: "Don't Just Be Exploiters and Culture Vultures" – Stanley Niaah', *Jamaica Observer*, 16 August 2020.

109 See 'Election Turnout by Percentage: 1962–2016', http://digjamaica.com, 25 June 2016, and '#JaVotes2020: JLP Trounces PNP 49 to 14 Seats', *The Gleaner*, 3 September 2020.

110 Tony Weis, 'The Rise, Fall and Future of the Jamaican Peasantry', *Journal of Peasant Studies*, XXXIII/1 (2006), pp. 61–88.

EPILOGUE

1 Simon Musasizi, 'Tugambire ku Jennifer Rubs Govt the Wrong Way', *The Observer*, 18 September 2012.

2 Alon Mwesigwa, 'Bobi Wine: I Refused to Sing for Museveni Regime', *The Observer*, 20 October 2017.

3 David Peisner, 'Uganda's "Ghetto President": How Bobi Wine Went from Dancehall Grooves to Revolutionary Politics', *Rolling Stone*, 25 April 2020.

4 See 'Deadly Uganda Protests over Bobi Wine's Arrest', www.aljazeera. com, 19 November 2020.

5 See 'Uganda Opposition Leader Bobi Wine Asks ICC to Investigate Rights Abuses', www.dw.com, accessed 8 January 2021.

6 See 'Uganda Election: Bobi Wine "Fearful for Life" after Museveni Win', www.bbc.com, 17 January 2021.

7 See 'Bobi Wine Sings from the Heart, Touches Hearts', www.newvision.co.ug, 21 December 2013.

8 Don Taylor, *Guns and Ganja: The Secret Life of Bob Marley* (London, 2003), p. 168.

9 Vivien Goldman, 'The Bush Doctor's Dilemma', *Melody Maker*, 9 December 1978.

10 See www.ghana.gov.gh, accessed 19 September 2019.

SELECT BIBLIOGRAPHY

Asserate, Asfa-Wossen, *King of Kings: The Triumph and Tragedy of Emperor Haile Selassie I of Ethiopia* (London, 2015)

Barrett, Leonard E., Sr, *The Rastafarians* (Boston, MA, 1997)

Barrow, Steve, and Peter Dalton, *Reggae: The Rough Guide* (London, 1997)

Bookman, Dutty, *Tried and True: Revelations of a Rebellious Youth* (Washington, DC, 2011)

—, *Selected Duttyisms* (Coral Springs, FL, 2015)

Bradley, Lloyd, *Bass Culture: When Reggae Was King* (London, 2000)

Caroll, Robert, and Stephen Prickett, eds, *The Bible: Authorized King James Version with Apocrypha* (Oxford, 2008)

Chang, Kevin O'Brien, and Wayne Chen, *Reggae Routes: The Story of Jamaican Music* (Philadelphia, PA, 1998)

Chevannes, Barry, *Rastafari Roots and Ideology* (Syracuse, NY, 1994)

Cooper, Carolyn, *Sound Clash: Jamaican Dancehall Culture at Large* (New York, 2004)

Crawford, Thomas, ed., *Selected Writings and Speeches of Marcus Garvey* (Mineola, NY, 2004)

Cronon, E. David, *Black Moses: The Story of Marcus Garvey and the Universal Negro Improvement Association* (Madison, WI, 1969)

Dawes, Kwame, *Bob Marley: Lyrical Genius* (London, 2002)

Daynes, Sarah, *Time and Memory in Reggae Music* (Manchester, 2010)

De Koningh, Michael, and Laurence Cane-Honeysett, *Young, Gifted and Black: The Story of Trojan Records* (London, 2003)

Ehrengardt, Thibault, *Reggae and Politics in the 1970s* (Paris, 2020)

Garvey, Amy J., *The Philosophy and Opinions of Marcus Garvey: Or, Africa for the Africans* (New York, 2021)

Garvey, Marcus, *Message to the People: The Course of African Philosophy*, ed. Tony Martin (Fitchburg, MA, 1986)

Gilroy, Paul, *There Ain't No Black in the Union Jack* (London, 1987)

—, *The Black Atlantic: Modernity and Double Consciousness* (London, 1993)

Grant, Colin, *Negro with a Hat: The Rise and Fall of Marcus Garvey* (London, 2009)

—, *I & I. The Natural Mystics: Marley, Tosh and Wailer* (London, 2011)

Grillo, Ioan, *Gangster Warlords: Drug Dollars, Killing Fields and the New Politics of Latin America* (London, 2016)

Gunst, Laurie, *Born Fi' Dead: A Journey through the Yardie Underworld*
(Edinburgh, 1995)

Hausman, Gerald, ed., *The Kebra Nagast: The Lost Bible of Rastafarian Wisdom
and Faith* (New York, 1997)

Hebdige, Dick, *Cut 'n' Mix: Culture, Identity and Caribbean Music* (London,
1987)

Hill, Robert, *Dread History: Leonard P. Howell and Millenarian Visions in the
Early Rastafarian Religion* (Chicago, IL, 2001)

Hope, Donna, *Inna di Dancehall: Popular Culture and the Politics of Identity
in Jamaica* (Kingston, 2006)

James, Marlon, *A Brief History of Seven Killings* (London, 2015)

Johnson, Linton Kwesi, *Selected Poems* (London, 2006)

Katz, David, *Solid Foundation: An Oral History of Reggae* (London, 2003)

Lewis, Rupert, *Marcus Garvey: Anti-Colonial Champion* (London, 1987)

Manley, Michael, *The Politics of Change: A Jamaican Legacy* (Washington, DC,
1975)

—, *Jamaica: Struggle in the Periphery* (London, 1982)

Murrell, Nathaniel Samuel, William David Spencer and Adrian Anthony
McFarlane, eds, *Chanting Down Babylon: The Rastafari Reader*
(Philadelphia, PA, 1998)

Niaah, Sonjah Stanley, *DanceHall: From Slave Ship to Ghetto* (Ottawa, 2010)

Potash, Chris, *Reggae, Rasta, Revolution: Jamaican Music from Ska to Dub*
(London, 1997)

Salewicz, Chris, *Bob Marley: The Untold Story* (London, 2009)

Seaga, Edward, *My Life and Leadership*, vol. 1: *Clash of Ideologies, 1930–1980*
(Oxford, 2009)

Stanbury, Lloyd, *Reggae Roadblocks: A Music Business Development Perspective*
(Mississauga, 2015)

Steffens, Roger, *So Much Things to Say: The Oral History of Bob Marley*
(New York, 2017)

Stolzoff, Norman, *Wake the Town and Tell the People: Dancehall Culture
in Jamaica* (Durham, NC, 2000)

Sullivan, Paul, *Remixology: Tracing the Dub Diaspora* (London, 2014)

Taylor, Don, *Guns and Ganja: The Secret Life of Bob Marley* (London, 2003)

Thompson, Dave, *Reggae and Caribbean Music* (San Francisco, CA, 2002)

Toynbee, Jason, *Bob Marley: Herald of a Postcolonial World?* (Cambridge,
2007)

Veal, Michael E., *Dub: Soundscapes and Shattered Songs in Jamaican Reggae*
(Middletown, CT, 2007)

Waters, Anita M., *Race, Class and Political Symbols: Rastafari and Reggae in
Jamaican Politics* (New Brunswick, NJ, 1985)

White, Timothy, *Catch a Fire: The Life of Bob Marley* (New York, 2006)

SELECT DISCOGRAPHY

1 'LOOK TO AFRICA': THE POLITICS OF THE RASTAFARI

Albums
Count Ossie and the Mystic Revelation of Rastafari, *Grounation* (1973)
Dadawah, *Peace and Love – Wadadasow* (1974)
Ras Michael and the Sons of Negus, *Nyabinghi* (1974)
Burning Spear, *Marcus Garvey* (1975)
The Abyssinians, *Satta Massagana* (1976)
Various, *Drums of Defiance: Maroon Music from the Earliest Black
    Communities of Jamaica* (1992)

Singles
Bob Marley and the Wailers, 'Redemption Song' (1980)

2 'MISS JAMAICA': MUSIC AND POLITICS, 1945-70

Albums
Symarip, *Skinhead Moonstomp* (1970)
Various, *Dance Crasher: Ska to Rock Steady* (1988)
Various, *History of Trojan Records, 1968–1971* (1995)
Various, *Studio One Story* (2002)

Singles
The Ticklers, 'Glamour Gal' (1952)
Clue J. and His Blues Blasters, 'Easy Snappin'' (1959)
Byron Lee and the Dragonnairs, 'Dumplins' (1960)
Folkes Brothers, 'Oh Carolina!' (1960)
Higgs & Wilson with Ken Richards and His Comets, 'Manny, Oh' (1960)
Laurel Aitken, 'Boogie in the Bones' (1960)
Laurel Aitken with the Boogie Cats, 'Boogie Rock' (1960)
Clancy Eccles, 'Freedom' (1961)
Clancy Eccles, 'River Jordan' (1961)
Al T. Joe, 'Independence Time Is Here' (1962)
Basil Gabbidon, 'Independent Blues' (1962)
Bob Marley, 'Judge Not' (1962)
Derrick Morgan, 'Forward March' (1962)

Jimmy Cliff, 'Miss Jamaica' (1962)
Joe White and Chuck, 'One Nation' (1962)
Lord Creator, 'Independent Jamaica' (1962)
Prince Buster and the Blue Beats, 'Independence Song' (1962)
Winston and Roy, 'Babylon Gone' (1962)
Prince Buster, 'Madness' (1963)
Bob Marley and the Wailers, 'Simmer Down' (1964)
Don Drummond and the Skatalites, 'Addis Ababa' (1964)
Justin Hinds and the Dominoes, 'Carry Go Bring Home' (1964)
Millie Small, 'My Boy Lollipop' (1964)
Roland Alphonso 'Lee Harvey Oswald' (1964)
The Skatalites, 'Fidel Castro' (1964)
The Wailers, 'Rude Boy' (1964)
Baba Brooks, 'Guns Fever' (1965)
The Skatalites, 'Guns of Navarone / Marcus Garvey' (1965)
The Clarendonians, 'Rudie Bam Bam' (1966)
Desmond Baker & the Clarendonians, 'Rude Boy Gone to Jail' (1966)
Hopeton Lewis, 'Sounds and Pressure' (1966)
Lloyd Williams, 'Rocksteady People' (1966)
Alton Ellis, 'Rocksteady' (1967)
Derrick Morgan, 'Court Dismiss' (1967)
Derrick Morgan, 'Tougher Than Tough' (1967)
Honey Boy Martin and the Voices, 'Dreader Than Dread' (1967)
Hopeton Lewis, 'Take It Easy' (1967)
Lee Perry and the Sensations, 'Set Them Free' / 'Don't Blame the Children'
    (1967)
The Valentines, 'Blam Blam Fever' (1967)
The Valentines, 'Stop the Violence' (1967)
Desmond Dekker and the Aces, 'Israelites' (1968)
Prince Buster, 'Judge Dread' (1968)
The Pioneers, 'Long Shot Kick de Bucket' (1969)
John Holt / The Wailers, 'Stranger in Love' / 'Jailhouse' (1970)
The Slickers, 'Johnny (Too) Bad' (1970)

3 'BETTER MUST COME': ROOTS REGGAE AND THE POLITICS OF JAMAICA IN THE 1970S

Albums
Max Romeo, *Let the Power Fall* (1971)
Various, *The Harder They Come* (1972)
The Wailers, *Catch a Fire* (1973)
The Wailers, *Burnin'* (1973)
Bob Marley and the Wailers, *Natty Dread* (1974)
Count Ossie and the Mystic Revelation of Rastafari, *Tales of Mozambique*
    (1975)
Bob Marley and the Wailers, *Rastaman Vibration* (1976)
Max Romeo, *War ina Babylon* (1976)

Peter Tosh, *Legalize It* (1976)
Prince Far I, *Psalms for I* (1976)
Tappa Zukie, *MPLA* (1976)
Third World, *Third World* (1976)
Bob Marley and the Wailers, *Exodus* (1977)
The Congos, *Heart of the Congos* (1977)
Culture, *Two Sevens Clash* (1977)
Junior Murvin, *Police and Thieves* (1977)
Peter Tosh, *Equal Rights* (1977)
Bob Marley and the Wailers, *Survival* (1979)
Black Uhuru, *Sinsemilla* (1980)
Bob Marley and the Wailers, *Uprising* (1980)
Various, *Churchical Chants of the Nyabinghi* (1983)

Singles
Laurel Aitken, 'Ghana Independence' (1957)
Laurel Aitken, 'Nebuchnezer' (1957)
The Four Gees, 'Ethiopia' (1967)
The Ethiopians, 'Everything Crash' (1968)
The Maytals, 'Do the Reggay' (1968)
Bob and Marcia, 'Young, Gifted and Black' (1969)
Bob Marley and the Wailers, 'Small Axe' (1970)
Max Romeo, 'Labor Wrong' (1970)
The Melodians, 'Rivers of Babylon' (1970)
Clancy Eccles, 'Rod of Correction' (1971)
Delroy Wilson, 'Better Must Come' (1971)
Junior Byles, 'Beat Down Babylon' (1971)
Max Romeo, 'Ginalship' (1971)
Max Romeo, 'Let the Power Fall on I' (1971)
Peter Tosh, 'Them a, fi Get a Beaten' (1971)
Clancy Eccles, 'Halilujah Free at Last' (1972)
Junior Byles, 'Joshua's Desire' (1972)
Junior Byles, 'Pharaoh Hiding' (1972)
Ken Lazarus, 'Hail the Man' (1972)
Junior Byles, 'When Will Better Come?' (1973)
John Holt, 'Up Park Camp' (1974)
Ken Boothe, 'Everything I Own' (1974)
Max Romeo, 'No, Joshua, No' (1974)
Jacob Miller, 'Roman Soldiers of Babylon' (1975)
Pluto, 'I Man Born Ya' (1975)
Derrick Morgan, 'Under Heavy Manners' (1976)
Joe Gibbs and the Professionals, 'State of Emergency' (1976)
Lord Laro, 'Budget Debate' / 'Foreign Press' (1976)
Neville Martin, 'The Message' (1976)
The Revolutionaries, 'Angola' (1976)
George Nooks, 'Tribal War' (1977)
Glenroy Richards, 'Wicked Can't Run Away' (1977)

Prince Far I, 'Heavy Manners' (1977)
Althea and Donna, 'Make a Truce' (1978)
Big Youth, 'Green Bay Killing' (1978)
Jacob Miller, 'Peace Treaty Special' (1978)
John Holt, 'Tribal War' (1978)
Lord Sassafrass and Debra Keys, 'Green Bay Incident' (1978)
Tappa Zukie, 'Green Bay Murder' (1978)

4 'INGLAN IS A BITCH': REGGAE CROSSOVER IN THE UK

Albums
The Clash, *The Clash* (1977)
Linton Kwesi Johnson, *Dread Beat an' Blood* (1978)
Sham 69, *That's Life* (1978)
Steel Pulse, *Handsworth Revolution* (1978)
The Clash, *London Calling* (1979)
Linton Kwesi Johnson, *Forces of Victory* (1979)
Madness, *One Step Beyond* (1979)
Misty in Roots, *Live at the Counter Eurovision 79* (1979)
PiL [Public Image Ltd], *Metal Box* (1979)
The Pop Group, *Y* (1979)
The Slits, *Cut* (1979)
The Specials, *The Specials* (1979)
The Beat, *I Can't Stop It* (1980)
Linton Kwesi Johnson, *Bass Culture* (1980)
New Age Steppers, *The New Age Steppers* (1980)
The Selecter, *Too Much Pressure* (1980)
UB40, *Signing Off* (1980)
UB40, *Present Arms* (1981)
Ruts DC, *Rhythm Collision, Vol. 1* (1982)
UB40, *UB44* (1982)
UB40, *Labour of Love* (1983)
Linton Kwesi Johnson, *Making History* (1984)

Singles
Louisa Marks, 'Caught You in a Lie' (1975)
Althea and Donna, 'Uptown Top Ranking' (1977)
Elvis Costello, 'Watching the Detectives' (1977)
The Clash, 'White Riot' (1977)
The Clash, '(White Man) in Hammersmith Palais' (1978)
Scritti Politti, 'Skank Bloc Bologna' (1978)
The Clash, 'Bankrobber' (1979)
Dennis Brown, 'Money in My Pocket' (1979)
The Bodysnatchers, 'Let's Do Rocksteady' (1980)
Madness, 'Embarrassment' (1980)
The Specials, 'Ghost Town' (1981)
Rhoda with the Special AKA, 'The Boiler' (1982)

UB40, 'Red Red Wine' (1983)
Smiley Culture, 'Cockney Translation' (1984)
Smiley Culture, 'Police Officer' (1984)
The Special AKA, 'Free Nelson Mandela' (1984)

5 'RING THE ALARM': THE 1980S AND THE DECADE OF DANCEHALL

Albums

U-Roy, *Version Galore* (1971)
Big Youth, *Screaming Target* (1972)
Herman Chin-Loy, *Aquarius Dub* (1973)
I-Roy, *Presenting I. Roy* (1973)
Lee Perry, *Upsetters 14 Dub* (1973)
Keith Hudson & Family Man, *Pick a Dub* (1974)
King Tubby, *Dub from the Roots* (1974)
King Tubby, *The Roots of Dub* (1975)
Tommy McCook and the Aggrovators, *Brass Rockers* (1975)
Augustus Pablo, *King Tubbys Meets Rockers Uptown* (1976)
Creation Rebel, *Dub from Creation* (1978)
Barrington Levy, *Englishman* (1979)
Prince Jammy, *Kamikazi Dub* (1979)
Ranking Slackness, *Slackest LP* (1979)
Sugar Minott, *Ghetto-ology* (1979)
Scientist, *Scientist Meets the Space Invaders* (1981)
Scientist, *Scientist Rids the World of the Evil Curse of the Vampires* (1981)
Dub Syndicate, *The Pounding System (Ambience in Dub)* (1982)
Lone Ranger, *M16* (1982)
Mad Professor, *Dub Me Crazy!!* (1982)
Scientist, *Scientist Wins the World Cup* (1982)
Sister Nancy, *One Two* (1982)
Yellowman, *Operation Radication* (1982)
Dub Syndicate, *One Way System* (1983)
Doctor Pablo and the Dub Syndicate, *North of the River Thames* (1984)
Dub Syndicate, *Tunes from the Missing Channel* (1984)
Yellowman, *King Yellowman* (1984)
Various, *Under Me Sleng Teng Extravaganza* (1985)
Barmy Army, *The English Disease* (1989)
Tackhead, *Friendly as a Hand Grenade* (1989)
Lieutenant Stitchie, *The Governor* (1989)
Shabba Ranks, *Just Reality* (1990)
Various, *Punanny* (2000)
Various, *Dancehall: The Rise of Jamaican Dancehall Culture* (2017)

Singles

Sound Dimension, 'Real Rock' (1967)
U-Roy, 'Rule the Nation' (1970)
U-Roy, 'Wake the Town' (1970)

U-Roy, 'Wear You to the Ball' (1970)
Trinity, 'Three Piece Suit' (1977)
Anita Ward, 'Ring My Bell' (1979)
Papa Michigan and General Smiley, 'Nice Up the Dance' (1979)
Barrington Levy and General Echo, 'Eventide Fire a Disaster' (1980)
Neville 'Struggle' Martin, 'No Mr IMF' (1980)
Sister Nancy, 'Papa Dean' (1980)
Barrington Levy, 'MI6' (1981)
Neville Valentine, 'MI6 Gunman' (1981)
Eek-a-Mouse, 'Operation Eradication' (1982)
Barry Brown, 'Politician' (1984)
Barrington Levy, 'Under Mi Sensi' (1985)
Tenor Saw, 'Ring the Alarm' (1985)
Wayne Smith, 'Under Me Sleng Teng' (1985)
Admiral Bailey, 'Punanny' (1986)
Admiral Bailey, 'Politician' (1986)
Al Campbell, 'Politicians' (1986)
Josey Wales and Admiral Bailey, 'Ballot Box' (1986)
Shabba Ranks, 'Love Punanny Bad' (1987)

6 'YUH NUH READY FI DIS YET': WOMEN AND THE POLITICS OF DANCEHALL AND REGGAE, 1990–2010

Albums

Sister Carol, *Liberation for Africa* (1983)
Sister Carol, *Black Cinderella* (1984)
Patra, *Queen of the Pack* (1993)
Lady Saw, *Lover Girl* (1994)
Patra, *Scent of Attraction* (1995)
Lady Saw, *Give Me the Reason* (1996)
Tanya Stephens, *Too Hype* (1997)
Lady Saw, *99 Ways* (1998)
Tanya Stephens, *Ruff Rider* (1998)
Lady Saw, *Strip Tease* (2004)
Tanya Stephens, *Gangsta Blues* (2004)
Tanya Stephens, *Rebelution* (2004)
Macka Diamond, *Money-O* (2006)
Ce'cile, *Bad Gyal* (2008)
Tanya Stephens, *Infallible* (2010)
Lady Saw, *Alter Ego* (2014)
Tanya Stephens, *Guilty* (2014)

Singles

Lady 'Mackrel' Worries, 'Don Girl' (1987)
Lady Saw, 'Hardcore' (1994)
Lady Saw, 'Stab Out Mi Meat' (1994)
Lady Mackrel / Queen Paula, 'Hot Girls Like We' (1996)

Lady Saw, 'What Is Slackness' (1996)
Tanya Stephens, 'Yuh Nuh Ready fi Dis Yet' (1996)
No Doubt, 'Underneath It All feat. Lady Saw' (2002)
Tanya Stephens, 'It's a Pity' (2002)
Ce'cile, 'Do It to Me' (2003)
Macka Diamond, 'Tekk Con' (2004)
Black-er / Macka Diamond, 'Bun Him' (2005)

7 'NOBODY CAN SING "BOOM BYE BYE" FOR ME': MEN AND THE POLITICS OF DANCEHALL AND REGGAE, 1990–2010

Albums

Shabba Ranks, *Raw as Ever* (1991)
Buju Banton, *Mr Mention* (1992)
Super Cat, *Don Dada* (1992)
Buju Banton, *Voice of Jamaica* (1993)
Beenie Man, *Blessed* (1995)
Buju Banton, *'Til Shiloh* (1995)
Capleton, *Prophecy* (1995)
Luciano, *Where There Is Life* (1995)
Anthony B, *Real Revolutionary* (1996)
Buju Banton, *Inna Heights* (1997)
Capleton, *I Testament* (1997)
Sizzla, *Black Woman and Child* (1997)
Buju Banton, *Unchained Spirit* (1999)
Sizzla, *Bobo Ashanti* (2000)
Capleton, *Still Blazin* (2002)
Buju Banton, *Friends for Life* (2003)
Buju Banton, *Rasta Got Soul* (2009)
Mista Majah P, *Tolerance* (2011)

Singles

Pan Head, 'Gun Man Tune' (1990)
Pan Head, 'Too Much Gun' (1991)
Buju Banton, 'Battyrider' (1992)
Buju Banton, 'Love Black Woman' (1992)
Buju Banton, 'Love Mi Browning' (1992)
Buju Banton, 'Murderer' (1993)
Capleton, 'Cold Blooded Murderer' (1993)
Beenie Man, 'No Mama No Cry' (1994)
Buju Banton, 'Driver A' (2006)

8 'DON'T TOUCH THE PRESIDENT': DANCEHALL AND THE TIVOLI GARDENS MASSACRE

Albums
Ninjaman, *Hardcore Killing* (1993)
Ninjaman, *Original Front Tooth Gold Tooth Gun Pon Tooth Don Gorgon!* (1993)
Bounty Killer, *Down in the Ghetto* (1994)
Bounty Killer, *The Mystery* (2002)
Elephant Man, *Higher Level* (2002)
Elephant Man, *Good 2 Go* (2003)
Vybz Kartel, *Up 2 di Time* (2003)
Vybz Kartel, *Timeless* (2004)
Mavado, *Gangsta for Life: The Symphony of David Brooks* (2007)
Various, *Power House Selector's Choice, Vol. 1* (2008)

Singles
Buju Banton, 'Bogle' (1992)
Alley Cat, 'Don's Anthem' (1998)
Beenie Man, 'Higher Level' (2001)
Buju Banton, 'Top A di Top' (2001)
Elephant Man, 'Passa Passa' (2001)
Beenie Man, 'Row Like a Boat' (2004)
Beenie Man, 'We Set di Trend' (2006)
Soltex 3000, 'Killa Walk, Prezzi Bounce' (2006)
Wayne Marshall, 'It's Evident' (2006)
I-Octane, 'Lose a Friend' (2009)
Bunny Wailer, 'Don't Touch the President' (2010)
Mavado, 'Change Right Now' (2010)
Twin of Twins, 'Which Dudus' (2010)

9 'NICE UP THE DANCE': THE REGGAE REVIVAL

Albums
Sean Paul, *Dutty Rock* (2002)
Damian Marley, *Welcome to Jamrock* (2005)
Buju Banton, *Before the Dawn* (2010)
Kabaka Pyramid, *Rebel Music* (2011)
Addis Pablo, *In My Fathers House* (2014)
Raging Fyah, *Destiny* (2014)
Protoje, *Ancient Future* (2015)
Hempress Sativa, *Unconquerebel* (2016)
Jah9, *9* (2016)
Raging Fyah, *Everlasting* (2016)
Chronixx, *Chronology* (2017)
Jesse Royal, *Lily of da Valley* (2017)
Kabaka Pyramid, *Kontraband* (2018)

Protoje, *A Matter of Time* (2018)
Jah9, *Note to Self* (2020)
Protoje, *In Search of Lost Time* (2020)

Singles
Protoje, 'Kingston Be Wise' (2012)
Jah9, 'Steamers a Bubble' (2013)
Inner Circle featuring Chronixx & Jacob Miller, 'Tenement Yard remix (News Carryin Dread)' (2015)
Kabaka Pyramid, 'Nice Up the Dance' (2020)

Election Dubplates
Beenie Man for Krystal Tomlinson
Christopher Martin for Robert Nesta Morgan
Christopher Martin for Alando Terrelonge
D'Angel for Juliet Cuthbert-Flynn
Dovey Magnum for Peter Phillips
I-Octane for Olivia Grange
Ishwana for Andrew Holness
Jahvillani for Karl Douglas
Jahvillani for Nigel Clarke
Jahvillani for Phillip Paulwell
Konshens for Tova Hamilton
Masicka for Andrew Holness
Masicka for Pearnel Charles Jr
Paparatzzi for Dwayne Vaz
Shenseea for Andrew Holness
Shenseea for Lisa Hanna
Skillibeng for Andrew Holness
Spice for Lisa Hanna
Stylo G for Peter Bunting
Teejay for Floyd Green
Wayne Wonder for Jodian Myrie

ACKNOWLEDGEMENTS

Thanks to all at Writing on the Wall in Liverpool for their guidance and support, especially to Madeline Heneghan and Mike Morris for reading an early draft and also to Emma Hulme for her encouragement. Particular thanks to David Katz for kindly reading a draft of the book and for providing such a generous endorsement and helpful list of essential corrections. Thanks to Shelley Bridson for her advice and guidance from the beginning of this project to the end ('From Genesis to Revelation'). Special thanks to Kofi Kulcha in Jamaica: your practical support was invaluable. I would like to thank all of our friends in Ghana, including Korby and Liz Gaere, Bobo Amuah, Asif and Paulina Kwofie (and their lovely family) and everyone that we know in Accra, Ampenyi and at Ko-Sa. Thanks also to Tony Rebel and all at Rebel Salute – when I turned up at your gate and your staff asked, without prompting, 'Are you with Reaktion Books?', I knew that I was in safe hands. Thank you to Rocky Dawuni, Jah9 and Bobi Wine for your time and your energy. Particular thanks to Rory Taylor at Positive Vibration in Liverpool – you are an inspiration and your festival and gigs are highlights of the year. Thanks to Jayne Casey and Eric Gooden at District, a fantastic venue. Thanks to Elliot Leib of Zion High Productions for his words of advice. Thanks to Levi Tafari in Liverpool for his advice and inspiration. To Nick Ellis: thanks for the upliftment. Thanks to my editors Dave Watkins and Amy Salter for keeping me in line and on track. Thanks to Gareth 'Taff' Taylor for listening to my sporadic DJ sets and to David Colbran for his expert advice on photography. Thanks to Tim Wells for providing such a useful archive of news articles on reggae. Thanks to Paul Duhaney and the Africa Oyé team for providing me with access to artists at their wonderful festival. Thanks also to Jules Bennett at Liquidation, and to Ally Goodman, Dave McTague and Richie Vegas at One Fell Swoop and Mellowtone.

INDEX

2 Tone Records 125–36

Abyssinians, the 110
Adams, Reneto, Superintendent
   264–6
Admiral Bailey (Glendon Bailey)
   185, 193–4
Afrocentrism 11, 16–20, 32, 80, 90,
   108, 162, 186, 196, 345
Aggrovators, the 40, 105, 165, 184
Aidonia 309, 327
Aitken, Laurel 36, 43, 47, 109
Alcapone, Dennis (Dennis Smith)
   70, 157–8, 169
Althea and Donna 96, 97, 139, 172
Anderson, Beverley 70, 84
Andy, Bob 64, 80–81, 108
   see also Bob and Marcia
Andy, Horace 108, 141, 278
Anthony B (Keith Blair) 30, 226,
   235–6, 246, 249, 286–8, 291, 324
Anti-Nazi League 119–21
Asfaw, Menen, Empress 292–3
Aswad 103, 121–2, 140–41, 161
Atlantic Records 183–4, 208, 222, 312

Baby Cham (Damian Beckett) 200,
   246–9, 251, 323
Babylon 16, 26, 30, 32, 101, 282, 286,
   344
   in songs and lyrics 42, 46, 64,
      69–70, 73–4, 79–81, 94, 101–6,
      118, 143, 148, 247, 298, 326
Banton, Buju (Mark Myrie) 200,
   209, 216–28, 231–2, 238–42, 244,

247, 263, 276, 287–8, 290–91, 293,
   295, 303–7, 311, 314, 325
   'Til Shiloh 214, 223–5, 287–8
Barker, Dave 65, 315
Barrett, Aston 73, 78, 160, 179, 222,
   316
Barrett, Carlton 73, 78, 160
Barrett Sr, Leonard E. 27, 29–30, 32,
   107, 110
Beat and Commercial Records
   (B&C) 58, 59–62, 72
Beat, the 126–7, 176, 283
Beenie Man (Moses Davis) 198, 208,
   223, 227, 229–32, 239–41, 246–51,
   261–3, 268, 271–2, 295, 309, 314,
   325, 333
Bennett, Donovan 198, 294, 311
Bennett, Louise Fraser 210–11
Betteridge, David 58–9, 313, 315
Bible 20, 22, 26–8, 30, 104–7, 73,
   104–6, 225
Big Youth (Manley Buchanan) 90,
   95, 103, 158–9, 190
Black Atlantic 10, 123–5, 143, 201,
   280, 330, 341–5
Black, Kenneth 'Skengdon' 263–4
Black, Pauline 126, 140
Black Roses Crew 261
Black Star Line 17, 19, 102, 344
Black Uhuru 98–9, 141, 189
Blackwell, Chris 36, 46–7, 57–61,
   71–3, 86, 141, 180, 210, 227,
   310–12
   relationship with the Wailers
      76–80, 98

relationship with the Marley
   family 181, 316
Blackwood, Lloyd 'Coxsone' 142
Blake, Winston 'Burry Boy' 84, 261,
   264
Blue Beat Records 47, 57–8
Blue Mountain Music 311, 316
Blunkett, David 233, 307
Bob Marley and the Wailers 61, 78,
   83, 90, 94–5, 98, 100–101, 103, 105,
   108, 137, 316
   see also The Wailers
Bobo Ashanti 29–30, 235–6
Bogle 262–3, 268–9
Bogle, Paul 16
Bolt, Usain 268, 272
Bookman, Dutty 281–3
Boothe, Ken 70, 77, 137
Bounty Killer (Rodney Price) 185,
   198, 211, 217, 223, 229–30, 247–51,
   271–2, 283, 294, 301, 307, 309, 323,
   328
Bovell, Dennis 118, 132, 139, 162, 189
Breakspeare, Cindy 92, 189, 290, 301
Broadcasting Commission
   (Jamaica) 295
Brooker, Cedella 181
Brooks, Baba 55, 61, 149
Brown, Barry 184
Brown, Dennis 31, 43, 140
Bunting, Peter 325, 328
Burke, Sharon 211
Burning Spear (Winston Rodney)
   19, 78, 83, 98, 178, 236
   Marcus Garvey 15
Burrell, Philip 'Fatis' 288–9
Burru 108–9
Bustamante, Alexander 34–5, 41–2,
   45, 48, 50, 68
Buster, Prince 38, 45, 48, 49, 53, 56, 58,
   68, 109, 128, 171
Busy Signal (Reanno Devon
   Gordon) 251, 306–7
Byles, Junior 68–70, 73, 80, 103

Campbell, Al 184, 262–3
Campbell, Ali 137–9

cannabis *see* ganja
Cape Coast Castle 8, 337–9, 343
capitalism and capitalists 16, 70, 83,
   92, 114, 192, 344
Capleton 30, 198, 201, 206, 217, 223,
   226–7, 229, 235–7, 241, 246–50, 314
Carrington, Vernon 30, 96
Castro, Fidel 48, 91–2, 289
CBS Records 79, 118, 173–4, 183
Ce'cile (Cecile Charlton) 208–9, 276–7
Channel One 40, 81, 99, 161, 167–8,
   172, 176–8, 190
Charles, Pearnel 82, 89, 326
Chin, Chris 179–80
Chin, Joel 312
Chin, Patricia 178–9, 210
Chin, Vincent 'Randy' 178–9, 210
Christianity 16, 20, 22, 24–5, 30–31,
   147, 154, 196–9, 245, 303
Chronixx 284, 289–90, 310–11
   Chronology 279
Clarke, Johnny 97, 103, 108, 141
Clarke, Nigel 326
Clarks (shoe brand) 296, 326–7
Clash, the 115–17, 119–21, 161
clientelism *see* garrison politics
Cliff, Jimmy 9, 33, 44, 48, 64, 71–2,
   86, 108, 137, 290
Clue J. and His Blues Blasters 37
cocaine 144, 151–3, 258–9, 264, 277–8,
   293, 304–5, 307, 309
Cohen, Stanley 252–4
Coke, Christopher 'Dudus' 260, 263,
   267, 270–78, 293, 301, 309
Coke, Lester 'Jim Brown' 88, 100, 153,
   258–9, 260, 264, 301
Coke, Mark Anthony 'Jah T' 259
Cole, Allan 'Skill' 316
Collins, Ansell 65, 99, 171, 190
Colombia 151–2, 188
Communists and communism 70,
   91–3, 123
Conservative Party (UK) 35, 114, 136,
   239
copyright 41, 166, 313–17
   see also intellectual property
   rights

Count Ossie (Ossie Williams) 42, 90, 109–10, 129
Crawford, Damion 320
Creation Rebel 106, 162
crime 50, 107, 133, 142–4, 151, 178, 230, 264–6, 273, 276–8, 289, 300–309, 320, 328, 330
Crown Prosecution Service (UK) 230–33
Cuba 36, 49, 84, 91–2, 100, 129, 177–8, 186, 289
Culture (band) 96, 98, 102, 141
Cuthbert-Flynn, Juliet 325

D'Angel (Michelle Downer) 232
Dakar, Rhoda 134–5
dancehall 147–56, 167–80, 183–94, 195–213, 214–33, 237–54, 257–69, 271, 276–7, 280–88, 293–5, 299–300, 302–12, 317–24, 326–42
Dave and Ansell Collins 65, 190
Davies, Omar 262
Dawuni, Rocky 32
Dekker, Desmond 53–4, 61, 120
destabilization 79, 82, 93, 152, 271, 273
Digital B Records 184–5, 288–9, 291
Dillon, Phyllis 188
Dixon, Bobby 'Digital' 184–5, 226, 288
Dodd, Clement 'Coxsone' 37–40, 43, 46, 48, 56, 59, 69, 97, 110, 142, 154, 156, 168, 170, 182, 207, 310, 313, 329
dons 52, 84, 152–4, 205, 261, 263, 269–78, 308
Dovey Magnum (Simsky Harrison) 324, 326
dread 9, 56, 65, 83, 103, 105, 132, 134, 137
dreadlocks 30, 80, 105, 107–8, 118, 335
Driscoll, Clive, Detective Chief Inspector 229–33
drumming 25, 29–30, 38–9, 108–11, 158, 176–7, 186, 224, 320, 342–3
dub 11, 29, 98, 118, 121, 123–4, 131, 141, 155, 159–65, 177–8, 284, 312, 321
dub poetry 123–4, 131–3, 221, 298

Dub Syndicate 164
dubplates 37–8, 156
    election dubplates 318–32
Dunbar, Sly 90, 98–9, 124, 141, 168, 177, 179, 189, 222–3, 262, 290
    see also Sly and Robbie
Dynamic Sounds 48, 64, 71, 73, 76, 262, 341

Eccles, Clancy 42–3, 55, 70, 73–4, 76, 102, 207
Edwards, Emmanuel Charles (Prince Emmanuel I) 29
El General 187–8
Elephant Man (Oneal Bryan) 208, 217, 229, 242, 246–51, 263, 271–2, 276
Elizabeth II, Queen 45
Ellis, Alton 54–6, 90, 103, 108, 139, 157, 172
Elmina Castle 7–8, 338
Empire Windrush (ship) 57, 62, 65, 115
England
    Birmingham 114, 120–21, 124, 126, 131, 136, 138, 230
    Coventry 130
    London 17, 19, 23, 35–6, 46–7, 49, 578, 60–64, 72, 76, 87, 91, 96, 98, 101, 115–23, 128, 130–35, 141–4, 161, 163, 165–6, 178, 181, 189, 229–34, 285, 301, 316, 332
Ethiopia 16, 20–24, 26, 28, 30–32, 49, 73, 91–2, 101–4, 344
Ethiopian World Federation 30
Ethiopians, the 68, 89, 137, 148

Fante (tribe) 24, 343
fascism 22–3, 119–21, 128
Federal Records 36, 38, 77, 182
fire 52, 234–6, 287, 324
Folkes Brothers, the 58, 109
Fontana 59
Front Line 98, 158

Gabbidon, Basil 45
gangs, gangsters and gang warfare 51–2, 71, 81, 84–5, 88, 96–7, 125,

129, 142–3, 149–3, 158, 202, 231, 259–61, 264, 270, 272–4, 290, 298

ganja 29–30, 106–7, 157, 172, 174, 242, 264, 269, 286

garrisons and garrison politics 51–2, 81, 84, 93, 149–52, 172, 178, 184–5, 203, 258, 272, 274, 276, 278, 289, 309, 322

Garvey, Marcus 15–26, 28–9, 32, 49, 78, 85, 101–2, 194, 275, 289, 337–8, 340, 342–4
see also Universal Negro Improvement Association (UNIA)

General Echo (Earl Robinson) 141, 171–3, 178, 189–90, 262
see also Ranking Slackness

general elections (Jamaica) 34–5, 39, 42–3, 50–51, 67–70, 72–76, 81–3, 85, 88–90, 74, 96, 111, 147–50, 154, 172, 228, 231, 236, 242, 245, 259, 270, 287, 318–32

general elections (UK) 114, 134, 139

Germain, Donovan 184, 217, 223–4, 226, 327

Ghana 7–8, 19, 24, 32, 109, 337–40, 343–5

Gibbs, Joe 64, 83, 90, 141, 172, 201

Gilroy, Paul 10, 142–3, 345

Golding, Bruce 229, 235, 242–4, 268, 270–75, 277–8, 293

Goldman, Vivien 86, 116, 341

Goodall, Graeme 36, 40, 61

Gopthal, Lee 57–61, 315

Grange, Olivia 'Babsy' 82, 209–10, 212, 260, 273, 304, 320–21, 323, 327

Green, Floyd 326

Greensleeves Records 141, 165–7, 178, 180, 183, 194, 204, 206, 216, 226, 295, 306, 312–13

Griffiths, Marcia 64, 78, 148, 188–9, 211, 217

Grounation 29, 110

gunmen 82, 84–5, 88, 95–6, 149, 151–3, 222–3, 259–60, 265, 274, 276, 286–7, 302–3

guns 51, 55, 81–2, 87, 95–7, 101, 143, 149, 153, 158–9, 187, 195, 198, 218, 222–3, 248–50, 265–6, 274, 276–7, 289–90, 294, 296–7, 302–3, 308–9, 318, 327–8, 330, 342

Gunst, Laurie 84, 152

Haile Selassie I Theocratic Order of the Nyahbinghi Reign 29

Hall, Stuart 114

Hanna, Lisa 299–30, 324–5, 327

Harder They Come, The (film) 34, 70–72, 86, 290

Harlem Renaissance 17, 281

Harry J (Harry Johnson) 40, 60, 63, 160

Harry J All Stars 40, 60, 63

Hempress Sativa (Kerida Johnson) 292

Henzell, Perry 34, 70–71

Hibbert, Toots 141, 224
see also Toots and the Maytals

Holness, Andrew 273, 278, 284, 320, 323, 327

homophobia 11, 187–8, 200, 219–23, 226–54, 294–5, 305–7

Holt, John 95, 97, 156, 264

Hoo Kim, Joseph 40

Hope, Donna 192–4, 300

Howell, Leonard 22, 27–8, 31, 76, 289

I Threes, the 78, 188–9, 207

I-Octane (Byiome Muir) 327
'Lose a Friend' 257, 277

I-Roy (Roy Reid) 98, 158

independent record labels 47, 57–8, 99, 141, 161, 178, 180, 182–4, 209–10, 212, 224, 310–12

Ini Kamoze 289–90

Inner Circle 70, 78–9, 98–9, 141

International Monetary Fund (IMF) 94–5, 100, 148

Island Records 36, 46, 58–63, 71–2, 76–80, 86, 96, 98–9, 118, 132, 141, 170, 179–83, 208, 210, 224, 227, 308, 312, 316–17

Israel 26–7, 30–31, 96, 103

Israelites 25–6, 42, 68, 74, 120, 286
ital 29

Jagger, Mick 96, 340–41
Jah 26, 32, 80, 89, 97, 99, 102, 105, 108,
    121, 175, 216, 225
Jah Cure (SIccature Alcock) 217,
    302–4, 307
Jah Wobble (John Wardle) 123
Jahvillani (Dujon Edwards) 326
Jah9 (Janine Cunningham) 283–5,
    291–2, 311, 318
Jamaica 8, 10–11, 16–19, 22–9, 32,
    33–58, 60, 63, 65, 66–112, 114–15,
    117, 119, 123, 131–2, 134, 137, 140,
    142, 147–61, 164, 166, 168–81,
    183–94, 195–213, 218–29, 231,
    235–8, 242–5, 253, 258–78, 280–91,
    294–332, 333, 336, 338, 340–41, 344
  Arnett Gardens (Jungle) 84, 153,
    261–2, 268
  August Town 226
  Back o'Wall 43, 50–51
  Blue Mountains 86
  Cassava Piece 272, 308
  Caymanas Park 67, 87
  government of 36, 41, 68–9, 76,
    80–87, 90–95, 100, 107, 153, 195,
    228–9, 242–3, 264, 270–71, 275,
    276, 301, 304–5, 309, 320–21,
    323
  Green Bay 95
  Hope Road, Kingston 30, 83–4,
    86–8, 100, 153
  independence of 42–5, 47–9, 94,
    114, 150–51, 179, 286–7, 329, 332
  Jamaican Parliament 39, 41, 75,
    89, 258, 264, 270, 274–5, 332
  Kingston 30, 36, 39, 43, 46–7,
    50–53, 58, 64, 67, 71, 74–5, 78,
    82, 84–5, 93, 95–6, 100, 109, 114,
    126, 132, 134, 138, 150, 152, 153,
    160, 173, 177–9, 208, 217, 225,
    229, 258–63, 266–7, 270–78,
    283–4, 289, 302, 307–8, 311,
    321–2, 341
  Matthews Lane 269

Montego Bay 150, 195, 259, 302
National Heroes Park 19, 49, 85
Portmore (Gaza) 153, 265, 272,
    295, 297, 299
St Andrew 262, 284, 324–6
St Ann 16, 91, 228, 299, 323–4
St Mary 196
St Thomas 25, 27, 109
Tivoli Gardens 50–51, 84–5,
    100, 148, 152–4, 186, 257–60,
    262, 264–7, 270–78, 282–4, 293,
    342
Trench Town 39, 83–4, 92, 186,
    268
Up Park Camp 95
West Kingston 39, 43, 47, 50–52,
    74–5, 82, 84–5, 109, 153, 229, 261,
    266–8, 270–75, 284
Wilton Gardens (Rema) 258
Jamaica Broadcasting Corporation
    (JBC) 37, 40, 48, 193, 295
Jamaica Constabulary Force (JCF)
    see Police (Jamaica)
Jamaica Defence Force (JDF) 36, 95,
    153, 274–5
Jamaica Hotel and Tourism
    Association (JHTA) 321
Jamaica Labour Party (JLP) 51–2,
    67–70, 74–5, 82, 84–95, 99, 100,
    107, 111, 132, 147–53, 184, 198, 202,
    210, 212, 228–9, 242, 245, 259, 260,
    264, 266, 270–76, 291–2, 297–8,
    301, 315, 320–32
Jamaican Forum for Lesbians and
    Gays (JFLAG) 232, 243
Jesus Christ 30, 277
Joe, Al T. 44–5
Joe Gibbs and the Professionals 83,
    141
  State of Emergency 66
Joe Higgs and Roy Wilson 40
Joe White and Chuck 45
John the Baptist 21, 26, 102
Johnson, Linton Kwesi 113, 123, 129,
    131–4, 161
Joshua 68, 74–6, 89
Judaism 16, 24–6, 104

Kabaka Pyramid (Keron Salmon)
156, 283–4, 309–10, 311
Kay, Janet 189
Khouri, Ken 35–6, 69, 182
King, Diana 211
King Jammy (Lloyd James) 161, 166,
175, 178, 184, 193–4, 217, 222–3, 226
King Stitt (Winston Sparkes) 154,
157, 224
King Tubby (Osbourne Ruddock)
155–6, 160–61, 163, 165, 184
Koffee (Mikayla Simpson) 311
Kong, Leslie 36, 64, 67
Kumina 25, 38–9, 108–9, 186, 341

Labour Party (UK) 35, 131, 139, 148
Lady Saw (Marion Hall) 195–201,
203–5, 208–9, 211, 217, 249
Landis, Joya 158, 188
Lawes, Henry 'Junjo' 40, 165–7, 174,
177–8
Lee, Bunny 'Striker' 40, 55, 68, 91, 155,
158, 170
Lee, Byron 43, 47–8, 64, 148
Levy, Barrington 141, 149, 169, 171–4,
190, 208, 261, 296
Livingstone, Bunny *see* Wailer,
Bunny
Lone Ranger, the (Anthony
Waldron) 149, 173, 178, 179
Lord Creator 42, 138, 170
Luciano (Jepther McClymont) 201,
226–7, 284

Macka Diamond (Charmaine
Munroe) 205–7, 295, 313
McKenzie, Clyde 331–2
McKenzie, Desmond 228
Macmillan, Harold 35
Mad Cobra (Ewart Brown) 206, 216,
249–50
Mad Professor (Neil Fraser) 118,
161, 165
Madness (band) 128
Manley, Michael 51, 264, 330
as leader of the opposition
(1969–72) 67–70, 73–5

as leader of the opposition
(1980–89) 154
as prime minister (1972–80) 76,
79–82, 84–9, 91–7, 111, 114, 149,
261, 285–7
as prime minister (1989–92) 228,
259
Manley, Norman 34–5, 41–2, 45, 51,
67
marijuana *see* ganja
Marley Foundation 182
Marley, Bob 67, 79, 83–5, 96–100,
104, 116–17, 126, 137, 141, 148, 173,
180–82, 203, 217, 228, 235, 275, 281,
290, 341–2
as a member of the Wailers 48,
61, 72–3, 76–8
attempted assassination of 86–8,
153
death of 141, 154, 258, 262
estate of 180–82, 316
personal faith and politics 30,
67, 91–2, 152, 340
'Redemption Song' 22, 106
Marley, Cedella 210
Marley, Damien 290–91, 307
Marley, Rita 31, 181, 188–9, 283
Marley, Ziggy 260–61
Martin, Vincent 'Ivanhoe', 'Rhyging'
71–2
Martin, Neville 88, 148
Masicka (Javaun Fearon) 329
Massop, Claudie 84, 88, 96–100, 259
Mavado (David Brooks) 251, 271–3,
276, 283–4, 297, 301, 308–9
Maxi Priest (Max Elliot) 142
Melodians, the 104, 137, 157
Melodisc 36, 47, 57
mento 36, 38, 169, 341
Metropolitan Police *see* Police
(England)
Michigan and General Smiley 156,
166, 309
Miller, Jacob 79, 94–6, 99
Minott, Sugar 140–41, 168–9, 178, 217,
221, 264
Misty in Roots 120–22

MOBO Awards 229, 303, 306
mods 62, 252, 254
Montague, Robert 320
Moore, William 'Haggart' 261–3
moral panic 252–4, 283
Morant Bay Rebellion 16, 27, 52, 263, 275
Morgan, Derrick 44–5, 54–6, 60, 63, 81, 222
Morgan, Robert Nesta 326–7
Moses 21, 28, 68, 74, 81
Motta, Stanley 36
Mowatt, Judy 31, 78, 188–9
Murvin, Junior 81, 103, 116
Museveni, Yoweri 335–7
Mussolini, Benito 22–4
Myrie, Jodian 325

Nardo Boom 187
Neita-Robertson, Valerie 327
neo-liberalism 149–50, 330, 332
Nicaragua 16, 152
Ninjaman (Desmond Ballentine) 194, 215–16, 265–6, 294, 303–4, 327
Nkrumah, Kwame 19, 32
noise abatement 268, 318–24
Nyabinghi drumming 108–11, 158, 224
Nyahbinghi Order, the *see* Haile Selassie 1 Theocratic Order of the Nyahbinghi Reign

O'Gilvie, Edward 289
On-U Sound 161–4
one-drop reggae 176, 201, 225, 281, 287–8, 298, 343
One Love Peace Concert 95–7, 279, 285–6, 340
OutRage! 227–34, 241, 245, 253–4
overdubbing 63–5, 76–7

Pablo, Addis 311
Pablo, Augustus 29, 106, 160, 164, 179, 314
Pama 61
Pan Head (Anthony Johnson) 222–3
Pan-Africanism 19, 101, 121

Papa Michigan and General Smiley 156, 166
Paparatzzi (Akiem Bradbury) 329
Paragons, the 156–7
Passa Passa 266–9
Patra (Dorothy Smith) 204–5, 209–10
Patterson, P. J. 73, 228–9, 235–6, 264, 287
Paul, Sean 208, 229, 268, 280, 301, 312
People's National Party (PNP) 34–5, 39, 41–4, 51–2, 67–70, 73–6, 80–95, 99–100, 107, 147–53, 178, 184, 190, 198, 202, 215, 242, 245, 259–64, 268–9, 272, 275–6, 287–9, 291–2, 297–8, 320–32
Penthouse Records 184, 216–18, 224, 327
Pere Ubu 124
Penn, Dawn 188
Perry, Lee 'Scratch' 40, 55–6, 60, 64, 77, 79, 81, 105, 108, 116–17, 122, 155, 158, 160, 170, 180, 282, 314
Phang, George 190, 262, 274, 289
Phillips, Peter 324–5
Phipps, Donald 'Zeeks' 269
Phoenix Music International 314
Pioneers, the 64, 137
Pocomania 185–6
Police (England) 115, 121, 130–34, 144, 229–33, 252, 254
Police (Jamaica) 68–9, 76, 95, 99, 153, 172, 197, 259–68, 274, 286, 293, 297, 299, 303, 308–9, 318–23, 322–3
Police (USA) 258, 305
'politricks' 67, 89, 286, 291
Polygram 182–3, 216, 224, 226–7
Pop Group, the 121, 123–4, 162–3
Popcaan (Andre Sutherland) 280, 296, 307
Powe, Dylan 266–7, 269, 283
Presidential Click 267, 271, 276, 293
Pretenders, the 124,
Prince Emmanuel *see* Edwards, Charles
Prince Far I (Michael Williams) 81, 98, 105, 164, 190

Prince Jammy *see* King Jammy
Privy Council 181, 301–2, 332
Promised Land 26, 42, 68, 102
Protoje (Oje Ollivierre) 281, 283–4,
    289, 311, 329–30
Public Image Limited (PIL) 123
publishing rights and publishing
    companies 165–6, 178, 180–81,
    191, 310–11, 311, 313–16
    see also intellectual property
    rights
punanny lyrics 193–4, 196, 198, 289,
    309

Queen of Sheba, the 21, 104

R&B 11, 37–9, 43, 46, 57, 174, 201, 204,
    280, 330, 341
racial supremacism 16, 23, 28, 30, 285
Radio Jamaica Rediffusion (RJR) 36,
    40, 207
Ranglin, Ernest 37, 46
Ranking Slackness (Earl Robinson)
    169
    see also General Echo
Ras Michael and the Sons of Negus
    110
Rastafari 11, 15–32, 34, 42–3, 50, 65,
    67–9, 73–8, 80–81, 84, 89, 91–2,
    94, 97, 101–12, 113, 115–18, 121, 126,
    137, 139–40, 142, 147–8, 158–9, 170,
    184, 188, 218, 221, 223–6, 235–6,
    239, 244–5, 276, 281, 286–7, 289,
    290–92, 298, 327, 339, 342–4
Reagan, Ronald 137, 149
Rebel Salute 212, 283–4, 323–4, 333
Rebel, Tony 217, 221, 283, 288
redemption 20–22, 101, 106
Reggae Revival 11, 111, 279–93,
    302–18, 324, 329–30, 340, 342
Reggaeton 185
Reid, Arthur 'Duke' 37–9, 43, 46, 56,
    59, 156–7, 188, 222, 313, 329
Revolutionaries, the 40, 90, 95, 98,
    168
Richards, Keith 98, 341
Rihanna 191, 268, 280

Riley, Tarrus 217, 271, 290–91, 326
Riley, Winston 171, 190–91, 215, 217
Rock Against Racism 119–10, 128
rockers (music style) 176
rocksteady 34, 37, 54–6, 61–3, 67, 129,
    139, 155, 157, 167–72, 188
Rolling Stones, the 124, 340–41
Romeo, Max 64, 68–70, 78–81,
    170–71, 231, 284
Roots Radics 40, 164, 167–8, 171
roots reggae 46, 66–112, 115, 118, 120,
    126, 137, 140, 153, 158, 173, 175–8,
    180, 189, 193, 199, 212, 214, 224,
    227, 236, 258, 277, 281–2, 285–6,
    290–92, 310, 324, 330, 334–5, 342
Royal, Jesse 288
rude boys 52–6, 62, 65, 71, 84, 125–6,
    149, 152, 158, 222–3, 245, 290
Ruts, the 118–19, 121

Sangster, Donald 50, 67
Scientist (Hopeton Brown) 141, 161,
    165–7, 178, 312–13
Scott, Style 164
Scritti Politti 123
Seaga, Edward 39–43, 49, 87–8,
    99–100, 148, 259–61, 264, 285–7,
    329–30
    as MP for Kingston Western
        (1962–2005) 43, 82, 85, 264–6
    as music entrepreneur 46–8, 71
    as leader of the Jamaica Labour
        Party (JLP) 50–52, 74–6, 88–9,
        94, 96–7, 228–9, 235–6
    as prime minister (1980–89)
        149–50, 154
Selassie, Asfaw Wossen Haile,
    Crown Prince 24
Selassie, Haile, emperor of Ethiopia
    21–32, 73, 91, 94, 103–7, 184, 194,
    235, 275, 292, 299, 316, 342–3
    coronation of 21–2, 26–7,
        292–3
    death of 24, 91
    overthrow of 91
    visit to Jamaica 68
Selecter, the 125–6, 140

Shabba Ranks (Rexton Gordon) 185–7, 193–4, 197, 204, 210, 214–16, 219–21, 227, 251, 295, 301
Shaka, Jah 142
Shakespeare, Robbie 90, 160, 168, 189
  see also Sly and Robbie
Shalit, Emil 57
Shearer, Hugh 67–8, 76
Shenseea (Chinsea Lee) 311, 324–7
Shervington, Pluto 89
Sherwood, Adrian 161–5
Shower Posse 84–5, 100, 153, 258–61, 267, 270
Silk, Garnett 221–2
Simpson-Miller, Portia 229, 245
Sims, Danny 87, 180–82, 316
Sister Carol (Carol East) 207–8
Sister Nancy (Ophlin Russell) 189–91, 205, 208
Sizzla (Miguel Collins) 30, 198, 201, 226, 232–4, 237–42, 246, 248–51, 253, 290–91, 302–3, 307–9, 314
ska 34, 37–8, 40–49, 52, 54, 57, 61, 110, 117, 125–31, 135–6, 224, 341
Skatalites, the 38, 40, 48–9, 53, 61
Skillibeng 327
skin bleaching 218, 297
skinheads 61–5, 119–20, 126, 130
slavery 8, 9–11, 20, 22–5, 32, 45–6, 52–3, 89, 103, 106, 109, 185, 236, 285–6, 301, 320, 341, 345
Slickers, the 55, 137
Slim Smith and the Uniques 156, 169
Slits, the 118–19, 161–2
Sly and Robbie 99, 124, 141, 262, 290
Small, Millie 188
  'My Boy Lollipop' 33
Smile Jamaica concert 83–7, 290, 305
Smiley Culture (David Emmanuel) 46–7
Smith, Michael 67, 132, 298
Smith, Wayne
  Under Mi Sleng Teng 147, 175–7
socialism and socialists 70, 80, 83, 111, 114, 119, 178, 330

Solomon, King 21, 73, 103–4
Sony Music 185, 204, 215–16, 221, 311
Sound Dimension, the 156, 310
Soviet Union 49, 91, 100, 137
Spaulding, Anthony 83–4, 86
Specials, the 125–6, 129–31, 134–6
  The Specials 113
Spice (Grace Hamilton) 217, 272, 295, 324
State of Emergency 82–3, 96, 210, 258, 273–6
Steel Pulse 98, 120–22, 127
Steely & Clevie 185, 207
Stephens, Tanya 199–201, 204–9, 204–10, 217, 245
  Gangsta Blues 195, 202–3
Stitchie, Lieutenant (Cleveland Laing) 183–4
steppers (music style) 118, 148, 176–7
Stop Murder Music 229, 232–3, 237–45
Stowe, Maxine 211, 215
Studio One 38, 53, 59, 160, 168–9, 172, 188–9, 207, 217
Stylo G (Jason McDermott) 325–6
Super Cat (William Maragh) 215–16, 262, 264
Symarip 63

Tatchell, Peter 219, 229–30, 234, 241, 244
Tavares-Finson, Tom 260, 301, 308
Taylor, Don 78, 83, 85–8, 180, 340
Teejay (Timoy Jones) 311, 326
Tenor Saw (Clive Bright) 175, 190
Terrelonge, Alando 327
Thatcher, Margaret 127, 131, 149
Third World (band) 78–9, 96, 98
Thompson, Aston 'Bucky Marshall' 84, 96, 99
Thompson, Caroll 140
Thompson, Dudley 95, 99
Thompson, Linval 107, 108, 167, 178
Tippa Irie (Anthony Henry) 142
Tomlinson, Krystal 325
Toots and the Maytals 190, 223
Tosh, Peter 67, 70, 72–3, 78, 90–91,

96, 98, 105, 107, 188–9, 235, 279, 285–6, 289, 340–42
Treasure Isle 37, 48, 59–60, 157, 168
Trinity (Wade Brammer) 172
Trojan Records 57–65, 72, 77, 117, 129, 190, 313, 315, 317
Trooper, Ricky 309, 322–3
Twelve Tribes of Israel, the 30–31, 96

U-Roy (Hugh Roy) 98, 156–8
UB40 124, 135–9
Uganda 334–7
Union of Soviet Socialist Republics *see* Soviet Union
Universal Music Group 78, 310–11, 316, 324
Universal Negro Improvement Association (UNIA) 17–19, 21, 23
USA 149, 151–2, 175, 182, 199, 202, 211, 237, 259–60, 273, 280, 309, 330, 335
    Miami 35, 92, 238, 258, 264, 304
    New York 17–18, 20, 25, 39, 71, 87, 100, 163, 178–9, 181, 187, 207, 215, 219, 258, 272, 293
    Ohio 124

Valentines, the 55–6
Vaz, Daryl 273, 328
Vaz, Dwayne 329–30
Virgin Records 98, 141, 158, 178, 181
    see also Front Line
VP Records 177–80, 183, 196, 200–201, 203, 209–10, 216, 224, 226–7, 294, 306, 311–13
Vybz Kartel (Adidja Palmer) 205–6,

249–51, 271–6, 280, 283, 293–301, 303–4, 308, 327–8, 330, 332

Wadley, Earl 'Tek Life' 87, 96
Wailer, Bunny 48, 70, 72, 78, 98, 205, 182, 188–9, 194, 249, 277
Wailers, the 48, 53, 56, 61, 64, 69, 70, 72–3, 74, 76–8, 83, 117, 119, 170, 179–80, 182, 189, 329
    see also Bob Marley and the Wailers
Warner Brothers, Warner-Elektra-Atlantic (WEA) and Warner Music Group 183–4, 222, 280, 312
Waters, Anita 75, 148
Welsh, Milton 'Red Tony' 84, 96, 153, 262
West Indies Recording Ltd (WIRL) 39–40
Williams, Clive 'Lizard' 297–9
Wilson, Delroy 48, 55, 70, 97, 117
Wine, Bobi (Robert Kyagulanyi Ssentamu) 333–7
Witter, Earl 258, 274–5
Wonder, Wayne (Von Wayne Charles) 325

Xterminator Records 200, 218, 288–9, 291, 302

Yellowman (Winston Foster) 141, 147, 150, 173–4, 178, 184, 262

Zest Group 178, 312
Zion 26, 48, 102–4, 105
zionism 25–6
Zukie, Tappa 91, 98, 248